UNIX® Made Easy

LURNIX

Osborne **McGraw-Hill**
Berkeley   New York   St. Louis   San Francisco
Auckland   Bogotá   Hamburg   London   Madrid
Mexico City   Milan   Montreal   New Delhi   Panama City
Paris   São Paulo   Singapore   Sydney
Tokyo   Toronto

Osborne **McGraw-Hill**
2600 Tenth Street
Berkeley, California 94710
U.S.A.

For information on translations and book distributors outside of the
U.S.A., please write to Osborne **McGraw-Hill** at the above address.

Modular Guides is a trademark of LURNIX. UNIX is a registered
trademark of AT&T. VT100 is a trademark of Digital Equipment. Xenix
is a registered trademark of Microsoft Corporation.

UNIX® Made Easy

1234567890 DOC 89

ISBN 0-07-881576-2

•Contents at a Glance•

•Contents•

2 Basic Editing with the Visual Editor 59

3 Using UNIX Directories   117

4 Using Basic UNIX Utilities 171

6 Command Line Interpretation by the Shell 259

7   Setting File Permissions   331

8

The UNIX World of Directories   363

9   Advanced Visual Editing   385

10   Running Multiple Commands   439

13   Using the C Shell History   553

14   Creating Aliases   583

15   Setting the User Environment   611

16 Using a Network of UNIX Machines 651

17   Using the X Window System   681

18   Basic Text Formatting   717

20 Process Monitoring and Control 811

21   System Administration   861

B   Answers   941

Foreword

UNIX Made Easy was developed by a team of Lurnix teachers and educational design specialists. Our team created a list of skill objectives and developed exercises that carefully built the appropriate knowledge and skill. We then added text that guided the reader through the exercises and examined the needed concepts. Drafts were given to students, revisions made, the text was formatted, edited, checked, revised again, and so forth. Because the subject is complex, the commands extremely numerous, and the underlying concepts often difficult to master, the team invested literally thousands of hours developing these guides to the UNIX system. We trust learning UNIX is as an enjoyable and rewarding experience for you as developing these guides was for us.

—John Muster

Acknowledgments

The project manager for the book was George Woolley.

The authors were assisted in text formatting, management, index creation, and editing by Chloe Griffin and Gretchen Stude.

The principal authors who created first drafts or major rewrites of the chapters were:

Peter Birns	Patrick Brown	Dave Cottle
Herb Cowan	Kevan Garrett	Fil Machi
John Muster	Leo Pereira	Carl Pregozen
Sean Rouse	Scott Silvey	George Woolley
Mark Yatabe		

Introduction

UNIX is a powerful and flexible operating system/computing environment. It is available on more types of computer systems than any other operating system, and its use is expanding at a rapid rate. However, UNIX has a well-earned reputation for being difficult to learn.

Although there is already an abundance of on-line documentation and reference books about UNIX, we developed the modular learning guides in this book to give serious users and programmers a more efficient way to explore and master UNIX's wide range of features and programs. *UNIX Made Easy* offers you a series of focused chapters, each of which is a carefully crafted, comprehensive, hands-on, conceptually complete Learning Guide™ that will help you master a specific portion of the UNIX system.

ABOUT THIS BOOK

In the following chapters, each new UNIX feature is introduced with a brief explanation of its value to you, the user. You are then guided through carefully designed examples of the feature or program—examples that you make work on a functioning UNIX system. After the examples is a discussion of how the feature or program works. Because these concepts are discussed *after* you use the particular feature, the explanation is more meaningful to you. You already have experience with how it works.

After you master the basic skills, you'll explore the more complex features. Thus your knowledge of UNIX is carefully and efficiently constructed.

Thousands of students have found that by following the exercises and conceptual discussions in Learning Guides such as these, UNIX is actually easy to learn.

SCOPE OF BOOK

There are two major families of UNIX: System V, which was developed by AT&T, and BSD (Berkeley

Systems Distribution), which was created at the University of California. This book addresses both of these systems and notes the differences between them.

A UNIX system's primary user interface is called the shell. The two most widely used shells are the Bourne shell, which is a standard part of BSD and System V, and the C shell, which is included with most UNIX systems. This book explores both of these shells, emphasizing the C shell as the command interpreter, except in the chapter on shell programming, which emphasizes the Bourne shell.

HOW THIS BOOK IS ORGANIZED

UNIX Made Easy is divided into 21 chapters. Each chapter is a hands-on tutorial that examines a group of topics related to a single major subject, such as visual editing, using directories, changing file permissions, or writing shell scripts.

Some chapters, such as Chapter 2, "Basic Editing with the Visual Editor," and Chapter 3, "Using UNIX Directories," are essential to a number of later chapters and must be mastered before you proceed.

Figure I-1, "Chapter prerequisites," identifies the chapters that you need to complete before beginning other chapters.

Chapters 1 through 3 should be read in sequence. At that point, you will be prepared to examine three topics, **mail** (Chapter 5), utilities (Chapter 4), and text

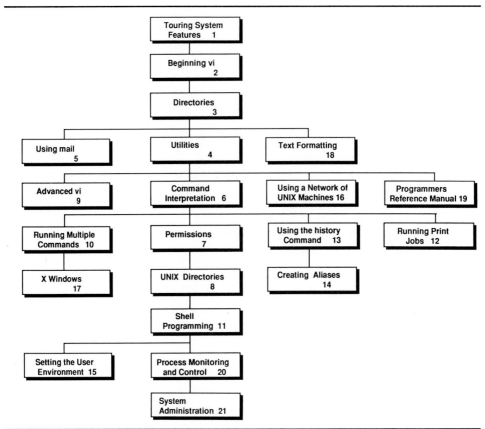

FIGURE I-1.   Chapter prerequisites

formatting (Chapter 18); you may choose the order of these three chapters. You must complete the examination of utilities in Chapter 4 before beginning the topics of Command Interpretation by the Shell (Chapter 6), Advanced **vi** (Chapter 9), Networks (Chapter 16), or the Reference Manual (Chapter 19). Examine these chapters in whatever order is of most interest to you; however, Chapter 6, "Command Line Interpretation by the Shell," contains concepts needed for mastery of the remainder of the book.

Some chapters describe capabilities available only on certain systems. Most UNIX systems have the C shell, but if you do not, you may wish to quickly pass through Chapter 10, "Running Multiple Commands," Chapter 13, "Using the C Shell History," and Chapter 14, "Creating Aliases." These chapters examine features available on the C shell, but not on the Bourne shell.

Only if you have X window will you be able to run the exercises in Chapter 17, "Using the X Window System."

Each chapter of the book includes:

- An introduction

- A Skills Check (a list of skills you need before starting the chapter, and a reference to the chapter that teaches those skills)

- An Objectives list (what you can expect to learn from the chapter)

- A set of examples to work through on particular topics, along with comments on the examples and summaries of the topic

- Exercises to test your progress, with answers at the back of the book

- A conclusion

- A Command Summary

These reference aids are explained briefly on the last page of the book:

- Utility Information Pages (UIPs)

- Index

A Brief Synopsis

Chapter 1, "Touring the System's Features," leads you on an introductory grand tour of the UNIX features and capabilities that are explored in greater detail in the subsequent chapters.

Chapter 2, "Basic Editing with the Visual Editor," introduces you to the commands you will need to edit files using the visual editor.

Chapter 3, "Using UNIX Directories," shows you how to use directories to organize your files, and how to change the current directory.

Chapter 4, "Using Basic UNIX Utilities," examines how utilities operate, and explores the operation of a number of often-used utilities.

Chapter 5, "Sending Messages to Other Users," guides you through sending and receiving mail on your UNIX system.

Chapter 6, "Command Line Interpretation by the Shell," explains how you communicate with the shell, and how it processes your instructions. The shell is the primary interface to the UNIX system. This chapter explores and compares the two shells you are most likely to use—the C shell and the Bourne shell.

Chapter 7, "Setting File Permissions," tells you how to grant and restrict usage of your files to three kinds of users: yourself, users assigned to the same group as you, and all others on the system.

Chapter 8, "The UNIX World of Directories," guides you through the contents of the UNIX system directories, and shows you how they are related to your work.

Chapter 9, "Advanced Visual Editing," gives you experience using the advanced editor features. You will perform tasks such as customizing the editing environment, editing several files at once, manipulating blocks of text, and assigning text strings to specific keys.

Chapter 10, "Running Multiple Commands," shows you how to execute and control many jobs at the same time, using a C shell capability called job control.

Chapter 11, "Shell Programming," explores the basics of Bourne shell programming and briefly introduces C shell programming. Shell script programming allows you to accomplish complex tasks quickly.

Chapter 12, "Running Print Jobs," guides you through the commands needed to print files on a printer, and to monitor and control your print jobs.

Chapter 13, "Using the C Shell History," demonstrates how to view, modify, and reissue commands you have previously executed.

Chapter 14, "Creating Aliases," describes how to create alternate names for existing commands, and how to build new commands out of combinations of old commands.

Chapter 15, "Setting the User Environment," shows you how to control various aspects of your user environment, including the names of commands, what type of terminal the system will assume you are using, where printer output will go, and so on. The chapter also examines the differences between the C shell and Bourne shell environments.

Chapter 16, "Using a Network of UNIX Machines," explains how to access other machines, how to transfer data between them, and how to send messages.

Chapter 17, "Using the X Window System," examines the basic user functions in an X Window environment, including how to get into and leave the environment, and how to create new windows.

Chapter 18, "Basic Text Formatting," teaches you how to use text formatting commands to create formatted files. It introduces formatting macros and gives examples of commands to create tables, pictures, and mathematical equations in your document.

Chapter 19, "Using the UNIX Reference Manual," shows you how to use the UNIX **man** (manual) pages, both on-line and hardcopy, to get information about the system.

Chapter 20, "Process Monitoring and Control," helps you to more precisely monitor your work through a capability called process control. It explains what a process is to UNIX, how it comes into being, what it does, and how it ends.

Chapter 21, "Systems Administration," explores the basic system administration utilities.

CONVENTIONS USED IN THIS BOOK

UNIX Made Easy uses the following conventions to aid your understanding of the book. *Fonts* within examples of command input are as follows:

- **boldface** type is used for fixed parts of the command, including the command name and its options

- *italic* type is used for variables

These same styles are used when the command or its parts are referred to within sentences.

A distinctive type of font is used for screen output, which looks like this:

```
This line is in monospace
```

Italics are used the first time a new term is introduced, and occasionally for emphasis.

- *Steps*   Each time you are asked to perform an action on the computer, the action will be in the form of one or more numbered steps, like this:

1. Type the following:

who

In most chapters, it is assumed that you will press the ⌜Return⌝ key after a command. Where there is some possibility of confusion, the ⌜Return⌝ is explicitly shown. In certain chapters, where the actions taken are not computer steps, numbered steps may also be used.

- *Special Keys*   Special keys are boxed; for example, ⌜Return⌝ means press the return key.

Control characters are also boxed, as in ⌜Ctrl-d⌝ . When you see these, hold down the Control key (usually marked **Ctrl** on your keyboard), and press the key shown after the dash once.

- *System V vs BSD*   When different commands are needed for System V and BSD, both will be shown. In most cases this is done as in the following example.

1. In order to view the file one screen at a time, type one of the following commands:

System V:
pg *filename*

BSD:
more *filename*

ADDITIONAL HELP FROM OSBORNE/McGRAW-HILL

Osborne/McGraw-Hill provides top-quality books for computer users at every level of computing experience. To help you build your skills, we suggest that you look for the books in the following Osborne series that best address your needs.

The "Teach Yourself" series is perfect for people who have never used a computer before or who want to gain confidence in using program basics. These books provide a simple, slow-paced introduction to the fundamental uses of popular software packages and programming languages. The "Mastery Skills Check" format ensures your understanding concepts thoroughly before you progress to new material. Plenty of examples and exercises (with answers at the back of the book) are used throughout the text.

The "Made Easy" series is also for beginners or users who may need a refresher on the new features of an upgraded product. These in-depth introductions guide users step-by-step from the program basics to intermediate-level usage. Plenty of "hands-on" exercises and examples are used in every chapter.

The "Using" series presents fast-paced guides that cover beginning concepts quickly and move on to intermediate-level techniques and some advanced topics. These books are written for users already familiar with computers and software who want to get up to speed fast with a certain product.

The "Advanced" series assumes that the reader is a user who has reached at least an intermediate skill level and is ready to learn more sophisticated techniques and refinements.

The "Complete Reference" series provides handy desktop references for popular software and programming languages that list every command, feature, and function of the product along with brief but detailed descriptions of how they are used. Books are fully indexed and often include tear-out command cards. The "Complete Reference" series is ideal for both beginners and pros.

The "Pocket Reference" series is a pocket-sized, shorter version of The "Complete Reference" series. It provides the essential commands, features, and functions of software and programming languages for users of every level who need a quick reminder.

The "Secrets, Solutions, Shortcuts" series is written for beginning users who are already somewhat familiar with the software and for experienced users at intermediate and advanced levels. This series provides clever tips, points out shortcuts for using the software to greater advantage, and indicates traps to avoid.

Osborne/McGraw-Hill also publishes many fine books that are not included in the series described here. If you have questions about which Osborne books are right for you, ask the salesperson at your local book or computer store, or call us toll-free at 1-800-262-4729.

OTHER OSBORNE/McGRAW-HILL BOOKS OF INTEREST TO YOU

We hope that *UNIX Made Easy* will assist you in mastering this fine operating system, and also pique your interest in learning more about other ways to better use your computer.

If you're interested in expanding your skills so you can be even more "computer efficient," be sure to take advantage of Osborne/McGraw-Hill's large selection of top-quality computer books. They cover all varieties of popular hardware, software, programming languages, and operating systems. We cannot list every title here that may relate to UNIX and to your special computing needs, but here are a few books that complement *UNIX Made Easy.*

Teach Yourself C, by Herbert Schildt, is a simple, hands-on introduction to C programming that leads beginners through the fundamentals of C. Mastery learning techniques that use exercises and skills checks make sure your programming abilities grow, lesson by lesson.

ANSI C Made Easy, by Herbert Schildt, is a thorough, in-depth introduction to the ANSI standard of the C programming language. Like all books in the "Made Easy" series, *ANSI C Made Easy* includes plenty of clear examples and hands-on exercises that facilitate quick and lasting comprehension. This book guides you from beginning- to intermediate-level programming.

C:The Complete Reference, also by Herbert Schildt, is now available in a second edition that covers ANSI C. It is for all C programmers—from beginners who are somewhat familiar with the language to veteran C programmers. This comprehensive reference discusses C basics and C library functions by category, including algorithms, C applications, the programming environment, and C's latest direction—C++.

Why This Book Is for You

If you are a new UNIX user, this book is especially designed for you. The order of presentation, the selection of examples, and the format of "experience first and explanation after" all represent a distillation of years of teaching UNIX to several thousand people by the staff at Lurnix. You can save yourself long hours of frustration by taking advantage of the authors' extensive experience in teaching UNIX.

If you teach UNIX at a university, or are a teacher at a company or other organization, this book will make your job easier. It provides you with a course strategy, and can function as a workbook for your students.

If you are an experienced UNIX user, but there are certain areas of the system you haven't mastered, you will find that you can quickly improve specific skills with this book.

LEARN MORE ABOUT UNIX

Here is an excellent selection of other Osborne/
McGraw-Hill books on UNIX that will help you build
your skills and maximize the power of the operating
system you have selected.

If you're looking for an intermediate-level book,
see *Using UNIX® System V Release 3*, by The LeBlond
Group. This is a fast-paced, hands-on guide that
quickly covers basics before discussing intermediate
techniques and even some advanced topics. If you're
using UNIX System V Release 2, see *A User Guide to the
UNIX® System*, Second Edition, by Dr. Rebecca
Thomas and Jean Yates.

For all UNIX users of System V Release 3.1 (from
beginners who are somewhat familiar with the operating system to veteran users), see *UNIX®: The Complete Reference*, by Stephen Coffin. This is the ideal
desktop resource; it discusses every command, as well
as text processing, editing, programming, communi-
cations, the shell, and the UNIX filesystem.

·1·

Touring the System's Features

One way to visit New York City for the first time is to start at the top of the Empire State Building, identify the major landmarks, and examine the orderly way streets and avenues are laid out. Next, visit the subway to examine the map and see how to get around the city. The first visit could also include a quick tour of the highlights, followed by an in-depth investigation of the most interesting parts of the city.

The purpose of this chapter is to take you on a guided, "hands-on" tour of the UNIX system in the same way, with a focus on how to get around and what the computing environment has to offer. Each feature is introduced by examples that you can try out.

You are not expected to remember everything in this chapter. The remainder of this book will help you explore the features of UNIX in greater detail.

SKILLS CHECK

Before beginning this chapter, you should

- Have access to an account on a UNIX system
- Be able to describe the formatting conventions presented in the Foreword

OBJECTIVES

After completing this chapter, you will be able to

- Create files using various UNIX utilities
- Copy, move, and remove files
- Communicate with other users
- Connect several utilities together
- Describe the filesystem of UNIX

1.1   ESTABLISHING COMMUNICATION WITH UNIX

The UNIX computing environment is designed to serve many users at the same time. Each user gains access to the system by specifying an *account name* or *login name,* and by providing the appropriate *password.* Failure to supply a corresponding login and password results in denial of access.

Before starting to log on to the system, you need several pieces of information:

- The name of the particular computer that you are assigned to use, if you are at an installation that lets you access several machines
- The login name for your account
- Probably a password for your login
- Possibly the abbreviation for the name of the type of terminal you are using

This information will be supplied from one of two sources. If there are people in charge of maintaining accounts on your system (systems administrators), one of them will give you the needed information. If you are the first user on a new machine and have no mentor to assist you, check the user's manual that is provided with your system. The section entitled "Getting Started," or its equivalent, includes instructions on logging in as *tutor, user, guest,* or some other login name that implies the account is for regular use, not for system administration.

Your user's manual will also include directions for logging in as **root**, the account for the system administrator. Because the powers associated with this account are extensive, it is unwise to log in as **root** until you have mastered the essential skills for using the system.

There are several steps to the login process. Each step must be successfully completed.

Selecting the System

On systems that use several computers linked together, you may be asked to identify the name of the
specific computer you are to access. On a single
machine system, or if your terminal is directly linked
to one computer, you probably will not be asked for
this information. In this case, you may proceed to the
next section, "Identifying the User Account."

   If you must identify the system to access, the first
prompt you see is similar to one of the following:

```
pad:
request:
system:
```

1. Type the identifying name of the computer to
   which you were assigned, and press $\boxed{\text{Return}}$. When
   you type a name that the program recognizes, you
   are connected to that computer.

   On some networking systems you can abbreviate the name of the computer using the first two or
   three letters of the name.

Identifying the User Account

Having selected the system, you are greeted with the
login banner. Now you can identify yourself by
specifying the name of your account, your *login* ID or
login name.

The following prompt is displayed:

```
login:
```

1. Type your assigned login name in lowercase letters.

2. Press the [Return] key.

Providing the Password

After you have typed your *login*, you must supply the correct *password*. This is the secret password that only you should know. For security reasons, as you type your password it is not displayed on the screen.

The following prompt is displayed:

```
Password:
```

1. Enter your password.

2. Press the [Return] key.

3. If you provided a corresponding set of *login* and *password* entries, you are moved on to the next step. If the *login* and *password* you supplied did not correspond, an error message appears, such as:

```
Login incorrect
```

Two common reasons for an incorrect login are

- You mistyped either the *login* or the *password* entry, or

- You accidentally typed the *login* in uppercase letters

4. If you simply made an error in typing, reenter the *login* and *password*.

5. If you used uppercase, the computer is now treating your terminal as a teletype terminal that will only work with uppercase letters. (When this happens, most ordinary terminals display a backslash in front of the password prompt.)

   To begin again, hold down the $\boxed{\text{Ctrl}}$ key and press the **d** key one time. This kills the login program. Another immediately starts up. A new login banner appears, and you can start over.

Identifying the Terminal Type

Because UNIX can accept many different vendors' terminals that work in different ways, the system must be informed of the type of terminal you are using.

   If the login program does not already have the information, it prompts you with the following:


```
Term:
```

1. This prompt often contains a default terminal setting in parentheses. If the default that is listed is correct, press $\boxed{\text{Return}}$.

2. If you need to inform the system of a different terminal type, enter the abbreviation for your terminal that is provided by your system administrator. Here are some commonly used terminal abbreviations for different terminal types:

h19
tvi925
vt100
wyse50

USING SHELL COMMANDS TO OBTAIN INFORMATION

1.2

When you have successfully logged in, a prompt is displayed. The prompt may be customized for your site, or it may be one of the default shell prompts, such as:

$
%
#

The prompt is displayed on the screen by a program that interprets each command line you type. This program, called the *shell*, accepts command lines issued by you, interprets what you type, and executes whatever other programs are specified.

The shell prompt means the shell is waiting for you to type a command giving it instructions.

If you make a mistake while typing a command, use the [Backspace] key to back up the cursor. Or, hold the [Ctrl] key down while you press the **h** key. Then retype the command.

Logging Off the System

You have learned to log on to the system; you must also be able to log off the system.

1. Once you are certain that you are ready to leave UNIX, type

   exit

   This will usually log you off your system.

2. If **exit** does not work, type

   logout

   You have now logged off your system.

Determining Who Is on the System

1. Log back on, following the procedure you just learned.

2. To determine who is logged on, type the following command:

   who

   Press the [Return] key.

3. This command line instructs the shell to execute a program called **who** that displays the login names of all users who are currently logged on. The display looks something like this:

```
michael    ttyh3     Jul 14 21:11
julie      ttyi1     Jul 14 17:58
isaac      ttyi7     Jul 14 11:35
```

Each line of output is for a single user and consists of several fields. The components of the entry for *isaac* are

isaac   login name of the user
ttyh7   user's terminal port
Jul 14 11:35   the month, day, and time of login

Each terminal is connected to the computer through a port that has a designation beginning with *tty*. When the **who** command is issued, the **who** utility searches specific system files to determine the login name, port, and time each user logged in. The **who** utility then formats the information and outputs it. In this case, the output from **who** is displayed on the screen. After **who** has completed its work, it dies and the shell displays a new prompt, indicating that it is ready for your next instruction.

Obtaining the Date and Time

Many programs on UNIX are time dependent. For instance, you just used **who** to determine the date and time current users logged in.

1. You can directly access the date and time information from the shell. To do this, type

date

and press [Return].

2. The output is displayed on your screen.

1.3   CREATING AND MANIPULATING FILES

When you requested a listing of current users, the **who** utility located the needed information and formatted the report. The output from **who** was, by default, sent to your screen.

1. You can also instruct the shell to *redirect* the output away from your screen to a file. Type the following shell command line:

who > *users_on*

2. Notice that nothing appears on the screen except the next shell prompt. In this command line, the > redirection character instructs the shell to create a new file (named *users_on*), and connect the output of **who** to the new file. The output is said to be *redirected* to a new file.

Listing Files in Your Home Directory

Because UNIX is a multiuser system, each user is given a separate workspace or "Home" directory.

When you log in, your *Home directory* is opened for a place to begin work.

On UNIX, information is retained in files. There are system program files, user-created files, and other kinds of files. You just created a new file named *users_on*. You created the file; you own it; you have access to it. The file is listed in your workspace or Home directory. You will learn more about files in later chapters in this book.

You can create additional new directories to keep files together that pertain to a given topic or task. The files and directories you create are accessible from your Home directory. Chapter 3 gives you details on how to work with directories on UNIX.

1. You can request the names of files listed in your current (Home) directory. Type the following command:

   ls

   and press $\boxed{\text{Return}}$.

   In this case, the **ls** utility obtains a list of the names of files listed in your Home directory and outputs that list to the screen. After the **ls** utility completes its work, the shell provides another prompt.

Viewing the Contents of Files

The UNIX system includes several utilities that display the contents of files on the terminal. Each one handles the task differently. One way is to display files a screen at a time.

1. Try each of the following commands:

pg *users_on*
more *users_on*

At least one command resulted in the file's display on the screen. The other probably resulted in the message:

```
Command not found
```

Although these commands work in similar ways, **more** is used on Berkeley Standard Distribution (BSD) systems, and **pg** on AT&T's System V. Some systems accept both commands. Use whichever one works on your system.

2. The contents of the file *users_on* are now displayed on the screen. The output appears one screen at a time. If a file is longer than one screen, press the Spacebar to view each successive screen. On some systems you may have to press Return.

After **pg** or **more** completes its work, the shell again displays a prompt.

Creating a Text File with cat

You will usually create text files using an editor such as the UNIX visual editor, **vi**. However, you can quickly create small test files without first mastering an editor, by using one of several other shell commands. You will become familiar with the **vi** editor in Chapter 2.

1. Type the following:

cat > *first_file*

And then press [Return].

   The cursor returns to the beginning of the next line. However, notice that the shell does not display a new prompt. You are no longer in communication with the shell, but with the **cat** utility. There is no **cat** prompt, but any line you enter is read by **cat**.

2. Type the following lines:

This is a line of text in the first-file.
This is another.

Press the [Return] key. The **cat** utility reads your input and writes it to a new file named *first_file*.

3. Inform the **cat** utility that you are finished adding text by returning to a new line, and then press [Ctrl-d].

   (To do this, hold down the [Ctrl] key, and press the **d** key once.) Make sure that you are on a new line. This [Ctrl-d] or end-of-file (EOF) character tells **cat** there is no additional input. The **cat** utility dies, and the shell displays another prompt.

   The **cat** utility takes its name from the word "con**cat**enate" because, as you will see, it can be used to splice several files together.

4. From the shell, obtain a listing of your files, using

ls

The files *users_on* and *first_file* are listed.

5. Examine the contents of *first_file* by typing

pg *first_file*

or

more *first_file*

The file consists only of the text you typed. Nothing else is added by the system.

6. Create another text file with

cat > *second_file*

Add some text, and return to the shell with [Ctrl-d].

7. Obtain a listing of your current files with **ls**.

8. Examine the contents of *second_file* with **pg** or **more**.

The command **cat** > *filename* is a shell command. It instructs the shell to connect the output from **cat** to the file *filename*, and to execute the **cat** utility. By default, the terminal keyboard is connected to the input of **cat**. Whatever you type is read by **cat** from your terminal and written to the file. The **cat** utility has a tough job; it reads input and writes output, making no modifications. How input and output are handled is the subject of Chapter 6, "Command Line Interpretation by the Shell."

Copying Files

You have thus far created several files by instructing the shell to create a file for the output of utilities like

who and **cat**. The files are listed each time you type the **ls** command. You can also create new files by copying files.

1. To make a copy of *first_file* and give it the name *first2*, type

   cp *first_file first2*

2. Examine the contents of *first2* by typing

   pg *first2*

   or

   more *first2*

   The file *first2* is an exact copy of *first_file*. Each file is a separate entity; one can be edited without affecting the other.

3. Create another copy of *first_file*, named *junk*, by entering the following:

   cp *first_file junk*

   In summary, to create *newfile*, an exact copy of *file*, enter the command **cp** *file newfile* from the shell.

Renaming Files from the Shell

As each file is created, it is given a name. Each file's name is used to access the file. The names are not permanent fixtures, but can be changed.

1. Examine the contents of your file named *second_file*, using **pg** or **more**.

2. Change the name of the file *second_file* to *phon*, by typing the following command:

   mv *second_file phon*

3. List your files with the **ls** command. The filename *second_file* is missing; *phon* is there.

4. Display the contents of the new *phon* file using **pg** or **more**.

The **mv** *file newfile* command changes the name of *file* to *newfile*. Although the name implies that it **moves** the file, it usually just changes the name where it is listed (in your Home directory).

Displaying the First Few Lines in a File

There are times when it is helpful to view the first few lines of a file to remind you of the contents.

1. On BSD systems and some others, you can look at the first ten lines of *first_file* by typing the following command:

   head *first_file*

2. To view the last lines in the file, use the **tail** command on BSD:

   tail *first_file*

Removing Files

1. To delete a file from your account, you **rem**ove it. Type

   rm *first2*

2. Type **ls** to confirm that the file is no longer listed.

Removing Files with Confirmation

There is a "silence" about the UNIX system that often disturbs people. For instance, when you instruct **rm** to remove a file, all you get in response is the next shell prompt. The system silently does as requested and then prompts for your next instruction. If you would like the opportunity to confirm before files are removed, use the inquiry option of **rm**.

1. A few steps back you created a file named *junk*. Request its removal with the following:

   rm -i *junk*

2. Next, you are asked if you really want it removed. Type **n** or press [Return] to abort the removal process.

3. Confirm that you still possess too much *junk* with

   ls

4. Again request removal of the *junk* file with

   rm -i *junk*

5. This time instruct **rm** that you *do* want *junk* discarded by responding to the inquiry with

y

6. Confirm that *junk* has been removed with **ls**.

Removing Several Files

The **rm** command accepts multiple filenames.

1. Use **cat** to create three files: *file1, file2,* and *file3.*
2. Remove them all at once, with

   rm *file1 file2 file3*

Creating a Combination File

In UNIX there are often several different ways to accomplish the same task—such as combining two files into a third. One way is to use the **cat** command.

1. Type the following command line:

   cat *first_file users_on* > *total*

   This command instructs the shell to do several things:

   • Create a new file, *total*

   • Connect the output of **cat** to *total*

   • Execute **cat**

The **cat** utility then reads the files *first_file* and *users_on*. It writes what it reads to the new file *total*. Hence, *total* consists of the contents of the two input files.

COMMUNICATING WITH OTHER USERS   1.4

There are several utilities on UNIX that allow you to communicate with other users. Two are introduced here.

Writing a Message to Another User

Often, terminals are located a great distance from each other. The system provides a means of communication. If you want to contact another user who is logged on, you can send messages to the correct terminals.

1. Use the **who** command to find a coworker who is logged on. Users' login names are the first field in the **who** output. Then use the login of your colleague in the following command. (If you do not know anyone who is logged on, send a message to yourself using your own login.)

2. Start the message-sending process by typing

    write *other_login*

This command line instructs **write** to connect to the port where *other_login* is located. The **write** utility sends a message to the screen there, telling *other_login* that you are sending a message.

3. Type a line or two of text. When you are finished, conclude the **write** session by returning to a new line and pressing Ctrl-d.

Writing a File to Another User

You can also send files to another user's screen using the **write** utility. Type the following command:

write *other_login* < *first_file*

The < *first_file* portion of this command line instructs the shell to connect the file *first_file* to the input of **write**. The **write** utility reads *first_file* instead of your terminal and displays what it reads on the terminal that *other_login* is using.

Sending Mail to Another User

The **write** utility can be used only when the target user is currently on the system. To send a message to a user who is not logged on, you can use **mail**, the UNIX postal service. For instance, to send mail consisting of the file *first_file* to *other_login*, type the following command:

mail *other_login* < *first_file*

You can also send messages and files to users on your system. The **mail** facility also permits you to send messages and files to other systems. These topics are explored in Chapter 5, "Sending Messages to Other Users."

EMPLOYING THE UNIX TOOLBOX OF UTILITIES

1.5

The UNIX operating system contains a variety of user programs called utilities. Each program performs a series of specific tasks. Each utility can be independently used, usually with a file as input. Utilities can also be connected to each other, to accomplish more complex tasks.

Printing a File

Of the commands that you have tried so far, only **more** and **pg** are specific to different UNIX systems. The command **more** usually only exists in BSD machines; **pg** is in System V.

The commands to send a file to a printer for printing are also system dependent. To print a file, type one of the following commands:

System V:
lp *first_file*

BSD:
lpr *first_file*

If the system responds to either of these commands with an error message about a lack of a destination printer, you will need to ask a colleague or your system administrator for the name of a printer available to you. Once you have the printer name, type

System V:
lp -ddest *first_file*

BSD:
lpr -Pdest *first_file*

The *dest* refers to the destination printer to which your file is being sent. Type in the printer name you obtained from your system administrator.

If you have several printers available, the **-d** option in System V and the **-P** option in BSD allow you to specify which printer you want to use.

Sorting Lines in a File

1. Use the **cat** utility to create a file called *names*, with the following content:

   joan   *7777*
   chuck   *3333*
   bill   *3576*
   mary   *1573*

   This file of names and phone extensions was created in the order in which the information was received. The file is not in alphabetical order. You can use a utility to obtain a version sorted in alphabetical order.

2. Type the following to sort the lines from the *names* file:

sort *names*

The **sort** utility reads the file *names* and rearranges its lines. The output is displayed on the screen.

3. Use **sort** to sort the lines from several of your other files. Examine the output. Lines beginning with uppercase letters appear alphabetically before lines that begin with lowercase letters.

Unless instructed otherwise, the **sort** utility sorts in ASCII order. ASCII is an acronym for the American Standard Code for Information Interchange. In ASCII order, nonalphanumeric characters are first, then numbers, followed by uppercase characters, and then lowercase characters. Therefore, lines beginning with nonalphanumeric characters are first, then lines that begin with numbers, followed by uppercase lines, then lowercase.

Employing an Option with sort

To sort a file in reverse order, you must invoke the utility instructing it to work in an optional way.

1. Type the following command:

sort -r *names*

Compare the output to that of the previous **sort**.

The **-r** is one of several options to the **sort** command that instruct the utility to change the way it functions. The options are examined in Chapter 4, "Using Basic UNIX Utilities."

Including Several Files as Input

The **sort** commands you have used thus far told **sort** to read a single file for input. Two or more files can be read and the lines sorted together. Type the following command line:

sort *first_file names* > *ordered_1*

The **sort** utility reads both files (*first_file* and *names*) and sorts all the lines that it reads. The resulting output is the contents of both files, merged together, sorted, and written to the file *ordered_1*. Neither *first_file* nor *names* is changed.

Counting Lines, Words, and Characters

It is often useful to count the lines, words, or characters in a file. There is a UNIX utility that accomplishes that specific task.

1. Type the following command:

wc *first_file*

This command instructs **wc** to read the file *first_file*. The output from the **word count** utility is similar to the following:

8   39   190 first_file

This output consists of the number of lines (8), words (39), and characters (19) in the file it read, followed by the filename.

2. Have **wc** determine the number of lines, with the **-l** option:

wc -l *first_file*

The **-l** option instructs **wc** to output only the number of lines it reads from the input file.

Selecting All Files for Input

The **wc** utility also allows you to count the contents of two or more files at the same time.

1. If you list several filenames with **wc**, as you did with **sort**, those files will be examined. You can also select all files in your current directory (your Home directory) by typing

wc *

The shell replaces the asterisk with the names of all the files in your directory and then executes **wc**. The **wc** utility examines all files listed, and displays output like this:

```
 8       39      190 first_file
 9       29      175 ordered_1
 8       39      190 phon
 4       20      120 users_on
29      127      675 total
```

The output from **wc** is a list of information pertaining to all input files, and then a total.

Locating Lines That Contain Specific Words

1. It is often useful to locate the lines in a file that contain a word or string of characters. Type the following command:

   grep *bill names*

   This command asks the **grep** utility to go through the *names* file line by line, searching for lines that contain the string of characters *bill*. It outputs only those lines that have a match.

2. You can also use the **grep** utility to search through all the files in your directory. Type the following:

   grep *the* *

   In this command line, the shell again replaces the asterisk with all the filenames listed in your current (Home) directory. The **grep** utility then searches all files for the string of characters *the*, whether in the word *the* or in ano*the*r word.

Printing a Listing of Misspelled Words

Many UNIX systems contain a spell-check program that examines files for misspelled words.

1. For instance, you can examine *users_on* for mis-spelled words with the following command:

   spell *users_on*

If there are any misspelled words in the file, they are displayed on the screen.

Determining Input and Output

Utilities get input, do some task, and write output. Some utilities get their information or input from the system (**date, who, ls**). In this tour of the system, you have been using the < and > redirection symbols to specify where utilities get their input and where they write their output. When you enter **cat** > *file1*, the output of **cat** is connected to *file1*. No input is specified, so by default input is connected to your keyboard.

With the command **write** *login* < *file2*, *file2* is connected to the input of **write**.

1. You can also connect files to the input of **cat**. For instance, type

   cat < *names*

   In this case, the file *names* is connected to the input of **cat**. Because no output destination is specified, the output is by default connected to your terminal. Thus, the file *names* is read by **cat** and displayed on the terminal screen.

2. You have also been instructing utilities to open files, with commands such as

   sort *names*

   The same approach works with the **cat** utility. Type

   cat *names*

   The file *names* is opened, read, and displayed on the screen.

The redirection commands are summarized as follows:

> *filename* establishes where output goes.
< *filename* establishes where input comes from.

Command	Input	Output	Effect
cat > *file1*	keyboard	*file1*	keyboard input goes into *file1*
cat < *file2*	*file2*	terminal	*file2* is displayed on the screen
cat *file1*	*file1*	terminal	*file1* is displayed on the screen
cat < *file1* > *file2*	*file1*	*file2*	contents of *file1* are written into *file2*
cat *file1* > *file2*	*file1*	*file2*	contents of *file1* are written into *file2*

The subject of redirection is examined more completely in Chapter 6, "Command Line Interpretation by the Shell."

Connecting Tools Together in Pipelines

In this chapter you have used utilities individually. An important feature on UNIX is the ability to combine utilities in command lines.

Before UNIX, the way to use several utilities in a row was to employ temporary files. For instance, to view a sorted list of who is logged on the system, type the following series of commands:

• Create a temporary file with the output of **who**:

who > *temp*

• Sort the temporary file and put the sorted output in a second temporary file, *temp2*:

sort *temp* > *temp2*

- Examine the contents of the output file, *temp2*:

pg *temp2*

- Remove the temporary files:

rm *temp temp2*

UNIX provides an easier way.

Sorting the Output of who Using Pipes

The display that **who** provides is not in alphabetical order. You can pass the output of **who** to **sort** for alphabetizing.

1. Type the command:

who | sort | pg

The **|** symbol is called the *pipe*. It is usually found on the same key as the backslash. The output of this command line consists of the lines from **who**, sorted in alphabetical order, displayed on the screen. No temporary files are created or have to be removed. The pipe connects the output of one utility to the input of another.

2. Pipes and redirects can be combined. Create a new file for the sorted output. Type the command:

who | sort > *sor_who*

3. Examine the file *sor_who*.

In this command line you are instructing the shell to connect the output of **who** to the input of **sort** and the output of **sort** to a new file, *sor_who*.

Determining How Many Times a User Is Logged On

The following commands use utilities, pipes, and options.

1. Type the following command line, substituting your login name for *logname*:

   who | grep *logname*

   The output of **who** is connected to the input of **grep**. The **grep** utility searches for lines that include the string of characters that is your login name. The output of **grep** consists of one line for each time you are logged in.

2. Pass the output of **grep** to the **wc** utility to count the number of lines that include your login name. Enter

   who | grep *logname* **| wc -l**

   The output is a number, equal to the number of lines in the output of **grep**, which is the number of times the selected user is logged on.

Selecting Fields from a Database

One of the most useful functions of modern computers is database management. The UNIX operating system provides several utilities that are used with databases.

1. Type the following command:

who I awk '{print $1}'

The **awk** utility extracts the first field from each line of the output of **who**.

2. Explore how **awk** works by changing the command to select the second field; to do this, change the **$1** to a **$2** in the **print** statement. The **awk** utility can be used to select and print specific fields, make calculations, and locate records by the value of specific fields.

Combining Database Files

Another utility, **paste**, is used to combine lines from different files.

1. Type the following:

paste *names ordered_1*

Notice that the **paste** utility reads the first line from both files, combines them into one line, and outputs that line. It then reads and combines the second line from each file, and so forth.

You will use other database utilities in Chapter 4, "Using Basic UNIX Utilities," including **cut** and **join**. The **cut** utility is used to select fields from a database. With **join**, specific records can be joined together to create a new record if the value in one field (such as a social security number) is the same in both original records.

Desktop Publishing

The UNIX operating system allows you to perform a wide variety of desktop publishing tasks—from simple business letters to books and large projects, complete with tables, footnotes, and numeric equations. The standard utilities are not "what you see is what you get" (*wysiwyg*), but rather are command driven. Applications that provide visual graphic displays are available and often added.

One of the most basic text processing tools is the formatter that arranges text into paragraphs and displays. The UNIX text processing tools are explored in Chapter 18, "Basic Text Formatting."

1.6   MODIFYING THE USER ENVIRONMENT

One of the strengths of the UNIX operating system is its flexibility. The system allows you to customize a variety of programs to your own liking.

Changing Your Password

One of the simplest ways to customize your account is to choose a secure but memorable password. This is not only convenient, but necessary for monitoring security of the data on the computer.

Before you begin the process of changing your password, decide on an appropriate new one. There are several words to avoid when choosing a password. Do not use

- Your login ID

- Your first or last name, or a child's or spouse's name

- Your address

- A word listed in a dictionary

These are all easily guessed.

Be sure to include both upper- and lowercase letters, and try to use a numeral or two.

With all these considerations, you may find it difficult to create a secure password. One way to choose a password is to use the first letters of every word in a memorable sentence. For instance, if you enjoy the work of a particular author, your password might be

MfaiMT47

This looks difficult to remember. It *is* extremely difficult to crack, but it is easy for you to remember if:

My **f**avorite **a**uthor **is M**ark **T**wain, and I am **47** years old

1. Once you have decided on a new password, type the following command:

   passwd

   You are prompted for your *old* password. To protect you, the program will not continue unless you identify yourself by correctly providing the current password.

2. Type your *old* password and press $\boxed{\text{Return}}$. You are now prompted for your new password.

3. Type your new password. The program asks you to repeat it to make certain that you type it correctly.

4. Type your new password again. When the shell prompt returns with no error messages, your password has been changed.

Changing the Prompt

Throughout the chapter we have talked about the shell prompt. The standard shell prompts are

```
#
$
%
```

This prompt, like much of your user environment, can be changed.

1. Type the following command *if you are using a C shell*:

set prompt = *"waldo "*

where *waldo* is whatever you want the prompt to be.

2. *If you are using the Bourne shell,* type the following:

PS1 = *'waldo '*

3. Your prompt is now reset. This prompt remains set until you log out.

In Chapter 15, "Setting the User Environment," you will permanently customize different aspects of your computer environment, such as the terminal type.

Renaming Commands for Personal Use

The C shell includes an **alias** feature that permits you to rename commands—for ease of memory or to save keystrokes.

1. Create an **alias** called **on** by typing the following command:

   alias *on* **"who I sort"**

2. Check to see if the **alias** command worked by typing

   on

3. To find out if any other aliases have been set, type the following:

   alias

   All aliases set automatically at login, or by you in this session, are displayed.

4. If your system does not have the command **rm**, aliased to the **i**nquire option, create the alias:

   alias *rm* **"rm -i"**

5. Attempt to remove a file with **rm** *filename* and observe the result.

Reissuing Commands Using history

1. Type the command:

cat *names*

2. Reissue the previous command by typing

!!

The **!!** command tells the shell to execute the last command line again. You can also select command lines by number, and make changes in commands. Chapter 13, "Using the C Shell History," is a complete description of the **History** mechanism.

1.7 USING UNIX SECURITY FEATURES

Examining Permissions

Earlier you changed your password to improve system security. Another very important aspect of UNIX security is file permissions. As the owner of a file, you can determine whether other users can read or write the file. If the file is a command file, you can specify who can execute the file.

1. To view the permissions of the *users_on* file, type the following command:

ls -l *users_on*

The **-l** option tells **ls** to provide a long listing of the file.

2. The output is something like this:

```
-rw-rw----   1 gretchen     453 Jul 18 11:17 users_on
```

The first field in the output, which consists of ten character places, shows the permissions set for that file. In Chapter 7, "Setting File Permissions," you will study permissions in much more depth. For now, however, look at the second, third, and fourth characters of the permissions field. The **r** and **w** indicate that you have permission to read and write to the file. (The second **rw** indicates that some other users also have read and write permission for the file.)

Denying Read Permission on a File

One of the security measures you can take is to make a file completely inaccessible by other users. (Since you own it, you can change it back at any time.) No user can read or copy your file if you don't grant them read permission.

1. Type the following command to remove read permission from the file *users_on.*

   chmod -r *users_on*

2. Examine the permissions field for *users_on* by typing

   ls -l

Where the previous permissions were **rw** for read and write permissions, the new permissions only include a **w**.

3. Check the file's permissions by trying to display the file with the following command:

cat *users_on*

You immediately receive an error message saying that you do not have permission to read the file.

4. Return the read permission to the file with the following command:

chmod +r *users_on*

The **chmod** command is used to **ch**ange the **mode** of a file.

1.8   PROGRAMMING WITH UNIX TOOLS

You can use UNIX to program in a variety of formats and languages.

Creating a Shell Script

One of the most basic and useful programming tools is the shell script. You are using the shell as an interactive command interpreter. It is also a programming environment.

1. Create a new file with the following command:

   cat > *new_script*

2. Type the following lines into the file, and press
   [Ctrl-d] when you are finished:

   ls
   pwd
   who
   date

   The contents of the file *new_script* now are a series
   of shell commands.

3. Examine the file to be certain it is correct, with:

   cat *new_script*

4. To make the file executable as a command, you
   must grant yourself execute permission. Type the
   following command to make *new_script* executable:

   chmod +x *new_script*

5. Look at the new permissions with the following
   command:

   ls -l *new_script*

   You now have read, write, and execute permission.

6. Execute the file by typing its name:

   new_script

   Each of the commands that made up the file is
   executed, and its output is sent to the screen. The
   shell is a powerful programming utility and is used
   throughout the system.

7. If you receive an error message such as "Command not found," enter the following:

./new_script

This command line tells the shell exactly where to find the shell script **new_script**.

In summary, to create and use a shell script:

- Create a file of shell commands
- Make the file executable
- Execute the file by entering the script name

Describing Programming Utilities

The UNIX operating system gives programmers a number of programming tools that either are packaged with the system or can be added.

UNIX is written in the popular C programming language. The C compiler is named **cc** and is available on most systems. The **make** utility allows programmers to control code development using several files at the same time. Various debugging tools are also used extensively.

Compilers are available for most major languages, such as COBOL, Pascal, FORTRAN, and BASIC. A variety of application languages and databases are used.

EXPLORING YOUR ENVIRONMENT   1.9

The shell program that interprets your commands is started at login. Several pieces of information are given to your particular shell process, so that your computing environment is appropriate. You can examine how the environment is set up.

1. From the shell, type

   set

   The output is a listing of the variables that are set at login for your account. Among the many lines displayed, you should find some like the following:

```
user  forbes
shell /bin/csh
home  /users1/programmers/forbes
path  (/usr/ucb /bin /usr/bin /usr/local /lurnix/bin /usr/new .)
```

   The *user* variable is your account name that you entered when you logged in.

   The *shell* line indicates which of several shell programs is interpreting the commands that you enter: **csh** is the C shell, **sh** is the Bourne shell, and **ksh** is the Korn shell. They all handle basic commands in essentially the same way, and for now it makes little difference which is running.

   The information to the right of *home* is the *path* to your workspace or Home directory. It is called a path because it is a list of directories from the top of the filesystem to your Home directory. Files in UNIX are organized into a hierarchical directory structure. The files you have created are listed in a directory—your Home directory.

Determining Your Location in the Filesystem

1. When you log on to the system, you are automatically connected with your Home directory. Another way to get a listing of the names of the directories, from the top to your Home directory, is to type the command:

pwd

This utility displays your **present working directory**. The output looks something like the following:

`/u1/staff/your_login`

This is the *full path* of your present working directory. Your Home directory is listed in a parent directory. That directory in turn is in one above it, and so forth, up to the topmost directory.

2. Obtain a listing of the files in your current, Home directory with the usual command:

ls

The output is a listing of files that you have created.

Viewing the Filesystem from the Top

The top of the UNIX directory system is generally referred to as *root,* or sometimes slash, because it is symbolized by the slash character.

1. Obtain a listing of the files and directories in the root directory with the following command:

   ls /

   The output of this utility is a listing of some of the system directories such as *dev, tmp, bin, and usr.* It also contains the first directory after **/** that was in your path when you typed **pwd** from your Home directory.

   You have used the **ls** utility before. When used without an argument, it outputs a list of files in your current directory. In this case you are giving the command an argument, **/,** which instructs **ls** to display the files listed in the root directory.

2. Check your present working directory by typing the following command:

   pwd

   Even though you generated a listing of the contents of the root directory, your current directory is not changed. It is still your Home directory. The **ls** utility allows you to obtain listings of other directories without actually changing directories.

3. You can also change directories. To change your present working directory to root, type the following command:

cd /

The command **cd** is the change directory utility.

4. Confirm that your current directory is now the root directory by typing the following command:

pwd

The output is not terribly descriptive:

/

Your current directory is now the root or slash directory, which is at the top of the UNIX filesystem.

5. Display a list of the files and directories in the root directory. Type

ls

The listing is the same as the **ls** / command that you typed earlier. The directories *dev, tmp, bin,* and *usr* are system directories, where the files that run the system reside.

Returning Home

1. In a later chapter (Chapter 8, "The UNIX World of Directories"), you will learn more about the directory system and how to move around within it. For now, return to your Home directory with the following command:

cd

No matter where you are on the system, the **cd** command with no argument will bring you Home.

2. Make sure you are in your Home directory with the following command:

pwd

Examining the Real Toolboxes

The *bin* directory in root contains some of the utilities available on the system in the form of binary files. Obtain a listing of these utilities with the following command:

ls */bin*

The / is important; do not omit it.

This command says to list the files in the directory */bin*. You may recognize some of the files in */bin*. They are the utilities you have already used, such as **cat, rm, who**, and **ls**. These are the actual programs that are accessed when you type a command of the same name.

The */bin* directory is not the only directory that contains executable code. You will examine others in Chapter 8.

Examining the Login Processes

An encrypted version of your password, and other information about you, resides in a file.

1. Type the command that is appropriate to your system:

pg *etc/passwd*

or

more */etc/passwd*

2. Press the ⎡Spacebar⎤ to get the next screen.

3. Type **q** to stop and return to the shell. This file */etc/passwd* is read whenever a user logs on.

4. Examine your entry in the */etc/passwd* file with the following command, substituting your login ID for *your_login:*

grep *your_login* */etcpasswd*

5. The file consists of seven fields separated by colons. Here is the general format of the file; compare your entry with it:

```
login:password:uid:gid:misc:home:shell
```

The fields of */etc/passwd* are as follows:

login	The login or name for your account.
password	Your encrypted password.
uid	The user ID, the number that is assigned uniquely to your account.
gid	Each user must be a member of at least one group. More about this later.
misc	The miscellaneous field need not be filled.
home	Your Home directory is listed. This is your current directory when you first log on.
shell	The program that is started when you log on. It is usually either the C shell (*/bin/csh*) or the Bourne shell (*/bin/sh*).

Identifying Devices

When a terminal is connected to the computer, it is connected at a *port*. Each port is assigned a *tty* (short for teletype), which is a special file that the system recognizes.

1. Obtain a listing of the system devices with the following command:

   ls */dev*

   The output contains a list of files in the */dev* directory that the system uses to communicate with the outside world. There is a group of files that begin with *tty*, such as *tty1* or *ttyh2*. These are the terminal ports.

2. Find out which port your terminal is connected to. Type the following:

   tty

   The output is the number and path of your port, such as */dev/tty03*. This is the port through which the computer talks to you.

Playing Games

Like all truly useful computer systems, UNIX usually includes games.

1. List the games available on your system with the command:

   ls */usr/games*

These games are generally not very complex in their graphics, but they can be fun. Some systems may not have a games directory because of space restrictions.

2. To play one of the games, type the following command. If your system does not have the game **worms**, substitute another game.

*/usr/games/***worms**

3. If you get stuck in a game that you don't want to continue, try pressing $\boxed{\text{Ctrl-c}}$ or $\boxed{\text{Ctrl-d}}$ to kill the game and return to the shell.

1.10   EXAMINING HOW UNIX DOES ITS WORK

Because UNIX is a multitasking system, it runs many programs at once. Each time you execute a utility, at least one new *process* is generated.

1. Obtain a listing of your current processes. Type one of the following commands:

System V:
ps

BSD:
ps -g

2. The output is a listing of the processes currently associated with your login name, along with some information about each process (*TT* is the *tty* number, *STAT* is the status of the process, and so forth). You will probably have at least two processes

running—a shell, the **ps** command, and maybe
more. Each process is a program you have running
on the system.

Listing Systemwide Processes

If your system is slow or busy, do not do the following
exercise. The **ps** command gave you the status of the
processes associated with your login. You can also
look at the processes running on the entire system,
including all the users currently logged on.

Type one of the following:

System V:
ps -ef

BSD:
ps -aux

This may produce more information than you really
want to know. The output is a list of the process status
of every process currently running on the system,
along with a plethora of information on each process.
This information can be very useful for troubleshooting the system.

Backgrounding a Process

Many of the processes running on the system are not
associated with a particular user, but are part of the

operating system. These processes are running *in the background* and are invisible to the user. You, too, can run a process in the background.

Type one of the following commands to create a new file:

System V:
ps -ef > *new_ps* &

BSD:
ps -aux > *new_ps* &

This command line tells the shell to run the **ps** command and redirect the output into a file named *new_ps*. The ampersand tells the shell to execute the whole process in the background, and return a new shell prompt so that you can continue working. The number that was displayed when you executed the command is the process number of the command line as it is executed. When the process is finished, a message is sent to the screen.

This feature allows you to run time-consuming programs in the background while you continue working in the foreground. Obviously, with a command as short as **ps**, backgrounding isn't so crucial; but there are times when it will save you time and work.

CONCLUSION

UNIX is a multiuser, multitasking operating system. It includes numerous utilities that can be linked together for greater effect. As you probably noticed from this whirlwind tour, UNIX is a complex, powerful, and occasionally unusual operating system. In this chapter you have been introduced to many commands and concepts, but you are not expected to completely remember and understand them all. These commands and concepts will be explored more completely in future chapters. By the end of the book, you will be very familiar with the UNIX system and all that it has to offer.

COMMAND SUMMARY

Logging In and Out

exit
Kills current C Shell (also see logout).

login
Logs user in.

logout
Logs user out.

passwd
Changes user's password.

Directories

(See Chapter 3, "Using UNIX Directories")

cd
Changes working directory.

ls
Lists current directory.

ls -l
Lists current directory with one file or directory per line.

pwd
Displays the name of the current directory.

File Information Utilities

(See Appendix A, "Utility Information Pages")

cat *file1* *file2*
Concatenates *file1* and *file2*.

COMMAND SUMMARY (*continued*)

grep *word filename*
Searches for lines containing a particular *word* (or pattern) in *filename*.

wc *filename*
Counts lines, words, and characters in *filename*.

Data Base Utilities

(See Appendix A)

awk '{print $x}' *file*
Prints the xth field of *file*.

paste *file1 file2*
Combines two files field by field.

sort *filename*
Displays *filename* in sorted order.

Other File Utilities

cp *file1 file2*
Copies *file1* to *file2*.

head *filename*
Displays the beginning of *filename*.

more *filename*
Displays *filename* one screen at a time (on BSD).

mv *file1 file2*
Renames *file1* as *file2*.

pg *filename*
Displays *filename* one screen at a time (on System V).

rm *filename*
Deletes *filename*.

COMMAND SUMMARY (*continued*)

rm -i *filename*
Same as **rm** *filename,* but ask the user to confirm the deletion.

spell *filename*
Checks the spelling throughout *filename*.

Other Utilities

tty
Displays the path and filename for this terminal.

who
Displays list of users currently logged on.

write *otherlogin*
Writes a message to another user's terminal.

Mail
(See Chapter 5, "Sending Messages to Other Users".)

mail *loginfilename*
Sends by electronic **mail** to *login.*

Command Interpretation
(See Chapter 6, Command Line Interpretation by the Shell")

command < filename
Makes *filename* the input for command.

command > filename
Sends the output of command to *filename.*

commandcommand
Makes the output of *command1* the input of *command2*.

COMMAND SUMMARY (*continued*)

Permissions

(See Chapter 7, "Setting File Permissions.")

chmod -r *filename*
Removes permission to read *filename*.

chmod + r *filename*
Gives permission to read *filename*.

Shell Programming

(See Chapter 11, "Shell Programming")

set
Lists the variables **set** in your login and their values.

scriptname
Executes the commands in the file *scriptname*.

Printing

(See Chapter 12, "Running Print Jobs")

lp*filename*
Prints *filename* on the lineprinter (System V).

lpr *filename*
Prints *filename* on the lineprinter (BSD).

History

(See Chapter 13,"Using the C Shell History")

!!
Executes the last shell command again (C shell).

COMMAND SUMMARY (*continued*)

Aliases

(See Chapter 14, "Creating Aliases") — BDS only

alias *string* "command"
Accepts *string* as equivalent of *"command."*

alias
Lists your **alias**es and their values.

User Environment

(See Chapter 15, "Setting the User Environment")

set *prompt* = *"string"*
Makes *string* the new prompt (C shell).

PS1=*"string"*
Makes **string** the new prompt (Bourne shell).

Process Monitoring

(See Chapter 20, "Process Monitoring and Control")

ps
Displays current processes for this login name.

·2·

Basic Editing with the Visual Editor

When writing programs or text it is necessary to create files, modify the content, rearrange material, and insert new lines. To accomplish these tasks, editors were developed. The UNIX visual editor, **vi**, is an extremely powerful, command-driven screen editor. All instructions are given by entering combinations of keystrokes. The visual editor is available on nearly all UNIX systems and is an essential tool. By using the **vi** editor, you can make changes and additions to text precisely and, with practice, easily.

The visual editor provides several ways of accessing files, moving through files, and making changes.

The various commands of the **vi** editor allow you to easily replace, delete, or move characters, words, paragraphs, data structures, or lines of code. Copies of the document in varying stages of development can be saved and later printed.

SKILLS CHECK

Before beginning this chapter, you should be able to

- Access and leave the system (Chapter 1, "Touring the System's Features")
- Execute basic shell commands (Chapter 1)
- Create a file using the **cat** command (Chapter 1)

OBJECTIVES

After completing this chapter, you will be able to use **vi** to

- Create and access files
- Modify files
- Select particular words or lines in a file

2.1   CREATING A PRACTICE FILE

Files are central to the UNIX computing environment. Letters, code, programs, output, and even utilities are files. The visual editor can be used to create new files as well as edit existing files. It is easiest to learn to use **vi** by starting with an existing file.

1. Log on to your UNIX account.

2. One of the many ways to create a file on UNIX is with the **cat** utility. Create a new file by typing

cat > *practice*

3. Type in the following lines. Don't worry about mistakes. In later exercises, you will use the visual editor to move around the file and correct spelling errors.

This practice file will be used
several times in this book.
Although I am creating this file with the cat command,
I will be editing it with the visual editor.
a b c d
1 2 3 4 5
1 2 3 4 5
A B C D E F G H
(This is not making too much sense.)
Hello, I will be sure add several more
lines of text before quiting:

4. Tell the **cat** utility that you are through entering text by pressing Ctrl-d . A shell prompt reappears.

You just used the command **cat** > *filename* to create a new file. The filename you assign to a file (like *first_file* or *practice*) becomes the identification label used by UNIX to locate the file when you want to work on it. Even though a file is created with one utility, it can still be identified by its name and accessed by other utilities.

2.2 EXAMINING AN EXISTING FILE WITH THE VISUAL EDITOR

You can access the existing file *practice* with the **visual** editor. Type the command:

vi *practice*

and press Return .

The cursor appears on the first line of the file. You are no longer in the shell, but in the *command mode* of the visual editor. At this point you can issue commands to move the cursor through the file.

Using Direction Keys to Move Around in a File

Often when editing a file, the task is to correct the spelling of a word, remove specific lines of text, or insert additional code at different places in the file. You must inform **vi** exactly where you want to add text, or which specific character, word, or line you want to change. The screen cursor is central to communicating with **vi** and must be moved to the appropriate location.

Moving One Character or Line at a Time

One way to move the cursor through a file is with the *directional keys*. On some terminals, these are the arrow keys:

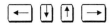

On other terminals you will use the **h, j, k,** and **l** keys, as shown in Figure 2-1.

1. With the *practice* file displayed, press the down arrow ⟨↓⟩ key or type **j** several times. The cursor moves down one line each time you press the down directional key. If the cursor does not move, press the key marked ⟨Esc⟩ and then try again.

2. Try each of the four arrow keys and the other directional keys. Move the cursor up, down, right,

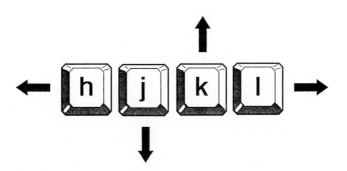

FIGURE 2-1. Directional keys

and left through the text. Blank spaces, whether between words or accidentally placed at the end of a line, are characters.

3. Attempt to move the cursor beyond the text — to the right and left, above the first line, and below the last line. Note that you cannot go beyond the existing text.

Augmenting the Directional Keys

The number keys (**1** through **9**) can be used as part of the directional key commands.

1. To have the cursor move four spaces down, type

4

and then press ⬇ or type

j

Preceding a directional key command with a number moves the cursor that number of lines or characters.

2. Move around the screen by typing commands such as:

2 ⬆
4 ➡
3 ⬇
4 ⬅

3. Many terminals will repeat a function if you press down a key and hold it. Hold a directional key down to see how it works on your terminal.

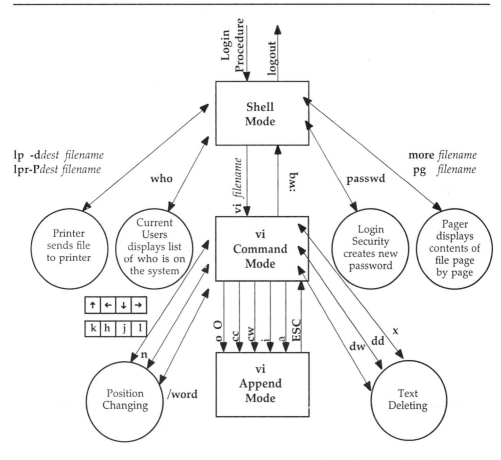

FIGURE 2-2. Conceptual map of editing with **vi**

EXAMINING THE EDITING PROCEDURE 2.3

Figure 2-2 is a conceptual map of editing with **vi**. Locate the box marked "Shell Mode." Find the arrow leading down from the shell, labelled "**vi** *filename*." In this case, *"filename"* is the file *practice*. According to the conceptual map, if you are in the shell mode and enter the command **vi** *filename,* you will move into another mode, the **vi** command mode. From the command mode you can move around and examine the file.

The command **vi** *filename* is a *one-way command* that moves you from the shell to the **vi** command mode and leaves you there. The shell is no longer interpreting the commands you enter, but the visual editor is. It is only from **vi** command mode that you can begin editing a file.

When you press the directional keys, the editor moves the cursor and then waits for your next command. You can enter one cursor movement command after another without ever leaving the command mode.

Find the directional key commands in Figure 2-2. The double-headed arrows indicate that the commands are *two-way commands.* These commands do not move you into another mode and do not require the use of the [Return] key. When the commands are issued they take effect immediately.

In summary, the cursor can be moved around the screen if you are in the command mode. The **h, j, k,** and **l** keys on all terminals, and the arrow keys on most terminals , are used to move the cursor a space or line at a time around the contents of a file. Each directional key can be augmented by entering a number key before it. The editor remains in the command mode when cursor movement commands are entered.

Ending an Editing Session

You must inform the editor when you want to leave and return to the shell. On the conceptual map

(Figure 2-2), locate the command that moves you from **vi** command mode back to the shell.

1. Leave the editor and return to the shell by typing

   :wq

   This instructs the editor to write the file and quit the editor.

Recovery from a Misspelled Filename

People often incorrectly type the name of an existing file. When this occurs, UNIX automatically begins the process of starting a new file. The editor provides a way of overcoming this difficulty. For instance:

1. Type the following command with its filename misspelled:

   vi *praztice*

   The editor searches for a file named *praztice*. Unable to find a file with that name, the editor starts to create a new file, using the misspelled filename.

2. You can get the correct file (*practice*) for **edit**ing, and throw away anything you have done in the misspelled file (*praztice*) by typing

   :edit! *practice*

   and pressing ⌐Return⌐.
       This abandons the misspelled file and starts **edit**ing the file named in the **:edit!** command.

2.4   MOVING TO SPECIFIED TEXT

Thus far, you have been moving around the file using arrow keys. An easier way to move the cursor to a specific word in the text is with the forward search command. In the file *practice*, you can quickly move the cursor to a selected location, such as the word "be."

1. From the command mode, type

   /be

   and press ⎡Return⎤. As you type the slash character (/), and the target word *be*, each character typed appears in the lower left corner of the screen. The text is *not* entered into your file. The editor is displaying your forward search command on the terminal so you can see what you are typing.

2. After you press the ⎡Return⎤ key, the cursor moves to the specified word (*be*) in the text. If it does not, press ⎡Esc⎤ and try again.

3. Use the forward search command to locate another word such as *text*.

   When you type (from command mode) */word* and ⎡Return⎤, the cursor moves to the next occurrence of *word* in the text. The forward search command only works if you are in the **vi** command mode. It is a two-way command. You do not leave the command mode.

Finding Other Instances of the Target

If the word "several" appears more than once in your file, the forward search command locates only the first appearance of the word after the cursor.

1. To locate the **n**ext occurrence of the word "several," type

   n

2. Keep typing **n**ext. When the editor reaches the end of the file, it loops back to the beginning of the file and continues the search. The **n** command is a two-way command; you do not leave the command mode.

Locating Characters, Not Words

The forward search command finds the string of characters that you specify. It can be used to locate characters other than single words. For instance, the /*the* command will locate words like this:

the
theatre
mother

You can also use the power of the forward search command to locate a string of several words. For instance:

1. Select and locate two words such as

   /*several times*

2. Locate some other strings in the file using the forward search feature of the editor.

2.5   MOVING THE CURSOR WORD BY WORD

So far, you have used the **h, j, k,** and **l** keys or the arrow keys to move the cursor one character or line at a time. The forward (/) search command moves the cursor to any specified word. The cursor can also be moved in word increments.

Moving Forward and Backward One Word at a Time

1. In the file *practice,* use the forward search (/) feature to position the cursor on any word in one of the first few lines of text.

2. Type the following lowercase command:

   w

   The cursor advances to the next word on the line.

3. Type the **w** command several more times. The **w** command advances the cursor forward to the *beginning* of the next word.

   In addition to moving forward to the beginning of the next word, the visual editor can move the cursor to the end of a word and backward to previous words.

4. Enter each of the following commands and observe their actions:

b

e

w

5. The word commands can be augmented to move through several words at a time. Type each of the following:

*3***b**

*2***e**

*3***w**

*4***b**

In summary, the **w** moves the cursor forward to the beginning of the next word. The **e** command moves the cursor forward to the next end of a word. The **b** command moves the cursor backward through your text one word at a time. All three commands can be prefaced with a number to move several words at a time. Figure 2-3 summarizes these commands.

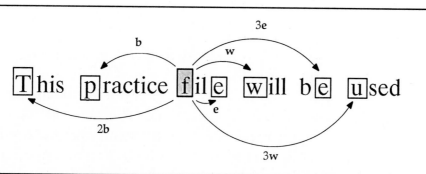

FIGURE 2-3.   Moving by Words

2.6   DELETING TEXT ELEMENTS FROM COMMAND MODE

Another important class of editing operation is removing text from a file. With the visual editor you can remove one or more lines, words, or characters. The next several steps will delete portions of your file. After using these procedures to explore the delete capabilities of the editor, you will leave the editor *without* writing the changes, so these deletions will not be permanent.

Removing Whole Lines from a File

One or more lines in a file can easily be deleted with the editor.

1. Move to the first line of text in your file, *practice*. Place the cursor on any character in that line and type

   dd

   You do not need to press the ⟨Return⟩ key. As soon as you type the second **d**, **vi** does what is requested: the line is removed.
      Blank lines, as well as text lines, can be removed with the **dd** command. The **dd** command is a two-way command. You enter it from the command mode, and after it does its work, you are still in the command mode.

Like the directional keys, the **dd** command can be prefaced with a number command to delete more than one line at a time.

2. Issue this **vi** command:

2**dd**

The cursor line and the one following it are deleted. Typing 3**dd** will delete three lines, beginning with the line where the cursor is located. If # is a number, typing #**dd** will delete # lines.

3. Go to the last line in your file and type the command

3**dd**

Nothing was deleted, because you asked **vi** to delete more lines than were available to delete.

Deleting the Remainder of a Line

The visual editor does not limit you to deletion of a whole line.

1. Move the cursor to the middle of a long line and enter the following:

D

2. Note that the remainder of the line is Deleted.

Deleting Words from a File

In addition to deleting lines from a file, the editor lets you delete specific words.

1. Move the cursor to the first letter of a word, and type the following **vi** commands:

   dw
   3 **dw**

   The **dw** command deletes words.

2. Place the cursor in the middle of a long word and type the **dw** command. The editor removes all characters from the cursor to *and including* the next space. To remove the whole word, place the cursor on the first letter.

3. Position the cursor on the beginning of one of the last three words near the end of a line of text. Type the **vi** command:

   4**dw**

   The editor accepts arguments that affect text on more than one line, unless there is a space at the end of the line.

4. Place the cursor on the (character. Request deletion of two words with

   2**dw**

   Note that the (is treated as a word and is deleted. The same is true for other characters that are not numbers or letters (non-alphanumeric).

Deleting Individual Characters

Specific single characters can also be deleted from a file.

1. Move your cursor to any character, such as the *H* in the word "Hello."

2. Delete the character under the cursor with this lowercase command:

x

The **x** (x-out) command deletes only the single character under the cursor. It is the delete-one-character-at-a-time command.

3. The command *6x* will do what you expect. Select a word with the forward search command and enter

6x

Spaces between words on a line are characters just like letters or numbers. Thus, the **x** can be used to delete unwanted spaces between words.

Table 2-1 summarizes the commands you have just used.

TABLE 2-1.   Summary of Delete Commands

Object to delete	Command
character	x
word	dw
line	dd
remainder of line	D

Quitting the Editor Without Saving Changes

In this chapter, you have been making quite a scramble of your *practice* file. It is possible to quit this editing session, return to the shell, and have the *practice* file remain as it was when you called up the file at the beginning of this section.

1. From the command mode of the visual editor, type

   :q!

   This command does not include a write, just a quit. It says: "Quit the editor program, but don't write the changes I have been making."

   Note that you are now back in the shell.

Exercise 2-A

Examine the conceptual map in Figure 2-2 and then answer the following questions before continuing with this chapter.

1. What command allows you to move the cursor one word to the left?

   _____

2. What command takes the cursor to the word "Administration"?

   _____

3. What command deletes one line of text?

_____

4. Where must the cursor be positioned to delete a line of text?

_____

5. What command moves the cursor forward five words of text?

_____

6. What command deletes three words of text?

_____

7. What command do you enter to leave **vi** without saving the changes to the file?

_____

ADDING TEXT RELATIVE TO THE CURSOR   2.7

Thus far you have been moving around in the file, but you have not been adding text. There are several ways to add text, including adding new text to the right of the cursor, opening a line below the cursor, and opening a line above the cursor.

Appending Text to the Right of the Cursor

You have been instructing the editor to move the cursor around the file by issuing specific commands in command mode. To inform the editor that you want to start adding text, you must also enter specific commands.

1. Call up the file *practice* with the visual editor. Type

   vi *practice*

   You are now in the command mode, where the keys have special meaning.

2. Move the cursor to a selected letter on the screen, and delete the letter by typing

   x

   The **x** tells the editor to delete one character when you are in the **vi** command mode.

3. Move the cursor to the end of the first line in the file.

4. Type the following command one time:

   a

   The **a** does not appear on the screen. Nothing appears to have happened. However, just as the **x** command instructs **vi** to delete one character, the **a** command tells **vi** to start adding everything you type to the file. You are no longer in command mode.

5. Type an *x*. Because you are no longer in command mode, *x* is not treated as a command. Instead of deleting a character, the *x* is simply a letter that appears on the screen and is added to the file.

Examine the conceptual map in Figure 2-2. Note that the **a** command takes you out of command mode and puts you into *append* or *insert* mode.

6. Type the following text:

I am now adding more text.
Therefore I must be in the append mode.
The a command moves me into the append mode,
and starts adding text to the right of the cursor.

Leaving Append Mode and Returning to Command Mode

In the last exercise you opened a file with the visual editor, moved the cursor around with specific commands, and then entered the **a** command. The **a** told the editor to leave **vi**'s command mode and enter append mode. You then added text. Remember that even though you might be finished entering text, anything you type in append mode will not return you to command mode; it just continues to be appended to the text. You need a way to instruct the **vi** editor to move you out of append mode and back into command mode.

1. Again examine Figure 2-2. Find the command that appears on the arrow that moves you from append mode back to command mode: it is the ⌈Esc⌉ key.

2. Press the Esc key now. Nothing appears to be different on the screen. However, try typing the x again. A character is deleted; x is now a command. You are again in command mode. By pressing the Esc key you moved out of append mode and back to the command mode.

3. To confirm, press the Esc key a second time. If a beep sounds, or the screen flashes, **vi** is telling you that you are already in command mode.

Inserting Text to the Left of the Cursor

The **a** command adds text *to the right of the cursor.* Another command is used to insert text *to the left of the cursor.* In command mode, move the cursor to the beginning of a line on the screen.

1. Type the insert command:

   i

2. Then type the following text:

   The difference between the
   i and a commands does not seem to be very
   obvious.

   Note how the existing text moves down. The **i**nsert command is particularly useful when adding text at the beginning of a line.

3. Add some additional text, and return to the command mode by pressing the [Esc] key. You must always return to command mode to issue cursor movement commands.

In Summary, the **i** command moves you from command mode to append mode. Every character you type after the **i** command is entered as text in your file, starting with the space to the *left* of the cursor.

Using Escape to Determine Your Present Mode

The [Esc] key is an essential component of the visual editor. Whenever you are in doubt about where you are in **vi**—command or append mode—press the [Esc] key. In the append mode, [Esc] moves you to the command mode. In the command mode, [Esc] produces a beep or flash indicating you are already in command mode. In either case, after you press [Esc] you are certain to be in command mode. From this point, you can decide what you want to do.

Comparing the a and i Commands

Both the **a** and **i** commands add text at the cursor. The following exercise demonstrates the difference.

1. Place the cursor in the middle of a long word. Note where the cursor is located (its "original location").

2. Now, type the *right of cursor* append command:

   a

   and add the following text:

   xx

3. Press ⌈Esc⌉ and use the arrow keys to return the cursor to its original location.

4. Type the *left of cursor* insert command:

   i

   Add the text:

   yy

5. Try both commands with the cursor in a variety of locations, such as beginning, middle, and end of a word, and of a line.

Opening a Line Below the Cursor

It is also possible to add text between two already existing lines.

1. Move the cursor to any location on a line in the middle of your screen.

2. Type the **o**pen command (lowercase):

   o

3. Add text such as this:

*There certainly are a lot of ways to move from
the command mode to append!
Each one starts adding text in a different place
with respect to the cursor.*

4. Return to the command mode by pressing the [Esc] key.

   The **o** command opens space for a new line below the cursor line, and before the next line in your file.

Opening a Line Above the Cursor

In addition to opening lines below the cursor, you can also open new lines above the cursor.

1. Move the cursor to a line in any location.

2. Open a line above this line with the **O**pen command (uppercase):

   O

3. Now add some text such as this:

   *It is probably useful to be able to place text above
   a line.
   Especially when I want to enter text before the first
   line in a file.*

4. Because you are now in the append mode, the way back to command mode is the usual. Return to the command mode by pressing the [Esc] key.

5. Move to the top of your file, and enter text above the first line. As with the other append commands, you can continue typing as many lines as you wish; you are not limited to that one line.

6. To make sure you are in **vi** command mode, press the Esc key. Then save the file as it is now written and return to the shell, by typing the command

   :wq

Summarizing Append Commands

You have now added (or appended) text on all four sides of the cursor. These commands are summarized in Figure 2-4. Remember:

i   inserts to the left
a   appends to the right
O   opens a line above
o   opens a line below

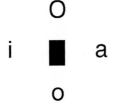

FIGURE 2-4.   Basic append commands

Inserting Text at the Beginning of a Line

1. Move the cursor to the middle of any line of text in your file and type the uppercase command:

I

The cursor moves to the beginning of the line. You are now in append mode, and anything you type is Inserted before the first character of the line.

2. Add some text such as this:

This is a useful new command.

3. Press the Esc key to leave the append mode and return to command mode.

The **I** command moves the cursor to the beginning of the line, and changes the editor to append mode. Every character you type is Inserted as additional text until Esc is pressed.

Appending Text at the End of a Line

Adding text to the end of a line can be accomplished with the cursor initially located anywhere on the line.

1. In command mode, move the cursor to the middle of a text line and type the uppercase command:

A

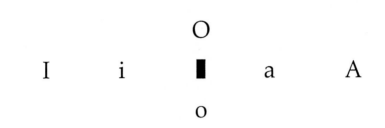

FIGURE 2-5.   Append commands summary

This command moves the cursor to the end of the line, and changes the editor to append mode.

2. Add some text such as the following, and return to command mode:

Adding text to the end of a line is a useful feature.

and press Esc .

All append commands move you into append mode until Esc is entered. The various append commands differ only in where they position the cursor before you begin to add new text. Figure 2-5 illustrates where each command instructs the editor to add text to a line in your file.

Moving Backward in the Append Mode

Whenever you are in append mode, you can press almost any key, resulting in that character being placed in your file and displayed on your screen.

A few keys have special powers. For example, keys you have already used that are not entered as text but instead cause an action to take place are $\boxed{\text{Esc}}$, which moves you from append to command mode, and $\boxed{\text{Backspace}}$, which moves the cursor back one space.

At times, the $\boxed{\text{Backspace}}$ key does not work properly. If you are on a terminal that does not respond properly when you press the $\boxed{\text{Backspace}}$ key, you can often use $\boxed{\text{Ctrl-h}}$. Try it:

1. Make certain that you are in the append mode.

2. Back up one space by pressing $\boxed{\text{Ctrl-h}}$.

   In the command mode of the editor, moving back one word at a time is accomplished with **b**. In append mode you can move back a word at a time without changing to the command mode, using $\boxed{\text{Ctrl-w}}$.

3. Enter the append mode, add a few words, and then press $\boxed{\text{Ctrl-w}}$. The $\boxed{\text{Ctrl-w}}$ key moves the cursor back through newly added text one word at a time.

4. Add more text. The new text replaces, or overwrites, what was there. For those of us who have trouble making up our minds, this is handy.

CREATING A NEW FILE WITH THE VISUAL EDITOR   2.8

Thus far you have been moving the cursor around, deleting text, and adding text to an existing file. The visual editor also creates new files.

1. Begin the process of creating a new file by typing

   vi *journal*

   The screen clears, a column of tildes lines up on the left of the screen, and you are placed in the command mode of the visual editor. There is no text to move around in. A clean slate awaits your wisdom.

2. Go into append mode, and add a few lines of text. Type

   a

   and then type your text.

3. Return to command mode, move around with arrows, and delete a word or two. Note that the editor acts the same whether you are creating a new file or editing an old one.

   The command to create a new file is exactly the same command you enter to edit an existing file: **vi** *filename,* where you supply *filename.* One of two things happens when you enter the **vi** *filename* command:

   - If the *filename* you type after **vi** is an already existing file, **vi** accesses that file for you to edit.

   - If the *filename* you select does not exist, a new file is created with that *filename.*

4. Write the file, leave the editor, and return to the shell with the usual command:

   :wq

SUMMARIZING MODE CHANGES — 2.9

Reexamine Figure 2-2. When you want to edit a file from the shell mode, with the shell prompt on your screen, you type **vi** *filename* and press Return.

This calls up the **vi** program to work on the file *filename*. You are placed in **vi**'s command mode. In the command mode, you can move around the file using the directional keys or the forward search command (*/word*). You can also use two-way commands like **x** to delete single characters.

To add text to the file, you must leave the command mode and go into the append mode. For this, you can use commands such as **a**, **i**, **o**, or **O**. Once you enter one of these commands, you are in the append mode. Whatever you type is added to the file until you press Esc to return to the command mode.

UNDOING AND REPEATING EDITING COMMANDS — 2.10

Two powerful features of the editor are its *undo* and *repeat* functions. What they do is determined by what command was last entered.

Undoing the Last Command

Mistakes happen. Lines are accidentally deleted; text is added that is no improvement. An essential tool for humans is the undo command, which undoes (rescinds) the most recent text-changing command.

1. Place your cursor on the first line in the file. Type

   8dd

2. Move the cursor to another line in the text.

3. Type the **undo** command:

   u

   The eight deleted lines return. The **undo** command affects only the previous text-changing command. You can only issue the **undo** command from the command mode of the visual editor.

4. Type **u** again. Because **u** undoes the preceding command, typing **u** a second time rescinds the undo. The eight lines disappear.

   The **u** command can undo only the most recent append or delete command. However, you can move the cursor without affecting the **u** command.

Undoing All Editing Changes on a Line

There is a second Undo command that undoes any number of changes that you made to the one line where the cursor is located, providing you have not moved the cursor off the line.

1. Select a line of your text and delete one word from the line.

2. Change the spelling of another word *in that same line.*

3. Without moving the cursor out of the line, type the uppercase command:

   U

   The removed word reappears, and the altered word returns to its original state.

4. Go through the same procedure again, but this time, after you make the two changes, move the cursor to another line before entering the **U** command.

5. When the **U** command fails, enter the lowercase command:

   u

   Only the last change can be undone this way, and only with the lowercase **u** command.

The undo commands are summarized in Table 2-2.

TABLE 2-2.   The Undo Command Summary

Command	Function
u	(Lowercase) undo the effect of the last command given
U	(Uppercase) Undo the effect of all changes made to the line, providing cursor has not been moved from the line

Repeating the Last Text-Changing Command

Frequently, an editing change has to be made to several locations in a file. For instance, assume you need to add the text "This is an addition" to the end of several lines.

1. Select a line in the file, move the cursor to any location in the line, and enter the command

   A

   The cursor moves to the end of the line; you are in append mode.

2. Enter this text:

   This is an addition

3. Press the [Esc] key to return to command mode.

4. Without making any other text changes, move the cursor to another line and type a period (.). Yes, just a single period. The last text-changing command is repeated; the addition is made to this line.

5. Make the same change to another line.

6. Delete a word, move the cursor to another word, type a period, and delete the second word.

   The period is the visual editor's "Play it Again, Sam" command. It instructs the editor to repeat whatever text-changing command was just accomplished.

DETERMINING WHEN THE EDITOR WRITES THE FILE

2.11

When you begin editing a file, the editor creates a *buffer* or workspace for editing. When you are finished and type **:wq**, you instruct the editor to **w**rite the file and **q**uit the editor.

Saving Both Copies of a File

Earlier in this chapter you quit the editor without writing the changes into a file, using the **:q!** command. In some cases, you may decide that you want to save both the original file and its new modified version.

1. Access the file *practice* and make a few changes to it.

2. To save a copy of the modified version of *practice*, type the following from the **vi** command mode:

:w *newfilename*

where *newfilename* is any name you want.

A message similar to the following will appear on your screen at the bottom of your file:

```
newfilename [New file] 18 lines, 15. characters
```

You instructed the editor to open and write the file and give it the name *newfilename*.

3. The next task is to protect the original version from being written over. The regular **write quit** (**:wq**) command would write the new version over the old. Your objective is to quit the **vi** editor *without* saving the changes to your file. So, enter

   :q!

4. Type the **ls** command to look at the latest listing of your files. You have accomplished your goal. Your directory now contains a copy of your original file *practice,* in addition to the modified copy listed under the new filename you chose.

Exercise 2-B

1. What command do you enter to add text to the right of the cursor?

   _____

2. How can you make sure that you are in **vi** command mode?

   _____

3. In what mode must you be to use the cursor movement directional keys?

   _____

4. What command must you enter to add text to the beginning of the line the cursor is on?

   _____

5. Suppose you are editing the file *view* with the visual editor. You have made a series of changes, but have not written the file. You decide that it would be best to keep the original version and keep the modified version in a file called *room*. What commands should you enter?

_____

6. What command do you enter to undo the effect of the last command that changed text?

_____

7. What command repeats the last text-changing command?

_____

MAKING SUBSTITUTIONS IN A FILE   2.12

The **vi** commands **dd, dw,** and **x** allow you to selectively delete lines, words, and characters. The **a, A, o, O, i,** and **I** commands add new text. However, at times what is needed is the *replacement* of text with new text.

Replacing One Character

The visual editor permits you to remove one character and replace it with another single character.

1. Enter the **vi** command mode by typing the following:

   vi *practice*

2. Move the cursor to any word you want by using the search forward command:

   /word

3. Replace the first letter of this word by typing the command

   r

   Follow the **r** with any replacement character.

4. As another example, place the cursor at the first *o* in the word "too." Type the **r** command, followed by the letter *w*. The *o* in the word "too" is replaced by a *w*. The word "too" becomes "two."

The command **r** replaces the character located under the cursor with the very next character that you type.

Breaking Up a Long Line

One important use of the replace command is to break one long line into two lines. If a line is too long, what is needed is for a Return to be placed in the middle, making it two lines.

1. Move the cursor to the space between two words in a long line.

2. Type the replace command (**r**) and then press the Return key. You are replacing the space character between the two words with a Return. As a result, the second part of the long line moves to a new line. This works because when you press the Return key, it enters a special character that indicates a new line.

   The **r** command is a two-way text-changing command. You are left in the command mode.

Joining Two Lines of Text

There are also times when you want to join two lines together.

1. Select two short lines in your file and position the cursor anywhere on the first line.

2. Type an uppercase **J**. The **J** command **J**oins the two lines into one.

Substituting Text for a Single Letter

You have learned how the **r** command **r**eplaces a single character with one other character. Often an author or programmer needs to remove one character and then substitute several characters for it.

1. With the cursor positioned over the first letter in a word, type the lowercase command:

s

The dollar sign ($) appears on the character. This dollar sign represents the character that is being replaced.

2. Add text such as this:

Is it true that I am now in the append mode?
I must be, text that I am entering
is going onto the screen,
and I expect into the file.

3. Signal that you are finished entering text by pressing the ⌈Esc⌉ key.

4. Select another place in the text and replace one character with another using the **r** command.

5. Likewise, select another letter and substitute a sentence for it using the **s** command.

Unlike the **r** command, the **s** command must be followed by ⌈Esc⌉ when you are finished entering text.

Both the **r** and **s** commands add text in place of a single character in your file. The **r** command replaces one character with a single new character. The **r** command makes the substitution and returns you automatically to the command mode. Because **r** is a two-way command, you are not left in append and you do not use the ⌈Esc⌉ key.

In contrast, the **s** command substitutes the character under the cursor with as much text as you enter until you press the ⌈Esc⌉ key. The **s** command allows you to substitute as many characters as you wish for the one removed character. You move from command mode to append mode and stay there until you use the Esc key to return to command mode. The **s** is a one-way command.

Substituting for a Word

It is also possible to change one word in your text into a multitude of other words.

1. Using the */word* command, place your cursor on any word and type the change word command:

   cw

   The dollar sign ($) appears at the end of the word, indicating the end of the text that is being replaced.

2. Add text such as this:

   XXX This is text entered
   after a cw command XXX

3. When you have finished, leave the append mode by pressing Esc.

   Typing the **cw** command removes one word and moves you into the append mode; everything you type is entered as text until you press the Esc key.

Substituting for Lines

The **s** and **cw** commands allow you to substitute text for a single character and for specific words, respectively. You can also substitute entire lines in your file.

1. Place the cursor anywhere on a line.

2. To substitute new text for the line, type the following command (in lowercase):

   cc

3. Add text such as this:

   And this is a new line of text!
   Well, actually two, taking the place of one.

   With the change line (**cc**) command, whatever you type is entered into the file in place of one line. You are not limited to entering only one line, but can append any number of lines at this point. The **cc** command deletes the line of text and moves you from command mode to append mode. You remain in append mode, adding lines of text, until you press Esc .

Exchanging the Remainder of a Line for New Text

1. Move the cursor to the middle of a line of text.

2. Type the following command (in uppercase):

   C

3. Add some text to replace the remainder of the line.

   The **C** command puts you in append mode and lets you **C**hange the part of a line from the cursor position to the end of the line. The characters from the left margin up to, but not including the cursor remain unchanged. Whatever text is typed (until [Esc] is used) is substituted for the remainder of the line.

Table 2-3 compares the two commands.

4. After you have explored the delete and substitution commands, write the file and return to the shell with

   :wq

COMPARING THE SHELL WITH APPEND AND COMMAND MODES 2.13

You have been issuing commands to the shell, and to the visual editor, both in command mode and in append mode. Each interprets your commands in a different way.

1. From the shell, enter the following three letters:

   who

TABLE 2-3.   Summary of Delete and Substitute Commands

	Character	Word	Line	Remainder of line
Delete	x	dw	dd	D
Substitute	s	cw	cc	C

A listing of current users logged on appears on your screen. To the shell, the three characters **w h o** are interpreted to mean, "Execute the utility named **who**." The utility determines who is logged on and formats a report that is output, in this case, to your screen.

2. Leave the shell, and call up the editor to work on the file *practice* that you have been using in this chapter:

vi *practice*

You are now in the command mode of the visual editor, editing a file.

3. Place the cursor at the beginning of a word in the text, and enter the following three characters:

w
h
o

The characters **w h o** have a very different meaning to the visual editor command mode:

- The **w** is interpreted to mean move to the right one word.

- The **h** tells the editor to move the cursor back one space.

- The **o** is the command for opening a line below the current line.

You are now in the append mode of the editor.

4. To complete the comparison, enter the same three characters again. The effect of entering **w h o** when

you are in the append mode is that three letters are added to the file.

The distinction between the two modes within the **vi** editor is a critical one. Whenever you leave the shell and enter the **vi** editor you always enter the command mode. A set of specific commands are understood and acted upon by **vi** in this mode. These result in moving the cursor, deleting text, or shifting into append mode.

When an append command is given (such as **a** or **cw**), the editor is programmed to start treating every character you type as input to the file. You are moved out of command mode and into append mode. Once in append mode, virtually every character you type is put in the file as text and is displayed on the screen. You remain in append mode until you press the Esc key.

Pressing the Esc key is necessary to return to the command mode, regardless of which command you used to enter the append mode. The Esc key is always the way back to command mode.

A common error is to try to move the cursor while you are in append mode instead of command mode. If you do this, a series of weird characters (^K ^K ^L ^L ^H ^H or ^[A ^[B ^[D ^[D) appear on the screen. The ^K or ^[A type characters are the *control characters* associated with the arrow keys. Because you are in append mode, the visual editor is happily adding the characters you type to your file. In this case, the added characters are the control characters. Should this happen, you need to press Esc and use the **x** command to delete the unwanted characters.

2.14   USING ADDITIONAL CURSOR MOVEMENT COMMANDS

The commands in the remainder of this chapter are presented according to the two kinds of functions they perform.

- **Cursor positioning commands**   These commands move the cursor to a particular designated position in your file.

- **Display adjusting commands**   These commands move the screen display forward or backward in the file relative to the cursor's current position and display a new section of text.

Using Line Numbers When Editing

It is often useful to know the line number for each line when you are editing a file. If you do not see line numbers while editing, type the following command, which instructs the editor to provide numbers for the current editing session.

:set number

This displays line numbers on the left side of the screen. They are not part of your file, just of the display.

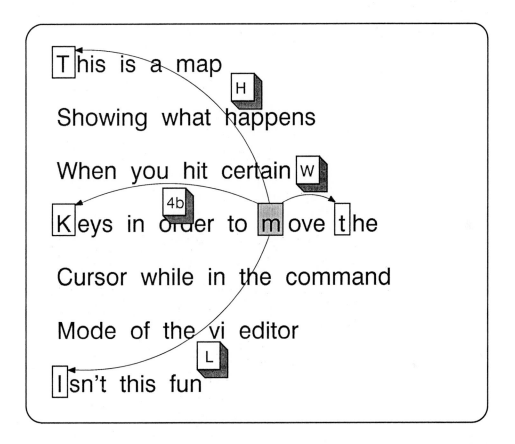

FIGURE 2-6.   Cursor movement

Moving the Cursor Around the Screen

Examine Figure 2-6. The shaded square in the center
is the cursor. To move the cursor to the top left (the *T*
in the word "This"), you type the uppercase command
H. In this figure, the arrow connecting the cursor to

this destination has the **H** key printed next to it. Three other cursor movement commands are depicted: **w**, **4b**, and **L**.

Returning to the Last Cursor Position

Often while editing you need to move to a distant location in the file to check on some specific concern. Once the task is completed, you must return to the original line to continue editing.

1. First, mentally note the line number where the cursor is currently located. Then reposition the cursor to some other line in your file. As an example, move the cursor to line 11 by typing the command

   *11***G**

2. Add a line of text. Now type two single quotation marks:

   ''

   You have entered the secret passage back to your original location. The two single quotation marks return you to your previous location in a file, no matter where it is.

3. Try entering the two-quotation-mark command again. You are moved to the most recent previous location, line 11.

4. Table 2-4 is a listing of new commands used to move the cursor without leaving command mode. Practice each command several times, making sure

TABLE 2-4. New Cursor Positioning Commands

Command	Function
0 (zero)	Moves cursor to the beginning of whatever line it is on.
$	Moves cursor to the end of the line.
42G	Moves cursor to line 42 (or another specified line).
G	Moves cursor to the last line in your file.
-	Positions cursor at the beginning of prior line.
+	Positions cursor at the beginning of next line.
42l	Positions cursor at *column 42* of current line (or another specified column number).
L	Positions cursor at lowest line displayed on the screen.
M	Positions cursor at midpoint on the screen.
H	Positions cursor at highest line on the screen.
f*b*	Moves cursor forward on the line to next *b* (or to another specified character).
?*word*	Moves cursor backward through text to prior instance of *word*.
n	Moves to the next pattern identified in a previously issued /*word* or ?*word*.
''	Returns cursor to the last line moved from.

to note the position of the cursor before and after you perform each command.

Adjusting the Screen's Visual Display of Text

The cursor movement commands you just used relocate the cursor to a new character, word, or line. They are line and text oriented, not display oriented. The commands described in Table 2-5 are used to adjust

TABLE 2-5. Display Adjusting Commands

Command	Function
Ctrl-d	Scrolls the cursor down a block of text in a file.
Ctrl-u	Scrolls the cursor up a block of text in a file.
Ctrl-f	Displays the next screenful of text in a file.
Ctrl-b	Displays the previous screenful of text in a file.
z#.	Displays on the screen only # lines of text. (z4. displays only 4 lines at a time; the number can be 1 to 23.) Type lowercase z, and remember the . (dot) is part of the command.
z.	Redraws screen. (This is similar to the previous command, except that it doesn't change the number of lines displayed.)

the terminal's visual display and move forward or backward to a different block or section of text, regardless of its context.

1. Read through the display adjusting commands in Table 2-5.

2. Try each of them several times.

Augmenting Display Commands

1. If you place a number before the commands Ctrl-d and Ctrl-u , it modifies the amount of text displayed on the screen. For example, type

   10

   and press Ctrl-d to scroll down through ten lines of text. From now on, until you change it to a different value, each Ctrl-d or Ctrl-u will scroll ten lines.

2. The command **z#.** specifies a specific number of lines to display when the screen is drawn. For instance, if you type

z3.

three lines appear on the screen. The dot after the *3* is essential.

You may want to use this command to save time when editing, because the terminal can display a smaller screenful of text more quickly. You might find that reducing the amount of information on the screen helps the eye to focus more easily, and is particularly helpful when locating certain words with the forward search command.

Exercise 2-C

1. What command allows you to replace a character without entering append mode?

   _____

2. What command allows you to change an entire line?

   _____

3. What command allows you to change all text from the cursor to the end of the line?

   _____

4. What command do you enter to see the line numbers of each line?

_____

5. What command moves the cursor back to the beginning of a word?

_____

6. What command moves the cursor to line 23?

_____

7. What command tells **vi** to display only six lines of text?

_____

CONCLUSION

The visual editor is a complex, command-driven screen editor available on essentially all systems. When you call up an existing or new file for editing, you are placed in the command mode. From this interpreter you can issue commands to move around the file and to enter the text addition mode, append. There are usually several ways to accomplish every editing objective. You should select a set of commands that meet your needs. More will be added to your repertoire as you work with the system.

The following pages contain command summaries of all commands examined in this chapter.

COMMAND SUMMARY

Cursor Positioning Commands

(h j k l)

⬅️ ⬇️ ⬆️ ➡️

Move cursor one line up/down or one space right/left.

0 (zero)

Moves cursor to the beginning of whatever line it is on.

$

Moves cursor to the end of the line.

42G

Moves cursor to line 42 (or another specified line).

G

Moves cursor to the last line in your file.

w

Moves cursor forward to the first letter of the next word.

e

Moves cursor forward to the next end of a word.

b

Moves cursor backward to the beginning of a word in your file.

-

Positions cursor at the beginning of prior line.

+

Positions cursor at the beginning of next line.

42l

Positions cursor at column 42 of current line (or another specified number).

COMMAND SUMMARY (*continued*)

L
Positions cursor at lowest line displayed on the screen.

M
Positions cursor at midpoint on the screen.

H
Positions cursor at the highest line on the screen.

f*b*
Moves cursor forward on the line to next *b* (or to another specified character).

F*b*
Moves cursor backward on the line to previous *b* (or to another specified character).

/*word*
Moves cursor forward through text to next instance of *word*.

?*word*
Moves cursor backward through text to prior instance of *word*.

n
Moves to the next pattern identified in a previously issued /*word* or ?*word*.

"
Moves the cursor to the previous location in the file.

Display Adjusting Commands

Ctrl-d
Scrolls the cursor down a block of text in a file.

COMMAND SUMMARY (*continued*)

[Ctrl-u]
Scrolls the cursor up a block of text in a file.

[Ctrl-f]
Displays the next screenful of text in a file.

[Ctrl-b]
Displays the previous screenful of text in a file.

z#.
Displays on the screen only # lines of text. (**z4.** displays only 4 lines at a time; the number can be 1 to 23.) Type lowercase **z**, and remember the . (dot) is part of the command.

z.
Redraws screen. This is similar to the previous command, except that it doesn't change the number of lines displayed.

vi Two-Way Commands
dd
Deletes cursor line of text.

#dd
Deletes # number of lines of text.

dw
Deletes one word from text.

#dw
Deletes # number of words from text.

x
Deletes the one character under the cursor.

COMMAND SUMMARY (*continued*)

#x
Deletes # number of characters from text.

r*c*
Replaces the one character under the cursor with the next character typed

u
Undo. Reverses last text-change action.

vi One-Way Text Changing Commands

a
(Lowercase) Inserts text starting with the space to the right of the cursor.

A
(Uppercase) Starts adding text at the end of the line.

i
(Lowercase) Starts adding text to the left of the cursor.

I
(Uppercase) Inserts text at the beginning of the line.

o
(Lowercase) Opens (or inserts) a line below the cursor.

O
(Uppercase) Opens a line above the cursor.

cw
Changes only the one word under the cursor.

s
(Lowercase) Substitutes for a single character.

COMMAND SUMMARY (*continued*)

S
(Uppercase) Substitutes for an entire line.

cc
(Lowercase) Substitutes for an entire line (same as **S**).

C
(Uppercase) Changes the rest of the line (from the cursor position forward).

Mode-Changing Commands

[Esc]
Escapes from text append mode and returns to **vi** command mode.

:q
Quits work on a file if no changes or additions have been made.

:wq
Writes changes made to a file during that editing session into the memory of UNIX, quits work on the file, and returns to the shell mode.

:q!
Quits work on a file, and returns to the shell mode, but does not write changes made during the editing session.

·3·

Using UNIX Directories

On UNIX, files are collections of information that are stored on the system and can be referred to by name. In the office environment, file cabinets, file drawers, and file drawer dividers let you group together files that pertain to the same topic or issue. Directories serve a similar function in the UNIX environment. In this chapter you will create, use, and remove new directories, called *subdirectories*, within your Home directory and you will access the files within these subdirectories.

The UNIX *file system* or *directory structure* allows you to create files and directories accessed through a hierarchy of directories. This structure facilitates organization of information. For instance, a letter to client Forbes on July 2, 1989, can be a file named *Forbes-7.2.89* listed in a directory named *Correspondence.* Such an arrangement is essential to locating information quickly on the system. The terminal is a small porthole through which you look into your collection of files. If a carefully designed hierarchical system of files is in place, you will be able to access the needed information.

SKILLS CHECK

Before beginning this chapter, you should be able to

- Access and leave the system (Chapter 1, "Touring the System's Features")

- Create, display, and print files (Chapter 1)

- Execute basic shell commands (Chapter 1)

- Use several shell commands in combination (Chapter 1)

- Name, copy, and remove files (Chapter 1)

- Access and modify files using the **vi** editor (Chapter 2, "Basic Editing with the Visual Editor")

OBJECTIVES

Upon completion of this chapter, you will be able to

- Utilize the UNIX directory hierarchy system

- Create and remove directories

- Change directories

- Move files to directories located throughout the file system

EMPLOYING DIRECTORIES TO CREATE ORDER

3.1

Using directories is a fundamental UNIX skill, because nearly everything on the system is a file and all files are accessed through directories. A directory contains a list of the names of files. Until now you have not needed to concern yourself with directories, because everything you have created has been listed in your Home directory.

1. Log on to your account.

2. Your Home directory is your *current directory.* All filenames you enter with commands refer to files available through your current (Home) directory. For example, type the command

   who > *f_name*

   The new file *f_name,* containing a list of current users, is created in your current directory.

3. Ask for a listing of the filenames in your current directory. Type

   ls

   The names of the files you have created appear on the screen. If you have only a few files, this listing is brief. However, if you have many files, this listing will fill up the screen and be difficult to read. By creating directories, you can store similar files together, and have short listings in each one.

4. If there is no file listed named *practice,* create one now, using an editor or the **cat** > *practice* command. Append a few lines of any content to the file.

Figure 3-1 illustrates the relationship between your Home directory and some of the files probably listed in your Home directory. The directory is symbolized by a large D, and the files by rectangles.

It is convenient to think of directories as *holding* files, like file cabinets hold files. This metaphor is commonly used. It is, however, not strictly accurate because directories do not actually contain files. Rather, they contain just a list of the names of files and other information, such as where the electronic file is located in memory. Your Home directory, in fact, is just a file of information about all the files

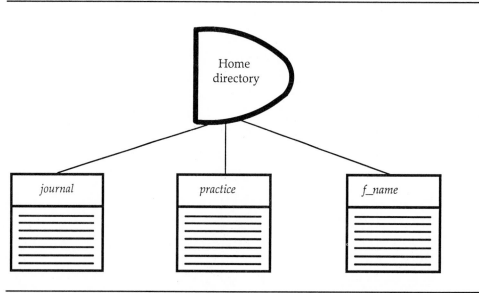

FIGURE 3-1.   The Home directory with three files

you have created "in" your Home directory. The **ls** command reads the names of the files listed in your current directory and then outputs those names.

Creating Directories

You can create new directories. New directories are listed in other directories, such as your Home directory. Each directory (often referred to as a subdirectory) can contain a list of files and other directories.

1. Create a new directory to be listed in your Home directory by typing the command

   mkdir *Projects*

   The command **mkdir** is used to **m**a**k**e a **dir**ectory. Use the name *Projects* for this first subdirectory because that is the name used in the following instructions and figures. You may wish to call future directories names like *Programs, Mail,* or *Memos.* The **mkdir** *Projects* command instructs the shell to make a new directory with the name *Projects,* and to list this new subdirectory in the current directory (your Home directory).

2. Request a display of the names of the files and directories that are listed in your Home directory by typing

   ls

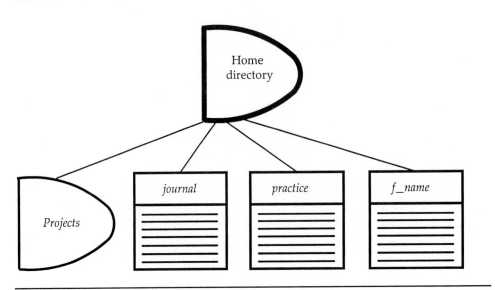

FIGURE 3-2.   The Home directory with a *Projects* subdirectory

The new directory, *Projects,* now exists and is listed in your Home directory.

Figure 3-2 is a depiction of your Home directory. The D associated with your Home directory is bolder than the D associated with the new *Projects* subdirectory, to indicate that your Home directory is still the one you are working in (your current directory).

Changing Directories

You can inform the shell that you want a different directory to be your working (current) directory.

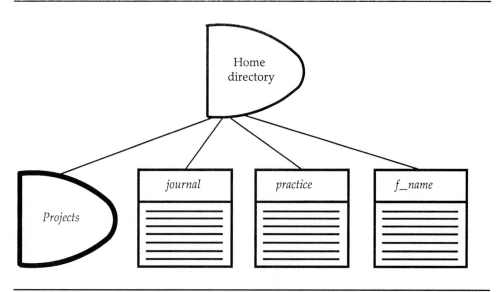

FIGURE 3-3.   The *Projects* directory as current directory

1. Change your current directory to the newly created *Projects* directory by typing

cd *Projects*

The command **cd** can be thought of as change directory or current directory. Figure 3-3 indicates that your current directory is no longer your Home directory; the subdirectory *Projects* is now current.

Examining the Path to Your Current Directory

Another UNIX command displays the *path* to your current directory.

1. Examine the path to your current directory, *Projects*, by typing

   pwd

2. The path is a list of directories separated by the / (slash) character. The last directory listed is *Projects*. The one before it is your Home directory. *Projects* is listed in your Home directory. Your Home directory is listed in some other directory.

The **pwd** command prints the path to your current or working directory from the granddaddy directory called *root*, which is symbolized by the first / in the path. You will explore paths further, later in this chapter.

Listing the Contents of a Subdirectory

The **ls** command lists the names of files in the current directory.

1. List the contents of the directory that is now your current directory (*Projects*). Type the command

   ls

2. Nothing is listed. You have no files in the new *Projects* directory. The files that appeared when you last entered **ls** still exist, but not in this directory. The **ls** command lists only the names of the files "in" your current directory. (You changed your current directory to be the new *Projects* directory by typing the **cd** *Projects* command.)

Creating Files Within a Subdirectory

1. With *Projects* as your current directory, create a new file named *test*. Use either

vi *test*

or

cat > *test*

2. Add a few lines of text to the new file.

3. Create another new file with the name *practice,* and add a line or two of text indicating that you are in a file in a new directory.

4. After you have created the two new files, list the filenames in this *Projects* directory with the usual

ls

The files *practice* and *test* appear, indicating that they are listed in the *Projects* directory.

Figure 3-4 illustrates the relationship between your Home directory and files listed in your Home directory, as well as the *Projects* subdirectory and the files you just created in it.

Returning to Your Home Directory

You used the command **cd** *subdirectory* (in this case **cd** *Projects*) to change your current directory from your Home directory, to the *Projects* directory. If you get lost in the file system, returning to your Home directory is simple.

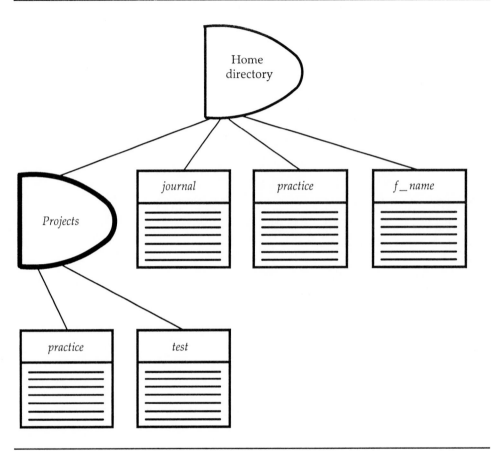

FIGURE 3-4. The Home directory, with the *Projects* subdirectory as the current directory

> **1.** To make your Home directory your current directory, type
>
> **cd**
>
> The **cd** command, when used without any directory name as an argument, changes your current directory back to your Home directory, no matter where in the file system you are currently working.

2. Confirm that your current directory is now your Home directory by typing

   pwd

   The display is the same output as before, except that your Home directory is the last one listed.

3. Get a listing of the names of the files in your current directory with the **ls** command. *Projects* appears, along with your other files, including a file named *practice*. Your Home directory is again your current directory.

4. Examine the contents of the file *practice* with **cat**, **pg**, or **more**:

   cat *practice*

   This file *practice* is not the one you just created in the *Projects* directory. *Files can have identical names if the files are listed in different directories.*

5. Although the names of subdirectories appear in listings of the Home directory, the names of the files listed in the subdirectories do not. These files are not listed in the current directory, and thus do not appear. However, if you request a listing of a directory that is listed in the current directory, the filenames are displayed. Type

   ls *Projects*

   The command **ls** *directory_name* displays the contents of the directory called *directory_name*, providing *directory_name* is listed in the current directory.

Distinguishing Between Files and Directories

In this book, directory names have an uppercase first letter, to distinguish directories from ordinary files. The system provides another way.

1. From the shell, type the command:

   ls -F

   The **ls** command with a **-F** option displays a list of all file and directory names listed in the current directory.

2. Examine the **-F** list. Directory names are listed with a / appended to the end. (If you have filenames displayed with a * at the end, they are executable files and will be discussed in Chapter 7, "Setting File Permissions.")

Moving Files into a Subdirectory

To impose order on the chaos of an untamed Home directory, you can move the listing of files from your Home directory to a subdirectory.

1. Move the listing of *f_name* from the current directory to the *Projects* directory by typing

   mv *f_name Projects*

   The command to move a file from the current directory to a subdirectory is

mv *filename subdirectoryname*

When you issue the **mv** command, the system does not move the electronic file itself. Rather, the listing of information about the file is moved. The new directory now lists the file's name and location information. It is convenient to describe this process of changing where a file is listed as "moving the file."

In the previous command, the file keeps its original name in the new directory listing. The command to move a file listing from the current directory to a new directory *and* change the filename is as follows:

mv *filename   subdirectoryname/newfilename*

2. List the files in your Home directory to see if *f_name* is still there by typing

   ls -F

   Confirm that the file has been "moved."

3. Make *Projects* your current directory by typing

   cd *Projects*

4. List the files in the *Projects* directory by typing

   ls -F

Your files *practice, test,* and *f_name* are listed. The listing for the file *f_name* was moved to your *Projects* directory.

Creating Subdirectories Within Subdirectories

Earlier in this chaper you created the *Projects* directory as a directory listed in your Home directory. You can also create a subdirectory to be listed in the *Projects* directory.

1. Check to see that the *Projects* directory is still your current directory by typing the command

   pwd

2. Create a new subdirectory called *Code* by typing this shell command line:

   mkdir *Code*

3. Leave the *Projects* directory, and change to your new *Code* directory by typing the command

   cd *Code*

4. Make sure the *Code* directory is your current directory, with

   pwd

   This time the output of **pwd** consists of the path to your Home directory, followed by */Projects/Code.* The new subdirectory, *Code,* is listed in the *Projects* directory. The *Projects* directory is listed in your Home directory, and your Home directory is listed in some other directory.

5. Create a file named *report3* in your *Code* directory.

6. List the files in the current directory by entering

ls -F

You now have the file named *report3* listed in the *Code* directory, which is listed in the *Projects* directory, listed in your Home directory. At this point your directory structure should look like the one in Figure 3-5.

Moving Through the File System

1. Change your current directory to your Home directory with

   cd

2. List the files and directories in your Home directory with

   ls -F

   A complete listing of all the files and directories located in your main or Home directory is displayed. The *Code* subdirectory and the file *report3* are not included, because they are not listed in your Home directory. Instead, they are listed in directories that are one or more levels beneath the Home directory.

3. Move through the path to the *Code* directory, and view the *report3* file by typing the following commands:

   cd *Projects*
   cd *Code*
   cat *report3*

   Your current directory is now your *Code* directory.

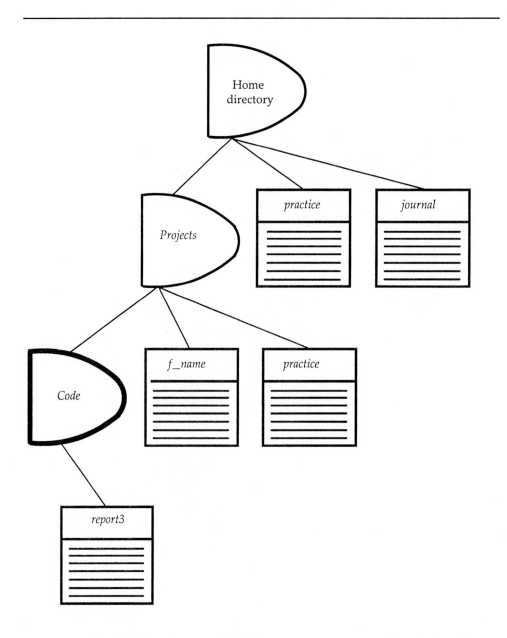

FIGURE 3-5. The Home directory and its two subdirectories, with *Code* as the current directory

Exercise 3-A

1. What is the command to make a directory named *Proposals?*

   _____

2. What command will change your current directory to the *Proposals* directory?

   _____

3. What command will change your current directory back to the Home directory?

   _____

4. What shell command can you enter to identify your current directory?

   _____

5. What list command will distinguish the files from the directories?

   _____

6. Your Home directory is your current directory, and you enter the command line **cd** *Projects.* You then create a file named *confused.* What directory will list the *confused* file?

   _____

7. How is it possible to have two files with the same filename in your account?

   _____

8. Your Home directory is your current directory. What command will move a file named *florence* to a directory named *Proposals,* which is a subdirectory of the Home directory?

_____

3.2   USING PATHNAMES

In the previous section, you moved through the directory system by entering a series of **cd** commands.

cd *Projects*
cd *Code*

You typed a **cd** command for each directory change. The system provides a shortcut that allows you to *directly* change your current (Home) directory to the *Code* directory with only one command.

Using Pathnames to Change Directories

1. Make your Home directory your current directory by typing the command

   cd

2. Examine Figure 3-5 again. Change your current directory from Home to the *Code* directory in a single step by typing the following command (leaving no spaces between the directory names and the / character):

cd*Projects/Code*

3. Check the path to your current directory by typing

pwd

Your current directory is now *Code*. The command **cd** *Projects/Code* is the efficient way to change your current directory to a subdirectory (*Code*) of a subdirectory (*Projects*).

The *Projects/Code* argument is a "list" of directories that describes where a directory or file is listed. *Projects/Code* is a *pathname*. In this case, *Code* is listed in *Projects*, which is listed in your current directory. The path to *Code* is from the Home directory through *Projects* to *Code*.

The system keeps track of your current directory. A single file or directory name refers to a file or directory within the current directory. Pathnames are the mechanism used to inform the system what path to follow to access a file or directory that is *not* listed in the current directory.

Using Pathnames with Utilities

Pathnames can also be used to make shell commands function on files not listed in your current directory.

After the previous procedure, your *Code* directory is your current directory. A few steps back, you created a file in the *Code* directory called *report3*.

1. Change directories to your Home directory by typing

cd

2. Type the command

vi *report3*

This command results in one of two events. The editor begins the process of creating a new file called *report3* in your Home directory. Or, if you already have a *report3* file in the Home directory, the editor will access that file. In either case, however, you do *not* access the *report3* file that is listed in the *Code* directory. Type **:q** to leave the unwanted file and return to the shell.

To get to the desired *report3* file, you must change directories to your *Code* directory and then edit the file. Or, you can use the more efficient pathname.

3. Use the visual editor to edit the *report3* file listed in your *Code* directory. You can do this without changing your current directory from your Home directory. Type

vi *Projects/Code/report3*

By using a pathname to a file, you can have any UNIX utility "reach through" the directory path to work on a file not listed in the current directory.

4. Make changes or additions to *report3,* leave the file, and return to the shell. Your current directory is still your Home directory. Even though you worked on the file listed in a different directory, you did not change your current directory from your Home directory.

Copying Files into Other Directories Using Paths

Pathnames are particularly useful with the **cp** and **mv** commands. You can copy or move files from one directory to another.

1. Make sure your Home directory is your current directory.

2. Type the following command (leave no spaces between the names and the /characters):

   cp *journal Projects/Code/journal2*

   With this command, you tell the shell to

   • Make a copy of the *journal* file listed in your Home directory

   • List the copy in the *Code* directory

   • Give the new copy the name *journal2*

   The general form of the **cp** command is

cp *filename Directory1/Directory2/newfilename*

where *filename* is a file in the current directory; *Directory1* is listed in the current directory; *Directory2* is listed in *Directory1;* and *newfilename* is the new name given to the copy of the file when it is listed in its new home, *Directory2.* You do not need to include the *newfilename.* Omitting the *newfilename* results in the copy having the same name as the original file. The same name is acceptable because the second file is in a different directory.

3. Confirm that *journal* was properly copied and listed in its new home. Change directories from your Home directory to the *Code* directory, and type the command

cd *Projects/Code*

In this case, an electronic copy of the file is made. The new directory listing includes information needed to locate this new copy. Both the original and the copy can be edited independently.

4. Examine the copied file by typing

cat *journal2*

The contents of the file *journal2* appear on the screen.

Listing the Contents of Subdirectories

1. Return to your Home directory by typing

cd

2. From Home, use the pathname to examine the contents of the *Code* directory by typing

ls *Projects/Code*

Any command that takes a filename as an argument will work with pathnames.

Exercise 3-B

1. What command changes your current directory from your Home directory to a directory named *Education,* which is listed in a directory named *Proposals,* which is listed in your Home directory?

   _____

2. From the Home directory what command allows you to edit a file *kirby* that is listed in the *Proposals* directory?

   _____

3. From the Home directory, how can you create a directory *Rejected* listed in the *Proposals* directory?

   _____

4. How could you copy a file *selquist* from the Home directory into the *Education* directory?

   _____

USING DIRECTORY SPECIAL CHARACTERS   3.3

UNIX has several characters that have special meanings in pathnames. Each character stands for a directory.

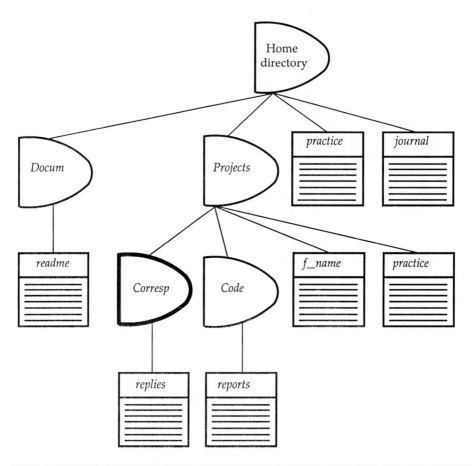

FIGURE 3-6. The completed Home directory structure, with *Corresp* as the current directory

Before exploring these special characters, create two new directories. First, locate the *Docum* directory in Figure 3-6. It is located below your Home directory. It is listed in your Home directory.

1. Make certain you are in your Home directory by typing

cd

2. Create the *Docum* directory by typing the command

mkdir *Docum*

3. Now type the command

ls -F

Your new directory *Docum* is among the files and directories listed.

4. Change to the *Docum* directory by typing

cd *Docum*

5. Create a file named *readme* in the *Docum* directory. Type

vi *readme*

6. Enter a few lines of text and write this new file; then return to the shell. The file *readme* is now listed in the *Docum* directory, which is listed in your Home directory.

Creating a Subdirectory Using a Pathname

1. Move back to your Home directory. Type the command

cd

2. One more directory must be made: the *Corresp* directory listed in the *Projects* directory. From Home, type

mkdir *Projects/Corresp*

3. Change to the *Projects* directory. Type

   cd *Projects*

4. Find the names of the files and directories listed in the current directory, *Projects.* Type the command

   ls -F

   The new directory *Corresp* that you created from your Home directory is listed.

5. Change to the new directory *Corresp* by typing

   cd *Corresp*

6. Create a file named *replies* in the *Corresp* directory, and include a few lines in it. Save the file and return to the shell.

7. Leave the *Corresp* directory and return to your Home directory. Type

   cd

   Your directory hierarchy now matches the structure in Figure 3-6. Look at Figure 3-6 and consider the following statements: You can change to directories located *below* the current directory, and you can change from a subdirectory *back* to your Home directory. However, you have not yet changed *from one subdirectory to another subdirectory* located on a different branch of a directory tree (from *Code* to *Docum,* for example). The special characters introduced in the next section allow changes of this kind. But first,

8. Make sure you are in your Home directory by typing

cd

Then change your directory to *Code* with

cd *Projects/Code*

Explicitly Calling Your Home Directory

One special directory character, the tilde (~), is only available on the C shell. If you are using a Bourne shell, use **$HOME** in the following exercises.

1. Your present working directory is *Code.* Change back to your Home directory by typing

   cd ~

2. Examine your current directory path by typing

   pwd

   Your current directory is now your Home directory. The ~ (tilde) is interpreted to be your Home directory.

Using Dot and Dot-Dot

There are even more efficient ways to move around the file system. The following features are useful when you are unsure of where you are within the directory hierarchy, and also when you want to enter more complicated commands.

1. Obtain a listing of **all** files in your current directory by including the **-a** option with the listing command as follows:

   ls -a

   Your listing looks something like this:

   ```
   .      ..          journal2 report3
   ```

   The files *journal2* and *report3* have appeared before. There are also dots listed.

2. Try the **more** or **page** command to figure out what kind of file the dot is. Type one of the following commands:

   System V:
   page .

   BSD:
   more .

   You receive a message indicating

   ```
   *** .: directory ***
   ```

3. Likewise, examine the dot-dot (..) file by typing

   System V:
   page ..

   BSD:
   more ..

   From the output, the .. file is also a directory.

4. Confirm that your current directory is the *Code* directory. Type

   pwd

5. Change directories to the dot (.) directory by typing the command

   cd .

6. Determine the path to the dot directory by typing

   pwd

   The output of **pwd** says that your current directory is still *Code*. But *Code* was also your current directory before you typed the **cd** command. The single dot (.) is the listing of your current directory. The dot (.) is your current directory, regardless of its name. You can use the dot in paths.

7. Change your current directory to the dot-dot directory by typing

   cd ..

8. Check where you are by typing

   pwd

   You are now in the *Projects* directory. In Figure 3-6, *Projects* is the directory *above* the *Code* directory where you were located. The command **cd ..** has changed your current directory to the *Projects* directory.

   The dot dot (..) is the listing for whatever directory is located *one level above* your current directory, called the *parent* directory. At any directory level (except for the highest directory) you can type **cd ..**

and you will change directories to the next higher (parent) directory.

9. Change directories back to the *Code* directory by typing the command

cd *Code*

In summary, it is possible to change directories in both directions within the file system. The command **cd** *subdirectory* changes directories from a directory to the subdirectory. The directory name must be specified because several directories may be listed in one parent directory. The **cd ..** command changes directories from a subdirectory to a parent directory. The dot-dot symbol can be used because each directory has only one parent directory.

Moving Files into a Parent Directory

1. Move a file from the *Code* directory into the *Projects* directory. Type

mv *report3* ..

Because .. is the parent directory, and the *Projects* directory is the parent of *Code,* you just moved the file *report3* from *Code* into *Projects.*

2. Return to the *Projects* directory by typing

cd ..

3. Confirm that the listing for *report3* was moved into *Projects* by typing

ls -F

Examining the Full Path to Directories

There is one other directory special character, the / (slash) character. The / by itself is also a directory.

1. Change to the / directory. Type

   cd /

2. Find the path to your current directory by typing

   pwd

   The output of **pwd** is

   /

3. The / directory is very special. Attempt to change directories to the parent of the / directory. Type

   cd ..

4. Find out what your current directory is by typing

   pwd

   Your current directory is still the / directory. Unlike any other directory, / is its own parent. The / directory is also called the *root* directory. Every file on the system is listed in the / directory or in one of its subdirectories. The / directory is called *root* because all other directories branch from it.

5. Change directories back to your Home directory by typing

cd

6. Examine the path to your current directory. Type

pwd

The output of **pwd** is a list of directories starting with the / character. This first / character is the / directory. The remaining / characters in the list are there to separate directory names. The output of **pwd** shows the path from the / directory to your current directory, called the *full pathname.*

3.4 SPECIFYING PATH STARTING POINTS

The directory special characters are used in path-names to access distant files or directories.

1. Change directories to the *Code* directory:

cd *Projects/Code*

2. Examine Figure 3-6 carefully and devise the correct command to change your present working directory from the *Code* directory to the *Corresp* directory. You must instruct the shell to follow the path up through the *Projects* directory and then down to the *Corresp* directory. Because *Projects* is the parent of your current directory *Code*, *Projects* is the .. directory.

3. Type the command

cd *../Corresp*

This command instructs the shell to change directories to the parent directory, and then change directories from there to the *Corresp* directory.

4. Your current directory now is the *Corresp* directory. Confirm this by typing

pwd

5. The Home directory can also be used as the starting point in pathnames. Type the command

cd ~*/Docum*

This command instructs the shell to follow a path beginning at your Home directory (~), and then change directories from there to *Docum*. Your current directory is now *Docum*. Regardless of your current working directory, a change-directory command that specifies the starting point of ~ changes your working directory to the specified directory. If you are using the Bourne shell, use **$HOME** instead of the tilde.

6. Confirm that you are in the *Docum* directory. Type

pwd

The output of **pwd** shows the full pathname starting from the root directory to your current directory, *Docum*. Note each directory listed, and the order in which they appear.

7. Make the / directory your current directory. Type

cd /

Your current directory is now the root directory.

8. The full pathname of your *Docum* directory should still be displayed near the top of your screen. Type the following:

cd *full_pathname*

where *full_pathname* is the full pathname of your *Docum* directory.

9. Check what directory you are in by typing

pwd

You are back in the *Docum* directory. Using **cd** with a directory's full pathname moves you into that directory, regardless of your current directory, since the full pathname is from the / directory. Every file on the system has a unique full pathname that can be used to identify the file.

Moving and Copying Files by Specifying Paths

Examine Figure 3-6, and decide how to move the file *readme* from your current directory, *Docum*, to the *Corresp* directory. Using the pathname of *Corresp* will allow you to make such a transfer. Find both *Docum* and *Corresp* directories on Figure 3-6.

1. To move the listing of the file *readme* to the *Corresp* directory, type

mv *readme* ~/Projects/Corresp

2. Confirm that *readme* was relocated into your *Corresp* directory by getting a listing of the *Corresp* directory. Type

   ls *~/Projects/Corresp*

   The *readme* file appears.

3. You can also use full paths to copy files. Change to your Home directory with

   cd

4. Find the full pathname of your Home directory with

   pwd

5. Change to the */tmp* directory. Type

   cd */tmp*

   The */tmp* directory is a temporary directory. All files listed in this directory are temporary and are removed regularly by the system.

6. Create a file named *tellme* by typing

   who > *tellme*

7. Use a full pathname to place a copy of *tellme* in the *Docum* directory. Type the command

   cp *tellme your_home _pathname/Docum*

   where *your_home_pathname* is the full pathname to your Home directory.

8. Confirm that the file *tellme* is in the *Docum* directory. Type

   ls *your_home_pathname/Docum*

The path *your_home_pathname/Docum* is the full pathname of the *Docum* directory. The full pathname of your Home directory is part of the full pathname of all the subdirectories of your Home directory.

Using Utilities by Specifying Paths

1. Change directories to *Docum* using the Home directory shortcut:

   cd *~/Docum*

2. You can also visually edit the file *readme* without moving from your current location in *Docum* by typing

   vi *~/Projects/Corresp/readme*

3. Edit the *readme* file as desired, and return to the shell. While you were editing a file listed in your *Corresp* directory, the *Docum* directory remained your current directory.

4. Change directories to Home, and find its full pathname by typing

   cd ; pwd

   Note the full pathname of your Home directory.

5. Change to the / directory. Type

   cd /

6. Examine the file *tellme* in the *Docum* directory by typing

   cat *your_home_pathname/Docum/tellme*

where *your_home_pathname* is the full pathname to your Home directory. Even though your current directory is /, you can look at a file listed in the *Docum* directory.

7. Move back to Home, and remove the *tellme* file by typing the following commands:

   cd ; rm *Docum/tellme*

Summarizing Pathnames

The file system makes possible three kinds of file and directory access within a directory tree. You can access files, change directories, or execute commands:

- Among directories listed in your current directory or in any subdirectories, through the use of directory names or pathnames, using commands such as

  cd *directory_name*
  cd *directory_name1/directory_name2*
  cat *directory_name/file_name*
  cat *directory_name1/directory_name2/file_name*

- In the parent directory, your Home directory, or the root directory, through the use of the special characters .. and / and ~:

  cd ..
  cd ~
  vi *../file_name*
  ls ~

> cat ~ /file_name
> cd /
> ls /

- Among parallel directories, using a combination of the above two methods in commands such as

> cd ../directory_name
> vi ../directory_name1/directory_name2/file_name
> ls ~/directory_name1/directory_name2
> mv ~/directory_name(s)/file_name /file_name
> cp ~/directory_name(s)/file_name .

There exists no direct way of changing directories between two subdirectories below the same parent directory, except by following the path through the parent directory and then to the subdirectory of interest.

3.5   LOCATING FILES IN THE DIRECTORY STRUCTURE

You have been moving files among subdirectories. To find a file, you have learned how to change to each directory, and see if the file is listed in that directory. If you have many directories, this can become tedious. There are other commands that allow you to easily search through directories.

Searching a Specific Directory

One way to locate a file is to search a specific directory. You can do this with the **ls** command.

1. Make sure you are in your Home directory. Type

   cd

2. As you have seen before, the command **ls** *directory_name* displays the list of filenames in the directory named in *directory_name*. For example, type the following command:

   ls *Projects*

   The command lists the names of files that are in the *Projects* directory—even though your current directory is your Home directory.

3. You can also search more than one directory at a time. Type

   ls *Docum Projects/Corresp*

   The contents of both *Docum* and *Projects/Corresp* are listed.

   By using **ls** *directory_name(s)* you can search each directory you name without changing directories.

Listing the Contents of Every Subdirectory

You can use **ls** to search specific directories. However, if a file is listed in a deep subdirectory, you'll have to enter a lot of commands to search each directory along the way. There is an option to **ls** that searches every subdirectory.

1. Change to your Home directory and type the following command:

ls -R

2. If the list is long, pipe the output through **pg** or **more** like this:

ls -R | pg

Lists of the filenames in your Home directory, and in each of its associated subdirectories, are displayed. For example, by examining the output of the command **ls -R**, you can see that the file *replies* is listed in the directory *Corresp*, which is listed in the directory *Projects*.

The command **ls** with the **-R** option reads the contents of each directory **Recursively**. It searches a directory, and all associated subdirectories. With this command, you can locate files that you know are in a subdirectory, without having to specifically list each subdirectory in the command line.

Using the find Command to Search for Files

You have seen how to locate a file using **ls** with the **-R** option to list the contents of every subdirectory. If the output of **ls -R** is long, however, a file is easily missed—even when the output is piped through **pg** or **more**. The **find** command is another useful, if awkward, tool for searching for a file.

1. Assume you forgot in what directory the file *readme* is listed. You can find *readme* by typing the following command:

find ~ -name *readme* **-print**

2. Now find the file *report3* by typing

find ~ -name *report3* **-print**

This command line translates as follows:

~	Search starting at the Home directory and proceed through all of its subdirectories.
-name *report3*	Search for a file **named** *report3*.
-print	Output the full path to that file.

3. Search for a nonexistent file *reporter3* by typing

find ~ -name *reporter3* **-print**

Nothing appears. The **find** command only displays the files it finds. If a file doesn't exist, **find** displays nothing.

In summary, to use **find** to search for a file, type

find *top_directory_name* **-name** *file_name* **-print**

where *top_directory_name* is the directory where you want to start searching, and *file_name* is the name of the file you want to locate.

3.6 MOVING DIRECTORIES

Just as you can move regular files, you can also move directories.

1. Change directories to your Home directory by typing the command

   cd

2. Move the *Docum* directory so that it is listed in the *Projects* directory. Type

   mv *Docum Projects*

3. Confirm that the *Docum* directory is no longer listed in your Home directory by typing

   ls

4. Check the contents of the *Projects* directory. Type

   ls *Projects*

   The *Docum* directory is listed in *Projects*.

The **mv** command allows you to move directories as well as regular files. To move a directory into another directory, type

mv *directory_name dest_directory_name*

where *directory_name* is the name of the directory that you want to move, and *dest_directory_name* is the name of the directory in which you want to list the first directory.

5. Create a file listed in the *Docum* directory called *indocum*. Type

   vi *Projects/Docum/indocum*

6. Add some text, write the file, and quit **vi**.

7. Move the *Docum* directory so that it is listed in your Home directory, changing the name to *Docs* by typing

   mv *Projects/Docum Docs*

8. Confirm the move by typing

   ls

   The directory *Docs* is now listed in your Home directory.

9. Make sure that the *Docs* directory lists the same files as *Docum* did. Type

   ls *Docs*

   The filename *indocum* is listed. Since *indocum* was listed in the *Docum* directory, this must be the same directory but with a different name.

10. Change the name of the *Docs* directory back to *Docum*. Type

    mv *Docs Docum*

11. Remove the file *indocum* from the *Docum* directory by typing

    rm *Docum/indocum*

In summary, to rename a directory, type

mv *old_dir_name new_dir_name*

where *old_dir_name* is the current name of the directory and *new_dir_name* is the name to be given to the directory. Again, you can use pathnames as part of a directory name.

3.7 REMOVING DIRECTORIES AND FILES

The commands to remove files are very useful. However, they do remove files thoroughly—unless you have a backup copy, there is little chance of recovery. Use the remove commands with care. Also, make sure you are in the appropriate directory for each of these activities.

Removing an Empty Directory

There are two commands you can use to **rem**ove a **di**rectory. The first command removes an empty directory—a directory with no files in it.

1. Move to your Home directory with

   cd

2. List the Home files and directories with

   ls

3. Change to the *Docum* directory by typing

   cd *Docum*

4. Check to see if there are any files in the *Docum* directory by typing

   ls

5. If there are any files in the *Docum* directory, remove or move them.

6. Return to your Home directory with

   cd

7. Remove the directory *Docum* by typing the command

   rmdir *Docum*

8. Confirm that the *Docum* directory is gone by typing

   ls

   The Docum directory has been removed.

   The **rmdir** command removes *empty* directories. The next section discusses another command used to remove directories that are either empty or contain files.

Removing a Directory and Its Files

To remove a directory containing files, you must first locate the directory you want to remove. Use the **cd** command to change to the appropriate directory, or use pathnames to execute commands from your current directory.

1. To remove the directory *Code* from the *Projects* directory, first change to the *Projects* directory. Type

   cd *~/Projects*

2. Double-check that you are in the proper directory and that *Code* is listed by typing

   pwd ; ls

3. Attempt to remove the *Code* directory. Type

   rmdir *Code*

You receive an error message:

```
rmdir: Code not empty
```

or

```
directory not empty
```

The directory cannot be removed with **rmdir** because it still contains files.

4. To remove the directory *and* its files, type

rm -r *Code*

The **-r** option of the command instructs **rm** to recursively remove files. The shell starts with the directory named, and removes everything in the directory—even if that directory contains other directories.

5. Confirm that *Code* has been removed by typing

ls

Not only was the *Code* directory removed, but so were all the files in the directory, *and* any subdirectories you might have created in *Code*.

Caution: The **rm -r** command is very powerful and should be used very carefully. Double-check that the directory you are removing doesn't contain subdirectories that you may need. Move anything you want to keep to another directory before you use the **rm -r** command.

REPEATEDLY CHANGING DIRECTORIES EFFICIENTLY

3.8

Suppose that you are doing work that requires you to move back and forth between two directories. You can use the **cd** command, specifying the path each time. There are two other C shell commands that allow you to change directories more quickly. If your machine doesn't have the C shell, you cannot do these exercises.

Saving Your Current Directory

An efficient way to repeatedly change directories is to have the shell save the path to your current directory before changing directories.

1. Change to the directory */tmp* by typing

   cd */tmp*

2. Make your Home directory your current directory by typing

   pushd ~

   The following response appears on your terminal:

   ~ /tmp

3. Confirm that your current directory is your Home directory. Type

   pwd

The **pushd** command performs two functions; it saves the name of your current directory and it changes to the new directory specified. The message on your terminal informs you of the saved directory name.

Recalling the Last Saved Directory

You have saved your current directory name before changing directories by using **pushd**. You can also change back to the saved directory.

1. Change back to the saved directory name by typing

   popd

   Then check to see that your current directory is */tmp* by typing

   pwd

   The **popd** command changes to the directory whose name was last saved by **pushd**.

2. Change to your Home directory and save the name of your current directory. Type

   pushd ~

3. Change to the *Projects* directory without saving the name of your current directory. Type

   cd *Projects*

4. Now type

   popd

5. Find out what your current directory is now by typing

   pwd

   Your current directory is the *tmp* directory. The **popd** command moved you back into the directory last saved with **pushd**.

6. Save two directory names by typing the following commands:

   pushd ~/*Projects*
   pushd /

   Your current directory is now */*. The last saved directory is ~/*Projects*, since that was the current directory when you executed the **pushd /** command.

7. Change to the last saved directory name. Type

   popd

   Your current directory is now the *Projects* directory. The next saved directory name is */tmp*.

8. Change directories back to the */tmp* directory by again typing

   popd

9. Recall the next saved directory name. Type

   popd

   You receive an error message like this:

   ```
   popd: Directory stack empty
   ```

This message indicates that there are no more saved directories. Visualize a stack of dishes. The last dish that you put on top of the stack is the first dish you remove later. Stacks on a computer work the same way. The last item saved on a stack will be the first item removed from a stack. The program says "stack empty" because each time you execute **pushd**, it saves (or pushes) the name of the current directory onto a stack. When you then execute **popd**, it takes the directory name from the top of the stack, removes it (or pops it off), and changes directories to that directory. If there are no more saved directory names, the stack is empty.

10. Move around some more using **pushd** and **popd** until you feel more comfortable with these two commands. Notice that each time you execute **popd**, you move back to the last directory from which you executed **pushd**, which follows the stacking concept.

11. When you feel ready to move on, keep executing **popd** until the stack is empty.

Exercise 3-C

1. What shell command would locate the lost file *atlantis*?

   _____

2. What command changes directories to the parent directory?

   _____

3. What command would you type to change to the *Marilyn* directory listed in your Home directory?

_____

4. Assume that directories *Programs* and *Letters* have the same parent directory. How would you change your current directory from *Programs* to *Letters*?

_____

5. What command would you enter to move the file *eakins* so that it is listed in your Home directory?

_____

6. What is the difference between the commands **rmdir** and **rm-r**?

CONCLUSION

You have now moved around the file system, and created and used directories. You have also accessed files using special directory characters and path-names. By storing files in subdirectories, you can organize and manage your files, keep old copies of files, and remove groups of useless files. Files are accessed by specifying the pathname of the file. If no pathname is specified, the current directory is searched. Root, the Home directory, the parent directory, and the current directory can all be used as starting points for the path to a file. The full pathname for a file is the list of directories, beginning with root, that must be traveled to access the file.

COMMAND SUMMARY

cd *pathname*
Changes to the directory specified by *pathname*.

pushd *directory_name*
Saves the name of the current directory on a stack, and changes directories to *directory_name*.

popd
Changes directories to the last directory saved by **pushd**.

pwd
Displays the full pathname of your current directory.

mv *filename path/newfilename*
Moves the file named *filename* into the directory specified by *path* and, if given, renames the file *newfilename*.

mv *directoryname path/new_directoryname*
Moves the directory named *directoryname*, into the directory specified by *path* and, if given, renames the moved directory *new_directoryname*.

cp *filename path/newfilename*
Puts a copy of *filename* into the directory specified by *path* and, if given, names the copy *newfilename*.

ls -a
Displays a list of files and subdirectories in your current directory, including your current directory (.) and your parent directory (..).

ls -F
Displays the names of files in your current directory and places a / after directory names. Executable files are displayed with an *.

COMMAND SUMMARY (*continued*)

ls -R
Displays the list of files in your current directory and in all directories below your current directory.

ls *options directory_names*
Performs the **ls** command with the given *options* on each directory named in *directory_names*.

find *directory* **-name** *file* **-print**
Starts searching recursively from directory named *directory*, locates all files named *file*, and displays their location in pathname form.

mkdir *directory*
Creates a new directory called *directory*.

rmdir *directory*
Removes *directory*, but only if it does not contain any files or subdirectories.

rm -r *directory*
Removes *directory*, as well as everything it contains.

·4·

Using Basic
UNIX Utilities

One of the most important aspects of UNIX is the wide variety of specific utility programs available to you. Some utilities perform simple, narrow tasks. For example, one utility simply sorts lines, another examines input for adjacent identical lines, a third counts lines, and yet another one coordinates printing files for multiple users. More complex utilities select fields and manipulate data from a database file, handle communication between users, and facilitate file editing. Most utilities have options that instruct the utility to modify the way it accomplishes its task.

Several utilities can be hooked together to accomplish very complex tasks. The output of the first utility becomes the input of the next. For instance, three utilities can be executed in sequence to sort a file, select a subset of the lines, and print the result.

This chapter begins with an investigation of how two utilities—one that sorts lines and one that is a page printing program—work. The Utility Information Pages that are located in Appendix A at the end of the book are introduced, and then several additional utilities are examined. Each Utility Information Page entry describes how to use a utility. After completing this chapter you will be able to use the Utility Information Pages to examine utilities.

SKILLS CHECK

Before beginning this module, you should be able to

- Log on to a UNIX system (Chapter 1, "Touring the System's Features")

- Issue shell commands to create, move, copy, and remove files (Chapter 1)

- Create and edit files with the visual editor (Chapter 2, "Basic Editing with the Visual Editor")

- Change and use directories (Chapter 3, "Using Basic UNIX Directories")

OBJECTIVES

Upon completion of this chapter, you will be able to use UNIX utilities that

- Select or alter specific portions of a file

- Order, count, and locate similar lines in a file

- Create files that are composites or joins of other files

- Perform mathematical calculations using the desk calculator

- Use the Utility Information Pages in Appendix A to examine utilities

SORTING FILES
4.1

The **sort** utility reads lines from input and arranges them in order. In the first chapter you arranged the lines of a file by typing

sort *filename*

The lines from the file *filename* are displayed in order on the screen. You also used the **-r** option to have **sort** produce a listing in reverse order.

Exploring sort

You can use the **sort** utility to arrange items in a specific order (reverse, numeric, or non-ASCII, for example), sort on a specific field, merge sorted files, and check if a file is already sorted. (These aspects of **sort** are described in the entry for **sort** in the Utility Information Pages (UIP).) Each UIP consists of several sections: a summary of what the utility does, a series of explained sample commands, a list of options, and other useful notes. Turn to the **sort** entry in the Utility Information Pages.

1. Type each of the sample **sort** commands in the UIP entry, using files that you have created.

2. Experiment further with **sort** by typing commands using each of the listed options.

4.2 PRINTING WITH SIMPLE PAGE FORMATTING

Thus far, you have been using either the **lp** or the **lpr** utility to spool files for printing. The **lp** and **lpr** printing utilities queue jobs and pass files to the printer. If the file is larger than a page, there are no header or footer margins separating the text into pages. When you want to affect how text is formatted, or paginate the output, you must invoke one of several formatting utilities to act on the file. Manipulating layout with one utility and printing with another is typical of UNIX utilities. Each utility has a focus, doing its job well and carrying no extra baggage. In this section, you will learn to use the simple **pr** utility that outputs a file in pages to the screen or printer. Although **pr** is a useful utility to learn, the main purpose of this section is to illustrate how to learn about UNIX utilities using this book and its Utility Information Pages in Appendix A.

Creating a Sample File

To examine how **pr** works, you need a long file.

1. If you have a text file that is over 100 lines, make a copy of it called *prtest* by typing

   cp *filename prtest*

   where *filename* is the name of your long file.

2. If you do not have a text file that is at least 100 lines long, create one in the following way:

   a. Create a file called *prtest* by copying your journal file:

      cp *journal prtest*

   b. Determine how long the file is by typing

      wc -l *prtest*

   c. If necessary, continue adding files or adding text until *prtest* is at least 100 lines long, by entering commands in this form:

      cat *filename* >> *prtest*

      where *filename* is any of your test files.

Printing and Paginating a File

You can paginate the long file for output.

1. Have **pr** paginate, and **pg** control the screen by entering one of the following commands, depending on your version of UNIX:

   System V:
   pr *prtest* **l pg**

BSD:

pr *prtest* **| more**

The **pr** utility reads the contents of a file and outputs the lines in separate pages. Each page is identified by header and footer margins, with the date, time, filename, and page number at the top. The **pr** utility is particularly useful in preparing a file for printing.

2. The output of **pr** can be piped to another utility such as the print spooler. Send the output of **pr** to the printer. Type one of the following commands:

System V:

pr *prtest* **| lp -d***dest*

BSD:

pr *prtest* **| lpr -P***dest*

The *prtest* file, when printed on the printer, includes the date, time, filename, and page number at the top of each page.

Printing and Paginating Multiple Files

As with many utilities, you can list several files to be read as input.

1. Print and paginate three of your files with **pr** by typing one of the following commands:

System V:
pr *journal prtest practice* **l lp -d***dest*

BSD:
pr *journal prtest practice* **l lpr -P***dest*

Each file is printed separately.

2. The **pr** utility can also accept piped or standard
   input. For example, print three files as one long file
   by having **cat** read the files first and pass its output
   to **pr**. Type one of the following commands:

System V:
cat *journal prtest practice* **l prl lp - d***dest*

BSD:
cat *journal prtest practice* **lprl lpr -P***dest*

Changing Page Headers

As with most utilities, you can instruct **pr** to work in
optional ways. In the output of **pr**, the default header
includes the name of the file at the top of each page.
You can replace the filename in the header with a
descriptive one-word title.

1. Change the header for the output of *prtest* by
   typing one of the following commands:

System V:
pr -h *MyFile prtest* **l lp -d***dest*

BSD:
pr -h *MyFile prtest* **l lpr -P***dest*

Instead of printing the filename *prtest*, the header and footer for each page now includes the string *MyFile*.

Using the **-h** option, you can indicate the contents of a file, or include the date or a copyright notice when you print a file.

Printing Multiple Files Side by Side

The **pr** utility includes an option for printing two or more files on the same page.

1. Print the files *prtest* and *journal* side by side. Type

pr -m *prtest journal*

The two files are printed side by side in the output. Unfortunately, lines that are longer than the width of the column are truncated.

By using **pr** with the **-m** option, you can quickly check two or more files for differences, or similarities.

Printing One File with Multiple Columns

In addition to printing several files, each in a separate column, you can print one file in several columns.

1. To print the file *prtest* in two columns, type

   pr -2 *prtest*

   By using **pr** with the -*number* option, you instruct **pr** to print the output in the specified *number* of columns.

Changing the Column Separation Character

Normally, **pr** separates output from two or more files with spaces between the columns. You can change the separation character.

1. Print the file *prtest* in three columns, separated by a column of # characters. Type

   pr -3 -s# *prtest*

The -**s** option instructs **pr** to separate the columns with a specified character, rather than the default space. Type the separation character immediately after the -**s** in the command line.

Changing Page Width

1. The width of the output of **pr** can also be modified. Type one of the following commands:

System V:
pr -w30 *prtest* | **lp -d**dest

BSD:
pr -w30 *prtest* | **lpr**

The **-w**30 specifies that the width of the page is to be 30 characters.

2. The column number and page width options can be combined by typing one of the following command lines:

System V:
pr -2 -w30 *prtest* | **lpr -d**dest

BSD:
pr -2 -w30 *prtest* | **lpr -P**dest

This command line instructs **pr** to produce two columns of output, each 30 characters wide.

Changing the Page Length

Normally **pr** produces pages that are 66 lines long. You can modify the number of lines by defining the length of the page.

1. Print the file *prtest* with a page length of 20 lines (small enough so that pages will fit on the terminal screen). Type one of the following commands:

System V:
pr -l22 *prtest* **| pg**

BSD:
pr -l22 *prtest* **| more**

The -l22 sets the page length to 22 lines. If you specify a page length that is too long to leave room for the header and footer, neither will be printed.

Skipping Pages from the Beginning

When examining very long listings, you can save time by passing over the first several pages. You can instruct **pr** to produce the output beginning with a specific page.

1. Tell **pr** to skip the first two pages of *prtest* and begin on page 3. Type

   pr +3 *prtest*

Deleting the Header and Footer

A standard feature of the **pr** utility is the inclusion of both a header and a footer. You can prevent these from being printed.

1. Remove the headers and footers from each page by typing

pr -t *prtest*

The **-t** tells **pr** not to print the headers or footers.

There are other changes to the standard format that you can make, but only on System V machines. If you do not use System V, go on to the "Combining Options" section.

Numbering Lines

On System V, you can tell **pr** to include line numbers in front of each line of the output.

1. Print the lines and line numbers of the file *prtest* by typing

pr -n *prtest*

You can align the line numbers by specifying the amount of digit space the numbers should take. You can also specify a character to separate the line number from the line.

2. Print the file *journal* using five digits for the line number, and separate the line numbers from each line with a letter *A*. Type

pr -n*A5 journal*

In summary, to number lines in the output of **pr**, with spaces and a selected separator character between line number and line, type

pr -n*ck file(s)*

The *c* is the single character separating the line numbers from the line of text, and *k* is the number of digits in the number.

Making the Output Double-Spaced

The output of **pr** is normally single-spaced. On System V, you can make the output double-spaced.

1. Print the file *prtest* in double-spaced format by typing

   pr -d *prtest*

The **-d** option instructs the utility to double-space output.

Changing the Offset

You can also change the offset (the number of blank characters before each line) on System V.

1. Print the file *prtest,* and change the offset to six characters by typing

   pr -o*6 prtest*

The **-o***6* tells **pr** to move the whole output to the right six characters. Lines are not shortened. When you employ the **-o***n* option, all lines are moved over *n* characters.

Combining Options

On both System V and on BSD you can combine several options to **pr** in one command line. For instance, the command

pr -n*A5* **-h** *name* **-2 -s***X* **-w***20* **+***4* **-l***30 filename*

instructs **pr** to do all of these things:

- Number each line, with the numbers separated from the lines by the *A* character, and each line number occupying five spaces.

- Print the word *name* in place of the filename in the header.

- Print the file in two columns.

- Separate the columns with *X*s.

- Use a page width of 20 characters.

- Print the file starting at the fourth page.

- Use a page length of 30 lines.

Summarizing pr

1. Locate and read the entry for **pr** in the Utility Information Pages.

2. Try each example, using different files.

3. Look at the brief descriptions for each option. You have used most of these options in this section.

UTILITIES THAT DISPLAY INFORMATION ABOUT FILES

4.3

One group of UNIX utilities displays information about files without modifying them. For example, there are utilities for counting words in a file, for comparing two files, and for searching for words or patterns in a file.

Making Sample Files

To see the function of these utilities you will need to create three sample files.

1. Using the visual editor, create a file called *rhyme1* that contains the following:

   This is a sample file
   Ole King Cole was a merry old soul,
   and a merry old soul was Old King Cole.
   Jack and Jill, went up the hill,
   to fetch a pail of water. [Space] [Space] [Space]
   Jack fell down, and broke his crown.
   and Jill came tumbling after.
   This file is listed in a Directory.

2. Copy this file to a file called *rhyme2* by typing

   cp *rhyme1 rhyme2*

3. Use the visual editor to make the three changes indicated by arrows.

This is yet another sample file.←
Tab This one will be similar to the last one. ←
Ole King Cole was a merry old soul,
and a merry old soul was Old King Cole.
Jack and Jill, went up the hill,
to fetch a pail of water.←
Jack fell down, and broke his crown.
and Jill came tumbling after.
This file is listed in a directory.

4. Write the file and return to the shell.

Counting the Characters, Words, and Lines in a File

The word count utility reads the contents of a file, counts the number of lines, words, and characters that are in the file, and outputs the results.

1. Determine the number of lines, words, and characters in the file *rhyme1* by typing

   wc *rhyme1*

2. Use another of your files as input for **wc**, such as:

   wc *practice*

Exploring the wc Utility Information Pages

There are ways to limit the output of **wc** so that only the number of words, number of lines, or number of characters is displayed, instead of all three.

1. Enter

   wc -l *practice*

2. Determine the number of users who are logged on by typing

   who I wc -l

3. Examine the entry for **wc** in the Utility Information Pages. Type each of the sample commands using the files that you have created.

4. Type **wc** commands using combinations of the listed options.

   The **w**ord **c**ount utility is a useful program that can be used in combination with other utilities and by itself to determine the number of words, characters, and lines contained in a file.

Combining Files with cat

In earlier chapters, you used the **cat** utility to display and create files.

1. One of the primary uses of **cat** is to con**cat**enate files together. Enter the following:

   cat *practice rhyme1*

   The **cat** utility reads both files as input. The output is sent to your screen.

   You can create new files that are concatenations of other files by specifying where the output is sent.

2. Enter

cat *practice rhyme1 > combo*

The greater-than sign takes the output from **cat** and redirects it into a new file called *combo.*

The **cat** utility is useful for displaying files, including combined files.

3. Examine how **cat** can be used to print nonprinting characters and line numbers, and examine the command syntax, by reading the Utility Information Pages for **cat**.

4. Type each of the sample commands using the files that you have created. Some of the commands create new files. You can use the **cat** utility to display the new files.

Comparing the Contents of Files

The **comm** utility compares two files and produces three columns of output: lines that are only in the first file, lines that are only in the second file, and lines that are in both files.

1. Create two files:

- *alpha1* with the following contents:

  a

  b

  c

  d

  e

- *alpha2* with the following contents:

d

e

f

g

h

Study this method of representing two files

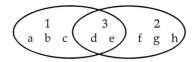

and note the following:

- The lines a, b, and c are unique to *alpha1*.

- The lines f, g, and h are unique to *alpha2*.

- The lines d and e are common to both files.

2. Compare the files *alpha1* and *alpha2* by typing
   comm *alpha1 alpha2*
   The following output is produced:

a

b

c

       d

       e

   f

   g

   h

Reading from top to bottom, the first group of letters (a,b,c) are lines unique to the first file and are not indented. The second group of letters (d,e) are lines in both files and are indented by two tab stops. The third group of letters (f,g,h) are lines unique to the second file and are indented by one tab stop.

The **comm** utility should only be used with sorted files.

3. Arrange the lines of the files *rhyme1* and *rhyme2* in order, and create two files called *rhyme1.sort* and *rhyme2.sort*. Type the following:

sort *rhyme1 > rhyme1.sort*
sort *rhyme2 > rhyme2.sort*

4. Compare the two sorted files by typing

comm *rhyme1.sort rhyme2.sort*

The following output is produced:

```
                This one will be similar to the last one.
                Jack and Jill, went up the hill,
                Jack fell down, and broke his crown.
                Ole King Cole was a merry old soul,
        This is a sample file
            This is yet another sample file.
                and Jill came tumbling after.
                and a merry old soul was Old King Cole.
            to fetch a pail of water.
        to fetch a pail of water.
```

Each line is indented as explained in Step 2, indicating whether the lines are unique to one file or common to both. The last two lines shown:

```
   to fetch a pail of water.
to fetch a pail of water.
```

appear to be the same. However, you will recall that this text line from the first file, *rhyme1.sort*, ends with three blank spaces, but the line from the second file, *rhyme2.sort*, does not.

Limiting the Output of comm

When the **comm** utility is invoked with no options, it displays all three columns. There are options that limit this display.

1. To display only the lines common to both *alpha* files, type

   comm -12 *alpha1 alpha2*

   The option **-12** forces **comm** to suppress the display of lines that are unique to *alpha1* or *alpha2*. Therefore, only the lines common to both files are displayed.

2. Read the Utility Information Pages on **comm** for information on how to select only the lines unique to one file.

3. Type each of the sample commands using the files that you have created.

Examining Differences Between Files

The **diff** utility indicates how two files are different. It reports the lines that are different, the location of these lines in their respective files, and what lines you need to add, change, or delete to convert one file to the other.

1. Find the differences between *alpha1* and *alpha2* by typing

diff *alpha1 alpha2*

The following output is displayed.

```
1,3d0
<a
<b
<c
6a4,6
>g
>h
>i
```

The display shows the differing lines in the files. Each line that is preceded by a < symbol is a line from the first file, *alpha1*; and each line that is preceded by a > symbol is a line from the second file, *alpha2*. The lines that are numbers and letters (*6a4,6* and *1,3d0*) indicate the locations of the differing lines in their respective files. For example:

```
1,3d0
```

indicates that lines 1-3 need to be deleted from the first file to make it look like the second file. The line

```
6a4,6
```

reports that lines 4-6 from the second file must be added to the first file after line 6, to make the files look the same.

Modifying diff

1. Examine the Utility Information Pages for **diff** to see a way to modify how trailing spaces are treated.

2. Type each of the sample commands using the files that you have created.

Exercise 4-A

1. How would you print and paginate the files *sample* and *sample.2* with one command?

   _____

2. Which option to **pr** produces double-spaced output?

   _____

3. What does the **sort** command do?

   _____

4. What information does the **wc** utility give you about a file?

   _____

5. What will the following command do?

   cat *lions tigers bears > oh.my*

   _____

6. Which two commands will find the similarities and differences between two files?

_____

4.4 LOCATING FILES THAT CONTAIN SPECIFIC PATTERNS

The **grep** utility searches a file and prints every line that contains a given string of characters.

1. Search the file *rhyme1* for all lines containing the word *old* by typing

   grep *old rhyme1*

   All of the lines containing *old* are displayed on the screen.

2. If you want to search for a target that is more than one word, enclose the target in quotations. For example:

   grep *"old soul" rhyme1*

   When the target is enclosed in quotes, **grep** searches through the input file for strings that exactly match whatever is between the quotes. It does not ignore blank spaces or tab stops.

Exploring grep

The **grep** utility can be used to search for a wide variety of targets. It can be told to display the line number of the line, and has many other useful features.

1. Read the Utility Information Pages for **grep**, and type each of the sample commands using the files that you created.

2. Experiment further by typing your own commands. Use each of the listed options and various patterns.

Exercise 4-B

1. What command should you type to number the lines of the file *joy?*

   _____

2. What does the following command do?

   pr -h *two_files* **-m -w50 -l22** *red yellow*

   _____

3. What are the differences between the **comm** and **diff** utilities?

   _____

4. What command do you type to print all the lines from the file *green* that contain the word *color?*

   _____

4.5   USING DATABASE UTILITIES

UNIX has a number of utilities for database manipulations. You can select fields, output records, and do numerical calculations.

Creating Sample Files

To examine the database utilities, you will need to create several sample files.

1. With the visual editor, create a new file called *names*, containing the following:

   Lewis,Maggie
   Adams,David
   Davis,Jane
   Smith,Susan
   Davis,Burt

2. Create the file *numbers*, containing the following text:

   112
   115
   111
   112
   117

3. Create a new file called *phones*, and type the following text:

555-1000
555-2000
555-3000
555-4000
555-5000

Using paste

The **paste** utility combines two or more files line by line.

1. Combine the files *names* and *phones* by typing

paste *names phones*

The following output appears on your screen:

```
Lewis,Maggie    555-1000
Adams,David     555-2000
Davis,Jane      555-3000
Smith,Susan     555-4000
Davis,Burt      555-5000
```

The contents of the files *names* and *phones* are merged together. The first line of output contains the first lines from both files. Thus, the first column is made up of all the lines from the file *names,* and the second column consists of the lines from the file *phones.* The columns are separated with ⌷Tab⌷ characters. The files *names* and *phones* are un-changed.

Exploring paste Further

You have used the **paste** utility to combine two files. You can also use **paste** to combine several files at once and separate columns with any character.

1. Read the entry for **paste** in the Utility Information Pages, entering each sample command using files you have created.

2. Experiment with each of the listed options by creating your own **paste** commands.

Creating Database Files with paste

You have used **paste** to combine files into columns. By combining files as columns, you can also create files that could be used as a database. Let's now create some database files to use with the next utility.

1. Create a file named *birthdate* with the visual editor, and include the following text:

    1/22
    4/6
    6/7
    5/3
    11/16

2. Using the visual editor, create another file named *zips*. Type in the following text:

31676
64251
59535
31412
95364

3. Combine the files *numbers, names,* and *phones* into a file called *name.phone* by typing

paste *numbers names phones* > *name.phone*

4. Combine the files *numbers, names, birthdate, zips,* and *phones* into a file called *everything.* Type

paste -d: *numbers names birthdate zips phones* > *everything*

The **-d** option instructs **paste** to separate the columns with a specified character rather than the default Tab . The **paste** utility uses whatever character is listed immediately following **-d**. In this case, it is a colon.

5. Using the visual editor, add the following line to the newly created file, *everything*:

This file contains everything

Both of the files you have created will be used in the next section.

Selecting Columns or Characters Using cut

The **cut** utility reads input and displays portions of each line as output. You can instruct **cut** to display characters that occupy specific positions in the lines, or request output of specific columns from the input data. The **cut** utility does the opposite of **paste**.

1. Display the contents of the file *name.phone.* Type

   cat *name.phone*

   The file contains three columns of data: three-digit numbers, names, and phone numbers.

2. Have **cut** select only the column of names from the file by typing

   cut -f2 *name.phone*

   The **-f2** in the command instructs the **cut** utility to display the second **field** (or column) from the file. It counts fields by looking for the field separator—in this case, the default Tab .

Exploring cut

You just used the **cut** utility to display a specific column of a file. You can also use **cut** to display specific characters, or to select fields that are separated by characters other than tabs.

1. Read the entry for **cut** in the Utility Information Pages. Enter each of the sample commands using the files *practice, name.phone,* and *everything.* Note the results of each command when using different files.

2. Explore the **cut** utility by creating different commands using the available options. You can create more sample files either by typing your own, or by combining existing files with the **paste** utility.

Creating Files with cut and paste

You can use both **cut** and **paste** to create additional specific database files. (The files you create will be used by the next utility, **join**.)

1. Create a new file called *region* with the visual editor, and type in the following text:

110 Tab *W*
111 Tab *NW*
112 Tab *N*
113 Tab *NE*
114 Tab *E*
115 Tab *SE*
116 Tab *S*
117 Tab *SW*

2. Combine the files *birthdate* and *names* into the file *birth.name* by typing

   paste *birthdate names > birth.name*

3. Create a file named *num.name.birth* from the file *everything* by typing

   cut -d: **-s -f**1-3 *everything > num.name.birth*

   The **-d** option specifies the column separator, informing **cut** to look for the colon when counting fields. The **-s** option tells **cut** to ignore all lines that have no delimiter characters. The **-s** option should only be used together with the **-f** option.

4. Create a file called *zip.num* by combining *zips* and *numbers.* Type

paste -d*: zips numbers > zip.num*

Using join

You have seen how the utility **paste** is used to combine files, using only line numbers. The first line from each file is pasted together in the output, regardless of the values in the respective fields.

In database work, however, records from different files often need to be joined based on the value in specific fields. The **join** utility allows you to combine columns (fields) of data from one file with columns from another file based on the value in an identified field.

1. Combine the two database files, *name.phone* and *region,* by typing

join *name.phone region*

The following appears on the screen:

```
112 Lewis,Maggie 555-1000 N
115 Adams,David 555-2000 SE
117 Davis,Burt 555-5000 SW
```

The **join** utility matches lines that have a common entry in the first field. The **join** utility requires that the common field be sorted. In this case, the entries of *name.phone* are not sorted on the first field, so not all of the entries are printed.

2. Arrange the entries of *name.phone* so that they are sorted properly, and type the following to store the output in *sorted.name.p:*

    sort -o *sorted.name.p name.phone*

    The **-o** option instructs **sort** to write the output to the file *sorted.name.p,* instead of passing it to the screen.

3. Instruct **join** to combine *sorted.name.p* and *region* based on the first field. Type

    join *sorted.name.p region*

    The following output is displayed:

    ```
    111 Davis,Jane 555-3000 NW
    112 Lewis,Maggie 555-1000 N
    112 Smith,Susan 555-4000 N
    115 Adams,David 555-2000 SE
    117 Davis,Burt 555-5000 SW
    ```

Since the first field of both files is an ordered list of numbers, the **join** utility is able to combine the two files based on the values in each field. Another feature of the **join** utility is that all possible combinations of common entries are printed. This way, both entries from the file *sorted.name.p* that have the first entry of *112* are matched to the same entry in the file *region*.

Exploring join

You have used the **join** utility to combine two files with common first fields. You can also use **join** to combine files in other ways, by specifying the fields to join, changing the field separation character, or specifying which fields to display.

1. Read the Utility Information Pages for **join**, typing each of the sample commands using the files you created. Be sure to identify which fields are being joined, and which characters to use as field separators.

    The **join** utility requires that the field being joined must first be sorted. Use the **sort** utility with the field sorting options to arrange the file properly.

2. Combine files in other ways by creating your own commands using the listed options.

Manipulating Database Information Using awk

The **awk** utility is very powerful. It allows you to find lines containing specific strings of characters, to manipulate the data, and to print selected portions.

1. Print all lines from the file *practice* that contain the word *hi* by typing

   awk '*/hi/*' *practice*

   Each line that contains the letter string *hi* is printed.

Exploring awk

The **awk** utility can do much more than locate a pattern. For instance, you can request the printing of the first field of the output of **who**. Enter the following:

   who | awk {print $1}

This example employs **awk** from the command line. You can also create command files that are utilized by the **awk** utility.

1. Create a file named *awk_prog* with the following contents:

   */112/{***print** $1, $2}

2. Have **awk** run the commands in the command file *awk_prog* on the input file *everything,* by typing

   awk -f *awk_prog everything*

   The **-f** option to **awk** instructs the utility to obtain its instructions from the file *awk_prog.* The output is a list of the first and second fields of all lines that contain the string *112.*

3. To further explore the **awk** utility, read through the Utility Information Pages on **awk**, and type in each of the sample commands using different files.

4. Experiment with other **awk** commands by changing the parameters in the sample commands.

4.6   UTILITIES THAT MODIFY FILES

Another set of utilities allows you to make modified copies of files.

Creating a Sample File

To see how these utilities modify a file, you need to create a sample text file.

1. Create a sample file called *bbunny* with the visual editor. Enter append mode, and type the following:

Eh. What's up doc?
What's up doc?
What's up doc?
What's up doc?
What's cookin?
What's up doc?
Hey look out! stop!
Are ya gonna give up quietly or will I mess ya up?
Are ya or aren't ya
You're gonna hurt someone

You're gonna hurt someone
with that old shotgun.
Eh? What's up doc?

2. Write the file and quit.

Using uniq

The **uniq** utility removes duplicate lines.

1. Remove duplicate lines from the file *bbunny* by typing

uniq *bbunny*

The following is the output of **uniq**:

```
Eh. What's up doc?
What's up doc?
What's cookin?
What's up doc?
Hey look out! stop!
Are ya gonna give up quietly or will I mess ya up?
Are ya or aren't ya
You're gonna hurt someone
with that old shotgun.
Eh? What's up doc?
```

Repeated copies of the line

```
What's up doc?
```

that are next to each other are removed from the output. To remove all duplicate lines, sort the file first, then pass it to **uniq**. The original file *bbunny* is not changed.

Limiting uniq

You can also control the output of **uniq** to print either the lines that are repeated or those that are not repeated.

1. Try these options after reading about them in the Utility Information Pages for **uniq**.

2. Type each command using the file *bbunny* and any other files you have created. Some of the **uniq** commands create new files, so be careful not to overwrite any existing files.

Translating Characters from a File

The **tr** utility translates specified characters in its input to other specified characters.

1. Display the file *bbunny* so that all uppercase *W*'s are printed as lowercase *w*'s. Type

   tr *W w* < *bbunny*

   The file is displayed, and all the uppercase *W*'s are output in lowercase. The utility **tr** has replaced each uppercase *W* with a lowercase *w* in the output displayed. The original file is not altered.

Exploring tr

The **tr** utility can also be used to translate more than one character at a time and to delete characters.

1. Try both of these options after reading the Utility Information Pages for **tr**.

2. Explore **tr** by typing each of the sample commands using any of the files you have created. Some of the commands create new files. Be aware that if you use the name of an existing file for the name of a file that will be created, the old file may be overwritten.

3. Experiment further with **tr** by typing your own commands using different characters and files.

Editing with the Stream Editor sed

The **sed** utility reads the input, makes specified changes, and outputs the changed version.

1. Display the file *bbunny* with the first and second lines deleted. Type

   sed *'1,2* **d***' bbunny*

   The entire file, except for the first two lines, is printed on the screen.

Exploring sed

The **sed** utility is an editor that lets you make changes to a file or the output of another utility. It edits the "stream" of data as it passes through. Like other editors, there are commands that allow you to replace text, delete text, and add text.

1. For example, to change how your login is spelled in the output from **who**, enter the following:

   who | sed '**s/***login***/***newspelling***/**'

   where *login* is your login name and *newspelling* is any other name you choose. The **sed** utility will use it to replace your login. The command you just entered passes the following program to **sed**:

   s/login/newspelling/

   This program consists of the standard line editor substitute command, telling **sed** to examine all lines of input and to replace the first occurrence of the string *login* with the string *newspelling* on each line where it finds *login*.

You can have **sed** read a file for instructions.

2. Create a file of **sed** commands called *sedscript* with the visual editor. Enter append mode and type the following:

   s/*Eh*/*Hey*/**g**
   /*look*/,/*You*/ **d**
   2 **a**
   I do not know

3. Save the file and return to the shell. You will use this file in the last example of the Utility Information Pages for **sed**.

4. Examine and explore the **sed** command in the Utility Information Pages, typing each of the sample commands and using the files that you have created. Use the file *sedscript* with the last example.

USING THE ON-LINE CALCULATOR 4.7

You can perform simple arithmetic using the on-line calculator utility called **dc** (short for **d**esk **c**alculator).

Accessing the Calculator

The **dc** utility reads in numbers and executes arithmetic commands based on the input. Unlike the previous utilities in this chapter, **dc** is an interactive command interpreter. Like the visual editor, **dc** has its own command mode separate from the shell.

1. Start up the **dc** utility by typing

   dc

   You are now in the **dc** command mode. Unlike **vi**, **dc** does not have any other modes. You can only execute commands.

Executing dc Commands

1. From the command mode of the desk calculator, attempt to add 1 and 2 by typing

   1 + 2

The error message

`stack empty`

appears on the screen.

Unlike some calculators, **dc** is a *postfix* calculator: it stores numbers in a list or on a *stack* until they are needed, removes numbers when an operation takes place, and stores the answer on top of the stack.

2. Add *1* and *2* again, this time with the following command:

1 2 +

Both the numbers *1* and *2* are pushed onto the stack. After the **+** is entered, the top two numbers on the stack (*1* and *2*) are removed from the stack and added together. Finally, the answer (*3*) is pushed onto the stack. The answer, however, is not printed. The **dc** utility has a strict set of commands. The **+** command only adds two numbers; it does not print the result.

3. Print the result of your addition by typing

p

The **p** command **p**rints the number that is at the top of the stack.

4. You can type the command so that the answer is printed right away, like this:

1 2 + **p**

The advantage of using a stack is that there is no need for parentheses or priority of operation within commands. A statement written in postfix notation can only be interpreted in one way.

If you are unfamiliar with a stack, think of a deck of cards that you can write on. Putting (or *pushing*) a number onto a stack is the same as writing a number on a blank card and putting that card on top of the deck. Removing (or *popping*) a number from the stack is the same as taking the top card from the deck and throwing it away.

5. Leave the **dc** utility by typing

q

You are now back in the shell.

Exploring dc

The **dc** utility can perform more complicated calculations. To explore **dc** further, read the Utility Information Pages for **dc**.

1. Start up the **dc** utility and type each of the sample commands. Try to determine the arithmetic answer before typing in the command.

2. Experiment further with **dc** by typing your own commands.

Exercise 4-C

1. Which two utilities display files side by side?

_____

2. What command would you type to see the first three fields (which are separated by # characters) of the file *data_base?*

_____

3. To join two files on the first field, what must you do first to make sure that **join** works properly?

_____

4. What command would you type to change all occurences of the character **+** in the file *add* to the character **-** ?

_____

5. How does the command structure of the **sed** and **awk** utilities differ from other utilities?

_____

6. What **dc** command would you type to print the result of 7 **+** 12?

_____

CONCLUSION

You have now used a wide variety of UNIX utilities. There are many more utilities on your system. You can find information about utilities and their functions by looking at the the UNIX manual and other system documents.

·5·

Sending Messages to Other Users

Maintaining the flow of information among all the users of a system is an essential component of a successful computing environment. Critical information such as changes that have taken place on the system, project schedules, and other corporate information must be given to system users quickly. The **mail** utility is a popular tool that can be employed by all users to communicate through a UNIX system. You can send specific messages or files to one person or to a group. Recipients are automatically notified that they have mail. The recipients may then read this mail, send a reply to it (if desired), and save or discard it.

Before beginning this chapter, you should be able to

- Access and leave the system (Chapter 1, "Touring the System's Features")

- Name, copy, and remove files (Chapter 1)

- Create, display, and print files (Chapter 1)

- Execute basic shell commands (Chapter 1)

- Access and modify files using the **vi** editor (Chapter 2, "Basic Editing with the Visual Editor")

OBJECTIVES

Upon completion of this chapter, you will be able to

- Send a mail message to another user

- Send mail to several users

- Send files to other users

- Receive mail

- Save messages

- Respond to mail messages

5.1   SENDING A MESSAGE TO A USER WITH THE MAIL UTILITY

UNIX electronic mail allows each user to send messages, including files, to other UNIX users, whether or not the other users are currently logged on to the system.

Initiating the Command to Send Mail to Yourself

To learn how to use **mail**, you will first practice by sending yourself messages. This way, you can send, as well as receive mail.

1. Because the objective of this exercise is to send mail to yourself, substitute your own login ID for *login* in the following command line. Type

   mail *login*

Using the Subject Line

On most systems, a user receiving mail is informed of both the sender and the subject of the message.

When you are sending a message, the **mail** utility may ask you to enter the title of your message, depending on how your account is set up. You may receive a prompt:

```
Subject:
```

1. If you receive this prompt, you can type a short (half a line or so) title for your message, and press Return. Or you can just press Return without entering a subject.

An entry in the *Subject*: line gives the recipient of your message the opportunity to easily choose which **mail** messages to read first. If you leave your *Subject*: line blank, some versions of the **mail** program will put the first few words of your message in the subject field of the message header.

Entering the Append Mode of mail

Locate the **mail** *login* command on the conceptual map (Figure 5-1). It leads from the shell to the **mail** append mode. After typing **mail** *login* (and possibly a Subject: line), you are in the append mode. The arrow is single-headed in the conceptual map, indicating that you are not automatically returned to the shell.

With **vi**, you are first placed in command mode. In constrast, with **mail**, you *automatically* start in the append mode. You do not have to type a command (like **vi**'s **a** or **i**) to go from command to append mode.

Entering the Message

The cursor is now at the beginning of a line. The **mail** program is waiting for input from the keyboard.

1. Type a short message such as this:

This is message number 1.

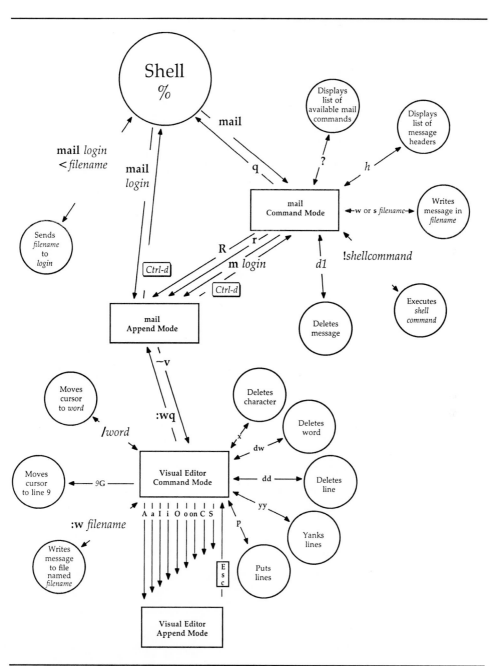

FIGURE 5-1. Using UNIX mail

and press Return .

2. Add another line or two, ending each line by pressing Return .

3. If you make a mistake, use the Backspace key or Ctrl-h to return to the point where you made the mistake. You can then correct it, as long as the cursor is still in the same line as the mistake. The task of correcting mistakes in previous lines is discussed later in this chapter.

Ending Your Message

Now that you have finished typing in your message, you have to inform **mail** that you are finished and want to send the message.

1. When you are ready to send your message, press Return to move the cursor to the beginning of the next line.

2. Then press Ctrl-d .

The shell prompt returns. Whatever you typed is sent as a message to the user to *login,* and you are returned to the shell.

Again examine the conceptual map in Figure 5-1. To exit the append mode of **mail,** you press Ctrl-d .

Receiving Your Message

The message you just sent will be delivered to your personal "mailbox" within a few minutes.

1. Check for the existence of mail, and start the process of reading it from the shell by typing

   mail

2. If your letter has not yet arrived, you will see the message

   ```
   No mail.
   ```

   and your shell prompt will reappear. It may take several minutes for the message to be delivered to your mailbox. Try checking again after a minute or so.

3. If you have mail, your terminal displays something like the following:

```
mail version 3.0 Type ? for help.
"/usr/mail/yourname": 1 message 1 new
>N 1 sender    Wed Jun 24 08 :13   13/315    Subject
?
```

The **mail** display includes a summary line, or header, describing the message you just sent yourself, followed by the **mail** prompt. The **mail** prompt is a **?** on System V, and an **&** on BSD. The summary line, which starts with the > symbol, indicates that a new

(N) **mail** message (new mail means unread mail), numbered 1, is in your mailbox. The new message has been received from *sender* on the indicated date. The subject of the message appears at the end.

4. If other users have sent you mail, you will see additional summary lines, one for each message.

5. Find the message number for your message (it is 1 unless you have other messages). To read the message, type

1

and press [Return].

The message you sent yourself earlier is displayed on the screen. If it is a long message, you may have to press the [Spacebar] or [Return] to see the next screenfull. After you examine the message a new mail prompt is displayed.

To see a particular message, you must type its message number at the **mail** prompt and press [Return].

Deleting a Message

Your mail file (mailbox) will become unmanageably large if you do not delete unneeded messages.

1. After reading your mail message, delete it by typing

d

and pressing Return .

2. End your session with **mail** by typing

q

and pressing Return , which returns you to the
shell prompt. Later you will use other commands
that read and save your mail.

Sending a Second Message

You just deleted the message you sent to yourself.
Send another one now, so you can explore more of
the **mail** command.

1. Type the following command, replacing *login* with
   your own login ID:

mail *login*

2. If you receive the *Subject*: prompt, type the following for your subject:

Here is my message 2.

3. Type the text of your message:

Here is the body of my message.
This is message number 2.

4. End the message by pressing Ctrl-d .

5.2

SENDING FILES THROUGH MAIL TO A USER

In addition to typing a **mail** message to be sent, you can send an existing file with **mail**. This way, you can easily edit the message (file) before sending it.

1. Use **vi** to create a file called *letter*. Write a few lines in it, including one mentioning that this is your third message.

2. Save the file and quit **vi**, so that you're back at the shell prompt.

3. Type the following command, again substituting your login ID for *login*:

   mail *login* < *letter*

   The shell prompt returns. You don't have to type the message. This command line sends mail to *login* just as before, only now the content of the message is taken from the file, *letter*.

   The less-than symbol < is used to tell the shell to open the file *letter* and connect it to the input of **mail**. If the input is not specified with a < *filename* on the command line, input is read from your keyboard just like the earlier two messages. When input is read from the keyboard, a [Ctrl-d] is used to end the input. That is why [Ctrl-d] is called "end-of-file" or "EOF." When a file is specified for input, the end of input is the end of the actual file.

   In summary, there are two ways to send mail.

- If you send mail by typing **mail** *login,* input is from the terminal and you conclude the message by pressing ⌐Ctrl-d⌐.

- If you type **mail** *login* < *filename,* the file is the input that is sent to *login.* The end of the file concludes the message.

SENDING MAIL TO MULTIPLE LOGINS

5.3

The **mail** utility can be used to send messages or files to several accounts at the same time. This function allows you to quickly send a memo or letter to a select group, or to every user on your system.

Sending a Message to Two Logins

For the fourth practice message, select a person you know, and use his or her login ID as *neighbor.login.*

1. Type the following command line, substituting your friend's login ID for *neighbor.login* and your own login for *login:*

   mail *login neighbor.login*

2. At the *Subject:* prompt, type

   Multiple mailings

3. After pressing ⌐Return⌐, type the following text:

   This is message number 4.
   I am sending it to more than one login.

4. End the message by pressing Ctrl-d . Now the same message is sent to both you and your neighbor.

   You can send a message to as many people as you want with this command line:

mail *login1 login2 login3*

where *login1, login2, login3,* . . . are the login ID's of each person.

Sending Files Through mail to Multiple Users

You can also use the standard input redirection symbol, <, to send a file to multiple recipients, like this:

mail *login1 login2 login3* . . . *loginx* < *file*

Exercise 5-A

1. What is the command to **mail** a file called *letter1* to a user whose login ID is *user1?*

_____

2. What do you type to indicate that you have finished typing a **mail** message?

_____

3. What is the effect of the following command?
   mail *andy fred joe* < *form.letter*

_____

RECEIVING MAIL ———————— 5.4

To be able to do the exercises in this section, send yourself five more messages. Be sure to put a message number in the text of each message, so you will be able to see the order in which they are displayed in the next section.

Whenever someone sends a **mail** message to you, it is put in your mailbox and saved for you to read at your convenience. Your mailbox is actually a file, stored in a different place on the system from most of your files. When you log in, your mailbox is examined. If there are any messages, the notification

```
You have mail.
```

appears automatically on your screen.

Depending on how your account is set up, the system looks at your mailbox every one to ten minutes. If someone sends you mail while you are logged in, you don't have to wait until the next time you log in to be aware of it. If there is mail for you, you will be told at the next shell prompt:

```
You have new mail.
```

Reading Mail

Earlier, you read the first message you sent to yourself. You later deleted it. After that, you sent yourself eight more messages, which you will soon read.

1. From the shell prompt, type the command

   mail

2. You have sent yourself eight new messages, and by now they should have arrived in your mailbox. You do not have to wait for the message telling you that you have new mail in order to read your mail. When you type **mail** with no arguments, you access your mailbox. A message header list similar to this one appears on your screen (it will have at least eight messages, rather than three):

```
mail version 3.0 Type ? for help.
"/usr/mail/yourname": 8 messages 8 new
>N 1 sender      Wed Jun 24 08:33    13/315      Subject
 N 2 sender      Wed Jun 24 08:55    13/315      Subject
 N 3 sender      Wed Jun 24 08:59    13/315      Subject
 ....
?
```

Interpreting mail Output

The message header display is rich with information. For each message, it tells you first whether the message has been read. The *N* means that a message is *New* and has not been read. In this display, all of your message headers are preceded by *N*.

Next is the message number. This reflects the order in which your messages were received. (The times of receipt correspond to the order of the message numbers.) You can use these numbers to refer to your messages.

The third field is the *sender* field. It tells you who sent the message. As you can see, you sent most, if not all, of your messages.

Then comes the date and time the message was received, and the length of the message. The length is in number of lines and characters, separated by a /.

Finally, each header has a Subject field. If the sender typed in a subject at the *Subject*: prompt, it will appear here.

The > that marks message 1 indicates that message 1 is your *current* message. Whenever you are reading your mail, one of the messages is the current message, and it is always marked with a >.

Examining the mail Command Mode

Whenever you type **mail** to read messages, you enter the **mail** command mode. The ? prompt at the end of the message list is your **mail** command mode prompt.

Examine Figure 5-1, and locate the box that says "**mail** Command Mode." The commands you type in **mail** from now on are two-way commands. They return you to the command mode prompt once they finish executing. You can see this represented on your conceptual map by the double-headed arrows that connect to the **mail** Command Mode box.

Getting a Listing of Commands in mail

You can request help from **mail** by typing either **help** or **?**. The resulting screen output contains many of the following:

```
mail Commands
```

print [msglist]	print messages
next	go to and type next message
edit [msglist]	edit messages
from [msglist]	give header lines of messages
delete [msglist]	delete messages
undelete [msglist]	restore deleted messages
save [msglist] filename	append messages to file
Reply [message]	reply to message, including all recipients
reply [msglist]	reply to the authors of the messages
preserve [msglist]	preserve messages in mailbox
mail user	mail to specific user
quit	quit, preserving unread messages
xit	quit, preserving all messages
header	print page of active message headers
!	shell escape
cd [directory]	chdir to directory or Home if none given
list	list all commands (no explanations)
top [msglist]	print top 5 lines of messages
z [-]	display next [last] page of 10 headers

[msglist] is optional and specifies messages by number, author, subject or type. The default is the current message.

There are numerous other commands available to you from the command mode. The list you see when you type ? is not exhaustive.

Using the header Command

After looking at the help screen of commands, the message header list that you had displayed when you first entered the command mode has disappeared.

1. Type

h

and press ⎡Return⎤. Once again, you see the list of message headers, and the **?** prompt.

    The **h** stands for **h**eader—whenever you can abbreviate a command in such a way that it does not conflict with the abbreviation of another command, **mail** will understand the abbreviation. To produce the header list, you can type **h, he, hea, head,** and so forth up to and including the entire word, **header**.

Using the print Command

In **mail**, the **print** command, or **p**, allows you to choose which of your messages you wish to read first.

1. At the **?** prompt, type

p*1*

and press ⎡Return⎤.
    This requests your first message to be printed on the screen. If you type **p** again, without an argument, your first message will be printed again,

because it is the current message. Whenever you read a message, that message becomes the current one.

2. Use the **print** command with the remaining messages. With the **p** command you don't have to view the messages in their order of arrival. For instance, you can type **p1**, followed by **p4**, followed by **p2**.

3. You can also simply press [Return] to make the next message current and display it on the screen.

Selecting Messages by Number

Another way of viewing your messages is to type just the message number, and press [Return].

1. To view message 3 at the ? prompt, type

   3

2. Then press [Return]. Message 3 is displayed.

Exercise 5-B

1. If you receive mail while you are logged in, do you have to wait until the next time you log in to find out you have mail?

   _____

2. If a user named *topaz* has sent you mail, what is the command to read it?

   _____

3. How do you display again the message that was just displayed?

   _____

4. How do you display the list of messages held for you in your mailbox?

   _____

DELETING MESSAGES _____ 5.5

As messages arrive from other users, they can pile up and become a nuisance. An essential skill is deleting messages. UNIX lets you delete the current message, a specific message, or a range of messages.

Deleting the Current Message

One way to delete a message is to read it first, and then delete it before reading another message.

1. Look at message 5 again. Type

   p5

   or

   _5_

   and press ⌐Return⌐.

2. When the message appears on the screen and you get your **mail** prompt (?), type

   d

after you read the message. This instructs mail to delete message 5, the current message, from the list of messages. Type **h** to verify that the header for message 5 is gone from the header list.

Deleting a Message That Is Not Current

In addition to deleting a message you have just read, you can delete specific messages.

1. Delete message 6 by typing the following:

d6

By specifying which message you want to delete, you avoid having to display it. The **mail** program deletes it, without first making it the current message.

2. Verify that message 6 was deleted by typing

h

Review the list of message headers; messages 2, 5, and 6 are gone.

Exiting mail Without Affecting the Mailbox

You have been reading and deleting mail. When you have finished, you need to get back to the shell.

1. One way to exit **mail** is to type a lowercase

x

This command is equivalent to **exit, xit,** and so forth.

2. Now that you have used **x** to get out of **mail,** return to the **mail** command mode again by typing

mail

Look carefully at the messages that are listed. The messages that you thought you had deleted from your mailbox are still there. That is because **x** tells mail to exit your mailbox without writing changes. It is left exactly as it was before you looked at it.

   Another way to leave the **mail** utility will be explained later in this chapter.

Deleting a Range of Messages

Besides deleting messages one at a time, you can delete groups of messages.

1. With the list of messages displayed, delete messages 2, 3, and 4 by typing

   d 2-4

   The dash (for minus sign) is used to specify a *range* of messages.

2. Look at the list of messages again with

   h

Messages 2 through 4 have been deleted from the list of message headers. However, as previously illustrated, they have not been deleted from the mailbox itself.

5.6　QUITTING THE MAIL PROGRAM

Another way to leave the **mail** program also writes your changes to the mailbox.

1. Type the command

q

or

quit

2. A message similar to the following appears on your screen:

```
Held 6 messages in /usr/mail/login
```

This message says the **mail** program is retaining (or holding) six messages that you have not yet read.

　The **q**uit command records all changes made to the mailbox through the **d**elete command, and returns you to the shell.

3. At the shell prompt, call up **mail** again and inspect the list of messages. This time messages 2 through 4 have indeed been deleted. If you started with nine messages, you are now left with six in your mailbox.

Several messages have a *U* (for *Unread*) at the left of the message number, whereas they were previously marked *N* (for *New*). This is because, when you quit **mail** with a **q**, the messages are marked according to what you did during the preceding session.

4. Examine the header list. The messages have been renumbered. At this point, what used to be message 5 has moved up to the number 2 position. The numbers now correspond to the current **mail** list.

USING THE UNDELETE COMMAND   *5.7*

It's possible you might accidentally delete a message. Fortunately, there is a **mail** command that will bring back deleted messages, until you use the **quit mail** command.

1. Remove message 2 by typing

   d2

   (The commands **d**2 and **d** 2 are equivalent.)

2. To bring back the message, type

   u

   The **u** command **u**ndeletes the last deleted message. All deleted messages are held until you type **quit**.

3. Verify that the last message is back. Type

p2

4. You can also **u**ndelete a range of messages. Delete messages 2 through 4 by typing

d 2-4

5. To undelete this range of messages, type the following:

u 2-4

6. Alternatively, even if you have deleted a range of messages, you can **u**ndelete a specific one. For instance, delete messages 2 through 4 again, with

d 2-4

7. Bring back message 3 by typing

u 3

8. Now check the results by typing

h

Message 3 is there, but messages 2 and 4 are still deleted.

With **mail**'s **u**ndelete command, there is no need to panic. It provides you with the power to restore a message that has been accidentally deleted.

When you **quit mail** after completing the **u**ndelete command, the message you have undeleted will remain in your mailbox. When you **quit mail** and leave messages deleted, you will *not* be able to undelete them in a later session.

CREATING AND ADDING TO MBOX

5.8

As you have seen, when you use the x command to exit mail after reading your messages, they remain in your mailbox, and any new messages that arrive are added to the existing ones. The size of your mailbox can thus reach enormous proportions.

On the other hand, if, after reading your messages you **quit mail**, all messages that you have read and not deleted are transferred to another file, called *mbox*, located in your Home directory.

Some systems are set up so that messages which have been read are retained in the mailbox, */usr/mail/login_ID*, or */usr/spool/mail/login_ID*, along with unread messages. If your system works that way, you may wish to skip the following exercise related to *mbox*.

Creating the mbox File

1. You should still be in the command mode of **mail**. If you are not, call up **mail**.

2. Read a message and then **quit**. A status message similar to the following appears on your screen:

```
Saved 1 message in mbox
Held 5 messages in /usr/mail/login_ID
```

where 5 indicates how many messages are left in your mailbox.

When you **quit** after reading one message, that message was added to the file *mbox*. Since *mbox* did not exist previously, the file was automatically created for this purpose. The other five messages were treated as unread mail. They were left in your mailbox, */usr/mail/login_ID*, and marked *U* for unread.

When **mail** responds with

```
Saved 1 message in mbox
```

it is telling you that one message was *added,* not that there is only one message in your *mbox* file. If you have an *mbox* that already has 15 messages in it, the new addition will make it a total of 16.

Reading Mail from mbox

When you want to read your letters, the *mbox* file can be accessed with the visual editor, like any other file. It can also be read using **mail**.

1. To read your messages from *mbox*, type

   mail -f *mbox*

   Your screen shows a message header list, just as when you ran **mail** earlier for new messages. The **-f** option instructs **mail** to treat the file *mbox* exactly as it treats your mailbox file—you can read messages in the same way: with the same commands.

2. Read the first few letters in your *mbox* by pressing Return or by selecting messages by number.

Deleting Messages from mbox

To manage the size of your *mbox*, you can delete messages held in *mbox* just as you did from your regular mailbox. As with **mail,** use the command **d**, or **d***n*, where *n* is a message number; or **d** *n-n*, where *n-n* is a range of message numbers.

Leaving mail with Different Effects on mbox

You can get out of **mail** and return to the shell by typing either **x** for exit or **q** for quit.

If you **quit,** you cause **mail** to alter *mbox*, removing from it those messages that you deleted in this session. Any messages not deleted remain in *mbox*.

If you use **x** to exit, the *mbox* file is untouched for this **mail** session, even if you requested that messages be deleted and they were removed from the header list.

Exit **mail -f** now by typing **x**.

SAVING MAIL MESSAGES AS FILES   5.9

If someone sends you an important file or program, you may want to save the information in a file of its own.

1. Return to the command mode of **mail** and inspect the list of message headers. Notice which message is marked as your current one (>).

242   UNIX Made Easy

2. At the prompt, type in the following:

s *saved*

This command puts your current message in the file called *saved* in the current directory.

3. If you want to save a message other than the current one, you must specify also the message number. Save message 2 in *saved* by typing

s 2 *saved*

You receive a message saying that the message was appended to the *saved* file.

Saving More than One Message

You can also specify a range of messages to be saved.

1. To save messages 3, 4, and 5, type

s 3-5 *saved*

2. When you save messages in a file, the contents of the file are not overwritten. The message is simply appended to the file, if it exists. If it doesn't, the file is created, and the message is saved.

3. Exit **mail** now, using the **x** command so that your saved messages are not deleted from your mailbox. (This is so you can continue with this chapter without depleting your mailbox. In a real mail session you probably would **quit**, thus avoiding the duplication of the same messages.)

READING SAVED MESSAGES   5.10

Now that you have saved messages in files, you can read your saved mail by reading the files. There are several ways to do this.

1. Look at the contents of *mbox* using one of the folloving commands:

   SystemV:
   pg *mbox*

   BSD:
   more *mbox*

   The *mbox* file holds the messages put there by **mail** after you read them without deleting them. All the messages retain their original headers, with sender, subject matter, and so forth.

      The headers make it possible for **mail** to treat *mbox* as your mailbox when you type **mail -f** *mbox*. Leave this header information intact if you want **mail** to be able to extract the messages later.

2. Examine the contents of the file *saved* by typing one of the following commands:

   System V:
   pg *saved*

   BSD:
   more *saved*

   Just as in *mbox*, the messages in the *saved* file retain their original headers.

3. Type

mail -f *saved*

The messages from the *saved* file appear as mail on your screen. You can read or delete these messages just as you could when you read other mailbox messages with **mail**. By giving a filename to the **-f** option of **mail,** you are instructing **mail** to read the *saved* file as if it were your own mailbox.

5.11   WRITING MESSAGES

You have been using the **s** command in **mail** to save messages in a file. In each case, the entire message, including the header, was saved. There is another **mail** command that saves messages *without* including the header.

1. From the command mode of **mail**, type

w *letters.mail*

You have just written the current message to the file *letters.mail.* Unlike the **s**ave command, **w** does not save the header of the message to the file. Only the body of the current message now exists in your current directory in *letters.mail.*

2. Exit **mail** and look at the contents of the file *letters.mail* by typing one of the following commands:

System V:
pg *letters.mail*

BSD:
more *letters.mail*

The header of the message has not been preserved;
the message exists alone.

3. To determine if **mail** can treat the file *letters.mail* as
another mail file, like *mbox* and *saved,* type

mail -f *letters.mail*

The **mail** prompt reappears, and the program waits
for your command. Now type

p*1*

The following message appears on your screen:

```
1: Invalid message number
```

Because the headers were not saved, **mail** is
unable to recognize *letters.mail* as a proper **mail** file.
It cannot find messages in the file even though you
are in **mail** command mode.

4. Exit **mail** with **x.**

REPLYING TO MAIL   5.12

When you receive mail, you will sometimes want to
reply to certain messages, to pose questions, or to
write answers or comments.

1. Mail yourself a message by typing

   mail *login*

2. At the *Subject*: prompt type

   RSVP

3. Type in the following message:

   I'm planning a party to celebrate
   my mastery of mail.
   Will you attend?

   and press Ctrl-d .

4. Let one minute pass, to make sure the message has time to arrive in your mailbox. Then call up **mail**.

Using the Reply Feature

Rather than going through the mail-sending process, you can reply directly to the sender of a message that you have received.

1. Read the message you just sent yourself, and then type an uppercase

   R

   The following information appears:

```
To: login
Subject: Re: RSVP
```

There is no prompt—you are already in the append mode of **mail**. It is waiting for your input, just as if you had invoked the program by typing **mail** *login*.

2. Type in a reply message accepting your party invitation, and press ⌐Ctrl-d⌐.

3. Look at Figure 5-1. Notice that the two reply commands, **r** and **R**, bring you into the append mode, and the append mode command ⌐Ctrl-d⌐ brings you back to the command mode.

4. Return to the command mode by pressing ⌐Ctrl-d⌐.

5. You will now see the **mail** prompt. Return to the shell by typing

    x

6. Type **mail** again. Your header list now includes a line which looks something like this:

```
N n login  Wed Jun 24 08:13  13/315   Re: RSVP
```

This is the header for a completely new message— your **R**eply to the RSVP message. Notice that the subject was retained, but that it was altered to indicate the message is a reply.

When a message goes to more than one login name, and you are included among the recipients of the message, using **R** to **R**eply allows you to reply privately to the author of the message. The other recipients of the original message do not receive copies of your answer.

Using reply and Reply

You have seen how you can use **R** to send a private reply to the author of a message that was sent to more than one user. If you wish to not only reply to the author of the message, but also to send a copy of your reply to all of the recipients of the original message, you can use the lowercase **r** command.

In summary you use **Reply** and **reply** in the same way. The only difference is that **R** directs your answer to the sender, but not to the other recipients of the original message; **r** directs it to the sender *and* all of the recipients.

5.13   INVOKING THE VISUAL EDITOR FROM MAIL

While creating a **mail** message, you can correct typing mistakes only on the line that you are typing. Going back to previous lines to make corrections is not possible. You can solve this problem by invoking the **vi** editor to edit the message you are creating.

1. From the shell, type

   mail *login*

   where *login* is your login ID. Then press ⏎ Return at the *Subject:* prompt.

2. At this point **mail** is waiting for your input. Type the following, on two separate lines:

This is a test
of the editing capabilities of mail.

3. Suppose you want to change

This is a test

to

This will be a test

You know that you cannot press Backspace or Ctrl-h to go back to your mistake. If you want to change previous lines in **mail**, you must call up the visual editor.

4. After the last word in the message, press Return. Then in a line by itself, type

　~**v**

and press Return.
　　First, your screen clears. Then you see your two lines of text at the top, and this message:

```
"/tmp/Re00727" 2 lines, 52 characters
```

at the bottom. You have invoked the visual editor and are now able to modify text, move around the file, add lines, and so forth—exactly as if you had written a file with **vi**.

5. Use **vi** commands to change the text so that the first line now says

This will be a test

When you are finished, press Esc.

6. Move to the last line and add some more text.

7. Once you are satisfied with the contents of your message, save and quit the file by typing

:wq

The following message appears:

```
"/tmp/Re00727" 2 lines, 57 characters
(continue)
```

Although you have quit the editor you are still in the **mail** append mode. You can add more text, make changes, or send the message. The command **~v** tells **mail** that you want to edit the message you are typing with **vi**. When you enter **:wq** to leave **vi**, you do not return to the shell, but back to **mail**—the place where your **vi** session started.

Now you are back in **mail** with the cursor on a blank line. The modified message does not appear on the screen. Whatever you add now will be appended to that message, as you are still in the append mode of **mail**. As you continue typing text, the **vi** information that you still see on your terminal will scroll up and disappear.

8. Type the lines

What can I say?
I'm impressed

Printing the Content of a Message

Since you can't see the beginning of a message after editing it with **vi**, there is a command that displays the entire message, up to the last line you have typed.

1. On the next line, all by itself, ask for a print of the file. Type

   ~p

   and press Return.

   This print command shows you the message you are writing. The following appears on your screen:

   ```
   Message contains:
   To: login

   This will be a test
   of the editing capabilities of mail.
   What can I say?
   I'm impressed
   (continue)
   ```

Getting Help for the Tilde Commands

So far you have used the ~p and ~v commands while typing a message. There are other tilde commands that you can use.

1. On a line by itself, type a tilde followed by a question mark:

   ~?

2. You will see this help message:

   ```
   The following ~ escapes are defined:

   ~ ~                        Quote a single tilde
   ~ c users                  Add users to cc list
   ```

~ d	Read in dead.letter
~ e	Edit the message buffer
~ h	Prompt for to list, subject and cc list
~ r file	Read a file into the message buffer
~ p	Print the message buffer
~ m messages	Read in messages, right shifted by a tab
~ s subject	Set subject
~ t users	Add users to to list
~ v	Invoke display editor on message
~ w file	Write message onto file
~ ?	Print this message
~ !command	Invoke the shell
~ |command	Pipe the message through the command

The following sections describe some of these tilde commands.

Reading In a File

While typing mail, you may want to include another file with your message. One way to do this is to edit the message you are typing with **vi**, use the **:r** *filename* command to read in the file, and then return to **mail** append mode. There is also a tilde command that allows you to read in files.

1. In the append mode of **mail** (rather than **vi**), on a line by itself, type

   ~r *letter*

and press ⌐Return¬.

2. You will see something like this:

```
"letter" 5/124
```

where 5 represents the number of lines, and 124 is the number of characters in the file *letter*.

   You have just read the text of the file *letter* into your message. You will not see the text of *letter* itself, but **mail** is telling you that it read the file, by displaying the indicator *"letter" 5/124*.

3. Now look at the whole message by typing the following on a line by itself:

   ~p

The content of the file *letter* is now part of the message you are creating.

Executing Shell Commands Within mail

While typing in a message, you might have to execute a shell command to check some information. To invoke the shell while in **mail**, use another tilde escape command.

1. In the **mail** command mode, type

   ~!ls

A listing of the contents of your current directory, including the filename *letter*, appears on your screen. The tilde and an exclamation mark preceding a shell command permit you to execute that shell command.

2. Now that we have used the contents of *letter*, we don't need it any more. Type

~ !rm *letter*

Your file *letter* is removed from your directory.

3. Make sure you removed *letter* by typing

~ !ls

The file *letter* is not listed.

Writing a Message to a File

You may decide that a message should be saved as a file in your own account. The tilde commands facilitate writing **mail** messages as files.

1. In **mail** command mode, on a line by itself, type the following:

~w *new.letter*

You have just written the contents of the message you are editing to a new file called *new.letter*.

2. Press ⌈Ctrl-d⌋ to send your message and return to the shell.

3. Now examine the contents of the file *new.letter* by typing

~ **!cat** *new.letter*

Notice that your message is there, but *without* the header. When you write the content of a message to a file, the header is eliminated.

At the end of this chapter you will find two summary tables of the commands you have used in this chapter. Use them for quick reference, or just to refresh your memory.

Exercise 5-C

1. What is the **mail** command mode command to save a message in the file *mbox?*

   _____

2. What is the command to use **mail** to review messages stored in a file called *letters?*

   _____

3. Which of the following commands to exit **mail** command mode will *not* remove deleted messages from your mailbox?

   Ctrl-d
   q
   x

   _____

4. What command will allow you to send a **mail** message reply to both the author of a message and to all of its original recipients?

_____

5. When creating a **mail** message, what will the ~v command accomplish?

_____

CONCLUSION

In this chapter, you sent electronic mail to other users on your system, and read mail you received. The **mail** program is augmented by a series of tilde commands that allow you to read a file, invoke the visual editor, and escape to the shell. With electronic mail, you and other users can efficiently exchange ideas, files, and information.

COMMAND SUMMARY

?
Prints a help screen of selected **mail** commands

p *message-list*
prints messages on screen

d *message-list*
deletes current message, or message list if specified

u *message-list*
undeletes deleted messages

R
Sends **R**eply to author of message

r
Sends **r**eply to all orginal recipients of the message, as well as its author

x
Exits, preserving all messages

q
quits, registering all changes (read, delete, and so on) made to the messages in the mailbox file

h
Prints active message **h**eader

s *message-list filename*
saves, header included, current message (or message list if specified) into *filename* (if specified) or into *mbox*

COMMAND SUMMARY (*continued*)

w *message-list filename*
Saves, without header, current message (or message list if specified) into *filename*, which must be specified

Tilde Command Summary

~?
Prints a summary of tilde escapes

~p
Prints the message being entered

~r
Reads in the named file

~v
Invokes **vi**, the visual editor, on the message being entered

~w*filename*
Writes the message being edited, without the header, to the named file

~!*command*
Executes the named shell command

·6·

Command Line
Interpretation
by the Shell

One of the strengths of the UNIX operating system is that it is composed of many utilities. These utilities can be easily combined to accomplish a variety of tasks. You have been introduced to many of these utilities already. The shell is also a utility. There are several shells that you can use, such as the C shell, the Korn shell, and the Bourne shell.

The shell is different from most utilities in that its main purpose is to act as an interface between the user and the UNIX system. Most shells follow the same basic pattern: the shell prompts for a command,

259

the user enters a command, the shell causes the command to be executed, and then the shell prompts for another command.

The shell is the primary "user interface" to the UNIX system. It allows the user to execute and control programs to accomplish tasks.

SKILLS CHECK

Before beginning this chapter, you should be able to

- Access and leave the system and execute basic commands (Chapter 1, "Touring the System's Features")

- Use basic UNIX utilities (Chapter 4, "Using Basic UNIX Utilities")

OBJECTIVES

Upon completion of this chapter, you will be able to

- Describe how the shell accomplishes its tasks

- Use multiple commands on a line

- Distinguish between and use various types of command options and arguments

- By entering appropriate characters in command lines, control the source of input and the destination of output for utilities

- Use shell variables in a command line

- Use various special characters in command lines

- Do simple C shell programming within a command line

EXPLORING THE SHELL

6.1

As an interface between you and the UNIX system, the shell has many features that help make your daily tasks both easier and more effective. Most of this chapter investigates the different features of the shell and how to use them. The last part of this chapter discusses how a command line is actually processed.

Executing Multiple Commands with One Command Line

Occasionally you will want to execute several tasks in order. Using what you have learned thus far, you could enter each command consecutively. For example, if you wanted to make a new file consisting of a sorted version of the information in the file *names* and then wanted to paste it together with the file *phones,* you could type the following two command lines:

sort *names* > *temp*
paste *temp phones* > *results*

However, within the shell it is possible to execute several commands on a single command line.

1. Enter the following line, which contains the above two command lines separated by a semicolon:

   sort *names* > *temp2* ; **paste** *temp2 phones* > *results2*

   The ; (semicolon) character is known as the *command separator.* It lets the shell know where one command ends and where the next one begins on the command line. The shell runs the first command to completion before beginning the second. If you didn't use the command separator, the shell would attempt to treat the list of commands entered above as a single command.

Interrupting a Utility

Often you will want to stop or kill a utility while it is running.

1. Enter the following command:

   cat */etc/termcap*

2. While the output is scrolling by, interrupt the **cat** command by pressing Ctrl-c .

   When you press Ctrl-c , an *interrupt* signal is sent to the utility that is currently running. Most utilities simply stop when they receive an interrupt signal. This is a good way to get yourself out of trouble when you want to quit a program that does not have some other obvious facility for quitting.

Executing Long Commands in the Background

Some utilities can take quite a while to finish their work. Fortunately, the shell has a way of running several processes at once.

1. Execute the following command in the background by putting an ampersand (&) at the end of your command line. Type

find / -print -name*phones* > *foundit* &

This is known as running a process in the background. When you press the [Return] key, a number is displayed on your screen and the shell prompt returns. The number on the screen is the process identification number and will be discussed in detail in Chapter 20, "Process Monitoring and Control." The ampersand at the end of the command line instructs the shell to run the command in the background, as explained in Chapter 10, "Running Multiple Commands."

2. Now type the following command using a command separator and an ampersand:

sort *names* > *temp3* ; **paste** *temp3 phones* > *results3* &

Both commands are run in the background.

A summary of all the special characters used in this section (plus some others) is given in Table 6-1, "Command Flow and Other Special Characters."

USING UTILITY OPTIONS AND ARGUMENTS   6.2

As you learned in Chapter 4, "Using Basic UNIX Utilities," the default task that the utility carries out

TABLE 6-1. Command Flow and Other Special Characters

Command	Function
&	Executes the command line in the background.
;	Command separator. Allows execution of multiple commands on a single line.
Ctrl-c	Interrupt character. Interrupts the current command.
Ctrl-d	End-of-file symbol. Acts like end-of-file character for terminal input.
$name	Substitutes the value of the variable *name*.

can be modified by including options on the command line after the utility name. In addition, many utilities such as **cat** or **sort** use filenames that follow the options.

Using Command Line Options

In Chapter 4 you used options to modify the function of a utility.

1. Sort the file *names* in reverse order by typing

sort -r *names*

The "words" that follow the command are its *arguments*.

The list of names in the file *names* appears on the screen sorted in reverse order. Normally, **sort** arranges the lines of a file in ASCII order; however, by using the **-r** option in the command line, the **sort** utility's task is now to arrange the lines of the file in reverse ASCII order. The way most utilities work can be modified with options.

2. Obtain a long listing of files in the current directory by typing

ls -l

The -l option to **ls** instructs the utility to display its output in a longer format, giving specific information about each file instead of just the names of each file.

3. List all files in the current directory. Type

ls -a

The -a option to **ls** tells the utility to list all files, including the normally hidden dot or control files that will be examined later.

4. Many UNIX utilities use the same options, but a particular option may mean different things to different utilities. For example, enter the following command:

wc -l *names*

In this case, the -l option instructs the **wc** utility to output the number of lines in a file. When used with **ls** in Step 2, the -l option had a different result.

Using Multiple Options

You can specify more than one option to a utility on a single command line.

1. Type the following multiple option command line:

ls -a -l

Not only are all of the filenames in the current directory listed, but they are also listed in the long format. You specified both options on the command line, and both were implemented simultaneously.

2. For additional flexibility, you can often specify two or more option flags on the command line using only one dash. For example, type

ls -al

This has exactly the same result as the previous command line.

3. Type the following command lines as another example of multiple options:

sort -r -d *results*
sort -rd *results*

Again the options are implemented simultaneously, and both approaches have the same effect.

Using Options with Arguments

Some utilities have options that take arguments.

1. In Chapter 4, you used the **-h** option to the **pr** utility to change the header title, and the **-l** option to change the page length. Type

pr -h *Names_Numbers* **-l20** *results*

Normally **pr** uses the name of the file as the title in the header and prints pages that are 66 lines long. In this command, however, the **-h** option takes *Names_Numbers* as its argument, and the **-l** option has *20* as its argument. These cause **pr** to use *Names_Numbers* as the header title for the file, and 20 lines for the page length.

Using Other Arguments for Various Utilities

So far, you have used options as arguments for various utilities. Filenames can also be arguments for a utility.

1. Type the following commands:

   sort *names*
   ls -l *names*

   Each command's argument includes a filename, *names,* which is entered after the utility name.

2. Not all arguments are options or filenames. For example, obtain a list of all the lines in the file *rhyme1* that contain the phrase *King Cole,* by typing

   grep *"King Cole" rhyme1*

   All the lines containing the phrase *King Cole* are printed. Here, the argument is neither a filename nor an option. It is a *character string.* Arguments to a command can include filenames, options, or character strings.

6.3

USING THE SHELL FILENAME EXPANSION FEATURES

The shell recognizes certain special characters, * ? . [and], called *expansion characters,* or occasionally called *wild cards.* The expansion characters make it possible for a single filename argument to match more than one actual filename.

Matching Single Characters in Filename Arguments

One expansion character allows you to match any single character in a filename with any other single character.

1. Copy the file *bbunny* into the file *rhyme3.* Type

   cp *bbunny rhyme3*

2. Display the three files *rhyme1, rhyme2,* and *rhyme3* by typing

   cat *rhyme1 rhyme2 rhyme3*

3. Display each file again, this time by typing

   cat *rhyme?*

   All three files are displayed, even though only one argument was listed in the command line. This is because, although the filename *rhyme?* does not exist as a filename, the **?** at the end of *rhyme* causes the shell to search the current directory for all filenames that begin with the string *rhyme* followed by any single character. The shell then replaces the string *rhyme?* in the command line with the list of matching filenames. Thus, the actual command executed by the shell is

cat *rhyme1 rhyme2 rhyme3*

4. Copy the file *rhyme1* to the file *rhyme11*, and copy the file *rhyme2* to the file *rhyme22* by typing

cp *rhyme1 rhyme11*
cp *rhyme2 rhyme22*

5. List all filenames that are made up of the string *rhyme* followed by a single character. Type

ls *rhyme?*

The filenames *rhyme1, rhyme2,* and *rhyme3* are listed. The filenames *rhyme11* and *rhyme22* are not listed, because their names have more than one character after the string *rhyme.*

6. You are not limited to just one expansion character in a string. List the filenames consisting of the string *rhyme* followed by two characters, by typing

ls *rhyme??*

This time only the files *rhyme11* and *rhyme22* are listed, because each of the two question marks is replaced by any one character that follows *rhyme.* In order to achieve a positive match, there must be two and only two characters after the string *rhyme.* Therefore, the filename *rhyme2* is not a match.

7. The ? expansion character can match any part of a filename. You can therefore place the ? at the

beginning, middle, or end of the target filename. To list all files that have five-character filenames, type

ls ?????

The five question marks can match any five characters, except filenames that begin with a dot (dot files). If a filename is five characters long and does not begin with a dot, it is listed.

Matching Multiple Characters in Filename Arguments

1. The **touch** command can be used to quickly create files with no contents. Create additional empty files by entering the following:

   touch *rhyme4 rhyme5 rhyme6*
   touch *rhyme7 rhyme8 rhyme9*

   There is another expansion character that matches any number of additional characters.

2. List all filenames that begin with the string *rhyme* by typing

   ls *rhyme* *****

   All filenames that begin with *rhyme* are listed. The asterisk (*****) matches any number of characters that follow the initial string *rhyme*.

3. The asterisk character is interpreted by the shell as a match for zero or more additional characters. For example, type the following:

   ls *rhyme1* *****

The shell matches *rhyme11* and the *rhyme1* filename. The *rhyme1* filename has zero additional characters, therefore it matches.

4. You can use the asterisk as shorthand for all files except dot files in the current directory. To count the number of words, lines, and characters in each non-dot file listed in the current directory, type

wc *

The shell substitutes all filenames for the * character then executes the command line. Here, the output includes a count of the lines, words, and characters of all non-dot files in your directory.

5. Like the **?**, you may include more than one * in a matching string. Type

ls -l **me**

All non-dot files with the string *me* as part of their filename are listed. These include the *rhyme* files, and if you had files named *metal, readme,* or *me,* these would also be listed.

6. You may also combine the * and **?** in matching strings. Type

paste **me?*

In this case, only non-dot files with names that end with the word *me* and a subsequent single character are matched. This includes *names, rhyme1, rhyme2,* and *rhyme3.*

Matching Specific Single Characters in a Filename Argument

You can also match specific characters instead of any single character.

1. For example, instruct the shell to match all filenames with the name *rhyme* followed by either of
   the characters *1* or *3*, by typing

   ls *rhyme[1,3]*

   The filenames *rhyme1* and *rhyme3* are listed. If you
   had a file named *rhyme13*, it would not be listed,
   because the brackets tell the shell to match only a
   single character.
       This process is very similar to the single-
   character matching you did with the **?** character,
   but it is more precise. The pattern *[1,3]* matches
   only the single characters *1* and *3*. Hence, with this
   command the shell lists the filenames *rhyme1* and
   rhyme3, but not *rhyme2*.

2. You can also specify a range of characters to match.
   Type

   ls *rhyme[0-9]*

   Many of the *rhyme* filenames are listed. If you had a
   file named *rhyme0*, it would be listed too. The
   expansion characters *[0-9]* are equivalent to the list
   [0,1,2,3,4,5,6,7,8,9].

3. You can also mix character ranges and individual
   characters. Type

   ls *rhyme[0-2,4,7-9]*

The list *[0-2,4,7-9]* is the same as the list *[0,1,2,4,7,8,9]*.

The commas used to separate the list within the brackets are optional and allow greater readability. The list *[0,1,2,3,4]* and the list *[01234]* are identical.

4. You can use more than one pair of brackets in a filename. Type

ls *[Rr]hyme[12]*

The filename *[Rr]hyme[12]* matches all filenames that begin with *r* or *R* followed by the string *hyme* followed by *1* or *2*.

You can combine brackets with the other file expansion characters as well.

Practicing with Filename Pattern Matching

Practice making pattern-matching strings. Use various combinations of the * and **?** and **[]** characters. Use the **echo** or **ls** commands to see which files are matched with your pattern. If you need to, you can make additional dummy files with the **touch** utility,

touch *file1 file2 file3*

Specifying Pathnames from Home Using C Shell Tilde Expansion

One other character is used by the C shell to abbreviate the path to a user's Home directory.

1. Change directories to the root directory. Type

   cd / ; pwd

2. List the contents of your home directory by typing

   ls ~

   The tilde (~) character is replaced by the pathname to your Home directory.

3. You can also access other users' Home directories in a similar manner. For example, list the contents of a friend's Home directory by typing

   ls *~friend*

   where *friend* is the login ID of your friend. If your friend's Home directory is readable, its contents will be displayed on the screen.

   The only difference between the two **ls** commands shown here is that to access someone else's Home directory, you must supply the login name of the user whose Home directory you wish to reference, right after the tilde. The command form is

   ls *~login_name*/directory_name

If the */directory_name* is included, the specified directory within *login_name* is listed. This feature greatly reduces typing on an open system where users often need to access one another's files.

4. Return to your Home directory with **cd**.

   A summary of special characters used in this section, is included in Table 6-2, "Shell Filename Expansion Characters."

TABLE 6-2.   Shell Filename Expansion Characters

Character	Function
*	Matches any number of characters, including zero.
?	Matches exactly one character.
[ ]	Matches exactly one of the enclosed characters.
[-]	Matches exactly one of the range of characters.
~	Expands to the path of the user's Home directory.
~l0ogin	Expands to the path of the Home directory of *login*.

Exercise 6-A

1. What single command line would you enter to get the date, time, and a list of who is on the system?

   _____

2. What command would you use to sort a file named *contacts,* redirect the output into a file that is called *sorted.contacts,* and have the whole thing run in the background?

   _____

3. What is the function of **sort, -r,** and *contacts* in the following command:

   sort -r *contacts*

   _____

4. Assume that a listing of your current directory looks like the following:

   chapter   chapter2   chapter3   newchapter1
   chapter1   chapter2a   intro

Which of these files would be listed with the following command?

ls *chapter*?

_____

5. What is the simplest command to list the contents of your Home directory when you are in another directory?

_____

6.4   REDIRECTING INPUT AND OUTPUT FROM THE COMMAND LINE

One of the truly powerful features of the UNIX shells is the ability to redirect the input and output of utilities (I/O redirection). The output from a utility can be sent to other utilities or to files. Input, too, can be obtained from other utilities or files.

Sending Output to a New File

The most basic input/output redirection step is to save the output of a utility, normally sent to your screen, into a file for later reference.

1. Before you practice output redirection, however, if you are working with the C shell, type the following command:

unset *noclobber*

This turns off an internal option of the C shell called *noclobber*, which is often set by default on many systems. It is important that you turn this option off, so that your system will respond as it is supposed to in the subsequent exercises. The *no-clobber* feature will be discussed in detail later in this chapter.

2. Many of the utilities that you have used thus far result in output displayed on your terminal. For example, type the following command:

sort *names*

The sorted list is printed on your terminal.

3. You can choose instead to have the output of the **sort** utility placed in a file. Type

sort *names > sorted_names*

The shell prompt is returned almost immediately, and no data appears on the screen.

4. List the filenames in the current directory by typing

ls

The filename *sorted_names* is included in the list.

5. Examine the contents of the file *sorted_names*. Type

cat *sorted_names*

The file contains the names from the *names* file, arranged in ASCII order—this is identical to the output of the command **sort** *names*.

The command you typed in Step 3, **sort** *names > sorted_names*, is the **sort** command from Step 2 with *> sorted_names* appended to it. The greater than symbol (>) tells the shell to send the output of the command before the symbol (in this case, **sort** *names*) to the file named after the symbol (in this case, *sorted_names*)—instead of to your terminal. Since the file *sorted_names* did not exist, it was created so that the output of the **sort** command could be placed in it. You are telling the shell to *redirect* the output intended for the terminal to a file. This process is called *output redirection*. The greater than symbol (>) is called the *output redirection symbol*.

6. Not all output is the same. Combine the file *names* and the nonexistent file *nothing* into the file *error* by typing

   cat *names nothing* > *error*

   An error message similar to the following will appear:

   ```
   nothing: No such file or directory
   ```

   This error message is sent to the screen and not to the file, because error messages are not normal output and therefore are treated differently. Even though you instructed the shell to send the output of **cat** to the file *error*, the error message is still printed on your terminal screen. The reason that error messages are treated differently is so you can see that an error occurred without having to examine the output files.

7. Using output redirection is very useful, but there is one danger. To study this danger, store the output of the **who** utility in the existing file *sorted_names:*

   who > *sorted_names*

8. Now examine the contents of *sorted_names* by typing

   cat *sorted_names*

   You can see that the original contents of the *sorted_names* file have been replaced by the output of the **who** utility.

   In summary, unless you have the C shell variable *noclobber* set, if you redirect the output of a command into an existing file, the contents of the file will be overwritten.

Adding Output to an Existing File

Just as you can create files with output redirection, you can also append (add) the output from a utility to the end of an existing file.

1. Create another file with the **date** utility by typing

   date > *testfile*

2. Append the output of the **who** utility to the end of *testfile*. Type

   who >> *testfile*

3. Examine the contents of *testfile*. If there are many people on your system, use either the **pg** or **more** utility.

The output of **who** appears in the file after the output of the **date** utility. Earlier, you used the greater than symbol (>) to send the output of a command to a file, but if the file existed, the contents were over-written. In this last **who** command, two consecutive greater than symbols (>>) cause the output to be appended to the file, instead of overwriting the file. The >> is used for *appending* data and is called the *append output* or *double redirect* symbol.

4. Examine what happens if you try to append output to a nonexistent file. Type the following command:

   who >> *nodate*

5. Look to see if the file *nodate* was created, and if it was, examine its contents.

   If you append output to a nonexistent file, the shell creates the file anyway.

Using the C Shell noclobber Feature

When redirecting output to a file, it is relatively easy for you to accidentally overwrite (or clobber) files that you wanted to save, possibly costing you hours of work. The C shell has a *noclobber* feature that helps you avoid the destruction of your files.

1. Instruct the C shell to protect existing files from output redirection by typing

   set *noclobber*

The **set** command is used to set shell variables. These variables will be discussed later in this chapter; however, the *noclobber* variable is special to the C shell and is rather useful. When the *noclobber* variable is set, the C shell will guard your files from being overwritten (or *clobbered*) by output redirection.

2. The file *sorted_names* exists and currently contains the output of the **who** utility. Attempt to overwrite the file with the output from the **date** utility. Type

date > *sorted_names*

An error message similar to the following appears:

```
sorted_names: file exists
```

The shell refuses to overwrite your file.

3. Verify, with the **cat** utility, that the contents of *sorted_names* were not overwritten.

   When you have the *noclobber* variable set, there may be times when you actually do want the shell to overwrite files. In this case, you can specifically instruct the shell to do so.

4. Overwrite the file *sorted_names* with the output of the **date** utility by typing

date >! *sorted_names*

5. Confirm, with the **cat** utility, that *sorted_names* was overwritten.

By placing the exclamation point (!) after the output redirect symbol (>), you instructed the shell to force the overwrite of the file, if it exists. If the file does not exist, the file will be created.

6. Having the *noclobber* variable set does not merely prevent you from accidentally overwriting files. Earlier, you created a file with the append output symbol (> >). Try now to append the output of the **who** utility to the nonexistent file *whosefile*. Type

who > > *whosefile*

The following error message appears:

```
whosefile: No such file or directory.
```

When the *noclobber* variable is set, the C shell will not create a file when you instruct it to append to a nonexistent file. To get around this, you can either use the normal file output redirection symbol (>), or you can put an exclamation point after the append output symbol, as shown in the next step.

7. Force the shell to create a file by typing the following append command:

who > >! *whosefile*

8. Verify that the file was created.

By including the ! after the >, you instruct the shell to append the output of **who** to the specified file if it exists, and to create a new file if the specified one does not already exist.

In summary, without the *noclobber* set, the > symbol instructs the shell to overwrite a file if that file already exists. The > > symbol instructs the shell to append the output to the end of the file if it exists and to create a new file if the specified file does not exist. However, if you set the *noclobber* variable, the > symbol will no longer overwrite existing files, and the > > symbol will not create new ones. If you wish to achieve the original behavior of these output redirection symbols while *noclobber* is still set, you must follow them with an exclamation point (!). The *noclobber* feature exists with the C shell, not the Bourne.

Using Files for Input to Commands

Not only does the shell provide a way for you to create files with the output from utilities but it allows you to use files for input, as well.

1. Send yourself a letter by typing

   mail *your_login*

   where *your_login* is your login ID.

2. Type several lines of text, and end the letter by pressing ⸤Ctrl-d⸥ on a blank line.

   Unless you instruct otherwise, the **mail** utility takes its input directly from your terminal. Just as you can redirect a utility's output to a file (instead of to your terminal), you can also tell a utility to read input from a file (instead of from your terminal).

3. Send yourself another letter, this time using the file *bbunny* as the input. Where *your_login* is your login ID, type

mail *your_login* < *bbunny*

Your prompt returns almost immediately. You will soon receive mail containing the file *bbunny* from yourself.

By using the less than symbol (<) in the **mail** command line, you instructed the shell to connect the file *bbunny* to the input for the **mail** utility, rather than taking input from your terminal. Because < redirects (or redefines) the input source from your terminal keyboard to some other source, it is called the *input redirection* symbol.

4. Many utilities can read from a file and from your keyboard. Type

cat

Nothing happens.

5. Type several lines of text. As you type each line of text and press the Return key, that line is reprinted on the screen. Because you did not supply a filename, the **cat** utility is getting its input from the default source, your keyboard. Tell **cat** you are finished with Ctrl-d.

6. You can redirect the input source to be a file. Type

cat < *bbunny*

The contents of the file *bbunny* are read by **cat** and output to your terminal.

7. Compare this output to the normal use of **cat** to display the file. Type

cat *bbunny*

There is no noticeable difference between this command and the previous one; exactly the same thing is accomplished in both instances—*bbunny* is read and output to your terminal. However, there are major differences between the two commands in terms of how UNIX accomplishes the tasks.

Examining How the Shell Redirects Input and Output

Whenever the shell executes most utilities it creates a new "process" that actually runs the utility program. When the process is created several pieces of information are passed to the new process, including your terminal **tty**, your Home directory, where to read input, where to write output, and where to write error messages. These three input and output locations are called *standard input, standard output*, and *standard error*. By default all three are set to your terminal.

When you enter a command line such as **cat** < *bbunny*, the shell opens the file listed and connects it to the standard input for the process that will run the **cat** utility. When **cat** reads from its standard input, it reads from the file *bbunny*. The **cat** utility then writes to its standard output. Because the command line did not instruct the shell to redirect output anywhere, the standard output is still connected to the default setting, your terminal. The utility reads from standard input and writes to standard output. It reads from a file connected to standard input and writes to your terminal connected to standard output.

When you issue the command **cat** *bbunny*, there is no instruction to the shell to redirect input or output. Both are left at the default setting, your terminal. One argument, the filename *bbunny*, is passed to **cat**. The **cat** utility is programmed to consider such arguments as filenames that it should open and read for input. It opens the file *bbunny* and reads it, writing to standard output, connected to your terminal.

1. Type the command

   cat < *bbunny* > *bbunny2*

   This command instructs the shell to open the file *bbunny*, connecting it to standard input, to open the file *bbunny2*, and to connect it to standard output. The utility reads from standard input (the file *bbunny*) and writes to standard output (the file *bbunny2*).

   When you use I/O redirection, the shell opens the appropriate files and connects them to the standard input and output for the utility before the utility is executed.

2. As a further example of the interaction between the shell and utilities in I/O redirection, type the following two commands:

   uniq *xyz*
   uniq < *xyz*

   These commands produce error messages complaining that the file *xyz* is nonexistent. On most systems, the two error messages are different. The first command produces something like

   ```
   cannot open xyz
   ```

   while the second command gives

```
xyz: No such file or directory
```

This subtle difference is important. The two messages come from different places. Since the **uniq** *xyz* command does not use I/O redirection, the shell pays no attention to the filename, *xyz*, but simply passes this word to the **uniq** utility as an argument, and then starts the **uniq** utility. When **uniq** starts up, it receives the argument and attempts to open the file called *xyz;* however, as you know, this file does not exist. The **uniq** utility informs you of this fact with the "cannot open" message.

The **uniq** < *xyz* command, however, uses input redirection, and so the shell attempts to open the *xyz* file before starting the **uniq** utility. The shell sees that the file is nonexistent, and the shell displays the "no such file" message.

The reason this clue shows up in the case of the **uniq** utility is that the programmers who wrote the **uniq** utility did not use the same UNIX error message as the shell uses. If your system produced the same error messages, it means that the makers of your version of UNIX modified **uniq** to use the standard error message.

Mixing Input and Output Redirection Within Command Lines

You can use both input and output file redirection on the same command line.

1. In Chapter 4 you used the **tr** utility to translate characters in a file and output the result to your screen. Now use **tr** to swap all the *c*'s and *d*'s in the input file *bbunny*, and store the output in the file *bugs*.

   tr *cd dc < bbunny > bugs*

   The shell opens the file *bbunny* for reading and the file *bugs* for writing, connecting them to standard input and standard output.

2. Verify that the contents of *bugs* are the same as the contents of *bbunny*, with each occurrence of *c* swapped with each occurrence of *d*.

Redirecting Output to Another Command

Another feature of the UNIX shells is the ability to "chain" utilities together on the command line by using the output of one utility as input for another utility.

1. Identify the unique lines of the file *bbunny* by typing the following commands:

   sort *bbunny > tempfile*
   uniq -u *tempfile*
   rm *tempfile*

   Since the **uniq** utility compares only adjacent lines, the lines of *bbunny* are first arranged in sorted order to group all identical lines together. So that **uniq** can scan the sorted lines, the output of **sort** is stored in the file *tempfile*. The second command line instructs **uniq** to read the *tempfile*. By using the **-u** option, you instructed **uniq** to print only the lines that were unique. The output is written to the default output, your terminal. Finally, since *tempfile* is no longer useful, it is removed. Making temporary files to hold output from one command as input for another can become tedious if you need to use complex commands.

2. Fortunately, you can use piping to eliminate the need to create temporary files. Type the following:

sort *bbunny* **| uniq -u**

You receive the same output with only one command line that you did with three commands in Step 1.

 The *pipe* symbol (**|**) instructs the shell to connect the output of the previous utility (in this case, **sort** *bbunny*) to the input for the utility after the symbol (in this case, **uniq -u**). A sequence of commands connected by pipe symbols is called a *pipeline*.

3. You can link more than one program together on a command line. Enter the following command where *logname* is your login name:

who | grep *logname* **| wc -l**

This command line tells you how many times the user *logname* is logged onto your system. There is no standard utility for counting the number of times a person is logged on. However, here you have created your own command by linking three different UNIX utilities together.

The shell connected the output of **who** to the input of **grep** and the output of **grep** to the input of **wc**.

Mixing Pipes and File I/O

Just as you can combine file input and output redirection, you can also combine file input and output redirection with pipes.

1. Save the unique lines of the file *bbunny* in the file *ubugs* by typing

   sort *bbunny* **| uniq** > *ubugs*

   In this command, the output of the **uniq** utility is sent to the file *ubugs*. This straightforward command works correctly. However, you can actually get yourself into some snags if you are not careful when mixing pipes and redirection.

2. One problem is ambiguous I/O redirection. Type the following command:

   sort | uniq > *ubugs2* < *bbunny*

   Here the shell is instructed to connect the output of **uniq** to the file *ubugs2;* however, it is not clear whether the **sort** utility or the **uniq** utility should read the file *bbunny* for its input.

   If you are using the C shell, you get an error message like this:

```
Ambiguous input redirect
```

However, if you are using the Bourne shell, this ambiguous command will be executed. The designers of the Bourne shell decided that since the first command (**sort**) is the only one not receiving input from a pipe, the file input must be intended for that command. Because the designers of the C shell decided this would not always be what the user intends, they elected to have the shell warn the user of possible problems with command line syntax, rather than to make a possibly incorrect assumption.

Capturing Output in the Middle of a Pipeline

Just as you can have the output of the last utility in a pipeline written to a file, you can also write the output of utilities in the middle of a pipeline.

1. Type the following:

   who | tee *who.unsorted* **| sort** > *who.sorted*

2. Examine the contents of the two files, *who.unsorted* and *who.sorted*. The *who.unsorted* file contains the unsorted output of **who**, and *who.sorted* contains the output of **sort**, which arranged the lines produced by **who** in ASCII order.

   The unsorted file was created by the **tee** utility. The **tee** utility reads its input and does two things with it. It writes to the file (named as an argument) and writes to the standard output. It is used in a pipeline to copy the output being passed along into a file and to the next command in the pipeline. You can find out more about the **tee** utility by consulting Appendix A, "Utility Information Pages."

Examining Standard Input, Output, and Error

As you know, UNIX utilities often send their output to your terminal screen and receive their input from your keyboard. Utilities that behave this way without requiring filenames on the command line are reading from the *standard input* and writing to the *standard output*. Error messages, as you saw earlier, are treated differently and are written to the *standard error*.

If not specifically redirected to a file by the user, the standard input is from your keyboard. Standard output and standard error are by default sent to your terminal screen. When you use the file redirection and pipe characters in the shell, you are changing the standard input and standard output. The programs that are being run send their output to the standard output and read input from the standard input. When you use the file redirection, it is the standard input and output that you are changing.

However, you cannot redirect the standard error so easily. This is so that a program can always send diagnostic output to your screen — even if the utility is in the middle of a pipeline or is sending its normal output to a file. Redirecting error messages is examined in the next section.

1. Type in the following command:

   cat < *names*

   In this command line you have connected the standard input for **cat** to the file called *names* and have left the standard output connected to your terminal (the default). The **cat** utility is not told that it is reading from a file. It was not provided with a filename argument, and so it assumes that it reads from the shell's standard input and writes its output to the standard output. Because you did not tell the shell to redirect standard output to anything, it is unchanged from the default, your terminal. The result is that you see **cat**'s output directly on your screen.

2. The following command accepts the default standard input, but redirects the standard output to a file:

   cat > *file1*
   This shows standard output redirection.
   [Ctrl-d]

   In this command line, you do not specifically connect the standard input, but you do connect the standard output to the file called *file1*. The result is that **cat** starts up and begins reading from the shell's default standard input (your keyboard). The **cat** utility reads everything you typed from the keyboard until the end-of-file character, [Ctrl-d], and then quits. As **cat** reads your input, it sends its output to the designated standard output, *file1*.

3. Examine *file1* to verify that it indeed contains all that you typed in Step 2.

4. Run the **cat** utility again, without connecting either the shell's standard input or standard output streams to anything. Type

cat
This uses no input
or output redirection

and press Ctrl-d.

Because the **cat** utility is reading by default from your keyboard, the end-of-file character Ctrl-d on a line by itself tells **cat** to stop reading input and quit. (The **cat** utility is simply sending what you type, line by line, to standard output, connected to your screen.)

In summary, you can control where a utility gets its input and where it writes its output by how you structure the command line. Utilities read input, perform an operation on the data, and write output. If you do not specify otherwise, the shell leaves both standard input and standard output set to your terminal. You can redirect where input and output are connected with redirection symbols. The < tells the shell to connect the input of the previous utility to the filename that follows. The I instructs the shell to connect the output of the previous utility to the input of the utility that follows, and the > is the symbol for connecting the output to a file.

Redirecting Error Messages

In an earlier example, you saw that error messages are treated differently and are sent to the terminal even though output is redirected. You can redirect the error to a file, just as you can with standard output.

1. Type the following command, which will produce an error message:

   cat *names nothing > err*

   The following error message is printed on your terminal screen, rather than sent to the file *err:*

   ```
   nothing: No such file or directory
   ```

2. Depending on your system, the file *err* may have been created. To see if it was created, try to examine it. Type

   cat *err*

   If the file was created, the error message does not appear in the file. If the file was created, remove it.

3. Combine the file *names* with the nonexistent file *nothing* into the file *err*, and save the error message. Type

   cat *names nothing >& err*

   Even though the file *nothing* does not exist, no error message appears on your screen.

4. Examine the contents of the file *err*. The error message is contained in this file. By adding the ampersand character (&) after the output redirect symbol (>), you instructed the shell to redirect standard error to the same file as standard output. The symbol >& is the *error redirect symbol*.

5. You can also pass error messages as output through a pipeline. Compare the output of the following two commands. Type

   cat *nothing names* **| sort**
   cat *nothing names* **|& sort**

   The first command results in the error message printing first. The second command has the error message sorted in order with the rest of the output. By including the ampersand after the pipe in the second utility, you instructed the shell to pass all error messages to the next utility as if they were normal output.

Reading from Standard Input

As you have seen, some utilities can read more than one file for input.

1. Display the two files *rhyme1* and *rhyme2* by typing

   cat *rhyme1 rhyme2*

   The two files are displayed one after the other.

2. You can also instruct the utility to read both a file and standard input. To display the file *names* followed by a sorted version of the file, type

sort *names* **|** **cat** *names* **-**

The unsorted version of the file *names* is displayed first, followed by the output of the **sort** command. In this command line the pipe instructs the shell to connect the output of **sort** to the standard input for **cat**. The **cat** utility is given two arguments, *names* and a minus sign. As the **cat** utility is executed, it first opens and reads the file *names;* then it interprets the - to mean, "read from standard input." It then reads the output of **sort**.

3. Reverse the order of the files displayed. Type

sort *names* **|** **cat** **-** *names*

This time the sorted version of *names* is displayed first, followed by the unsorted version.

4. The dash is required to tell **cat** to read the input coming from standard input. Confirm this by typing

sort *names* **|** **cat** *names*

Only the contents of the file *names* are displayed. The **cat** utility reads the *names* file but never reads the sorted version piped from **sort**. It is not instructed to read standard input.

Using a Utility's Output as Arguments for Another Utility

Thus far, you have used the pipe to connect the output of one utility to the input of another. There are times when you must include the output of one utility in the argument list of another.

1. For instance, type

   echo *"Today is: '**date**'"*

   The **date** utility is run and its output is written into the command line replacing the **'date'** section.

2. For example, type

   echo *"there are '**who | wc -l**' users logged on"*

   the command **who | wc -l** is run first. Its output (a number *n*) replaces that portion of the command line. The **echo** utility receives an argument list consisting of *there are n users logged on,* which it writes to standard output, your terminal. This process of replacing a command within backquotes with the text resulting from the command's execution is called *command substitution.*

3. You can use more complex commands for command substitution. Don't do the following unless you are on good terms with all users. If you had reason to send a message to each logged-on user, you could type the following:

   mail `who | awk '{print$1}'`
   message
   [Ctrl-d]

   The command enclosed in the backquotes (**who | awk '{print $1}'**) prints a list of all the login names of the users who are currently logged on. This output becomes a list of arguments for the **mail** command. By typing this command, you send a letter to everyone who is logged on to your computer.

TABLE 6-3. Shell Redirection Special Characters

Character	Function
>	Redirects standard output into a new file.
<	Redirects standard input.
> >	Appends standard output to an existing file.
>!	Forces standard output redirection.
I	Pipes output of utility on the left to input of the utility on the right.
>&	Redirects standard error and standard output (C shell).
I&	Pipes standard error and standard output (C shell).
2>	Redirects standard error only (Bourne shell).
2I	Pipes standard error only (Bourne shell).

Table 6-3 gives a summary of the special characters used in this section.

USING C SHELL VARIABLES IN THE COMMAND LINE

6.5

There will be times when the arguments to certain shell commands will be long or difficult to remember—for example, a long pathname. Both the C shell and the Bourne shell allow the declaration and use of *variables* that can be used in place of arguments and for other purposes. First, we will explore the C shell. The C shell maintains a list of variables. Each variable may have a list of zero or more words as its value.

Setting and Displaying C Shell Variables

Suppose you had reason to move files from your current directory to a remote directory on the system.

For this exercise the remote directory is */tmp*, where temporary files are written.

You might want to enter commands such as: **ls**/*tmp* or **mv**/*file* /*tmp*/*file* or **cd**/*tmp*. Variable assignment makes such tasks easier.

1. To assign the variable *t* the value /*tmp*, type

   set *t* = /*tmp*

2. To confirm the assignment of the variable, type

   echo $*t*

   The output from the shell is the value of the variable *t*:

   / tmp

   You can now use the *t* variable in commands. For instance, enter

   cp *bbunny* $*t*/*bbunny*
   ls $*t*
   ls $*t* **l grep** *bb*

   The shell makes the variable substitution before executing the command line.

3. To remove a variable, type

   unset *t*

4. Confirm this by typing

   echo $*t*

The response is displayed:

```
t: Undefined variable.
```

The variable *t* is now undefined.

Turning Variables On and Off

In the C shell, you can **set** and **unset** variables.

1. Begin by trying to display the value of an undefined variable. Type

   echo $*doe*

   The shell complains with this message:

   ```
   doe: Undefined variable.
   ```

   The variable *doe* has not yet been defined and so the shell has no value for it.

2. To create the variable *doe,* type

   set *doe*

   The shell completes this task with no complaints.

3. Examine the value of this variable you have just created, by typing

   echo $*doe*

   The shell completes its task with no message and displays only the prompt, indicating its readiness for a new command. Because the variable *doe* still has no value associated with it, the shell has no output to display. However, since the variable does exist, the shell does not display an error message.

Testing the Existence of Variables

It is useful to make certain that a shell variable exists before you attempt to use it.

1. To determine the existence of a variable in the C shell, type

echo $?*doe*

The shell responds with this curt message:

1

When a **?** precedes the variable name in the **echo** command, the shell displays the value 1 if the variable is defined, and 0 if it is not.

2. Now, to remove the variable *doe*, type

unset *doe*

3. Once again, try to display the value of *doe*. Type

echo $*doe*

The rebuke that you expected from the C shell is displayed:

```
doe: Undefined variable.
```

4. Now type

echo $?*doe*

The response is

0

The variable *doe* is no longer part of the C shell's list of variables.

Avoiding Command Line Parsing Problems with set

When attempting to assign values to variables with the **set** command, take care in the placement of the equal sign (=) separating the variable and its value. The following examples will help:

1. First, type the **set** command with a space between the equal sign and the value for the variable, like this:

   set *doe*= *billy*

   There is no response from the shell.

2. Examine the list of shell variables by typing

   set

   Included in the list of variables will be

   ```
   doe
   billy
   ```

Instead of the variable *doe* having the value *billy*, as you intended, the incorrect placement of the equal sign causes the creation of two variables, *doe* and *billy*, neither of which has a value.

3. Remove both variables by typing

   unset *doe billy*

4. Now place a space after the variable name, and no space before the value. Type

   set *doe* = *billy*

   The shell responds with

   ```
   set: Syntax error
   ```

5. Again, examine the list of variables by typing **set**. You may be surprised to see that the variable *doe* is in the list of variables—even after the shell announced a syntax error. Note, however, that the variable *doe* has no value in the list:

   ```
   doe
   ```

6. Once again, remove both variables by typing

   unset *doe billy*

7. This time, type the **set** command with no spaces separating the equal sign from either the variable or the value, like this:

   set *doe*=*billy*

8. Examine the value of the variable *doe* by typing

set

The output will include:

doe billy

This means that *doe* is defined and has the value *billy*.

The key to correctly assigning values to variables is to enter spaces before *and* after the equal sign:

set *name* = *value*

or to have no spaces before *or* after the equal sign:

set *name*=*value*

Mixing Shell Variables with Other Text

It is sometimes useful to append text to the end of shell variables. One example is when you wish to add a filename to the end of a variable that represents the pathname to that file.

1. First, create a variable by typing

   set *bin* =*/usr/ucb/*

2. To add the filename *vi* to the end of the *bin* variable, type

   echo ${*bin*}*vi*

The output is

```
/usr/ucb/vi
```

With this variable assignment, you can type ${*bin*}*vi,* and the shell will execute */usr/ucb/vi* as it replaces the variable *bin* with its value.

3. You can also place the curly braces around the filename appended to the variable. Type

echo $*bin*{*vi*}

The output is

```
/usr/ucb/vi
```

Examining All Variables

1. To see a list of all variables that are currently defined, enter the following command:

set

This command lists on a separate line each currently defined variable and its value.

Using Shell Array Variables

It is also possible to have shell variables that are *arrays* of information.

1. To create a variable that is an array of values, type

set *list* = (*alpha beta gamma*)

2. Examine the values of the variable *list* by typing

echo $*list*

The output is this list of values:

```
alpha beta gamma
```

3. You can refer to each entry of the array. To display the first item in the array *list*, type

echo $*list*[1]

The output of this command is

```
alpha
```

In this way, you can refer to any item in the array separately.

4. To discover the number of entries in the array, type

echo $#*list*

The output is

```
3
```

Passing Command Output to Variables

UNIX also allows you to assign the output of certain commands to a variable.

1. To begin, type

   set *list* = 'ls -F'

   The backquotes surrounding the **ls** command cause the shell to execute everything between them when the variable is being assigned.

2. Try to display the variable by typing

   echo $*list*

   The output is the entire contents of your directory displayed on one line, instead of the **ls -F** string that you probably expected. This is because the shell attempts to execute as commands everything it finds between backquotes.

3. Change your working directory and type

   echo $*list*

   Instead of the contents of the current directory, the value of the variable is still the contents of the previous directory. This is because the C shell executes the commands it finds between the backquotes only once, when the variable is set. The output for the variable remains unchanged until it is set again.

6.6 USING VARIABLES IN THE BOURNE SHELL

Variables are as useful in the Bourne shell as in the C shell. The syntax of variable creation in a Bourne shell is a little different.

Setting and Displaying Bourne Shell Variables

1. Get into a Bourne Shell by typing

sh

2. To assign the variable *t* the value */tmp,* type

t=/tmp

It is important that there are no spaces between the variable name and the equal sign, and also none between the equal sign and the value for the variable.

3. To examine the value of the variable *t,* type

echo $*t*

The output is

/tmp

Assigning Variables on the Command Line

It is also useful to assign the output of certain commands to variables.

1. To assign the output of the command **tty** to the variable *mytty,* type

mytty='**tty**'

2. Now examine the contents of the variable *mytty.* Type

echo $*mytty*

The output is your *tty* device file. In this way, you can assign the output of a long command to a variable.

Examining All Variables

1. To display a list of all variables currently defined within your Bourne shell, type

   set

   The output is a list of all defined variables and their values.

2. To end your session with the Bourne Shell, press Ctrl-d .

Exercise 6-B

1. In the C shell, which variable can you set to keep from destroying an existing file with the redirect symbol?

   _____

2. How are each of the following symbols used to redirect I/O?

   >
   <
   >>
   >&

3. What command mails a file called *letter* to a login named *terry*?

   _____

4. How would you sort the output of the **who** command and display it on the screen?

   _____

5. How would you set the variable _city_ to the value _Boston_ in the C shell? In the Bourne shell?

   _____

6. In the C shell, how would you set the variable _datem_ to the current date and time using the **date** command?

   _____

7. Which command lists your variables and their values?

   _____

QUOTING SPECIAL CHARACTERS ON THE COMMAND LINE

6.7

Many of the sample command lines you have used thus far make use of special shell capabilities like filename expansion, I/O redirection, and others. You instructed the shell to perform these special functions by including certain characters at appropriate places in the command line. For example, to indicate filename expansion, you used one or more of the expansion characters: asterisk (*), question mark (?), or square brackets ([and]).

Each of these these characters has a special meaning to the shell, and for that reason they are known as special characters. Sometimes you will not want the shell to interpret these characters as special. Instructing the shell to interpret a special character as an ordinary character is called *quoting* a character. There are three ways to quote or remove special powers from special characters.

Using the Backslash to Quote Special Characters

You can instruct the shell to treat a single special character as an ordinary character.

1. Type the following two commands, and note the difference in output:

echo *
echo *

The first command prints the names of all of the files in the current directory, but the second command just prints an asterisk.

When the shell encounters an asterisk in a command line, the shell replaces the asterisk with a list of all filenames listed in the current directory. In the first command line the shell makes the filename expansion for *. As a result, **echo** is given an argument list consisting of all filenames. It then echoes that list to your screen. In the second command line, the backslash (\) is a special character that tells the shell to treat the character that immediately follows it (in this case, the asterisk) as an ordinary character. The shell passes this character on to the **echo** utility as a string argument. The **echo** utility then performs its function and prints out its argument list, resulting in the lone asterisk being displayed.

2. The backslash (\) itself is a special character. To have the shell ignore the special property of the \, you must precede the \ with another \. Confirm this by typing the following command:

**echo **

The output is a single backslash. The shell interprets the first backslash as "treat the next character as an ordinary character." It then removes the first backslash and passes the second backslash on to the **echo** utility as a string argument. The **echo** utility faithfully sends it to standard output, connected to your terminal.

3. To have the shell ignore a ⌈Return⌋, type the following, where *login* is your login ID,

who I grep *login* **I **

and press ⌈Return⌋; type

wc -l

and press ⌈Return⌋ again.

Although you entered the command on two lines, the shell ignored the special nature of the first ⌈Return⌋ because it was preceded by a backslash. Only when the second ⌈Return⌋ was pressed did the shell interpret the input. This is a convenient way of entering long command lines.

4. There are other special characters in the shell. Try using various commands with these characters, first without quoting the characters. Then type the commands again, with quoting.

Using Double-Quotes to Quote Special Characters

The output of **ls -l** consists of a long listing of information concerning each file and directory listed in the current directory. The output can be passed to **grep** to select specific entries.

1. For instance, enter the following, where *login* is your login ID:

   ls -l | grep *login*

   This command line produces output consisting of all files owned by you.

2. To select all directories owned by you, enter the following:

   ls -l | grep *^d.*login*

   The argument to **grep** is

^d	locate lines that have a *d* as the first character on the line;
.*	followed by any number of any character
login	followed by your login ID.

   The \ is needed to instruct the shell not to interpret the * as a filename expansion character but instead to pass it as a * character to **grep**. The **grep** utility interprets .* to mean any number of any characters that is, any text.

3. The same result occurs when you enter the following command line:

   ls -l | grep *"^d.*login"*

In this case the asterisk is intepreted as an ordinary character because it is inside quotation marks (double-quotes, in this case).

When the shell, interpreting a command line, comes across a double-quote character, it interprets many (not all) special characters as ordinary characters, until it comes to the next double-quote character; then it turns interpretation back on.

3. For programming reasons, using double-quotes does not prevent the shell from interpreting all characters. Type each of the following commands, and note which ones return the expected output, error messages, or unexpected output:

echo "*this prints*"
echo "*$TERM*"
echo "*who*"
echo "*quote 'stuff' this*"
echo "*!echo*"

The backslash and enclosed single-quotes print, but the other characters do not. The double-quotes do not prevent the shell from interpreting the dollar sign, backquote, or exclamation point (in C shell). You can therefore use variables, command substitutions, and history inside double-quoted arguments.

Using Single-Quotes to Quote Special Characters

Double-quotes are used to prevent the shell from interpreting special characters in a string; however, double-quotes do not mask all characters. One last way to quote characters is to use single-quotes.

1. Try each of the **echo** commands you used in the previous exercise, using single-quotes instead of double-quotes. Type the following:

echo '\this prints'
echo '$TERM'
echo 'who'
echo 'quote 'stuff'this'
echo'!echo '

If you are using the Bourne shell, each of these commands prints what is inside the single-quotes as ordinary, not special, characters. If you are using the C shell, the last command, which includes the exclamation point, prints the previous **echo** command line. The history mechanism is not protected by single-quotes.

As you can see, single-quotes mask almost all special characters. There are two exceptions. One is the exclamation point for C shell users, as demonstrated in the preceding **echo** command. The other exception is illustrated in Step 2.

2. The other character that single-quotes do not mask is the single-quote itself. Try the following command:

echo 'it's mine'

You receive the error message:

`unmatched '.`

Because the argument for the **echo** utility begins with a single-quote, the shell matches the first single-quote with the next one, which occurs in the word *it's*. Thus, the last single-quote is left un-matched.

3. The single-quote can be masked with the double-quote. Type

echo *"it's mine"*

Determining Which Quote Character to Use

- Using single-quotes instructs the shell to interpret almost all special characters as ordinary characters, *except for* the exclamation point (!).

- Using double-quotes instructs the shell to interpret most special characters in a string as ordinary characters except for the dollar sign ($), backquote (`), and exclamation point (!).

- Using a backslash (\) in front of any special character instructs the shell to interpret that character as an ordinary character. In a string, each special character must be preceded by a backslash. The backslash is the only character that instructs the C shell not to interpret the exclamation point (!).

For a summary of special characters used in this section, see Table 6-4, "Quoting Special Characters."

TABLE 6-4. Quoting Special Characters

Character	Function
\	Do not interpret the next character as a special character.
' '	Single-quotes. Hide all special characters in this string from the shell (except ! in C shell).
" "	Double-quotes. Hide everything in this string from the shell, except $ and backquotes (and ! in C shell).
'command'	Backquotes. Run the enclosed command in a subshell and place output here.

6.8 PROGRAMMING THE C SHELL ON THE COMMAND LINE

In this book you have been using the shell to access different utilities. There are other commands available that are not utilities, but built into the shell itself. Some of these *built-in commands* consist of control structures that allow you to program within the shell, either in programs or from the command line.

One of the built-in programming structures is the **foreach** loop. Type the following **foreach** command at the shell prompt, and then type the **cp** and **end** commands in response to the question mark prompt you receive after the **foreach** command:

foreach *fn* **(*)** [Return]
cp $*fn* $*fn.bkup* [Return]
end [Return]

After entering the first line, you are greeted with a question mark. This is the shell's **foreach** prompt. The

foreach command is waiting for instructions. Whatever commands you enter before **end** will be executed once for each file specified. In the preceding example, a backup file is created for each file in the current directory. These backup files have the same name as the original files, with *.bkup* added to the end of the filename.

There are three parts of the first line of input:

- The **foreach** command instructs the shell to perform a series of commands for each file specified.

- The variable name (*fn*) sets a variable equal to the list of files specified.

- The list of files you want to specify is surrounded by parentheses. You can use expansion characters to specify a range of files. Here an asterisk is used, which the shell expands to be all the files in the current directory.

In this example, you are calling a built-in shell command to manipulate other utilities.

There are other built-in shell commands that can be used from the command line, such as **while** and **repeat** loops and **if/then** statements. These are examined in Chapter 11, "Shell Programming."

Exercise 6-C

1. How would you echo the following sequence to the terminal without using any quotes?

_____

*~\abc.

_____

2. How would you echo the following to the terminal?
it's mine

_____

3. How would you echo the following five characters to the terminal without using any backslashes?
"$20"

_____

4. How do you end a **foreach** loop?

_____

5. In a **foreach** loop, what happens to the commands between **foreach** and the **end** command?

_____

6.9   EXAMINING HOW THE SHELL EXECUTES COMMANDS

Thus far, you have used the shell to execute utilities and used filename expansion characters to save typing. You have used I/O redirection symbols to direct output to a file or a command, and direct input from a file or a command. You have also used shell variables in a command line. Each time you execute a utility, you type the command line, the utility executes, and then the shell prompts you for another command. Actually, much more than this happens inside the system.

Each command you type is interpreted and then executed by the shell, which itself is a utility. Because the shell is a utility that interprets commands, it is called a *command interpreter.* Any utility that interprets commands and then executes them is a command interpreter. Other command interpreters include **dc** and **mail**.

Command construction for the shell is done line by line. The basic unit of information transfer from you to the shell is the *command line.* Due to all the features that both shells have to offer, the command interpretation process is actually rather complicated.

When the Shell Starts Up

When a C shell starts up, if you are logging in, two initialization files, *.login* and *.cshrc,* are read and executed. If you are simply creating a subshell and not logging in, only the *.cshrc* file is read. If you are using the Bourne shell, its initialization file *.profile* is read and executed only upon log in. The commands in the initialization files are discussed in detail in Chapter 15, "Setting the User Environment."

The *.cshrc, .login,* and *.profile* filenames begin with a dot (.), so that they are normally not listed by the **ls** utility. This keeps them out of your way, since you will not need to change these files very often.

Shell Prompt

After the shell has finished setting up, it then prompts you for a command. The prompt used is stored in a shell variable that you may change. For the C shell, the prompt is in the variable *prompt.* For the Bourne shell, the prompt is in the variable *PSI*. This variable value is simply printed (usually on a line by itself), and your terminal's text cursor is placed after the prompt. The shell is ready for you to issue a command.

1. Examine the contents of your prompt variable. Enter one of the following commands:

   C shell:
   echo $*prompt*

   Bourne shell:
   echo $*PS1*

   Your prompt appears.

User Enters Command Line

The part of the operating system that handles reading from your keyboard is the *terminal driver*. When you type in a command, the terminal driver reads what you type and displays it on your screen. The shell does not see a single character until you press [Return] at the end of the command line. When you do this, your command line is passed on to the shell, and the shell commences its interpretation procedure.

This process is appropriately called *line oriented input*. When you are typing a command line, you are not actually interacting with the shell, but rather communicating with the terminal driver. During the time that you are typing in your command line, the shell is in a "sleeping" state; it is waiting for your command. Once you press [Return], the terminal driver stops editing your command line, allows the shell to "wake up," and passes the command line to the shell to process.

Shell Processing of the Command Line

Once the shell has your command line, it breaks it down and interprets it in order to properly accomplish what you want done. The command line interpretation procedure is complex and varies from shell to shell. However, many of the basic steps are common to all versions of the Bourne and C shells. All the following steps are performed by the shell to process the command line. The order in which they are presented is approximate and differs not only between shells but also between commands.

1.   Shell Parses Command Line into Words   The first and most basic step is that the shell breaks the command line into individual *words* (actually called *tokens* in computer jargon). The concept of a word is really dependent on what application is looking at the sentence, but with the shell, there are some specific rules that apply.

For example, the command line

sort -r *names*

is made up of three words or tokens (**sort, -r,** and *names*).

The command line

grep *"this is a word?" chapter5*

also contains three words (**grep,** *this is a word?,* and *chapter5*). Strings of words that are contained inside quotes are treated by the shell as single words.

Command lines can contain many words. Words are not necessarily separated by spaces, as in

who;ls -la

which contains three words (**who**, **ls**, and **-la**).

2. Shell Parses Quoted Strings   As you saw in Section 6.7, "Quoting Special Characters on the Command Line," parts of the command line that are contained inside quotes are usually interpreted in a special way.

When the shell encounters a quoted string, it searches the string for special characters that are not hidden by the quotes. For example, single-quotes (*'string'*) hide all characters except for the exclamation point (!). Double-quotes (*"string"*) hide all characters except for the exclamation point (!), dollar sign ($), and backquote (`` ` ``).

3. Shell Does Command Substitution   As you saw in Section 6.4, "Redirecting Input and Output from the Command Line," the shell replaces all sections of a command line enclosed with backquotes (`` ` ``) with the output of the commands inside the backquotes. The string inside the backquotes is a command line itself and must be interpreted separately so that the rest of the command may be understood properly. When the shell completes execution of the command inside the backquotes, the output of the command replaces the backquoted string in the original command line.

4. Shell Performs Variable Substitution   As you saw in Section 6.5, "Using C Shell Variables in the

Command Line," words or tokens that are preceded by an unprotected dollar sign (such as $TERM$) are interpreted by the shell as variable names, and their values are substituted in place.

5. Shell Sets Up Redirection   After performing command and variable substitution, the shell connects the standard input, standard output, and standard error for each utility or command named in the command line to either the default, which is your keyboard (for input) or your terminal (for output and error), or to the file or command specified by an I/O redirection symbol.

In the command line

tr *"[A-Z]" "[a-z]"*   < *data* **|** **tee** *data.nocaps* **|** **wc** -l

the standard error for each utility is connected to the terminal. The shell opens the file *data* and connects it to standard input for the **tr** utility. The output for **tr** is passed to the **tee** utility, which writes a copy to the file *data.nocaps* and writes to standard output, which the shell passes as input to the **wc** utility. The output from **wc** is sent to the default standard output (the terminal).

If the shell attempts to connect standard input from a nonexistent file, the shell stops processing the command line and sends an error message to its standard error (connected to your terminal) saying that the file is nonexistent. It then prompts you for a new command.

6. Shell Expands Filenames   As you saw in Section 6.3, "Using the Shell Filename Expansion

Features," you can use special characters such as * and ? in a filename. When the shell encounters these characters, it matches the given string to the names of files and then substitutes all matching filenames into place in the command line.

7. Shell Creates and Clobbers Files If the standard output for a command is connected to a file, the shell opens that file for writing. If the file does not exist, it is created. However, if the file does exist, the current content is overwritten (or *clobbered*), unless the file is being appended to, or the C shell variable *noclobber* is set. If *noclobber* is set and you did not instruct the shell to ignore it, an error occurs. The shell quits interpreting the command line, prints an error message saying that the file exists, and prompts you for a new command.

8. Shell (Bourne) Assigns Variable Values In Section 6.6, "Using Variables in the Bourne Shell," you saw how the Bourne shell allows a user to assign variables on the command line. The value of the assigned variable is then inserted into the proper location.

9. Shell Locates Commands Before the shell can execute a command, it must locate where that command is in the filesystem. There are three types of commands: *utilities*, *built-ins*, and *shell scripts*. A utility is a binary file containing instructions that the machine can understand directly. (Most commands you use, including the entire shell, are utilities.) A built-in command is *built into* the shell itself. (One command built into the C shell is the **history** command.) A shell script is a file that contains one or more command lines that the shell must interpret.

If the command is not built in, the shell searches for the utility or shell script in the filesystem. Since the filesystem is so huge, the shell only looks in certain specified directories for these programs. These directories are named in your *PATH* shell variable.

Print your *PATH* variable. Enter one of the following commands:

C shell:
echo $*path*

Bourne shell:
echo $*PATH*

Given the **ls** utility, for example, the shell looks in the first directory named in your *PATH.* If the shell does not find the command there, it then goes to the second directory, and so on. If the shell cannot find the program in any of the directories in the *PATH* variable, it prints the error message:

```
ls: Command not found.
```

10. Shell Replaces Command Names with Pathnames   After the shell finds the pathnames for all appropriate commands, the shell replaces the command names with their pathnames.

11. Shell Executes Utility Passing Remaining Arguments   Once the shell has done everything it understands in the command line, it executes each command that is not built in, by using the **fork** system call. For each command that is a utility or shell script, the shell **fork** creates a process and passes the arguments, standard input, standard output, standard error, and environment variables to that process.

Utility Executes

After all this shell processing of the command line, the utility is executed in the properly set up process. It has its own argument list (checking for options, filenames, and so on). It executes, and if there are no errors, accomplishes the task you set out to do.

Shell Prompt Returns

After all of these steps have been completed, the child process dies and your shell wakes up and displays the prompt for the next command. When you type another command, the entire process begins again.

Exercise 6-D

1. What is the function of the *.cshrc, .profile,* and *.login* files?

   _____

2. What is the name of the variable containing your prompt in the C Shell? In the Bourne shell?

   _____

3. What part of the system receives the typed input from the keyboard?

   _____

4. What are the three steps the shell performs that relate directly to files and filenames?

_____

5. Does the shell or the utility determine the validity of arguments to a command?

_____

The shell is a complex command interpreter capable of interacting with humans and with other programs. It provides you with file expansion, redirecting input and output, piping, quoting special characters in command lines, and doing simple programs in the command line. Using these capabilities well will make you a more effective user of UNIX.

CONCLUSION

COMMAND SUMMARY

Special Shell Commands and Characters

set
Displays list of shell variables.

set *name* = *value*
Sets the shell variable *name* to *value* (C shell).

set *name=value*
Sets the shell variable *name* to *value* (C shell).

name=value
Sets the shell variable *name* to *value* (Bourne shell).

unset
Deletes a variable from the shell (C shell).

touch *name*
Creates an empty file called *name*. Also updates the access time of an existing file.

set *noclobber*
Does not allow files to be clobbered by redirection (C shell).

unset *noclobber*
Allows files to be clobbered by redirection (C shell).

·7·

Setting File Permissions

UNIX systems today hold files that vary greatly in their importance — from state secrets to casual notes. If a file contains company secrets, only a few users should be able to read the file. Its availability must be fairly restricted. In contrast, a memo that everyone should read must be very accessible. Files on a UNIX system need different levels of protection.

UNIX treats essentially everything as a file. It stores information in files; it reads program files. Whether or not a user has access to each file is determined by a *set of permissions* attached to the file. By changing a file's permissions, you determine who can read, modify, or use the file. Basic UNIX security, for users and for the system, is based on carefully prescribing who has access to each file, through the permissions attached to files and directories. This chapter investigates how the UNIX file permissions work and how to modify them.

SKILLS CHECK

Before beginning this chapter, you should be able to

- Access and leave the system (Chapter 1, "Touring the System's Features")

- Create and display files (Chapter 1)

- Name, copy, and remove files (Chapter 1)

- Execute basic shell commands (Chapter 1)

- Use several shell commands in combination (Chapter 1)

- Access and modify files using an editor (Chapter 2, "Basic Editing with the Visual Editor")

- Use the UNIX directory hierarchy system (Chapter 3, "Using UNIX Directories")

OBJECTIVES

Upon completion of this chapter, you will be able to

- Determine who has access to a specific file

- Change permissions for a file

- Change how the system assigns default permissions to new files

- Determine who is permitted access to a specific directory

- Change permissions for who can access a directory

- Change the default permissions for new directories

USING READ AND WRITE PERMISSIONS

7.1

A person working on a UNIX system issues commands, enters data, writes programs, changes directories, and obtains information. All these activities are accomplished by accessing files. There are three ways files are accessed:

- When you examine the contents of a file with utilities such as **pg**, **cat**, and **vi**, you are **read**ing the file.

- When you have completed editing and enter **:w**, you **write** the file.

- When you issue a command, you **execute** a command file located on the system.

If you own a file, you may either allow or deny permission to read, write, or execute, or any combination of these three. You can modify the permissions on a file for three classes of users: the owner or user (yourself), other members of the owner's group, and all other users.

Demonstrating Read and Write Permissions

Any time you examine the contents of a file you must have read permission for that file. To modify a file with **vi** you need read and write permission for the file.

1. Call up an old file such as *practice* with the visual editor:

   vi *practice*

   You are able to read the file. Its contents are displayed on the screen.

2. Make a change in the file by adding lines, such as:

   These are two new lines I am adding to practice in this permissions chapter.

3. Write the file and quit the editor with the **:wq** command. You are able to make changes to the file because you have write permission.

Changing Permissions for a File To Be Read Only

You may wish to restrict access to a file. For example, suppose you want a letter to be available to read but not to change in any way. This is possible by removing the write permissions for that file.

1. Currently, the permissions attached to the *practice* file allow you to both read and write the file. Change the permissions to remove write permission by typing

   chmod -w *practice*

The **chmod -w** *filename* command tells the shell to change the **mode** (permissions) for the file to remove write permission (minus **write**).

2. Use the visual editor to call up the *practice* file again, and make some other changes to its contents.

3. Attempt to write the file with the **:wq** command. The resulting error message is like

```
File is read only
```

You cannot write the changes. You are able to read the file, but you cannot alter the file's contents because you do not have write permission.

4. To return to the shell, you must quit the editor. Quit without attempting to write by typing the editor command **:q!**.

Changing Permissions for a File To Be Write Only

You can change the permissions for the *practice* file to add write permission and deny read.

1. Type the command

chmod -r+w *practice*

2. Attempt to read the file using one of the following commands:

System V:
pg *practice*

BSD:
more *practice*

The shell responds with an error message:

```
practice: Permission denied
```

You do not have read permission on the file, hence you cannot read its contents. However, you do still have write permission for the file. It is possible to write to a file, even if you cannot read it.

3. The **cat** command can be used to add lines to the end of a file. Type

cat >> *practice*

This command specifies the output of **cat** to be appended to the *practice* file. No input file is specified, hence **cat** gets its input from your terminal.

4. Type several lines of text, then press $\boxed{\text{Ctrl-d}}$ to signal the end of the input. Because you have write permission for the file, the addition is made.

Adding Read and Write Permissions to a File

1. After the previous exercise you have write only permission for the file *practice*. To reset the permissions for *practice* to allow reading, type

chmod +r *practice*

2. Call up the file with the visual editor, **pg**, or with **more** to confirm that you are able to read the file.

3. If initially a file has neither read nor write permission, you can allow for both by typing

chmod +r+w *practice*

USING EXECUTE PERMISSIONS

7.2

In UNIX it is possible to place shell commands into a file and run them at one time. Creating command files or *shell scripts* can make work more efficient and error free.

Creating a File of Shell Commands

Shell scripts are created just like any other file, usually with an editor.

1. Ensure that you are in your Home directory by typing

   cd

2. Create a new file named *info* by typing the command

   vi *info*

3. Place the following lines in the *info* file:

   date
   pwd
   echo 'You have the following files'
   ls

4. Write the file and return to the shell.

5. In UNIX, to run a command you enter its name. From the shell, type

   info

Instead of executing the *info* command, you receive an error message:

```
info: Permission denied.
```

or

```
cannot execute
```

The file contains a valid shell script. But the shell does not execute it, because you do not have permission to execute the file even though you created it. Once you have written a file of commands, you must set the file's permissions so that it will be an *executable* file.

Changing Permissions to Make a File Executable

The error message you just received lets you know that the shell attempted to execute the file *info,* but found that you did not have permission to execute it; it is only a plain, ordinary, nonexecutable file. You have to change the permissions for *info* to be executable.

1. To make *info* executable, type

chmod +x *info*

The **+x** option grants execute permission for the file.

2. Execute the new *info* shell script by typing

info

You will see the name of your current working directory, the path to your current directory, and a listing of all files in your current directory. The shell commands placed within your *info* file are all run. The script was executable and the shell executed it. To make a file executable, the owner must change its permissions (or file mode) to include execute permission.

EXAMINING THE LONG LISTING FOR FILES

7.3

It is often useful to find out what permissions are presently attached to your files. UNIX provides options to the **ls** command for that purpose.

List the files in your Home directory by typing

System V:
ls -lg

BSD:
ls -l

This command outputs a long listing on your screen similar to the following:

```
total 9
drwxrwxrwx 4 mark staff    544 Nov 13 17:04 Projects
-rw-rw-rw- 1 mark staff   1452 Sep  7 11:58 info
-rw-rw-rw- 1 mark staff   1452 Sep  7 11:58 journal
```

```
-rw-------  1 mark staff 1064 Sep  2 21:14 practice
-rw-rw-rw-  1 mark staff 6100 Oct 12 11:32 practiceA
```

The first piece of information seen here ("total 9") indicates that the total number of data blocks used by the current directory is nine. Each line that follows contains a long listing of information for each file or directory in your current directory.

Identifying the Fields in a Long Listing Entry

The information for each file or directory is divided into seven fields. In this example, the first entry's fields are

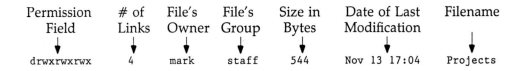

Permission Field	# of Links	File's Owner	File's Group	Size in Bytes	Date of Last Modification	Filename
drwxrwxrwx	4	mark	staff	544	Nov 13 17:04	Projects

Permission Field   The first field is ten characters long and looks like either

```
drwxrwxrwx
```

or

```
-rw-rw-rw-
```

If the first character is *d*, this denotes that the listing is for a directory. The remaining characters specify the permissions for the directory.

The listing for the file *info* has a minus sign in the first position of the first field. *info* is not a directory, but an ordinary file.

Links   The second field in each record is a number, such as 1, 2, 3, or 4. This number indicates the number of directory entries that refer to that file. In Chapter 3, "Using UNIX Directories," you made the *Projects* directory your current directory. There are four directory entries that refer to the *Projects* directory: the parent directory lists *Projects*; the *Projects* directory lists itself; and the two subdirectories of *Projects* each have a listing for the parent directory. Files generally have a 1 in this field, indicating that they are listed in that directory only.

Owner   The third field of the long listing is the login name of the owner of the file (remember, in some contexts the owner is called the user). In this example, *mark* is the name of the file owner.

Group   The fourth field is the name of the group
to which the file belongs. In this example, the group is
staff. Groups are used to gather together various users
who need to share access to the same files.

Groups in UNIX are like departments in a company—the group is a name for several users working
on a similar project. Every user belongs to at least one
group. Access to a file can be granted for all users in a
group and denied to all other groups.

Size   The fifth field of the listing is the length of
the file in bytes.

Modification Date   The date and time the file
was last altered is displayed in the sixth field.

Filename   The last field is the name given to the
file.

Examining the Permissions Field

Let's reexamine the permissions for the files in your
Home directory with the command **ls -l**.

In the permissions field there are ten slots for each
file, for example:

```
-rwxr-x--x
```

Every slot is occupied either by a minus sign (-), or by one of a few specific letters. The presence of a minus sign in a slot indicates that the particular permission is denied. The presence of an *r*, *w*, *x*, or *d* indicates a permission is allowed. (For some files you might also see the characters *b*, *c*, *l*, *p*, *s*, or *S*.)

Directory

The first slot indicates whether the listing is for a directory, a plain file, or a special UNIX file. A *d* indicates a directory; a - specifies a file other than a directory. The first character in the permissions field for the file *info* is a minus sign, indicating that *info* is a regular file. The file *Letters* is a directory, as indicated by the *d* in the first character location. In addition to the *d*, this location will also hold a *b*, *c*, or *l* for some files. These characters tell several UNIX programs when there is something different or special about a particular file so it can be treated accordingly.

File Permissions

The remainder of the permissions field is divided into three sets of three characters each. Depending on how your account is set up, the record for practice could look like this:

```
rw- r-- r--
```

The first set **rw-** determines what you as owner (user) of the file can do with the file. If the first of these three slots contains an *r*, the owner has read permission and can view the contents of the file; read permission is allowed. A minus sign (-) in this position indicates that read permission is denied.

If the second slot is a *w*, the owner has **write** permission and can alter the contents of the file. A minus sign in this position will prevent the owner from altering the file.

The third slot indicates whether the file can be executed. An *x* indicates that the owner has execute permission. A minus sign here means that the file does not have execute permission set for the owner.

In summary, the presence of an *r*, *w*, or *x* in the first set of characters in a permission field indicates that the associated permission is allowed; a minus sign (-) indicates that this permission is denied.

7.4   USING NUMERALS TO CHANGE FILE PERMISSIONS

There are two ways to change the mode or permissions for files. One method uses **chmod** and mnemonic codes such as **-w**, **+x**, and **-r** to add or remove permissions. There is another method that allows you to specify permissions with numerals.

1. Examine the permissions of the *info* file by typing

   ls -l *info*

2. Change its mode to be read and write only using

   chmod -x *info*

3. Examine the permissions field with

ls -l *info*

The field is probably

```
-rw-r--r--
```

indicating that the file is not a directory (minus sign in the first position), and that the user (you) has read and write permission (*rw-* in positions 2-4).

Until now you have changed a file's mode by explicitly telling the system what change you want by using a command, such as **chmod +x** *filename* to add execute permission. You can also use numerals to change permissions, as shown here:

4. Type the following:

chmod 700 *info*

5. Examine the permissions now granted by displaying a long listing for the file:

ls -l *info*

The resulting permissions field indicates the user has full read, write, and execute permission for the file, but that the group and other users have no access.

Using the numeral approach (**chmod 700**) to specify the permissions for a file allows you to specify the exact permissions you want to be granted, regardless of the current permissions.

Granting Specific Permissions with Numerals

You can specify read only permission using the numeral approach.

1. Type the following:

   chmod 400 *info*

2. Again examine the long listing for the file. Only an **r** is present in the owner permissions field.

   Examine the meaning of the numbers following **chmod**. In the following list of numbers, note that the numbers 1, 2, and 4 are used in combinations that add up to produce 3, 5, 6, and 7. Each of these combinations adds together to produce a number that no other combination yields.

   1
   2
   3 = 2+1
   4
   5 = 4+1
   6 = 4+2
   7 = 4+2+1

This set of unique numbers is used with **chmod** to establish the permissions for files. The numbers 1, 2, and 4 are assigned these permission values:

1 allows execute permission
2 allows write permission
4 allows read permission.

These primitives (1, 2, and 4) can be added together to grant any combination of permissions. The basic permissions for a file are

0   grants no permissions
1   grants execute permission only
2   grants write permission only
3   grants write and execute permissions (1 + 2)

The sum of 1 + 2 = 3 means that execute and write permissions are both granted, but read permission is denied. Additionally,

4   grants read permission only
5   grants read and execute (1 + 4)
6   grants read and write (2 + 4)
7   grants read and write and execute (1 + 2 + 4)

Thus the three numbers 1, 2, and 4 can be used to express the eight possible states involving combinations of execute, write, and read permissions.

Granting Combinations of Permissions

The following is a list of owner permissions and their corresponding meanings:

000   no permissions
100   x
200   w
300   wx
400   r

500	rx
600	rw
700	rwx

1. Use the **chmod** command plus an owner permission combination number to grant one of the eight permission states for one of your files.

2. After each permission change, examine the permissions field using the **ls -l** command.

Examining File Permissions for Group and Others

When you create a file of any kind, you are the owner of that file. As owner, you are responsible for setting permissions for yourself (often referred to as user), for others who are in the same group as yourself, and for any others who might have access to the system.

In the records of the long listing, the name of the owner and group are the third and fourth fields. The three sets of characters in the permission field (the first field) determine file access for three different types of users on the system: user, group, and all others.

| *user* | *group* | *others* |
| rwx | r-x | --x |

The same permission field rules for user (explained earlier in this chapter) apply for group and others.

The middle three positions determine the read, write, and execute permissions for members of the group with which the file is associated. This is done so that people working on the same project can have access to the same files and resources, and also place different restrictions on the rest of the system's users. The last three slots determine permissions for everyone else who has an account on the system.

For example:

```
rwx r-x - -x
```

In this example, the user has read, write, and execute permission for the file. Other members of the same group have read and execute permission, but not write permission. They can see and execute the file, but they cannot alter it. All others have permission to execute, but not to read or write to the file. Every file has an associated permission field for user, group, and all others on the system.

In most cases these three permission fields have the following meaning:

- User's permissions determine what you can do with the file if you own it.

- Group permissions determine what people in your group can do with your files, and what you can do with files owned by members of your group.

- Others' permissions determine what other users can do with the files you create, and what you can do with files owned by users not in your group.

Changing Permissions for Group and Others

You have learned how numeral values specify the permissions granted to files. The same mode-changing values are used to specify the permissions for any of the three sets (user, group, others) in the permissions field.

The **chmod 700** command you entered earlier granted full access to the owner and no access to group or others. The **700** code has three fields (7,0,0), representing the numerical permission code for owner, group, and others.

1. Add full permission to your group by typing

   chmod 770 *info*

2. Check the permissions for *info*. Type

   ls -l *info*

   Both the user and the group have read, write, and execute permission for the file. Others are denied access.

3. Type the following command, which grants full permissions to everyone:

   chmod 777 *info*

4. Check how you have changed the permissions for *info* by typing

   ls -l *info*

   The permissions now show read, write, and execute for user, group, and all other users.

5. Try out the following permission changing commands, first by changing the *info* file's permissions, then examining permissions with **ls -l**, and finally trying to execute *info*.

chmod 751 *info*
chmod 640 *info*
chmod 000 *info*
chmod 700 *info*

Exercise 7-A

1. What command gives you a long listing of your filenames, including the permissions attached to each file?

_____

2. What permissions are granted, to which classes of users, for a file with the permissions field -r-x------?

_____

3. What command would you use to change a file's permissions to include read, write, and execute for the owner of the file only?

_____

4. What would the permissions field be for a file after you changed its mode to include read, write, and execute permission for the user only?

_____

7.5   USING DIRECTORY PERMISSIONS

When you enter **ls -l**, the output reveals that directories have the same kind of permissions field as regular files, except for the *d* in the leftmost position. Directory permissions are much the same as for files. The owner can change the permissions; they determine which users have access to the directory and its files; and they use the same numerals for assigning permissions.

Controlling Directory Access

As with files, the owner of a directory has the responsibility for setting permissions for access to it. Directory permissions, like file permissions, include read, write, and execute.

1. Create a subdirectory *Mybin* in your Home directory by typing

   mkdir *Mybin*

2. Examine the specific permissions attached to *Mybin* by typing

   System V:
   ls -ld *Mybin*

   BSD:
   ls -l *Mybin*

3. Modify the permissions attached to *Mybin* by using the **chmod** command. Type commands such as

chmod 700 *Mybin*
chmod 400 *Mybin*

4. After each change mode command, check the permissions with

SystemV:
ls -ld *Mybin*

or

BSD:
ls -l *Mybin*

Examining the Need for Execute Permissions

Determine whether the *Mybin* subdirectory has read, write and execute permission allowed for you.

1. If it doesn't, type

   chmod 700 *Mybin*

The *Mybin* subdirectory now has read, write, and execute permission granted to you, the owner.

2. Create file *info1* in the new subdirectory. Type

   cp *info Mybin/info1*

3. Change the mode of *Mybin* to read and write only.

   chmod 600 *Mybin*

4. Attempt to change directories to *Mybin* by typing

   cd *Mybin*

The shell returns this error message:

```
Mybin: Permission denied
```

To change directories, you must have execute permission for that directory.

Exploring Read and Write Permissions for Directories

Change the permissions for *Mybin* to each mode listed at the top of Table 7-1, which follows. Then try each of the commands listed at the left of the table, and write in whether or not you can execute each command for each mode.

TABLE 7-1.   Effects of Changing Directory Permissions

COMMAND	700 Mode	400 Mode	200 Mode	100 Mode	000 Mode
List files: **ls** *Mybin*	yes				
Change Directories: **cd** *Mybin*	yes				
Read File: **pg** *Mybin/ info1* or **more** *Mybin/ info1*	yes				
Create File: **vi** *newfile*	yes				
Execute Script: **Mybin/info1**	yes				

These exercises reveal that

- Read permission is needed to list the contents of a directory with **ls**.

- Write permission must be granted to create files in, or remove them from a directory (or to write to the directory file).

- Execute permission is needed before you can make a directory your working directory with **cd**, or pass through it as part of a search path.

This last point has important consequences. Say there is a file for which you have execute permission, located in a directory that gives you read permission; you could look at the file's attributes with **ls**. However, if you do not have execute permission for the directory in which the target directory is nested, you cannot get through it to execute the file in the lower directory. In the previous example, you changed the permissions on *Mybin* to 600. Even though you have execute permission for the file *info1*, you cannot now execute *info1* because you do not have execute permission for the directory *Mybin*.

Establishing Directory Permissions for Group and Others

The permissions on directories are specified for user, group, and all others, in the same fields of the listing as for file permissions.

1. Restore full permissions to owner by typing

   chmod 700 *Mybin*

   No one but you can obtain a listing of the files in *Mybin* using **ls**, **cd** to that directory, or execute any of your executable files in that directory, regardless of the execute permissions for any individual file.

2. Allow all users in your group permission to execute your files in *Mybin.* Type

   chmod 710 *Mybin*

   Because of the 7 in the first position, this command allows only you total access to your own directory. It does not allow group users to **ls** or write files in your directory. Other users who are not in your group are still denied all access.

3. To allow read, write, and execute permission to all users on the system, type

   chmod 777 *Mybin*

7.6   DETERMINING PERMISSION SETTINGS WHEN FILES ARE CREATED

In UNIX you can create files three ways: when you copy files, when you request the creation of a new file using an editor, and when you specify a new file using redirection in a shell command.

Examining the Default Permissions

When you create new files, UNIX assigns predetermined default permission settings. When you created the command file *info,* the operating system set the user permission to read and write. Hence, you could not execute the file. Because most files are not programs, UNIX treats new files as ordinary files, not command files. The owner is granted read and write permissions. For security reasons, the initial file restrictions are generally set to read only for group and others. Hence the permissions are 644. For directories the default settings are full permissions for user, read and execute permissions to all other users (755). On some UNIX systems the directories are created with default mode of 754. These default settings are determined by the **umask** value.

Setting the Default Permissions

Suppose you need a customized set of file access restrictions for the files in your account. For example, you might not want anyone to be able to read certain files. If you only have a few files, you can always use **chmod 644** on all of the affected files. Or you can make your Home directory nonexecutable. However, if you still want other users to be able to list your directory, this would be inconvenient. Another solution is to change the default settings by modifying the **umask** system variable (*file creation mode mask*).

1. From your Home directory, type

   umask

   Unless you have already customized your file creation mode mask (**umask**) system variable, your terminal will display something like this:

022

or its equivalent:

22

2. Create a file *info2* with the **vi** command. Check the mode of *info2* by typing

ls -l *info2*

If your **umask** is set to 022, the mode of the new file is read permission for everyone, and write permission for user (owner). The **umask** value of 022 tells you that a new file will be created with the permission number 644.

$$
\begin{array}{rl}
666 & \text{read and write for file} \\
\underline{-022} & \textbf{umask} \\
644 & \text{granted}
\end{array}
$$

3. Set your **umask** to 077 by typing

umask 077

4. Create another file called *fact3*. Then check the permissions of *fact3* with

ls -l *fact3*

The permissions are read and write for owner only (600). The **umask** value determines the default owner, group, and other permission fields for each new file created.

5. Create a new directory while you have **umask** set at 077. Type

mkdir *Mydir2*

6. Make it your current directory by typing

   cd *Mydir2*

7. To examine the permissions list, type

   ls -ld

   Note that the mode of the new directory is 700 (777-077 equals 700).

8. Change the **umask** to other values, such as 066. In each case, create a directory, and then examine the permissions for that directory.

A table complementary to the permissions numerals table can be made for umask values. Consider the following table for **umask** values to set the permission for the other (non-owner, non-group member) users field:

000 grants all the default system permissions
001 restricts execute permission only
002 restricts write permission only
003 restricts write and execute
004 restricts read permission only
005 restricts read and execute (1 + 4)
006 restricts read and write (2 + 4)
007 restricts read, write, and execute (1 + 2 + 4)

A similar table can be made for **umasks** for group and owner permissions.

Inheriting Permissions When Files Are Copied

You created a new file *info* that contained several shell commands. You made it executable, and then executed it.

1. Make a new file by copying the *info* file:

   cp *info info3*

   Because you have read permission for *info*, you can copy it into *info3*.

2. Attempt to execute the new file.

   info3

   This new file is executable. The file *info3* inherited the same permissions as *info*. When you copy a file, the new copy of the file will have the same permissions as the original.

Exercise 7-B

1. What permissions are granted on a directory with the permissions field drwxr-xr--?

   _____

2. What command would you enter to set the permission fields of all newly created files to read and write for owner, and read only for everyone else?

   _____

3. What command would you enter to set the permission fields of all newly created directories to read, write, and execute for owner, and execute only for everyone else?

———————————————

UNIX is a collection of files. Some are essential for system operation, others contain valuable information, and still others are powerful programs that should be employed only by certain users. Many files are simply useful to one or more users.

CONCLUSION

Each file has an associated set of permissions that determine which users can read, write, and execute it. The owner of the file is responsible for managing its permissions.

Two methods of changing the file's mode, or permissions, are available: a mnemonic approach (**chmod +x**) and a numeral code (**chmod 700**).

COMMAND SUMMARY

ls -l
Produces a long listing, including permissions, of the files contained in the current directory.

chmod *mode filename*
Changes the permissions on *filename* to those represented by *mode*.

chown *owner filename*
Changes the owner associated with *filename* to *owner*.

chgrp *group filename*
Changes the group associated with *filename* to *group*.

umask *mode*
Changes the default permissions on new files to a permission value equal to 777 minus *mode* for directories and a permission value equal to 666 minus *mode* for plain files.

Mode Summary

r
Allows read permission for designated user.

w
Allows write permission for designated user.

x
Allows execute permission for designated user.

4
Allows read permission for designated user.

2
Allows write permission for designated user.

1
Allows execute permission for designated user.

·8·

The UNIX World of Directories

To manage files, you create new directories that are subdirectories of your Home directory. In the same sense, your Home directory is a subdirectory of some higher directory. Utilities, data files, and all other system files are listed in directories, and those directories are in turn listed in other directories. Essentially, everything on UNIX is part of a complex directory tree. In this chapter you will explore the major directories that are part of the UNIX filesystem.

SKILLS CHECK

Before beginning this chapter, you should be able to

- Access and leave the system (Chapter 1, "Touring the System's Features")
- Create and display files (Chapter 1)
- Name, copy, and remove files (Chapter 1)
- Use several shell commands in combination (Chapter 1)
- Execute basic shell commands (Chapter 1)
- Access and modify files using an editor (Chapter 2, "Basic Editing with the Visual Editor")
- Utilize the UNIX directory hierarchy system, sub-directories, and parent directories (Chapter 3, "Using UNIX Directories")
- Set file permissions (Chapter 7, "Setting File Permissions")

OBJECTIVES

After completing this chapter, you will be able to

- Move around in the UNIX filesystem
- Describe the UNIX filesystem structure
- Identify system directories and their contents

8.1   EXPLORING THE UNIX FILESYSTEM

On a UNIX system, there are many different files that are listed in directories. You have been using your

Home directory and various subdirectories to organize your own files.

1. Log onto your UNIX account.

2. Make sure your current directory is your Home directory by typing

   cd

Examining Files in the Home Directory

A long listing of the contents of your Home directory provides useful information about each file.

1. Obtain a long listing of your current directory by typing

   ls -l

   The **-l** option for **ls** requests a display of the permissions associated with the files. It also provides you with the size of each file, the owner of each file, and the date and time the file was last modified.

2. UNIX also gives you a command for discovering the type of a particular file. Type

   file *practice*

   The **file** command helps identify different kinds of files. In this case, *practice* is a text file.

3. Examine **file**'s report of all the files in your Home directory. Type one of the following commands:

System V:

file * I pg

BSD:

file * I more

There may be a number of different types of files listed, such as *ascii text, English text* and *roff, nroff* or *eqn input text*. There may also be directories and even executable files. You may also see other kinds of system files such as symbolic links, character special, block special, and so forth, which you will soon learn about.

Moving Up and Down in the System Hierarchy

Thus far in your exploration of UNIX, you have created subdirectories listed in your Home directory with the **mkdir** *directoryname* command. You have changed your current directory with the **cd** *directoryname* command. With these commands, you created a subdirectory in your Home directory and changed directories between the subdirectory and the parent directory.

1. To pinpoint your current location (and your Home directory) in the directory tree, type

pwd

The output is something like this:

`/users/staff/yourname`

The last name in the list is the name of the current (Home) directory (in this case, *yourname*).

2. Move into the parent directory of your current directory by typing

   cd ..

   No matter where you are below the *root* level in the branching scheme, UNIX recognizes .. (dot-dot) as the name of the directory just above your current one. A directory can have many subdirectories, but only one parent directory. Each subdirectory has its parent listed as the .. directory.

3. From this new vantage point, type

   pwd

   The output of this command is again the name of your current working directory. The list is now one name shorter; the name of your Home directory has dropped off. You are therefore located in the parent directory of your Home directory.

4. Examine the contents of your current working directory by typing

   ls -l

   Your Home directory name appears in the list of files in this current directory.

5. Examine the contents of this directory by typing one of the following commands:

System V:
file * | pg

BSD:
file * | more

Notice that most of the listed files are other directories that may be the Home directories of other users on this UNIX system. As these other Home directories are simply branches of the tree, just like your own Home directory, you can change into these directories (if you are *permitted* to do so).

6. Examine the contents of your Home directory without changing directories. Type

ls -l *yourloginname*

where *yourloginname* is your Home directory as listed in the current directory. From your current directory, you are looking into your Home directory.

Making root Your Working Directory

There are two ways to move to the top of the directory hierarchy; both use the **cd** command.

1. To move up *one step at a time* until you come to the topmost directory level, type

cd ..

2. Confirm your current directory status with

pwd

3. If you are not at the *root* directory yet, repeat the command **cd ..** until you get there.

4. Once at *root,* return to your Home directory and confirm that location, by typing

cd; pwd

5. To move to the *root* directory *in one step,* type

cd /

The / is the UNIX designation for the *root* directory. (It is also the character used to separate directory and filenames when you use a full pathname.) All of the directories in the UNIX filesystem branch from *root.*

6. Make certain your present working directory is *root,* by typing

pwd

The path is now rather short: / appears on the terminal.

7. To get a listing of the contents of *root*, type

ls -l

EXPLORING THE NATURE OF FILES AND DIRECTORIES

8.2

1. Type the command

ls -F

The output is a list of names, nearly all of which are subdirectories of *root*. These directories are the major functional subdivisions where files are stored on the UNIX system. Branching from the major directories are more directories and files. Every little part has its particular role to play; in any complex operation, organization is a paramount requirement.

Files are the basic organizational divisions for the UNIX system structure. A file is a package of information with a name, and its contents can be accessed using its name.

A directory is a file that contains filenames and a way to obtain information about the listed files. You may have files that contain words that make sentences, or a list of phone numbers. The words or phone numbers appear on your screen if you look at these files. When you type **ls**, the system actually looks at a special file called the directory and finds a list of "pointers" which lead to the other files. In effect, a directory is a road map to the files. One pointer leads to another directory, which in turn is another list of names and pointers to other files. In this way, a tree-like structure is created, with branches growing downward from the first list of pointers—the *root* directory.

Identifying Essential Files

Applying the upside-down tree analogy to the organizational scheme of the UNIX system allows us to visualize the layout of UNIX and provides for functional comparison as well. Some branches might even be removed, but the tree still flourishes.

For example, when a person leaves the company and is no longer needed to work on the UNIX system, the branch (in other words, the subdirectory) that is the Home directory might be removed. All the subdirectories created would disappear; however, the remainder of the UNIX system would probably not suffer.

On the other hand, there are some directories that the system must have in order to function. These major system directories may be located anywhere within the UNIX hierarchy. The subdirectories you are about to examine contain files, as well as other subdirectories that contain more files. The system needs these files to run properly and to keep track of all its various functions and information.

Both the operating system and its users need to know that all of a certain type of files are located in a specific subdirectory or set of subdirectories. This organization makes the system and the user much more efficient. Moreover, the UNIX system, as well as many of its commands, expects to find specific files in familiar places every time they are needed. These expectations are literally "programmed into" many commands.

Examining the Contents of the System Directories

1. Obtain a listing of the files in your *root* directory. First change to the *root* directory by typing

cd /

2. To see the list of files listed in the *root* directory, type

ls

The *root* directory lists the major system directories. Although there is some variation among systems, you will see directories such as */bin, /dev, /etc, /lib, /lost+found,* and */tmp.* There is also a directory for users' Home directories, whose name can change from system to system. It may be called */z,* or */u,* or */usr,* or some other appropriate name.

In addition, *root* contains the system *kernel,* a file called *unix* or *vmunix* (this name may also contain a version number). The kernel is loaded into memory when the system is *booted* (started up); it stays in memory until the system is shut down. The kernel manages and controls all the system's resources.

The *lost+found* directory may contain files from many system directories, including *root.* Whenever a filesystem check is run on your system, there will sometimes appear files that for some reason have become disconnected from their directories. The system lists these files in the *lost+found* directory, so that they can be located by their owners when they are missed.

3. Examine the permissions on the files and directories present in *root* by typing

ls -l

Not all of the files in *root* are accessible by everyone on the system. Certain files, like *mbox,* are only for the user **root**. The *root* directory is the Home directory of the user **root**, and there are files listed there that are not for public use.

4. Differentiate between the types of files by typing one of the following commands:

System V:
file * I pg

BSD:
file * I more

The major difference between the *root* directory and all other subdirectories is that *root* has no parent directory.

The /bin Directory

The directory name *bin* was originally derived from "binary," because the files in this directory were binary (executable code) files. Many of the commands with which you are familiar are executable files.

1. Change your current directory to */bin*, by typing

   cd */bin*

2. Make certain your present working directory is */bin;* type

   pwd

3. Examine the contents of */bin* by typing

   ls

The files for **ls** and **pg**, and other commands that you have used before, are files located in the */bin* directory. When you type the name of a command like **ls**, the instructions within the command file are executed by the system. These commands are often referred to as *utility programs,* and the */bin* directory is the place where you find the most important ones.

4. Now type one of the following:

System V:
file * | pg

BSD:
file * | more

The output from this command may say the files *ls* and *mkdir* are "demand paged pure executable." This is the UNIX way of telling you that these files are executable.

5. If you are on a BSD system, and have permission, you can look at the strings of characters in an executable file. For example, type

strings *vi*

Some of the command files may also be symbolically linked to other files. This means that when you type in a filename, you actually access the file located elsewhere. They are linked.

The /usr/bin Directory

There is also a directory below */usr,* called */usr/bin,* where more utility programs are stored. For now, think of these two /bin directories as the primary locations of the commands you use on the system. Examine /usr/bin by typing one of the following:

System V:
ls -l /usr/bin | pg

BSD:
ls -l /usr/bin | more

The /dev Directory

The /dev (device) directory contains all of the *device special files.*

1. Change to the /dev directory by entering

   cd /dev

2. Examine the contents of /dev by typing

   ls -l

The entire UNIX system is made up of files. Every structural unit in the operating system is treated like a file. Units like your terminal, the storage disk, or a tape drive are all handled as files by the operating system.

One example of a device special file is the interaction between the operating system and your terminal. UNIX considers terminals to be device files. To display a character on a screen, it writes the character to the terminal's device file; the character is then displayed on the screen. Each terminal has an associated file in the /dev directory.

3. Determine the file associated with your terminal by typing

tty

The command **tty** returns the device special file in the /dev directory that is associated with your screen and your processes. The output of **tty** provides the filename of your device file.

4. Connect the output of the **cat** utility to the device file for your terminal. Type

cat /etc/passwd >/dev/your_tty_file

The expected result of this command is the output of the **cat** utility that is connected to the file /dev/your_tty_file. The output is displayed to your screen. The file /etc/passwd was written to the device special file that is associated to your screen.

Just as the system can read from an ordinary file, it can also read information from a terminal or even a storage disk treating it as if it were a file. The same "as if" situation is true when you write information to a disk. When it reads or writes information, the system always writes from one "file" to another.

It is in this manner that all the different devices— the tape drive, disk drive, console, and others—are handled.

5. Once again list the contents of */dev*:

ls -l

Disk drives are listed with names such as *rsd0c* or *rsmd0a*.

Be aware, however, that all devices, including the tape drive, disk drive, and console are not accessible by everyone. Accessibility is controlled by the file permissions on these device special files. You have permission to write to your *tty* file, but you cannot write to the console, disk drive, or line printer. You often cannot write to another *tty*.

The /etc Directory

1. Make the */etc* directory your current directory by entering

cd */etc*

2. Type

ls -l

to view the contents of this directory.

The */etc* (etcetera) directory contains maintenance commands and essential data files used primarily for system administration. Maintenance commands are for periodic system chores, such as making and reading magnetic tape backups of what is on the system's storage disk(s). An example of an essential data file is the file *passwd*, which contains the encrypted passwords for each user, and is an important element of system security and login verification.

3. Now change back to *root,* so you can examine the directories described in the next few sections. Type

cd /

4. As you read the following descriptions, examine each directory with

ls *directory*

where directory is the name of the directory you are studying.

The **/lib** Directory

The */lib* (library) directory contains files crucial to the compilation of programming languages on UNIX. It is an archive for machine and programming information, in the same way a real library is an archive for a wide range of human knowledge. In addition, there is a */usr/lib* directory nested in */usr*. It contains the same sorts of files, but with a wider variety.

The **/tmp** Directory

The */tmp* (temporary) directory is where many programs running on the system keep temporary copies of files or data. Users often write temporary files to the */tmp* directory. No permanent files are stored here. Each time the system is rebooted, */tmp* is cleaned out.

The /usr Directory

The */usr* (users') directory has the most general purpose of all the major system directories. You have
already examined two of the subdirectories of */usr*, the
*/usr/***bin** and */usr/lib* directories. There are several
others, among them */usr/adm* (administrative information) and */usr/man* (on-line manual pages). You will
also often find in */usr* the directories for software
packages that were added to the system.

1. Make */usr/bin* your working directory by typing

   cd */usr/bin*

2. Now examine the contents of */usr/bin* with

   ls -l

3. There is a file called *calendar* that you should have
   permission to read and to execute. To make sure
   that the file contains readable text before you examine it, type

   file *calendar*

4. Since *calendar* is in *command text* form, it can be read
   with no adverse effect to your screen. On the other
   hand, if you were to **pg** or **more** through an
   executable file like */bin/ls*, the contents of the file
   would not be correctly displayed by the terminal.
   This could cause the screen to lock up, or at times to
   log the user off the system. Type one of the following commands:

   System V:
   pg *calendar*

BSD:
more *calendar*

As you can see, the file *calendar* is simply a collection of commands to the shell interpreter. When you run the command **calendar**, all the instructions contained in the file are executed.

The mail Directory

Below the */usr* directory is the directory *mail*. The *mail* directory contains unread mail to all users on the system.

1. Change to the *mail* directory by typing one of the following:

   System V:
   cd *mail*

   BSD:
   cd */usr/spool/mail*

2. Find out what is in the *mail* directory. Type

   ls

3. If your login name is not in the listing, send a short **mail** message to yourself.

4. Repeat the **ls** command until your login name appears in the listing.

5. Once your name is in the listing, find out what is in the file. Type

cat *your_login_name*

You should see the **mail** message that you just sent and other messages that you might not have read. The *usr/mail* directory is where the system stores unread mail.

6. Change back to the *usr* directory. Type

cd */usr*

The **/usr/spool** Directory

List the contents of the */usr* directory. One of the listings is the *spool* directory.

1. Change to the *spool* directory by typing

cd *spool*

2. Determine what files and directories are in *spool*.

ls -F

3. Notice the *uucp* directory, and examine its contents.

ls *uucp*

The *uucp* directory is where the system stores jobs that will be executed in batches at a later time. They include files to be sent between systems using the UUCP program.

4. One of the directories in */usr/spool* is the directory where unprinted files are stored before they are printed. It is named *lp* or some other name associated with your printers. Examine the directory.

There are probably more directories in your *usr/spool* directory; these vary from system to system. You can explore these directories, and you should find that each is similar to the directories mentioned above.

The users' Directory

We have now come full circle. The *users'* directory holds the Home directories for most, if not all, users on the system. This is the directory we moved into previously, when we began to explore the system hierachy. Think of this directory, with its many Home directories, as the place where the system users store the work they do on the system. Its name can be */z1, /u1, /user,* or any other assigned name.

Exercise 8-A

Complete the following exercises before proceeding to the next chapter.

1. What shell command will move you directly to the *root* directory?

   _____

2. Which directory contains the device special files?

   _____

3. Which two directories contain utility programs?

_____

The UNIX system is a collection of files. Each utility, user directory, terminal, and even the kernel is a file located in the filesystem. Directories are files that include the filename and a number that leads to information about the file and its disk address. Terminals are devices, as are tape drives and other equipment included in the system. Addition of new files, users, equipment, and commands is accomplished by extending the filesystem — adding the appropriate file.

The general layout of the root directory is reasonably consistent throughout the various flavors of UNIX although some names may be different and proprietary commands may be added by each vendor.

You move throughout the system by changing directories and using pathnames.

CONCLUSION

·9·

Advanced Visual Editing

The visual editor is used to create and edit files. Thus far, you have been entering commands that perform operations such as adding text, deleting text, and opening new lines. Each of these operations takes place relative to the position of the cursor. The editor also permits addressing text by line number. Blocks of text can be moved, deleted, and written to another file.

Other available **vi** features are choosing where in a file to begin editing when you execute **vi** from the shell, marking lines for editing, and customizing your editing environment with specific editing features, such as line numbers, word wrap, and auto indenting.

SKILLS CHECK   Before beginning this chapter, you should be able to

- Access and leave the system and execute basic commands (Chapter 1, "Touring the System's Features")
- Create, display, and print files (Chapter 1)
- Access and modify files using the **vi** editor (Chapter 2, "Basic Editing with the Visual Editor")

OBJECTIVES   Upon completion of this chapter, you will be able to

- Use the line command features of **vi** to set the editing environment
- Copy, move, delete, and write lines of a file using line numbers, marked lines, or special characters in **vi**
- Read another file into the current file
- Use buffers for cutting and pasting lines

9.1   ACCESSING A FILE FOR EDITING AT SPECIFIED LOCATIONS

There are several ways to use **vi** to access a file. Thus far in this book, you were instructed to type **vi** with a *filename* argument. Editing begins with the cursor at the first line of the file. There are also ways to instruct the editor to begin editing at other locations in the file.

Starting to Edit a File at a Specified Line

For example, begin editing with the cursor at the eighth line of the file.

1. Type the command line

   vi *+8 practice*

   A single space separates the **vi** command and the *+8*, and another space separates the *+8* from the filename. This command tells the editor to open the file and place the cursor at the beginning of the eighth line.

2. Make some changes in the file, such as adding a new line of text.

3. Return to the shell by pressing [Esc] and typing

   :wq

   The general format of the command is

vi *+n filename*

where *n* is a line number.

Accessing a File at a Specified Word

You can also instruct the editor to begin editing a file on the first line that includes a specific word or string of characters.

1. Type the following command:

vi +/*the practice*

If the file *practice* contains the string *the* as a word, or within some other word, the file is displayed with the cursor positioned on the first line containing that pattern.

The general format of the command is

vi +/*string filename*

Accessing a File for Reading Only

On some occasions, you will want only to examine a file using the power of **vi** commands. To prevent accidental changes, you can use the visual editor to only **view** a file.

1. Examine the file *practice* by entering

view *filename*

2. Move through the file using /*word*, ⌷Ctrl-d⌷, and ?*word*.

3. Even though you intended to just read the file, attempt to make a change or two to the text. Then enter the usual **:wq** to save and exit.

You are informed with an error message that the file is read only.

4. Exit **view** by quitting the editor without writing. Type

   :q!

   With **view** you can insist that you really do want to make changes by using the **:w!** command.

5. Call up the *practice* file again with **view**, and make some changes.

6. Write the changes to the file by typing

   :w!

   The **view** command functions like **vi**, except that changes cannot be written to disk unless you force a write with the **!** character. The **view** command is very useful to prevent accidental changes to important files.

MODIFYING THE EDITING ENVIRONMENT

9.2

You can tailor how the editor works for you, using a series of commands that customize your visual editor environment. You will use line number, auto indent, special character listing, wrap margin and other features in the next few sections. First, bring up the file *practice* by typing

vi *practice*

and make certain you are in **vi** command mode.

Employing Line Numbers

1. If you do not have line numbers, request them by typing

   :set number

   and pressing ⎡Return⎤.

2. To remove the numbers, type

   :set nonumber

   and press ⎡Return⎤.
       You may abbreviate the **number** command as **nu** in **vi**. Reset numbers using the abbreviation. The abbreviation for **nonumber** is **nonu** in the editor.

   The **number** command option is a typical **set** option in the visual editor. To make a **set** option take effect, you type

:set *option*

and press ⎡Return⎤.
    To turn off the feature, that is, return to the state before the option was set, you type

:set no*option*

and press ⎡Return⎤.

Setting Automatic Indenting

The **autoindent** command indents a new line the same amount of space as the line above it.

1. Identify a line in your file and insert a [Tab] or several blank spaces at the left margin.

2. Press [Return] and add another line. The new line is at the left margin.

3. Leave append mode with [Esc] and from command mode, type

   :set autoindent

   and press [Return].
      The abbreviation for **autoindent** is **ai**.

4. After you have set automatic indent, enter append mode.

5. Add another line beginning with a [Tab] or spaces. Press [Return] and add more lines.

Escaping autoindent

Occasionally **autoindent** becomes a nuisance.

1. Add another line of text that is **autoindent**ed, and press [Return].

2. Move the cursor back to the left, cancelling the **autoindent** for this one line while still in append mode, and press [Ctrl-d].
      This moves the cursor one shift width to the left.

If this doesn't move you back far enough, you can press Ctrl-d again.

3. To shut off **autoindent**, enter command mode by pressing Esc, and then type

:set noai

Ignoring Upper- and Lowercase in Searches

To the editor, *Father* and *father* are different strings of letters because of the uppercase *F* and lowercase *f*. The **ignorecase** option makes the editor ignore case during searches.

1. Following the same procedure as in the previous section, set **ignorecase** by typing

:set ignorecase

You can abbreviate **ignorecase** as **ic**. With **ignorecase** in effect, you can find any word, whether it is capitalized or lowercase, even when you have specified a search for lowercase.

2. Search for all instances of the word *the* by typing

/tHe

Even though the letter *H* is capitalized in the search command, all instances of the word *the* are found.

Listing Special Characters

The editor will display special characters, such as tabs, in a readable format.

1. While in the command mode, type this command:

   :set list

   A $ appears at the end of each line in the text. It is the code for the end-of-line character. Tabs are displayed as ˆI throughout the text.

Matching Programming Constructs

The **showmatch** option causes right (closing) parentheses and right brackets to be matched with their matching left (opening) parentheses or brackets.

1. While in command mode, type

   :set showmatch

2. Start typing text with a few left parentheses scattered throughout.

3. Once you have a few lines, type one or two right parentheses. As you "close off" each pair of parentheses, the cursor flashes on the matching open left parenthesis that is being closed.

4. Keep adding right parentheses until you close off all the open left parentheses. The first open right parenthesis you type causes your terminal to beep, flash, or in some way notify you that there isn't a matching open left parenthesis.

   This feature is useful when you are writing programs in a variety of programming languages.

Setting the Size of a Window

Thus far you have used the basic toggle mechanism for on-off **set** options in the visual editor. There is another type of feature which requires that you set a value.

1. To change the terminal window size definition, type the command

   :set window=12

   Make sure there are no spaces around the equal sign.

2. Now type

   z.

   The dot is essential to redraw your screen.

   Because the **window** option is now *12* instead of the usual *23*, there are only *12* lines displayed on the screen. As your screen scrolls, the upper portion will fill, but every time you invoke a command that causes the screen to be redrawn, only *12* lines will be filled.

   The following commands change the display on your screen and are affected by window size: **z.** for redraw, Ctrl-f for forward screening, and Ctrl-b for backward screening.

3. Reset your window to *23* lines by typing

   :set window=23

Setting Tab Spacing

The **tabstop** option allows you to set the number of spaces used when **vi** displays the tab character.

1. In command mode, type

:set **tabstop** = *4*

2. Press the Tab key. The editor now puts a tab stop at every four spaces, all the way to the right margin, whenever you press the Tab key. The **tabstop** abbreviation is **ts**.

3. Change the **tabstop** setting to *10* and try it again.

Setting the **tabstop** option only affects the visual display of the text while you're in **vi**. When the file is printed, the printer will use its own settings for tabs, and the file output may be spaced differently from the display you see in **vi**.

Automatically Returning to a New Line

The **wrapmargin** option allows you to set the position of the screen's right margin, which determines the maximum number of characters the editor can display on a line. Once that limit is reached, the lines will automatically "wrap" to a new line. The smaller the value, the closer to the right side of the screen you can type.

1. In command mode of the visual editor, type

:set **wrapmargin** = *50*

and press Return.
You can abbreviate **wrapmargin** as **wm**.

2. Enter the append mode and type several random lines. You cannot type lines longer than about 30 characters. After this point the editor will automatically return the cursor to the beginning of a new line.

A more reasonable **wrapmargin** value is 5. When you use the **wrapmargin** option, the system determines the line length by subtracting the value of **wrapmargin** from the standard line length of 80 characters. To shut off the **wrapmargin** option, give it a value of 0.

Reporting the Value of One Option

1. From the command mode, type

:set window

Observe at the bottom of your screen that the editor displays

```
window=23
```

2. When you want to see the current value for an option that has been set, you can type

:set *option*

and the option name and its value will be displayed.

Reporting the Value of All Options

1. To find out how all options are set, type

   :set all

2. The report indicates what options are on or off and the current values for options that accept values.

   If you forget the name of one of the **set** options you can use the **:set all** command to obtain a listing.

Exercise 9-A

1. How would you call up the file *practice* with the cursor at line 50?

   _____

2. What command line would you use to begin editing the file *practice* at the first occurrence of the string *help*?

   _____

3. What command calls up the full screen editor in read only mode?

   _____

4. What is the command that moves you back one word while you remain in append mode of **vi**?

   _____

5. What command enables you to view special characters (for instance, a tab) while editing a file?

_____

9.3   CUTTING AND PASTING WITH YANK AND PUT

One of the most useful functions of the **vi** editor is its ability to move and copy chunks of text to another location in a file.

Yanking and Putting Lines of Text

1. Make sure you are in the command mode, and then move the cursor to a line partway down the screen.

2. Now type

   yy

   Although it appears that nothing has happened, the **vi** editor has "yyanked" and made a copy of this line and is holding the copy in its memory. The line being copied is not deleted or otherwise affected by this command.

3. Move the cursor to a different place in your text. Type a lowercase

   p

   The line that was **yyanked** (copied) now also appears as a new line in the new location.

4. The yank feature is most useful for copying blocks of text. For instance, to yank seven lines of text, beginning with the cursor line, type

7yy

5. Move the cursor to a line where you want the yanked lines to be put, and type

p

A copy of the seven yanked lines of text now appears inserted as seven new lines below the cursor location.

Putting Lines in Several Places

1. Yank another line of text.

2. Move to a new location, and **p**ut the line of text there.

3. Move the cursor to another location, and **p**ut the line of text there, too. The yanked line of text now appears in three places, including its original location in the file.

Determining Placement of Put Lines

Try both the uppercase **P** and the lowercase **p** with the same portion of yanked text.

1. Type first the **P** and then the **p**, and notice where the line is placed with each command. **P** places the copied text on the line *above* the cursor location, and **p** places the copied text on the line *below* the cursor location.

Deleting and Putting Lines

The delete commands can also be combined with the put command in a fashion similar to the **yank** command.

1. Select a line to move somewhere else in your text.

2. Position the cursor on any character on the line to be moved, and type

   dd

3. Move the cursor to the line above the one where you want this text inserted, and then replace the deleted text by typing

   p

   To move a line of text from one location to a new location, delete a line of text, then move the cursor to a different location in your text, and use the **put** command to reposition the deleted text.

When you use either the **yank** or **delete** command, you must put the yanked or deleted text in a new place before using any text-changing commands; otherwise, you will lose it. You can use only cursor movement commands between **yank/delete** and **put** commands; you cannot save yanked or deleted text while you alter some other part of the text. For example, if you delete text, and then do another text changing task before repositioning the deleted text, the deleted text is lost. You will not be able to reinsert it in your file with the regular put command, you must use buffers, the subject of the next section.

USING NUMBERED BUFFERS 9.4

Whenever you delete one or more whole lines of text, the editor automatically saves the text in a buffer—a temporary holding area for your text. These buffers are numbered from 1 through 9. Individual words and characters that are deleted are not saved in a buffer. Numbered buffers are essential for retrieving deleted lines if you have made editing changes more recently than the deletions.

Placing Text in Buffers

1. From the command mode of the visual editor, delete one line of text, using

   dd

2. Reposition the cursor on a new line and delete two lines of text with

   2dd

3. Reposition the cursor on a new line and delete three lines of text using

    3dd

Retrieving Text from Buffers

You have now deleted three text blocks that are one, two, and three lines long, respectively.

When a text block is deleted, the deleted block is placed in buffer 1. Any old, deleted text that was in buffer 1 is shifted into buffer 2; old, deleted text in buffer 2 is shifted to buffer 3, and so forth. This process of shifting deleted blocks of text from buffer to buffer continues up to buffer 9, saving your last nine text blocks. The most recent text block deletion always resides in buffer 1.

1. You can now retrieve the two-line block of text you deleted in the previous procedure. Position the cursor just above where you want the lines from buffer 2 to appear and type the following using the double quote:

    "2p

2. In this command, the " instructs the editor to access a buffer, the 2 indicates which buffer, and the **p** indicates where to put the text—in a line *below* the cursor. If no text existed in buffer 2, you would receive a message saying

    ```
    Nothing in register 2
    ```

You may use either the lowercase or uppercase **P** commands, depending upon your needs. **P** places a copy of the buffer text *above* the current line; **p** places a copy of the buffer text *below* the current line. For example, the command "2**P** would copy the deleted text in buffer 2 to the line above the current cursor position.

Deleting and Putting Words or Characters

The **P** and **p** commands can also be used to put deleted characters or words in a different location in your file even though single characters and words are not saved in a buffer.

1. Move the cursor to the beginning of a word and delete the word with

   dw

2. Now move the cursor to the space between two other words, and type the lowercase command

   p

   The (lowercase) **put** command, combined with the **x** command, can quickly transpose characters in your text.

3. Move the cursor to the first letter of any word in your text and type

   x

4. Now type

   p

   and notice that the two characters are transposed.

Table 9-1 describes the two-way text-changing commands. Read the table and try each command

TABLE 9-1. Two-Way Text-Changing Commands

Command	Function
x	Erases (x out) only the letter under the cursor.
dw	deletes only the word under the cursor.
dd	Deletes the entire line.
D	Deletes the rest of the line (from the cursor position on).
r*b*	Replaces the letter under the cursor with the letter *b* (r*w* replaces character under cursor with letter *w*).
J	Joins cursor line with the next line in your text by appending the next line onto the end of the cursor line.
yy	Yanks the cursor line.
3yy	Yanks the specified number (3) of lines. For instance, 6yy is the "make a copy of the next 6 lines, remember them, and put them where I tell you to" command (see **put** commands).
P	(Uppercase P) Puts the yanked or deleted line(s) just above the cursor line.
p	(Lowercase p) Puts the yanked (or deleted) text just below the cursor line.

several times. The table summarizes commands introduced in this and earlier chapters.

EDITING BLOCKS OF TEXT _____ 9.5

There are several commands that allow you to copy a
single line or many lines of text from one place to
another in a file. These commands perform many of
the same functions you learned previously with the
two-way text-changing commands, but they are easier
to use in many circumstances.

Copying Blocks of Text

1. If you do not have line numbers on your screen, use
   the **:set nu** command to display them.

2. From **vi** command mode, in the *practice* file, type the
   following command, including the colon:

   :2 **copy** 4

   and press Return. A copy of line 2 was placed after
   line 4 in your file.

   With the **copy** command, the first number following the colon is the line number of the text that is
copied. The number following the word **copy** is the
target line number. The copied text is placed *after* the
target line.

3. The change made using the last command (copying a line) can be reversed by using the **u**ndo command:

u

4. You are not limited to copying one line of text at a time. Several lines can be copied to a specific location in a single operation. Type the command

:1,4 **copy** *7*

A copy of lines *1* through *4* is placed after line *7*. The original lines remain in place, but a copy is added to your text after line *7*.

5. Examine Figure 9-1. It depicts the effect of the following **copy** command:

:1,8 **copy** *17*

Using Line Addresses

Editing commands beginning with a colon (such as **:copy**) operate on a block of text that is identified by its beginning and ending line numbers, which are separated by a comma. Hence, *1,4* represents lines 1, 2, 3, and 4.

Likewise, *57,62* represents the lines beginning with 57, up to and including 62 . Be sure to type the lower

:1,8co 17

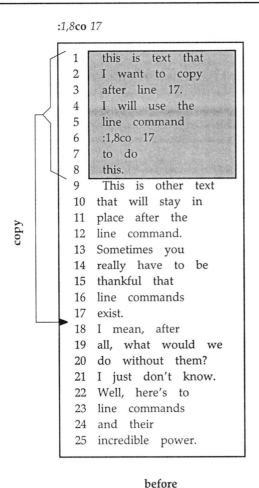

```
     1   this  is  text  that
     2   I  want  to  copy
     3   after  line  17.
     4   I  will  use  the
     5   line  command
     6   :1,8co  17
     7   to  do
     8   this.
     9       This  is  other  text
    10   that  will  stay  in
    11   place  after  the
    12   line  command.
    13   Sometimes  you
    14   really  have  to  be
    15   thankful  that
    16   line  commands
    17   exist.
    18   I  mean,  after
    19   all,  what  would  we
    20   do  without  them?
    21   I  just  don't  know.
    22   Well,  here's  to
    23   line  commands
    24   and  their
    25   incredible  power.
```

copy

before

```
     1   this  is  text  that
     2   I  want  to  copy
     3   after  line  17.
     4   I  will  use  the
     5   line  command
     6   :1,8co      17
     7   to  do
     8   this.
     9       This  is  other  text
    10   that  will  stay  in
    11   place  after  the
    12   line  command
    13   Sometimes  you
    14   really  have  to  be
    15   thankful  that
    16   line  commands
    17   exist.
    18   this  is  text  that
    19   I  want  to  copy
    20   after  line  17.
    21   I  will  use  the
    22   line  command
    23   :1,6co      17
    24   to  do
    25   this.
    26   I  mean,  after
    27   all,  what  would  we
    28   do  without  them?
    29   I  just  don't  know
    30   Well,  here's  to
    31   line  commands
    32   and  their
    ...  incredible  power.
```

after

FIGURE 9-1. The copy command

number first; the editor does not understand line addresses such as *62,57* or *9,2.*

1. The **copy** command can be abbreviated to **co**. For instance, type the command

   :10 **co** *4*

   The system makes a copy of line *10* and places it after *4.*

2. There are a few special characters that can be used with line commands. Try copying text to the very beginning of the file, with

   :10,14 **co** *0*

   Here, the lines *10* through *14* are copied and placed after line *0* (just before line 1).

3. To copy lines to the end of the file, type

   :10,14 **co** *$*

   The dollar sign $ is the last line, so lines *10* through *14* are copied after the last line of the file.

4. Finally, suppose the cursor is in line 55, and you want to copy lines 55 through *65* to immediately after line *80.* Type the command

   : .,65 **co** *80*

   The dot means "the current line," that is, the line where the cursor is currently positioned.

Moving Blocks of Text

The **copy** command lets you copy text to different locations in your file. You can also **move** the text from one location to another.

1. Type

   :1,8 **m** *17*

2. Examine Figure 9-2 to see the effect of this command. The lines *1* through *8* are moved to the new location, not copied. (The command **move** is abbreviated to **m**.)

The same conventions used for selecting a block of text for the **copy** command are also used for the **move** command.

Deleting Blocks of Text

There are numerous ways to delete blocks of text in your file.

1. To delete the first eight lines from a file, you can move the cursor to the first line and type

   *8***dd**

   or, *regardless of the location of the cursor,* you can type

   :1,8 **d**

   This command means "find lines *1* through *8* and delete them." Examine Figure 9-3 for a graphic depiction of the previous **d**elete command.

Writing Out Blocks of Text

It is often useful to create new files with portions of the file you are editing. To write a block of text from

:1,8 **m** *17*

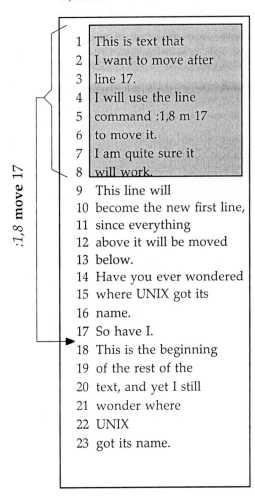

before   after

FIGURE 9-2.   The **move** command

:*1,8* **d**

	before			after
1	this is text that I want		1	This is more text that
2	to delete. I will use		2	will stay in
3	the line command		3	place even after
4	:1,8d to do		4	I delete lines 1 through
5	this.		5	8.
6	I must be in command		6	Later on tonight,
7	mode first,		7	I plan to forget
8	though.		8	all about vi, but
9	This is more text that		9	right now, it is
10	will stay in		10	very important
11	place even after		11	that I learn how to use
12	I delete lines 1 through		12	commands effectively.
13	8.		13	Yow! Maybe by the
14	Later on tonight,		14	end of the week
15	I plan to forget		15	I will know everything
16	all about vi, but		16	about UNIX.
17	right now, it is		17	
18	very inportant		18	
19	that I learn how to use		19	
20	commands effectively.		20	
21	Yow! Maybe by the		21	
22	end of the week		22	
23	I will know everything		23	
24	about UNIX.		24	

delete ◄

before   **after**

FIGURE 9-3.   The **delete** command

your current file out to a new file, you need two pieces of information:

- The line numbers for the first and last lines of the text you want to write out
- A new filename for this material

1. From **vi** command mode, type

   :*1,7* **write** *newfilename*

   where *newfilename* is a name you create for the new text.

2. The lines specified by the line address (*1,7*) are copied and written into *newfilename*. The text now exists in two places—in the file you are currently editing (*practice*), and in *newfilename*.

Writing Over an Existing File

Sometimes the **write** (abbreviated **w**) command is used to overwrite, or replace, an existing file. Depending on how your account is set up, the shell may not allow the command

:*1,7* **w** *report.2*

to overwrite *report.2* if it already exists. The following command will work whether *report.2* exists or not:

:*1,7* **w!** *report.2*

Adding to a File

Another type of **write** command appends text to a file. The command

:5,8 **w** *>> report.2*

writes lines *5* through *8* to the end of the file *report.2*.

Exercise 9-B

1. What **vi** command places lines 1 to 33 of your current file in a new file named *report.10*?

   _____

2. What **vi** command overwrites the contents of an existing *report* file with lines 29 through 200 of your current file?

   _____

3. What **vi** command appends lines 36 through 74 of your current file onto the end of the file named *report1*?

   _____

4. What mode must you be in to use the colon commands?

   _____

5. What command do you type to move lines 17 through 93 of your file to the end of the file?

_____

6. What colon command deletes everything in a file following line 117?

_____

7. How can you move a paragraph beginning on line 32 and ending on line 57 to the beginning of your file?

_____

9.6   USING TEXT MARKING IN A FILE

It is possible with the visual editor to mark a place in a file and then later return to it. You can thus specify text to be deleted, moved, written, or copied.

Marking Your Place in a File

In a file, the line number assigned to a particular line of code or text changes if lines are added or removed between that line and the beginning of the file. During editing, you often need to return to a particular line of text, but if the number has changed, it can be difficult to find the line you want.

With the **vi m**ark command, several positions in a file may be marked. Once a line of text is marked, you can easily return to that line, even if its line number has changed during the editing session. Your markings last only for the current editing session.

1. Make certain line numbers are displayed for the *practice* file. (If they are not, type **:set nu** and press Return .)

2. Go to a line in the middle of your file and note its line number. With the cursor on that line, type

   m*b*

   This command **m**arks the line and assigns it the label *b*. You can replace the *b* with any letter from *a* through *z*.

3. Move the cursor to another location near the beginning of the file. Remove or add a few lines of text at this new location.

4. To return to the line of text that you marked, type a single quote, followed by the letter you used in the **m**ark command. In this case, type

   'b

   The cursor moves to your original marked location, even though its line number is clearly different.

Deleting Lines from the Current Position to a Marked Spot

Sometimes you need to delete all text from the current line to a marked line.

1. Place the cursor on any line of text, and mark the line:

   m*a*

   where *a* is any letter from *a* to *z*.

2. Now move the cursor a few lines above or below the line just marked, and type the following:

   d'*a*

   The text between your present location and the marked line is deleted.

Deleting, Moving, or Copying Marked Blocks

You can use the **m**ark command to simplify the tasks of deleting, moving, or copying large blocks of text.

1. Move the cursor to the first line of text to be deleted. To mark that line, type

   m*a*

2. Next, move the cursor to the last line of the text to be deleted. To mark that line, type

   m*b*

3. To delete the marked text from *a* to *b*, type the command

   :*'a,'b* **d**

All text between and including lines $'a$ and $'b$ is deleted. This is just like the following delete line number command:

:16,32 **d**

Both commands identify lines and call for action.

4. Undo the previous command, so that the deleted text reappears.

Marked lines can be used to specify lines for all colon commands: **c**opy, **m**ove, **d**elete, and **w**rite. Lines in a file can be identified by either line numbers or by marks, and all colon or line commands can be used with lines identified by either method.

5. Practice using marks to move, delete, and write blocks of text.

READING IN FILES OF TEXT   9.7

A writer or programmer is often editing one file and needs to read in the contents of a different file. Pieces of text or programs that are used frequently can be kept in specified files and read into another file when needed.

In order to read text into the current file, you need to know two things:

- The *name* of the file containing the material you want to copy into your current file

- The *location* (line number) in your current file where you want the new material to appear

1. From **vi** command mode, type the following:

:8 **read** *filename*

where *8* is the line number of the current file after which you want material from *filename* to be read in, and where *filename* is the name of another file in your current directory.

 If you do not specify a line number in the **read** command, the new file will be read in after your current cursor location. The **read** command can be abbreviated **r**. Only a copy is made of the file to be read, leaving the original unchanged.

2. Because the **read** command is a text-changing command, you can **u**ndo it. If, after reading in a file, you decide you don't want to insert it after all, you can type

u

The lines you just read in will be deleted from your current file.

 At the end of this chapter are two command summaries of the colon or line commands you have learned so far. Practice these commands until you feel comfortable using them.

USING LETTERED BUFFERS

9.8

The **vi** editor maintains a set of lettered (*a* to *z*) buffers where you can store yanked or deleted blocks of text. Text blocks placed in these buffers remain there during the entire editing session, and can be accessed at any time through the use of the appropriate command.

Unlike the numbered buffers described earlier in this chapter — where deleted text is *automatically* deposited for safekeeping — you must direct the editor to save text in a lettered buffer.

Placing Lines in Lettered Buffers

1. Move the cursor to a line of text. Use the yank command to copy this line into the lettered buffer *b*. Type

   *"b***yy**

   In this command:

"	is the double quotation mark (not two single quote marks)
b	is the lettered buffer *b*
yy	is the yank command, which copies a line of text into the lettered buffer

2. In the following command, five lines of text are yanked and saved in lettered buffer *q*. Try it:

   *"q*5**yy**

If you yank lines to a buffer that already contains text, you overwrite the old entry.

Accessing a Lettered Buffer

1. Move the cursor to a different line in the file, and type the following to access the text, stored in the buffer *a*.

*"a*p

This command is

"	the double quotation mark
a	the lettered buffer *a*
p	the put command

Text in the *a* buffer is thus copied to the line just *below* the current cursor location.

Saving Deleted Text in a Lettered Buffer

You can also use lettered buffers to save text blocks that you have deleted.

1. To delete a line of text and place it in lettered buffer *b*, type

*"b*dd

2. To delete five lines of text and place them in the lettered buffer *g*, type

*"g*5dd

3. Move your cursor to the end of the file, using the **G** command, and recover the text you stored in lettered buffer *g*. Type

"*g***p**

HAVING KEYS ACCOMPLISH SEVERAL TASKS

9.9

Like many editors, the UNIX visual editor allows you to connect one or more commands to a single key, so that you can perform a repetitive editing task with a single keystroke. In the command mode of **vi**, this is called *mapping*.

Entering Control Characters in Text

You will soon use commands that include control characters such as ˆM for [Return] or ˆ[for [Esc]. It is possible to include them in text files.

1. In **vi** append mode, press [Ctrl-v]. Notice that the screen displays only the ˆ symbol.

2. Next, press [Return]. Displayed now on the screen is

ˆM

which is the control character for [Return].

3. Still in append mode, press Ctrl-h . As expected, the cursor moves back one space. You can also insert the control character for Ctrl-h in your text. Try the following sequence:

A ˆH has been added to your screen. Whenever you wish to insert special characters in your text, use Ctrl-v .

Mapping Keys in the Command Mode

There are many different uses for mapping in **vi**. Many programming languages include a basic if-then-else statement similar to the following:

```
if X
   then a
   else b
```

When you are writing a program, instead of typing these lines over and over, you can simply map them to one key.

For this example we will use the @ key as the key to be mapped. In the previous section you learned how to enter control characters.

1. From the command mode of **vi**, type the following **map** command (on one line):

:**map** @ o*if* X `Ctrl-v` `Return` `Tab` **then** *a* `Ctrl-v` `Return` `Tab` **else** *b* `Ctrl-v` `Esc`

Then press `Return`.

2. Move the cursor to a line where you would like to add an if-then-else statement, and type

@

Examining the Command Syntax

The **map** command takes two arguments: the first argument is the key you would like to map, and the second argument is what you want the mapped key to symbolize.

We started the previous map with an **o**, which is the visual editor command to **o**pen a new line below and move into the append mode. Everything from the **o** until the `Esc` character (^[) is entered in the append mode.

The text that is appended is interpreted by the append mode. The words *if* x, *then* a and *else* b are interpreted as text. The `Ctrl-v` allows you to enter the `Return` and `Esc` keys into the command sequence. The resulting ^M and ^[produce a carriage return and escape command respectively.

Using Abbreviations in the Append Mode

In the command mode, you can use mapping to cut down on the amount of time spent on repetitive editing. From the append mode, you can use **ab**breviations to accomplish the same thing.

1. From the command mode of **vi**, type the following (on one line), using the same symbolism as above:

:**ab ift** *if* X `Ctrl-v` `Return` `Tab` **then** *a* `Ctrl-v` `Return` `Tab` **else** *b*

Then press `Return`.

2. Move into the append mode with the **o** command, and type a few words, including the abbreviation **ift**. The abbreviation **ift** is expanded to

```
if X
    then a
    else b
```

9.10   EDITING MULTIPLE FILES

There are times when you need to edit two or more files at once. Every time you type **vi** *filename*, you start up the **vi** program. You can avoid this by instructing the editor that you want to edit several files, hence, the **vi** program is started only once.

1. Type the following shell command line:

vi *file1 file2 file3*

substituting names of files from your directory. You will see the message:

```
3 files to edit
```

2. The first file accessed is *file1*; make some changes and add text to this file using **vi** editing tools.

3. When you are finished editing *file1*, type

   :w

   which writes all the changes that you made in the buffer copy of *file1*. Notice that this command does *not* include the **q** for quit.

4. The first file has been written; the editor is still active. Now type

   :n

   The **:n** instructs the editor to open or access the **n**ext file for editing. It follows the series of filenames that you listed when you typed the initial **vi** command.

5. Make changes and write this second file.

6. Continue using the **:w** and **:n** commands as you edit your way through the series of files. When you reach the last file and type **:n**, you will see the message:

   ```
   No more files to edit
   ```

   You have now edited all the files that you named when you started **vi**.

7. If at this point, you want to reedit all the files in the

   sequence, type

   :rew

   This **rew**inds all the files originally edited and places you at the beginning of the series of files again. You do not, however, have to be at the end of the series of files to enter the **:rew** command. It can be entered at any time during an editing session.

8. When you are finished with this editing session, terminate it by typing

:q

Exercise 9-C

1. What **vi** command reads in a file named *report2* after line *4* of your current file?

   _____

2. What command line would you use to call up for editing the files *practice1*, *reminders*, and *practice2*?

   _____

3. While in **vi**, with four files queued up for editing, what command moves you to the next file?

   _____

4. What is the command to place three lines of text into the lettered buffer *a*, starting at the current cursor position?

   _____

9.11   CHANGING THE ORDER IN WHICH FILES ARE EDITED

As you are editing a series of files, you can get a list of the files you chose.

1. Pick four files from your Home directory, and call them up for editing using

   vi *file1 file2 file3 file4*

2. To check the names and order of files to be edited:

   :args

   In a line at the bottom of the screen, the editor displays the names of the files you requested to edit. These are the arguments to the **vi** command you entered.

3. Add to or reorder the entire editing series:

   :n *newfile1 newfile2 newfile3*

   where the three *newfiles* are filenames you want to include, whether or not they were among the initial **vi** command arguments. These new filenames replace the previously entered ones.

Ending an Editing Session Early

You can instruct the editor to quit, even when there are more files remaining to be edited.

1. Write the current file (if open) with the **:w** command, and then type

   :q

   You will see a message

   ```
   n more files to edit
   ```

where *n* is the number of files (arguments) left in your editing sequence.

2. Type **:q** again to end the editing process.

Storing Text for Use in Editing Other Files

One advantage of editing several files at once is that the editing program is initiated only once, saving time and resources. In addition, an editing environment spans several files. For instance, text saved in lettered buffers and environment settings remains in memory as you move to another file.

1. Call up a series of practice files with the command

   vi *file1 file2 file3*

2. Use the following command to save any four lines of text from the first file into buffer *a*:

   "a4yy

3. Put that file away, and call up the next file with the two colon commands

   :w
   :n

4. Move the cursor to any line on the screen and type

   "ap

   The text stored in the *a* buffer from the first file is now placed in the second file.

ACCESSING SHELL COMMANDS
FROM WITHIN THE EDITOR

9.12

Often while you are editing a file, you need to access the shell for information from a command such as **who, date,** or **ls**. It is possible to access the shell without leaving the editor.

Performing a Single Shell Command

1. Select and open a practice file with **vi.**

2. From the command mode, type

   :*!date*

   The shell command **date** is executed. Once the command is completed, the message

   [Hit return to continue]

   appears at the bottom of your screen.

3. When you press the [Return] key, you are returned to the editor.

   You can execute any single shell command from within **vi** by typing

:*!command*

where *command* is the desired shell command. The **!** is the shell escape character in the visual editor.

Creating a New Shell

You can instruct the visual editor to call up a new shell for you to use.

1. From **vi** command mode, type

   :sh

   You are greeted by a shell prompt indicating that you have created a temporary shell. You can now invoke any number of shell commands.

2. Type some shell commands, such as **date**, to check the current date, or **who**, to find out who is logged on.

3. To terminate this shell and return to the editor, press ⌑Ctrl-d⌑.

   The screen clears, and your practice file reappears. If ⌑Ctrl-d⌑ doesn't work, type **exit**.

9.13   INCORPORATING THE OUTPUT OF A SHELL COMMAND

You can incorporate the output from any shell command into a file that you are editing.

1. To get the results of a **spell** command to appear at the top of the file, from the **vi** command mode, type

   :0r !spell *filename*

   where *0* is a zero, and *filename* is the file you are editing.

2. To have the output of **spell** added to the end of your file, type

    :**$r** !**spell** *filename*

    Anytime you want the output of a shell command to be read into your file, you can use the command

:**r** !*command*

Exercise 9-D

1. What is the command to obtain a listing of your current directory without leaving **vi**?

    _____

2. How would you start a new shell while still in **vi**?

    _____

3. What command would you use to read the result of the **date** command into a file you are editing?

    _____

4. You have a number of files queued up for editing. You have just typed :**q**, and the message "3 more files to edit" is displayed. What do you enter to terminate the session?

    _____

5. If, after entering the command **vi** *first second*, you decide you want to move to the file *other*, what would you enter?

    _____

9.14 SAVING THE EDITING ENVIRONMENT

You have modified the editor environment by issuing a variety of set commands. All these changes will be eliminated when you leave the editor. You can have the shell remind the editor how you want your environment set up each time the editor is executed by setting environment variables.

1. If you are using the C shell, add the following line to ignore case in searches:

   setenv EXINIT 'set number autoindent ignorecase'

2. If you are using a Bourne shell, add the following two lines to your *.profile* file:

   EXINIT 'set number autoindent ignorecase'
   export EXINIT

For more information in environment variables, see Chapter 15, "Setting the User Environment."

CONCLUSION

You have examined some powerful features of **vi**. With the **vi** editor, you can access a file at any desired line or word; use many different methods of deleting, moving, copying, or changing blocks of text; and move blocks of text between files. Furthermore, you can customize your editing environment to suit your specific application, such as for writing large documents or creating programs.

COMMAND SUMMARY

:set *option*
This is the basic format of the **set** option command.

:set no*option*
This is the basic format to turn off the **set** options.

:set number
Puts line numbers on your screen. You can also use **set nu**.

:set nonumber
Removes line numbers from your screen. You can also use **set nonu**.

:set window = *value*
Defines the amount of lines drawn on your screen.

:set autoindent
Automatically indents each return. You can also use **ai**.

:set noai
Turns off the automatic indent.

:set tabstop = *value*
Sets the number of spaces used to display a tab. You can also use **ts** = *value*.

:set ignorecase
Tells the editor to ignore upper- and lowercase. You can also use **ic**.

:set shiftwidth = *value*
Sets the distance for the < / > shift text left/right commands, and the ^D (shift width back) and ^T (shift width forward) cursor commands.

COMMAND SUMMARY (*continued*)

:set wrapmargin=*value*
Sets the right margin of the display.

:set
Shows you all the options you have set.

:set all
Shows you all the **set** options available.

Line Command Summary

:1,26 **mo** *82*
Moves lines *1* through *26* after line *82*. (You select the line numbers.)

:1,26 **co** *82*
Copies lines 1 through 26 and places them after line 82. (You select the line numbers.)

:1,26 **d**
Deletes lines 1 through 26. (You select the line numbers.)

:1,6 **w** *newfile*
Creates a new file named *newfile* and copies text lines 1 through 6 from the current file into *newfile*. (You select the line numbers.)

:1,6 **w** >> *oldfile*
Appends copy of lines 1 through 6 to end of an existing file named *oldfile*. (You select the line numbers.)

COMMAND SUMMARY (*continued*)

:*1,6* **w!** *oldfile*

Overwrites (replaces) *oldfile* with contents of lines 1 through 6. (You select the line numbers.)

:*8* **r** *report.old*

Reads in the file named *report.old* after text line 8 in the current file. (You select the line numbers.)

Append Mode Special Characters

Ctrl-h

Backspaces one character.

Backspace

Backspaces one character.

Ctrl-w

Backspaces one word.

Ctrl-v

Allows input of control characters.

Esc

Escapes to command mode.

COMMAND SUMMARY (continued)

Selected Editing Environment Variables

Name	Default value
list	(nolist)

Tab characters appear as ^I and ends of lines are marked with $.

showmatch   (noshowmatch)

Closing parentheses and brackets are matched with their opening parentheses and brackets.

wrapmargin   (wrapmargin = 0)

Defines the distance between the right margin and the right edge of the terminal display.

Two-way Text-Changing Commands

x
Erases (x out) only the letter under the cursor.

dw
Deletes only the word under the cursor.

dd
Deletes the entire line.

D
Deletes the rest of the line (from the cursor position on).

rb
Replaces the letter under the cursor with the letter b (**r**w replaces character under cursor with letter w).

COMMAND SUMMARY (*continued*)

J
Joins the cursor line with the next line in your text by appending the next line onto the end of the cursor line.

yy
Yanks the cursor line.

3yy
Yanks the specified number (3) of lines. For instance, **6yy** is the "make a copy of the next 6 lines, remember them, and put them where I tell you to" command (see **put** commands).

P
(Uppercase P) Puts the yanked or deleted line(s) just above the cursor line.

p
(Lowercase p) Puts the yanked (or deleted) text just below the cursor line.

·10·

Running Multiple Commands

In the C shell, when you enter a command you are telling the shell to perform a task. In UNIX, tasks are called *jobs*. The UNIX C shell gives you the ability to execute several jobs simultaneously. The coordination of multiple jobs within the C shell on the Berkeley System is called *job control*. This section examines the job control features that enable you to manage several tasks at once.

SKILLS CHECK   Before beginning this chapter, you should be able to

- Access and leave the system (Chapter 1, "Touring the System's Features")

- Name, copy, and remove files (Chapter 1)

- Create and display files (Chapter 1)

- Access and edit files using an editor (Chapter 2, "Basic Editing with the Visual Editor")

- Use the **find** command to search for files (Chapter 4, "Using Basic UNIX Utilities")

- Redirect standard output and standard error to a file (Chapter 6, "Command Line Interpretation by the Shell")

OBJECTIVES   Upon completion of this chapter, you will be able to

- Run programs in the background

- Suspend and restart programs in either the foreground or the background

- Kill programs running in the background

10.1   RUNNING JOBS IN THE FOREGROUND AND BACKGROUND

A manager who has only one employee working can give instructions to the employee, be available to answer questions when necessary, and keep track of the employee's progress. When a job is finished, the employee can immediately inform the manager and wait for another task. This is analogous to executing one command at a time:

- You type a command line.

- The shell processes the command line and then executes the appropriate utility.

- When the utility has completed its work, the shell prompts you for another command.

However, managers usually have several employees to oversee. The manager schedules projects and communicates needs to each employee. Each employee is assigned a task. They each do their work and talk to the manager when they need to ask a question, or when they have results to report. Other employees are working or are placed on hold until the manager can get back to them.

This process is similar to the use of job control. The employee or job that has your attention is in the *foreground*. All other jobs are either in the *background* or *suspended*.

Running a Job in the Foreground

So far, you have only run commands in the foreground. Normally, when you give the shell a command, it runs that job in the foreground. All attention is paid to the job. Even the shell sleeps.

1. Run a simple UNIX program in the foreground. Type

more */etc/termcap*

When you request a new screenful of text by pressing the Spacebar, the space character you type is read and processed by the job that is running in the foreground. The shell sends the output from the foreground job to your screen. This job is called the *current job.*

Killing the Current Job

The shell provides a convenient method for killing the current job.

1. Start a program that will take a long time to execute, such as

   find / -name *temp* **-print**

   This command will print a list of the pathnames of every file in your system that has the name *temp.* On most systems, this will take a very long time to run. This will give you the opportunity to practice killing the current job.

2. Kill the **find** job by pressing Ctrl-c. (Hold the Ctrl key down and type **c** once.)

   Shortly after you press Ctrl-c, the shell prompt appears. The current job has been killed.

Because the special character produced by Ctrl-c kills or *interrupts* the current job, it is called the *interrupt character*. If Ctrl-c is not the interrupt character on your system and does not kill the current job, try using the Del key. A detailed discussion on displaying and setting the interrupt character is in Chapter 15, "Setting the User Environment."

Typing the interrupt character will not kill all jobs. Some utilities do not accept the interrupt character.

Running a Job in the Background

When you need to run a long job, you can run the job and wait for it to finish, or you can run the job and log onto another terminal. Better yet, you can run the job *and* work on another task, at the same terminal.

1. First, start up the **find** utility to locate all the files on your system with the name *temp*. Type

   find / -name *temp* **-print &**

   The ampersand (**&**) appended to the command line tells the shell that the command should not be run as the current job, but should be run in the *background*. A program that is running coincidentally with the current job is said to be *running in the background*.

   When you type this **find** command, a message similar to the following appears:

   [1] 11407

Then the shell prompt reappears.

The bracketed number [1] in the response message shows that you are running a single job in the background; this number is called the *job number*. The rest of the response is a unique five-digit number; this is the job's *process identification number*. It is the same identification number you see when using the **process** status utility. The **ps** utility lists the processes currently being executed.

2. Confirm that the **find** command is running by typing

ps

The terminal displays

```
PID     TT   STAT TIME   COMMAND
11407   h6   T     0:00   find / -name temp -print
17353   h6   R     0:00   ps
```

The process identification number and the number in the *Process ID*entification or *PID* field of the **ps** display are identical.

Here and throughout this chapter, the PID numbers you see on your terminal will probably be different from those shown in the text.

Running Multiple Jobs in the Background

You now have one job running in the background. The UNIX system allows you to run multiple jobs in the background.

1. Search for all files with the name *practice*. Type

find / -name *practice* **-print &**

As before, the shell responds with the job number and PID:

```
[2] 12414
```

2. Add another job to the background processing. Type

wc */etc/passwd* **&**

The shell responds with the job number and the PID, the prompt, and (after a few moments) the result of the word count command, as shown here:

```
133    244   4937 /etc/passwd
```

3. To redisplay the prompt, press the [Return] key.

In addition to the prompt, the following message is displayed:

```
[3]    Done              wc /etc/passwd
```

Thus, the shell notifies you that the job has finished. The other two jobs are probably still running.

4. Check the status of the two **find** jobs by typing

jobs

A list of jobs similar to the following appears:

```
[1]    +   Running find / -name temp -print
[2]    -   Running find / -name practice -print
```

The **jobs** command is a C shell command that lists all jobs that are either stopped or running in the background. (You will learn about stopped jobs shortly.) The **jobs** output is in four columns: the job number; the order (the + marks the lead job and the - marks the second job); the status (in this case, both are running in the background); and the command being executed.

Moving a Job from the Background to the Foreground

There are now two jobs running in the background. Also, several messages have probably been displayed, like these:

```
find: cannot open < /usr/bin/src >
find: cannot open < /tmp/TEMP >
find: cannot open < /usr/andy/Mail >
find: bad status < /sys >
```

As error messages are produced by utilities running in the background, the messages are sent to standard error, which is your terminal by default. In addition, background utilities send their output to standard output—also your terminal. The resulting screen interference can be disturbing, especially when you are using a text editor.

1. Verify that jobs are still running by typing

   jobs

   Unless the number of files on your system is small or your computer is fast, you should see both **find** commands running. As mentioned, the + sign marks the lead job.

2. Move the lead job into the foreground. Type

   fg

   You see the message

   ```
   find / -name temp -print
   ```

   In this way, the shell informs you that the **find** command, which is looking for *temp*, is running in the foreground and is the current job. It is not starting over, but is continuing as the foreground job.

3. Kill the current job by pressing [Ctrl-c].

4. Verify that the current job is no longer running with **jobs**.

5. Follow the same procedure to kill the remaining **find** command.

10.2 MANAGING A JOB

A manager must be able to switch from one task to another. Suppose you need to print a file, but you are in the middle of writing a long letter in the **mail** utility. If you are running one program, you cannot start a new program without terminating the first program. You could either kill the letter, or finish the letter before printing the file. Rarely is either alternative desirable.

To move from one program to another without killing the current program, you must first *suspend* or stop the current job.

Suspending a Job

1. Begin by starting to send a **mail** message to yourself. Type

   mail *your_login*

   and then type the following line into your message:

   This is a test.

2. Press ⎡Return⎤ so the cursor is on a new line.

3. Suspend the job by pressing ⎡Ctrl-z⎤. (Hold the ⎡Ctrl⎤ key down and type **z** once.)

   The terminal responds with the message:

   ```
   Stopped
   ```

The shell now displays a prompt on the terminal, showing it is ready for new instructions. The **mail** utility is now suspended. A suspended (stopped) job is not running, but it is not killed either. The system keeps track of the point where the program execution stopped and can restart it at the same point when instructed to do so.

4. Check that the **mail** utility is still there by typing

   jobs

   The **mail** job is listed as stopped.

Putting a Suspended Job into the Foreground

While your job is suspended, you can give any instructions to the shell. You can edit files, run other utilities, or even send other mail messages.

1. Check the date and time by typing

   date

2. When you are finished with other tasks, you can start your **mail** job again. Do this by typing

   fg

   The system responds with

   ```
   mail your_login
   (continue)
   ```

You are back at the same place in your **mail** message. The **mail** program does not redisplay your previous input.

3. To see all of the letter you have written so far, redisplay it by typing

~p

4. Add the line:

This is another line in my test letter.

5. Suspend **mail** again by going to a separate line and pressing Ctrl-z . The terminal displays

Stopped

Putting a Suspended Job into the Background

You have the **mail** utility suspended.

1. Run the utility in the background by typing

bg

The shell responds with:

[1]   mail your_login &

The bracketed number [1] is the job number. You are now running the **mail** utility in the background. The second part of the response to your **bg** command is the name of the command and argument list that has been moved into the background. The & character denotes that the command line is being run in the background.

The terminal then prints the message:

```
[1]  + Stopped (tty output) mail your_login
```

The job number is the first number in brackets. It is the same number you saw previously.

The remainder of the response message tells you that the job (**mail** *your_login*) needs to access your terminal keyboard but cannot do so unless it becomes the current job. Normally, **mail** utilizes the terminal keyboard for its input. However, if the operating system allowed a background process, such as your **mail** job, to use the terminal for input you would be unable to give input to the program you have running in the foreground. So, the operating system stops or suspends the background **mail** job.

2. Verify that the **mail** process is still present by typing

ps

MANAGING MULTIPLE JOBS   10.3

One of the essential qualities of a good manager is the ability to smoothly switch between different tasks. To do this, you need to know what projects are underway and what projects need reviewing. The good manager is able to switch between tasks smoothly.

Stopping Multiple Jobs

Currently, your **mail** job is the only one suspended in the background.

1. Begin a few more jobs by typing the following commands:

   vi *testfile* **&**
   find / -name *temp* **-print** > **&!** *tempfile*

2. Suspend the **find** job by pressing Ctrl-z.

3. Check the status of the jobs by typing

   jobs

   As usual, the lead job is marked with a plus sign. You can move the lead job into the foreground (with the **fg** command) or background (with the **bg** command). In this case, the most recent job is the suspended **find** command.

4. Run the **find** command in the background by typing

   bg

5. Check the job status again. Type

   jobs

   Now a different job is the lead job. Usually the lead job is the most recently suspended job, but if only background jobs are running, the lead job is the one that has been continuously in the background for the longest time.

Recalling the Most Recent Jobs

Thus far, you have manipulated only the lead job. To access any other job, you must either kill the lead jobs one by one, or let them run to completion. There is, however, a simple method of accessing the job following the lead job.

1. Make sure you have more than two **jobs** pending by typing the **jobs** command and checking for both a + and - in the second field. You will see something like this:

```
[1] - Stopped (tty input) mail your_login
[2] + Stopped (tty input) vi testfile
[3]   Running            find / -name temp print >& temp2
```

The **vi** job is the most recent suspended job (marked with a +). The **mail** job is the next most recent (marked with a -).

2. If your **find** job has finished, start another.

3. Previously, you have brought the lead job into the foreground by typing **fg**. You can also **foreground** the lead job in a different way by typing

   fg %+

   The %+ in the command line is another symbol for the lead job. Since the **vi** job was the lead job, it is brought to the foreground (and is now the current job). You are now editing the same file in the same state as when you left the job suspended.

4. Add a few lines of text.

5. Stop the job by pressing [Ctrl-z].

6. Check the jobs status again by typing

jobs

The lead job is marked with the plus, and the second lead job is marked with the minus sign.

7. Foreground the second lead job. Type

fg %-

The %- is a symbol for the job following the lead job; thus, the command brings the job following the lead job to the foreground. In the example, the suspended **mail** job followed the lead job and is now in the foreground.

8. Resuspend this job by pressing [Ctrl-z].

Recalling Jobs from the Jobs List

You have recalled the lead job and the one following it. You can also arbitrarily bring other jobs into the foreground.

1. Have the shell display a list of the current jobs by typing

jobs

A listing of all of your stopped or background jobs is displayed, for example:

```
[1]   +     Stopped mail your_login
[2]   -     Stopped vi testfile
```

```
[3]        Running find / -name temp -print >& temp2
```

Jobs that require the user's interaction will become stopped jobs if you attempt to run them in the background, as in the **vi** job you requested.

2. Place the job with the job number 1 in the foreground. Type

fg *%1*

The *%1* is the symbol for job number 1 (in this case, the stopped **mail** job). This job is brought to the foreground.

3. Resuspend the **mail** job.

4. Next, bring the third job to the foreground by typing

fg *%3*

Job number 3 is brought to the foreground. In the example, the **find** job that was running in the background is brought into the foreground.

5. Suspend the **find** utility.

In general, to recall any job into the foreground, you type

fg *%job_number*

where *job_number* is the job number of the chosen command line from the **jobs** command listing.

Moving a Specific Suspended Job to the Background

You can also move specific jobs into the background. The procedure is similar to the one for bringing a job into the foreground.

1. List the jobs by typing

   jobs

2. Move the **find** job into the background. Type

   bg %3

3. Use the **jobs** command to verify that **find** is running in the background.

   In general, to move a specific suspended job into the background, use the command

bg %*job_number*

where *job_number* is the job number of the chosen command line from the **jobs** command listing.

Killing a Job

Previously, you learned to kill the current job using ⌞Ctrl-c⌟, or another interrupt character. In this section you will examine how to terminate or kill stopped jobs and jobs in the background.

1. To complete the procedures in this section, you will need to add a few more jobs to your list. Type the following command lines:

   sort */etc/passwd* > *wordfile*
   Ctrl-z
   find / **-name** *temp* **-print** > &! *tempfile2* &

2. Determine what jobs you have pending by typing

   jobs

   The terminal display is similar to the following:

   ```
   [1]  - Stopped   mail your_login
   [2]    Stopped   vi testfile
   [3]    Running   find / -name temp -print >& tempfile
   [4] + Stopped   sort /etc/passwd
   [5]    Running   find / -name temp -print >& tempfile2
   ```

   The output indicates that the **sort** job is no longer pending.

3. Kill the most recent (lead) job in the example by typing

   kill %+

4. Examine the list of jobs again using the **jobs** command. The output is

   ```
   [1] + Stopped   mail your_login
   [2] - Stopped   vi testfile
   [3]   Running   find / -name temp -print >& tempfile
   [4]   Exit 1    sort /usr/dict/words > wordfile
   [5]   Running   find /-name temp -print >& tempfile2
   ```

The output indicates that the **sort** job is no longer pending.

5. Alternatively, you can kill a job using the job number. To kill job number 3, type

kill %3

6. Examine the list of jobs. The entry for job number 3 should be

```
[3]      Terminated    find / -name temp -print >& tempfile
```

The job has been killed.

In summary, the **kill** command takes the same arguments as the **fg** and **bg** commands. To kill the most recent job, use **kill** %+; to kill the second most recent job, use **kill** %-. To kill a specific job, you type **kill** %*job_number*, where *job_number* is the job number of the chosen command line from the **jobs** utility.

7. To avoid killing the wrong jobs, use **jobs** to first check what jobs are running before using the **kill** command. Type **jobs** now.

8. Kill the second job by typing

kill %2

9. Now attempt to examine the contents of the file you have been editing. Type the command

cat *testfile*

The shell responds with:

```
testfile: No such file or directory
```

Since you never did write the *testfile*, the file was never saved. Consequently, when you killed the editor, all the data you typed in **vi** was lost.

As a precaution, avoid indiscriminate use of the **kill** command on jobs involving text editors, database programs, **mail** programs, or any other program that has a large amount of user interaction. The **kill** command terminates a job without saving any of the user input or program results.

Determining Changes in Job Status

Whenever any sort of system event occurs while UNIX is running, the shell is informed of the change immediately. When a program is moved from the foreground to the background, from the background to the foreground, or suspended, the shell is alerted of the change in the process status. Normally, the shell informs you of a process status change only when a job becomes blocked so that no further progress is possible. The most common example of this is when the process is waiting for input. Notification does not necessarily occur immediately, but rather just before the next prompt is printed.

1. Use **sort** to alphabetize the entries of the file /etc/passwd, and throw the output away by writing the resulting sorted file to /dev/null. Sort the file in the background by typing

   sort /etc/passwd > /dev/null **&**

   The shell prints the job number and process identification followed by the prompt, but you are given no indication when the process is done.

2. Press Return. The shell prints

   ```
   [6]   Done        sort /etc/passwd > /dev/null
   ```

   You are now informed that your job has finished.

3. Set the *notify* variable by typing the following command:

   set *notify*

   Setting the *notify* shell variable informs the shell that you want to be alerted immediately of any changes in status of background jobs.

4. Try the **sort** command line again. Once again, the shell prints the job number and process identification followed by the prompt. However, when the process is done, the shell immediately informs you of the process status change by sending a message to your terminal screen:

   ```
   [6]   Done        sort /etc/passwd > /dev/null
   ```

Normally, the notification of a status change will occur at the next display of a new prompt. Setting the *notify* variable will tell the shell to inform you of the status change as it occurs.

Leave *notify* set for the rest of the exercises in this chapter. But if you want to disable the *notify* variable, type

unset *notify*

You can also set the *notify* shell variable automatically when you log in, if the command to set it is in your *.cshrc* or *.login* file. If so, the variable is set when the *.cshrc* and *.login* files are interpreted. When you want *notify* to be set automatically, add the following line to the end of your *.cshrc* file:

set *notify*

Suppressing the Output from Jobs

In a previous section, backgrounded jobs produced output that was displayed on your terminal. Output from jobs running in the background occurs *asynchronously* — that is, whenever the program has output ready. This terminal display of output can become very frustrating — especially if it appears in the midst of the output from another command such as **vi** or **ps**. There is a way of suppressing program output until you want it.

UNIX has a special set of generic *terminal options*, used for configuring the type of input and output the shell will accept.

1. To see what your terminal options are, type

   stty

Entered without arguments, **stty** (set **t**eletype options) prints a list of terminal option settings. The name set teletype options comes from the days when all computer input was done using typewriter-like teletypes.

2. Type the following line:

stty *tostop*

When **stty** is entered with arguments, it sets the terminal options. The *tostop* option forces background jobs to stop when they try to produce output.

3. Repeat the **find** command from the last section:

find / -name *testfile* **-print &**

The shell responds with:

```
[2] 14752
```

4. Make sure that **find** is still running by typing **jobs**.

As the **find** utility discovers files with the string *testfile* in their name, or encounters unreadable files, it tries to write its output to the terminal. The shell then prints

```
[2]  + Stopped (tty output) find / -name testfile -print
```

5. To reset the *tostop* terminal option to accept output from a background process, type

stty *-tostop*

In some cases, you will find that using the *tostop* option causes the output for the background job to be discarded. Therefore, in most cases it is better to *redirect* the program's output to a file, by using the >&! or >>&! shell operator.

LOGGING OUT WITH STOPPED JOBS   10.4

Job control is a very useful method for managing processes. Because background jobs and stopped jobs are invisible to the user until they need to write to the terminal or are finished, users may forget that processes other than the current one are running. Job control provides a method of warning a user during logout that stopped or running background jobs exist.

1. Type **jobs** to make sure there are jobs running in the background or stopped.

2. If you do not have any stopped jobs, type

   vi *testfile* **&**

3. Try to log out by typing

   logout

   The shell responds with an error message:

   ```
   There are stopped jobs.
   ```

In addition, you are not logged out. The shell is reminding you about your stopped jobs. This gives you a chance to decide whether to kill any of the unresolved jobs. Text editors and database programs are good examples of programs you do not want to kill.

If you were allowed to log out and these stopped programs were not ended, they would continue to exist. When you log in again, you would not be able to access these processes from your new shell. You would then have to kill them and lose any work done.

4. Check your jobs by typing **jobs**.

5. If you do wish to log out even though the jobs continue running, you can ignore them by typing **logout** a second time. Type

logout

The system will now kill the jobs and let you log out.

Logging Out with Jobs Running

Suppose that you want to run a job in the background that should continue running even after you log out. This is called running a job independent of your controlling terminal.

1. Log back into your account.

2. Start a process in the background, and then log out by typing

find / -name *temp* **-print** > & **/dev/null &**
logout

The **find** job continues to run, even after you log out.

3. Log back into your account.

4. Confirm that **find** is still running by typing **ps**.

5. Kill the **find** job with the **kill** utility.

There are some problems with this technique of running jobs independent of your terminal. The main problem is that once you log out, there is no way to resume control over backgrounded processes within the shell. Each shell can only manage jobs that it starts. Hence, independent jobs are ignored by all shells other than the one that creates them. Although there are more advanced ways of managing independent jobs, they don't involve features provided by the shell. To manage independent jobs, you have to resort to *process control*, which involves using some of the more complex features of the UNIX operating system. These are examined in Chapter 20, "Process Monitoring and Control."

Exercise 10-A

1. What command would you use to start up a **ps** in the background?

_____

For the next three questions, refer to the following listing:

```
[2]       Stopped    sort /etc/termcap
[3]   -   Stopped    vi .cshrc
[4]   +   Stopped    more .login
[5]       Running    find / -name foo
```

2. What command would you use to bring the **vi** editor to the foreground?

_____

3. What is the command to kill the **more** job?

_____

4. What is the command to get this listing?

_____

CONCLUSION

The UNIX C shell job control facilities can be used to greatly increase your productivity by allowing the computer to adapt to the way you work. A savant user can switch between the **vi** text editor, the **mail** program, and the **talk** communication program on a UNIX system as easily as switching from the telephone to correspondence or project memos in an office.

COMMAND SUMMARY

`Ctrl-c`
Kills the current job.

`Ctrl-z`
Suspends the current job.

`Ctrl-y`
Allows the current job to run until input is needed; then suspends the job.

command_name **&**
Runs the command *command_name* in the background.

fg *%job_number*
Brings the job with number *job_number* into the foreground. Without an argument, **fg** brings the most recently stopped job into the foreground.

bg *%job_number*
Puts the job with number *job_number* into the background. Without an argument, **bg** moves the most recently stopped job to the background.

jobs
Prints a listing of all of the stopped and background jobs.

kill *%job_number*
Kills the job with job number *job_number*. Without an argument, **kill** kills the most recently stopped job.

COMMAND SUMMARY (*continued*)

stty *tostop*
Informs the shell that the user wants background job output suppressed. The shell will stop any background program attempting to write output to the screen.

stty *-tostop*
Informs the shell that the user does not want background job output suppressed.

set *notify*
Forces the shell to notify the user of any change in the status of background jobs.

unset *notify*
Tells the shell not to notify the user of changes in the status of background jobs.

·11·

Shell Programming

In previous chapters you used many UNIX utilities by typing a command line at the shell prompt. You have also gained experience with some of the basic aspects of the Bourne shell. In this chapter you will create Bourne shell scripts that contain programming statements along with commands that invoke UNIX utilities. These scripts can be used to instruct the shell to perform complex or repetitive and routine tasks for you.

You will also use some new Bourne shell commands interactively (entered at the Bourne shell prompt), and within small Bourne shell scripts. You will be guided through development of a Bourne shell menu program and a program for accessing a phone list.

C shell programming is very much like Bourne shell programming. However, the Bourne shell is most often used for programming. Also, the C shell is not available on all UNIX systems, and the Bourne shell is. Once you are proficient at Bourne shell programming, you will find it relatively easy to learn C shell programming. The end of this chapter briefly examines the differences between the two.

SKILLS CHECK

Before starting work on this chapter, you should be able to

- Create and modify files with the visual editor (Chapter 2, "Basic Editing with the Visual Editor")

- Access and change variables (Chapter 6, "Command Line Interpretation by the Shell")

- Set file permissions to allow the execution of a file (Chapter 7, "Setting File Permissions")

OBJECTIVES

After completing this chapter, you will be able to

- Access Bourne shell variables from within a script

- Write a Bourne shell script that will get input from and write output to the user

- Utilize looping and branching control structures within a script

IMPLEMENTING SHELL SCRIPTS THAT WRITE OUTPUT

11.1

This section reviews the basic steps involved in creating and running a simple shell script that writes output to your screen.

Creating a Simple Script

A shell script is simply a file containing shell commands. One use of a script is to run several utilities by typing a single command.

1. Make sure that you are logged in to a Bourne shell before proceeding. If you are using the C shell, type

   /bin/sh

   This starts up a Bourne shell. Notice that your prompt has changed.

2. Use **vi** to create a new file named *dir_script* containing the following lines:

   pwd
   ls -l
   date

Making a Script Executable

To run a script you must first make it executable.

1. Make the script *dir_script* executable by typing

chmod +x *dir_script*

This command adds execute permission to your script.

Running Your Script

1. Run your new shell script by typing its name:

dir_script

The output is the same as if you had typed the commands individually from the command line.

Adding a New Command to Your Shell Script

Using **vi**, you can add a new command line to your shell script.

1. Add this line to the end of the script

alias *bye logout*

Determining Which Shell Has Been Interpreting Your Script

The C shell and the Bourne shell differ in some ways, so it is useful to be able to identify which one is interpreting your script.

1. Run the script again. You don't need to change the file permissions again; just type

   dir_script

   You get an error message:

   ```
   dir_script:  alias:  not  found
   ```

   This message occurs because the Bourne shell doesn't have a command called **alias**.

   The Bourne shell is normally used to interpret shell scripts if you do not specify otherwise.

Forcing the Bourne Shell to Interpret Your Script

You can ensure that the Bourne shell interprets your script by inserting a special request as the first line in the script.

1. Use **vi** to insert the following as the first line of your script:

   #!/bin/sh

2. Before leaving **vi**, delete the line that starts with **alias**. Run the script again by typing

   dir_script

The characters **#!/bin/sh** in *dir_script* tell the system that your script should be interpreted by a Bourne shell even if your current shell is the C shell (**/bin/sh** is the full pathname of the file containing the Bourne shell).

It is a good idea to *always* start a script file with **#!/bin/sh** when you want it to be interpreted by the Bourne shell.

Speaking Out with the echo Command

It is often useful to be able to display some fixed text from within a shell script. To accomplish this you need a command that can be used to display its arguments on your terminal. For example, from the shell type the command

echo *hi there*

The following appears on your terminal:

```
hi there
```

The utility **echo** writes its arguments to the standard output, which, by default, is connected to your terminal.

Speaking Out from Within a Shell Script

1. Use **vi** to edit the file *dir _ script* so that it looks like the following:

```
#!/bin/sh
echo Your current directory is:
pwd
echo The files in this directory are:
ls -l
echo The date today is:
date
```

2. Run this shell script again:

dir_script

The messages that were arguments to **echo** are sent to your screen.

Speaking Out with a Personal Touch

Most people prefer to be addressed by name, even in a form letter or computer screen. You can add a personal touch to your script by using **echo** to access the value of the Bourne shell predefined variable *LOGNAME* or *USER,* which is automatically set to be the user's login name.

1. Have the shell print the contents of the variable *LOGNAME.* From the shell type

echo $LOGNAME

Your login name is printed on the screen. If your login name is not printed, your system may use the predefined variable *USER.* Test this by typing

echo $USER

Your name is printed on the screen.

The value of the variable *LOGNAME* or *USER* (which is your login name) was accessed and displayed on your screen. (Accessing the value of a variable is known as *evaluating* a variable.) The shell knew that the word following the **echo** command was special, and was to be evaluated, because there was a dollar sign ($) immediately before the variable's name.

Using a Variable's Value from Within a Shell Script

1. Use **vi** to insert the following line as the second line of your script, immediately after the **#!/bin/sh** line. (If your system uses *USER* instead of *LOGNAME*, use the appropriate variable.) Type

   echo *Hello $LOGNAME*

2. Run this shell script again. Type

   dir__script

   Your shell script now addresses you by name.

Reviewing How to Define a Variable

To set the value of variables, use the = symbol.

1. At your Bourne shell prompt, type

   name="your name"

   where *your name* is your full name. (Notice that there can be no spaces around the equal sign.) The double-quotes (" ") around the *your name* value caused the Bourne shell *not* to interpret special characters such as the spaces within the string. Instead, the Bourne shell ignored the space characters and wrote your full name as one word for the value of the variable *name.*

Evaluating a User-Defined Variable

1. Just as you used **echo** and the $ symbol to evaluate the predefined variable *LOGNAME,* you can evaluate the new variable, *name,* that you just created. From the shell, type

   echo $*name*

   The value of the variable *name* is displayed on your screen.

Inserting a User-Defined Variable in a Shell Script

These same methods for setting and evaluating user-defined variables can be used within a shell script. In fact, anything you can do from the command line can also be done within a script, and vice versa.

1. Use **vi** to insert the following line into *dir_script,* entering your full name in place of *yourname:*

   name="yourname"

2. Now edit the line

   echo *Hello $LOGNAME*

or the line

echo *Hello $USER*

so that it reads

echo *Hello $name*

3. Run this shell script again. Type

dir_ script

Now this script will call anyone who runs it by your full name. Since this is not very friendly, the next section shows you how to have your script ask individual users to enter their names.

11.2   IMPLEMENTING AN INTERACTIVE SCRIPT

You have written a shell script that produces output. This section introduces a method for writing shell scripts that prompt a user for input, and uses the response to determine what actions should be taken. Shell scripts that can get input from users, as well as write output to users, are called *interactive* scripts.

Setting the Value of a Variable to the User's Input

To bring user input into a shell script, set the value of a variable equal to whatever the user enters.

1. To set a value for the variable *name,* type the following command:

   read *name*

   Nothing happens. The command is waiting for your input.

2. Pretend you have been prompted for your name, and type your full name followed by [Return].

3. To check that the variable *name* has indeed been set to your input, type

   echo $*name*

   The value of the variable *name* (which you entered in Step 2) is displayed on your screen.

   When you wish to assign user input to a variable, use this command:

read *variable*

The **read** command simply waits for a single line of input, followed by a return character, reads that line, and then places the result into the named *variable.*

Creating and Running an Interactive Script

1. Use **vi** to create a new shell script named *script2* containing the following lines:

   ```
   #!/bin/sh
   echo "hello, my name is script2, what is your name? "
   read name
   echo glad to meet you $name
   ```

This script contains the minimum components of an interactive script. The line after **#!/bin/sh** prompts the user for input. The next line **read**s the standard input (up to a [Return]) and then sets the value of a variable *name* equal to what is entered. The last line uses that input in a command.

2. Add execute permission to this file, then run it by typing the following commands:

chmod +x *script2*
script2

3. When you are prompted for input, do as the script requests and type your full name followed by a [Return]. Observe the message that is displayed, resulting from your input.

Creating a Simple Menu That Prompts for Input

A common use of interactive scripts is to present menulike interfaces for users so that they need not directly face the complexities of the shell. Menus are much like the above script, in that they prompt you for input, set the value of a variable equal to your input, and then perform some action based on the value of that variable. One difference is that the prompt from a menu is significantly longer than in the above script. Many menus display a prompt similar to the following example:

```
                    MAIN MENU
        1) Print current working directory
        2) List all files in current directory
        3) Print today's date and time

    Please enter your selection dave:
```

1. Create a script that will present this type of menu interface. Use **vi** to create a new script named *menu* containing the following lines. (If your system uses *USER* to store the name of the user, replace *LOG-NAME* with *USER*.)

   #!/bin/sh
   cat <<++

   MAIN MENU

   1) Print current working directory
   2) List all files in current directory
   3) Print today's date and time

   Please enter your selection $LOGNAME :
   ++
   read *selection*
   echo *Your selection was $selection*

2. Use **chmod** to add execute permission to this file.

3. Run your menu by typing

   menu

4. When you are prompted for input, do as the script requests and type either a *1,2,* or *3*, followed by a Return .

   In this script, you did not use the **echo** utility to print the menu. Instead, you used the **cat** utility.

When you are using a command that reads the standard input (such as **cat**), you can tell the command to get its input from the lines that follow the command in the script, rather than from an external file. The advantage to using **cat** in this way, instead of using multiple **echo** statements, is that it is more efficient and it permits greater flexibility. You can arrange the text that is **cat**ted any way you want.

This kind of redirection is known as receiving standard input from a *here document*. The way to indicate this redirection of standard input is by appending the < <*tag* construct after the command name, followed by the lines of input, and then the closing *tag*. In the above example, the two plus signs (++) serve as the *tag*. Tags need not be plus signs—they can be any string—but the two occurrences of these tags must match exactly. Also, the second tag must appear alone on a line, with no spaces or tabs before it. The string **EOF** is often used as a tag, signifying **End Of File**.

Exercise 11-A

1. What should be the first line of all Bourne shell scripts?

_____

2. How do you access the value of a variable in the Bourne shell?

_____

3. What is the best way to assign a user's input to a variable in the Bourne shell?

_____

4. How do you utilize a *here document*?

_____

USING CONTROL STRUCTURES — 11.3

The parts of a programming language used to control what a program does based on some condition are called *control structures*. This section presents several Bourne shell control structures that improve the previously presented menu script.

Handling Multiple Choices with the case Statement

For your menu to actually accomplish some work, you need to be able to control which one of several possible courses of action will be taken based on the value of the variable *selection*.

1. Use **vi** to edit your *menu* script and replace the line

    echo *Your selection was $selection*

    with the lines:

```
case $selection in
    1)
        pwd
        ;;
    2)
        ls -l
        ;;
    3)
        date
        ;;
esac
```

2. When you have added these lines, run the script again with **menu**.

3. When prompted, enter one of the three choices. The action specified after the **case** segment matching your selection is performed for you.

Explaining the case Statement

You have just used the Bourne shell control structure called **case**. The **case** control structure is used to select which one of several possible courses of action will be taken based on the value of a variable. Control structures such as **case**, that determine a course of action, are often referred to as *branching* structures. Figure 11-1 contains an English language translation of the **case** structure you just used in your *menu* script.

case $selection **in**	based on the value of the variable *selection*	
1)	in the case where it is 1	
pwd		print working directory
;;		the end of this course of action
2)	in the case where it is 2	
ls -l		list the files in this directory
;;		the end of this course of action
3)	in the case where it is 3	
date		run the date utility
;;		the end of this course of action
esac	the end of this **case** control structure	

FIGURE 11-1.   Annotated case statement

A complete **case** control structure should always include at least three major components:

- The **case** statement itself is used to indicate the beginning of the control structure, and to specify the variable to be evaluated.

- The condition segment is begun with a character followed by a **)**. It specifies a string (a series of letters and/or numbers) to be compared to the value of the variable specified in the **case** segment. If the value matches the specified string, the *actions* specified following the **)** are performed.

- The **esac** segment indicates the end of this **case** structure. (**esac** is **case** spelled backwards.)

All conditions must be terminated with two semi-colons (**;;**). This part of the **case** structure indicates the end of a course of action. When the **;;** is encountered, execution skips to the line after the **esac** that ends the **case** structure.

Making a Script Loop Continuously Using while

You'll notice that once your script performed the requested action, it returned you to the shell prompt. In most cases, however, you want the menu script to perform the desired action, and then redisplay the menu. Repeating actions within a program is called *looping*, and can be accomplished with the **while** loop.

If you are going to make the menu loop, you also need to provide a selection for users to choose when they wish to exit.

1. Use **vi** to edit your script so it looks like the following. Be careful to include all five critical spaces in the **while** statement:

#!/bin/sh
leave = no

while [$*leave* = *no*]
do
cat <<++

MAIN MENU

  1) Print current working directory
  2) List all files in current directory
  3) Print today's date and time
  x) Exit

Please enter your selection $LOGNAME :
++
read *selection*

case *$selection* **in**
   1)
     pwd
     ;;
   2)
     ls -l
     ;;
   3)
     date
     ;;
   x)
     leave = yes
     ;;
esac
done
exit *0*

You have added two statements at the top, a new menu item, a new condition statement, and two statements at the end of your *menu* script.

2. Once your modifications are complete, run the

Explaining the while Loop

Call up your script again to examine the lines of the program (the *code*). The **while** causes the shell to continue performing the actions between the **do** and its associated **done** as long as the expression on the **while** line evaluates as *true*. The expression for this is

while [$*leave* = *no*]

In other words, **while** the variable *leave* has the value *no*, repeat the actions that follow the **do** statement up to the **done** statement.

The new condition section for menu option *x* changes the value of this variable to *yes*. When *x* is selected, the value of *leave* is no longer *no*, so the **while** loop concludes, allowing the Bourne shell to continue with the statements following the **done**. In this example, the only command following **done** is **exit**. So, choosing **x** exits the program.

In this case, the **exit** statement does not accomplish much, because there is an automatic, implicit **exit** at the end of every program. If your code lets the interpreting Bourne shell reach the bottom of the file, it **exits** automatically. It is better, however, to call **exit** explicitly with an argument of *0*. This is a way to indicate specifically how the shell script ends. The UNIX convention for exiting is that *0* means "everything was okay." Any other number usually means something went wrong.

Here is the format of the **while** loop being used here:

```
while [ expression ]
do
        statement 1
        statement 2
        .
        .
        .
done
```

Clearing the Screen

You may have noticed that it would be a lot nicer if the screen were cleared before each display of the menu.

1. Call up your script and add a **clear** statement, like this:

```
#!/bin/sh
leave = no
while [ $leave = no ]
do
clear
cat <<++
```

This new statement will clear the display before printing the menu.

2. Save your file, then run the menu again. Make a few selections, then exit.

Making a Script Pause

The displays are neater now. Unfortunately the results of each choice go by very quickly, sometimes too quickly to see; but you can fix that, too.

1. Change your file to add a **sleep** statement, like this

   esac
   sleep *2*
   done
   exit *0*

2. Run the script again and make a few selections to see if the **sleep** command helps. The **sleep** utility causes the Bourne shell that is reading this script to stop and take a breather. The argument to **sleep** is the number of seconds this little coffee break should last.

Waiting for User Response

You can see that **sleep** slows things down, but if the user is a slow reader, or if there's a lot of output, it may not be slow enough. Next you'll learn how to make the script wait until the user wants to continue.

1. Modify your file again, replacing the **sleep** statement with two new statements

   esac
   echo *"Press Return to continue"*
   read *hold*
   done
   exit *0*

2. Run the script again to check the results of your modifications. Make two or three selections. After each selection, you must press $\boxed{\text{Return}}$ to get back to the menu.

The **echo** statement with no argument produces a blank line. The **echo** with an argument produces the prompt. The **read** statement waits for input; **read** writes to a variable which is the variable *hold*, the value of which is never accessed.

This version is even friendlier, since the user can move as quickly or slowly as desired.

Choosing an Unavailable Option

So far, your menu has performed actions based on four possible entries. However, what if you enter some other value? Try it and see.

1. Run your script and, in response to the prompt, type *8.* You are prompted to press ⌐Return⌐ to continue, and the menu is simply redrawn, with no action taken.

It would be better if some explicit action were taken, such as display of a message indicating an invalid entry.

Declaring a Default Condition

1. Exit from the script, and then use **vi** to add a new condition

```
    x)
        leave=yes
        ;;
    *)
        echo "Invalid choice. Try again."
        ;;
esac
```

2. Run your script again, entering some value other than *1,2,3,* or *x.* This time the script alerts you about your wrong input.

   The * (default) condition contains statements that will be performed if any value occurs *other* than those already mentioned in previous condition statements. In this case, an appropriate message is displayed.

Including Multiple Values in a case Segment

As you know, your script will terminate when a lowercase *x* is entered by the user. You can let another character have the same result.

1. Run your script and see what happens when you type *X* as your selection. You are told that you have made an invalid choice.

2. Exit the script by typing *x.*

   You can modify the script so that the user can exit with either an upper- or lowercase *x.* One way to do that is to have two **case** segments that perform the same action. There is an easier way.

3. Using **vi**, modify the exit condition statement so that it looks like this:

x|X)
   leave = yes

4. Run the script, and exit by typing an uppercase X.

5. Run it again, and exit with a lowercase x. Both x and X now work.

When you want any one of several user entries to result in the same action, use the pipe symbol (I) in the condition statement. This symbol is the *or* symbol and indicates that the statements coming next should be executed *if* the variable being tested contains one of the listed values. You are not limited to two possibilities, but may include many values, each separated from the others with a pipe symbol. Step 3 contains an example of the *or* symbol.

In summary, the complete **case** statement has the following format. Note the proper indentation.

```
case $variable_name in
    string)
        statement(s)
        ;;
    string)
        other statement(s)
        ;;
    .
    .
    .
    *)
        default statement(s)
        ;;
esac
```

Adding a Selection to Display a File

Another selection you can include in your menu is one that lets the user display the contents of a file.

1. Edit your script to add a new menu item. First, change the menu display to look like this:

   1) Print current working directory
   2) List all files in current directory
   3) Print today's date and time
   4) Display contents of a file
   x) Exit

2. Next, add a condition statement to deal with the new option. Use **pg** instead of **more** if you are using System V.

   4)
       echo *"Enter a file name "*
       read *fname*
       more *$fname*
       ;;
   x|X)
       leave = yes
       ;;

3. Run your new script and select the new option. When prompted, type the name of an existing file.

4. Find out what happens if you give the name of a nonexistent file. Select option 4 again, but this time give it a fictitious filename. You get an error message from **more** or **pg**.

Avoiding Errors with if

You can modify the script to check if a file exists before trying to display it.

1. Call up the script file and change the condition statement for the new option to look like this:

```
4)
    echo "Enter a file name "
    read fname
    if [ -f $fname ]
    then
        more $fname
    fi
    ;;
```

2. Run this version of the script, again selecting the new option, and again typing a fictitious filename. This time there is no error message from **more** or **pg**.

The **if** statement is another example of a branching structure. It is more versatile than **case,** because it can use expressions to test for many conditions other than simple string comparisons.

In the previous example, the construct

if [*-f $fname*]
then
     more $fname
fi

can be translated as, "**if** the contents of the variable *fname* is the name of a regular (text) file (**-f**), **then** run the **more** or **pg** command; otherwise forget it."

Note that an **if** statement is ended with **fi** (**if** spelled backwards).

When you entered a nonexistent filename, **more** (or **pg**) was not executed, so you did not get an error message.

Taking Actions When the if Is Not True

You can further modify the script so that it alerts users about nonexistent files.

1. Modify your script so that condition 4 looks like this:

   4)
        echo "Enter a file name "
        read fname
        if [*-f $fname*]
        then
             echo The contents of $fname:
             more $fname
        else
             echo $fname does not exist
        fi
        ;;

2. Run this version of the script, again selecting the new option, and again typing a fictitious filename.

This time you are told that the file does not exist. The **else** statement made this possible. The **else** statement is used to specify a list of one or more commands to run if the condition specified in the **if** statement is evaluated as false.

One simple form of the **if** statement is

if [*expression* **]**
then
    statement(s)
fi

This format makes no provision for action when the **if** statement is evaluated as false.

A more complex form of the **if** control structure introduced in this chapter is

if [*expression* **]**
then
    statement(s)
else
    other statement(s)
fi

Here there is a provision for what should be done when the **if** statement is evaluated as false.

Repeating an Action with for

Thus far you have used the **while** looping control structure. The **while** structure is used to repeat a sequence of actions as long as some condition remains true. Another type of looping is to repeat a sequence for actions on a specified list of objects (filenames, variables, and so forth).

1. The following will make backup copies of a number of files in your current directory.

   - First, type the following command, replacing *file1* and *file2* with the names of two files in the current directory:

   for *fn* **in** *file1 file2*

   You are greeted by a > prompt. Because you entered the **for** from the command line, the shell prints this secondary prompt (>) to let you know that it is expecting more instructions.

   - Give the shell what it is waiting for. Type the following lines in response to the prompts you receive:

   do
   cp *$fn $fn.bak*
   done

   The **for** command you typed first specifies that the statements between **do** and **done** are to be repeated **for** each filename specified after the word **in**. Together, these statements create a copy of each indicated file, giving it the same name as the original, with the added extension .bak.

2. Use **ls** to take a look at the files in your current directory. Included in the list should be several files with the .bak extension, created with the preceding **for** command.

3. Remove the .bak files (unless you want to keep them) by typing

rm *.bak*

The general format of the **for** command is

for *variable* **in** *list*
do
    statement(s)
done

The **for** command takes a *variable* name and a *list* of words, and performs the same *statement(s)* for each word in the *list*. (The words may or may not be filenames.) File expansion characters can be used to generate a list of filenames in the word *list*. The value of the named variable (in this case, *fn*) is set to the first word in the word *list*. Then, the statements between the **do** and **done** are executed. Next, the value of the variable is set to the second word in the *list*, and the statements are executed again. This process is repeated until the end of the word *list* is reached.

The **for** command must begin with the word **for** followed by a variable name, the word **in**, and a word list. The word **do** alone on a line starts the body of the loop, which is ended with **done**, also alone on a line.

Within the body of the loop, you may specify as many statements as you wish, and they should all be indented when used in a script. Since the name following the word **for** is a variable, accessing its current value is achieved with the dollar sign ($). As with any other variable, it is a good idea to use a name that indicates what it will contain.

Using for in Your Script

Since **for** is a Bourne shell command, you can use it in your script.

1. Use **vi** to edit your *menu* script, and modify the menu display so that it looks like this:

   1) Print current working directory
   2) List all files in current directory
   3) Print today's date and time
   4) Display contents of a file
   5) Create backup file copies
   x) Exit

2. Add the following condition statement:

   5)
       echo Enter file names
       read fnames
       for *fn* **in** *$fnames*
       do
           cp $fn $fn.bak
       done
       ;;

3. Run a test of this version of the script, creating two or three backup file copies. In this loop, the word list is the contents of the variable *fnames*, which has been set from user input. Be sure not to confuse *fnames*, which is serving as the word list, with *fn*, which is the variable that will be set to each word in the list.

Exercise 11-B

1. What are the three major components of the Bourne shell's **case** structure?

   _____

2. If you wanted to write a Bourne shell script that performed a series of actions as long as some condition evaluated as true, what control structure would you use?

   _____

3. What is the best way to have a script pause so that a user has time to read what is on the screen?

   _____

4. What is the * used for within **case** structures?

   _____

5. How can you get **case** to accept several alternatives as acceptable conditions for the same set of actions?

   _____

6. What is the closing part of an **if** structure in the Bourne shell?

   _____

FINISHING UP   **11.4**

Your script is now a fully functional menu. In this section you will make a small modification to your code that will make the menu a little friendlier. You will also be introduced to an alternative method for exiting a **while** loop.

Eliminating Returns from the echo Statements

Until now, every time you used an **echo** command the cursor was placed on the following line. A nice touch in menus is to have the cursor remain on the prompt line until the user enters a response and presses the Return key.

1. Use **vi** to edit the *menu* script and modify all lines in this format:

    echo *prompt string*

    to look like this on System V:

    echo *"prompt string*: \c"

    and this on BSD:

    echo -n *"prompt string: "*

    The **\c** in System V and the **-n** in BSD eliminate the return at the end of the line, and the quotes produce a blank space between the end of the prompt and the cursor.

2. The first prompt for input, at the end of the menu display, also needs some modification. Use **vi** to remove it from the input to **cat**, and then include it in an **echo** statement, so that you end up with

1) Print current working directory
2) List all files in current directory
3) Print today's date and time
4) Display contents of a file
5) Create backup file copies
x) Exit

++

echo -n *"Please enter your selection $LOGNAME : "*
read selection

System V users should use this form of the **echo** statement:

echo *"Please enter your selection $LOGNAME :* **\c***"*

3. Make a few selections, then exit.

Having the cursor wait at the prompt for user input is friendlier than using **echo** without the **-n** option (BSD) or the **\c** option (System V).

Using an Alternate Exit

Thus far, you have been using the method of exiting a **while** loop within a menu that includes an explicit exit condition within the **while** structure itself. There is another method of exiting that uses a loop with no exit condition (an infinite loop), and an explicit call to the Bourne shell built-in **exit** to exit the loop.

1. Use **vi** to edit *menu*. First, replace the **while** statement and the statement preceding it:

> *leave = no*
> **while** [*$leave = no*]

with the single line:

while :

2. Replace the condition statement:

> *x|X)*
> > *leave = yes*
> > *;;*

with the lines:

> *x|X)*
> > *exit 0*
> > *;;*

3. Delete the **exit** statement following the final **done**.

The expression : (colon) or the word *true* is always considered to be true, and the expression *false* is always false. Thus, **while :** causes an infinite loop.

The *exit 0* in the **case** statement causes the current shell to terminate.

4. Make a few more selections to verify that the changes work.

11.5 MAKING THE FINISHED PRODUCT EASIER TO READ

Now you have a working Bourne shell menu script. In the world of programming, it is important for a script to be readable, as well as to run smoothly. No program is ever really complete, and someday you or someone else may need to modify a program you wrote. Modifying programs is considerably easier when you can read what is already there, and figure out what each line of code does and what each variable will contain. To assure that your program is readable, always perform the following finishing touches:

- Verify that each variable has a name that describes its content.

- Check your indentation and use of blank lines between sections.

- Add comments where they might be helpful to another reader—including a header message.

Selecting Variable Names

The variable names you have used so far are words or derivatives of words. They describe the data that they contain. This is a good practice for you to observe in your programs as well. For example, when giving a name to a variable that will contain a filename, call it *filename* or *fname* or *filnme*, but not *x*.

Some Notes on Indentation

Review the indentation of the exercises you've done so far. Consistent indentation is very important for maintaining the readability of your code. Here are some rules to follow:

- In general, the components of a control structure should begin in the same column, and the body of the structure should be indented one level. For example, the associated **if, then, else** and **fi** statements should all start in the same column, as should a **while** statement with its associated **do** and **done**.

- Do not indent unnecessarily; only indent within control structures and loops.

- All steps of indentation should be the same distance. For example, always use equally spaced tabs, or always use four spaces. Be consistent.

Using Bourne Shell Comments

Good programming practices include placing comments inside your programs that explain what the various parts of your code do. Each line of a script that begins with a # is ignored by the Bourne shell and can include helpful comments for future readers of your code.

There is one exception to this rule. You will remember that the first line in your *menu* script begins with a **#**, followed by a bang (!), which indicates that the script should be interpreted by the utility that is named following the bang. (In this case, it is **/bin/sh**, the Bourne shell.) This is *not* a comment line.

As a later section demonstrates, the C shell interprets any script that has a # as the first character in the file, not followed by **!/bin/sh**. Any other first character other than # indicates a Bourne shell script. For this reason, many programmers replace the line

#!/bin/sh with a colon (:) by itself on the first line. (Remember, in the Bourne shell, a colon simply evaluates as true.) Either a colon or the **#!/bin/sh** will work. The method used in this chapter explicitly indicates the desired shell.

   Comments should be used to explain the parts of your code that might be less understandable to other people (or yourself) after some time has passed. Comments should also be used to put a header at the beginning of your program. This header can specify the name of the program, the program's author, its date of creation, and its function. See Figure 11-2 at the end of the chapter for a full listing of the *menu* program.

CREATING MORE SHELL SCRIPTS 11.6

You can create shell scripts to perform various tasks. One useful task for a script is to search a phone list.

Designing a Shell Script That Searches a Phone List

The Bourne shell script that follows can be used to search a phone list by name or phone number. It is invoked from the command line by typing the name of the script followed by an argument that provides the search pattern.

1. Create a script called *phone* with the visual editor, and type the following lines:

```
#!/bin/sh
grep $1 phone.list
```

2. Make your script executable. Type

chmod +x *phone*

3. Create a file called *phone.list* with the visual editor, containing the phone list. Type the following lines in the file:

abc 123-4567
rpq 234-1029
rpq 543-9681
sjl 567-4823
xyz 123-4567

4. Test your script. Type

search.phone *xyz*

The output is

```
xyz  123-4567
```

5. Try one more. Type

phone *123*

The output is

```
abc  123-4567
xyz  123-4567
```

These two lines were printed because **grep** displays all matching lines from the file *phone.list*.

The following line-by-line description demonstrates how the script works. Later, you will add more capability to this script.

The script begins with

#!/bin/sh

which instructs the system to have the file interpreted by the Bourne shell.

The only other line is

grep $1 *phone.list*

It consists of the command line for running the **grep** utility, including *$1* and *phone.list*, the two arguments. The first argument, *$1*, represents the first argument on the command line you typed to run this script. For example, when you typed

phone *xyz*

the first command line argument was *xyz*, and that was the pattern *$1* represented for the duration of the run. The second argument to **grep** is *phone.list*, which appears only within the shell script. You do not have to type *phone.list* on the command line that runs the *phone* script.

Using Quoted Arguments

As it stands now, the script is mildly useful. It saves you from having to type the name of the file to be searched with **grep**. However, it has more than one flaw, which you might not notice for a while.

1. Type the following command:

phone *"rpq 234"*

Instead of the expected output:

```
rpq 234-1029
```

you get something like this

```
grep: can't open 234
phone.list:rpq 234-1029
phone.list:rpq 543-9681
```

Here is what happened. When you typed the command line **phone** *"rpq 234"*, your login shell started the *phone* script and passed it the pattern "rpq 234" as a single argument. In other words, within the script *phone*, the value of $1 was *rpq 234*. The Bourne shell running the script then processed the commands in the script according to its evaluation rules.

One of the first processing steps consists of expanding shell variables, which means each variable is replaced with its value. In this case there was one shell variable, the positional parameter *$1*. Positional parameters are variables that contain the arguments from the command line that the shell passes to a command. Each argument is represented by its numerical position in the argument list ($1 represents the first argument, $2 the second, and so on). In this case, the first argument was *"rpg 234"*, so the variable, *$1*, was expanded to this value. Once this variable was expanded, the **grep** command line from the script effectively looked like this:

grep *rpq 234 phone.list*

Two parameters were expanded to three. The shell started the **grep** utility and passed it these three parameters. To **grep**, the three parameters mean

rpq	the pattern to search for
234	the first file to search
phone.list	the second file to search

When **grep** searches through more than one file for a pattern, it prefaces each line of its output with the name of the file in which it found the match. This is why the output contained the name of the phone list file. The first file, named *234*, does not exist, so **grep** reported the error message:

```
grep: can't open 234
```

Notice that because **grep** used *rpg* for the search pattern, it found two matching lines instead of the expected one line.

The *phone* script would be a more useful utility if it did not have this behavior for arguments containing embedded blanks, such as *rpq 234*. You want the script to treat the value of *$1* as a single word, and not split it into two. You can use quoting to accomplish this.

2. Change the **grep** line of the *phone* script to read

grep *"$1" phone.list*

3. Try the **phone** command again. Type

phone *"rpq 234"*

This time you get the correct output

```
rpq 234-1029
```

Quoting the positional parameter *$1* fixed the earlier problem. Now when the Bourne shell expands the variable *$1*, it produces (internally) the intermediate command line:

grep *"rpq 234" phone.list*

The double-quotes now force the shell to treat the value of *$1* as a single word. (Recall from Chapter 6, "Command Interpretation by the Shell," that double-quotes do not prevent the shell from interpreting the dollar sign as a variable identifier.)

Performing Multiple Searches

You can use looping to make your script search for several patterns.

1. Modify your script to look like the following:

   #!/bin/sh
   for *i* **do**
      grep *"$i" phone.list*
   done

   Make sure that the first argument to **grep** is *$i*, and not *$1* as it was before.

2. Try the modified *phone* script. Type

phone *rpq xyz*

You get the output:

```
rpq  234-1029
rpq  543-9681
xyz  123-4567
```

The **for** statement in the script loops over all the command line arguments, setting the variable *i* to each one in turn. For each value of the variable *i*, the shell runs the **grep** utility, substituting the current value of the variable *i* for **grep**'s first argument. The outputs of all the **grep** runs appear concatenated together, as you would expect.

Removing Duplicate Output Lines

The *phone* script is more useful than it was before, because it now accepts multiple search patterns. The patterns do not have to be names; any characters will do.

1. For example, type

phone *rpq 102*

You get the following output:

```
rpq  234-1029
rpq  543-9681
rpq  234-1029
```

The first line of the output appears twice. It appears the first time because the argument pattern *rpq* matched it. Its second appearance was caused by the match with the pattern *102.* The output is entirely consistent, but to show lines from the phone list more than once is unnecessary. The output can appear even more cluttered if several entries are repeated.

2. There is yet another undesirable effect. Type the following:

phone *xyz rpq*

You get the output:

```
xyz  123-4567
rpq  234-1029
rpq  543-9681
```

The output does not appear in alphabetical order, even though the phone list file is sorted. This is because the output is the result of two runs of the **grep** utility: the first run uses the argument *xyz* to pick up the first line of the output; the second run uses the argument *rpq* to pick up the remaining two lines. The pattern arguments were not in alphabetical order, so the output is not alphabetized, either.

3. Both problems—duplicate output and unsorted output—can be fixed with a minor addition to the *phone* script. Change the **done** line of the script to the following:

done | sort -u

This illustrates an important property of the Bourne shell control constructs: they can be treated just like commands. In this case, you can think of the **for** construct (everything from the keyword **for** through the keyword **done**) as a single command. Its output is the output that prints on your screen. The modified **done** line now takes the output of the **for** command and pipes it to the **sort** utility to alphabetize it. The **-u** option to the **sort** utility causes **sort** to produce **u**nique output lines.

4. Execute the new version on the two earlier examples. First type

phone *rpq 102*

The output is now

```
rpq 234-1029
rpq 543-9681
```

5. Try the other example. Type

phone *xyz rpq*

The output is

```
rpq 234-1029
rpq 543-9681
xyz 123-4567
```

Both commands now produce sorted output with no duplicates. This version of the *phone* script is

considerably more useful than the first one you created, yet it is not much more complex. The revised
script uses a few features of the Bourne shell programming language to significantly increase its capabilities.

11.7 SETTING BOURNE SHELL VARIABLES FOR C SHELL USERS

As mentioned earlier in this chapter, the file *.profile* is
only read for users that have the Bourne shell at login.
If your initial shell is the C shell, but you wish to have
Bourne shells make use of preset variables, you will
have to use a different strategy. Two methods are
available.

Using Your Own Version of *.profile*

You may create a new file, and call it *.profile* or any
other name you want. Include in that file the variables
you want to use. Then, whenever you create a new
Bourne shell with the command

sh

you can simply activate your version of an intializing
file by typing

. *filename*

where *filename* is the name of your version of *.profile*. This makes your variables available to the Bourne shell because the dot (.) instructs the Bourne shell to read the file.

If your version of *.profile* is located in your Home directory, and you want to read it from a directory other than your Home directory, use the command

.   *$HOME/filename*

Setting Environment Variables for the Bourne Shell

You may set variables in your *.login* file so that they are also available to the Bourne shell. For instance, if you want your Bourne shell primary prompt to be

```
Bourne Shell ==>
```

type the following in your *.login* file:

setenv *PS1 "Bourne Shell = => "*

This sets *PS1* as an **environment** variable, and as such it will also be available to the Bourne shell. The **setenv** command places variables in the system data region.

Although this second method is a bit faster than the first, be cautious. If you set too many environment variables, you may slow down the execution time of your shell.

11.8   COMPARING C SHELL PROGRAMMING WITH BOURNE PROGRAMMING

C shell programming is similar to Bourne shell programming in the following ways:

- Most of the same control structures exist in both Bourne and C shells.

- Variables may be set in both Bourne and C shells.

  Some of the differences between the two shells are

- The syntax to set a variable is different in the two shells.

- Certain built-in commands do not work in both shells. For example, **alias** only exists in the C shell.

- Certain variables are treated in a special way in only one of the two shells. For example, *noclobber* is not recognized by the Bourne shell.

- There are three ways to execute a C shell script.

  Most of what you learn about Bourne shell programming will apply to C shell programming. If you become proficient at Bourne shell programming, you will find it relatively easy to do C shell programming.

Executing a C Shell Script

The three ways to execute a C shell script are demonstrated in the following procedure.

1. Create a simple C shell script, called *simple,* with the visual editor. Include the following lines:

   #!/bin/csh
   echo *Hello*

2. Make this script executable by typing

   chmod +x *simple*

3. Execute the script by typing

   simple

   The script executes and prints

   ```
   Hello
   ```

   A subshell executes the command while your current shell sleeps.

4. Another way to execute the script is with the **source** command. Experiment by typing

   source *simple*

   Again the script executes and produces the same output.
   There is no visible difference between the two forms of execution, other than what you type. To the system, however, there is a difference. The first method (strict execution) creates a new shell that executes the script. The second method (**source**) causes your current shell to interpret the commands in the script.

5. The third method is to execute the script by having your current process overwrite the shell with the script. The following will log you out because when the script is finished, there is no shell to wake up—it was overwritten. Type

exec *simple*

The script executes again, and prints
```
Hello
```
You are then logged out.

Exercises 11-C

1. What does the colon (:) on a line by itself mean to the Bourne shell?

   _____

2. What command is most often used within a script to terminate a **while** loop with a condition that is always true?

   _____

3. List three features of a well-written program that make the program easy to understand.

   _____

4. Are C shell and Bourne shell control structures similar?

   _____

5. Which shell allows the **alias** command and treats the *noclobber* variable in a special way?

_____

The Bourne and C shells provide you with a powerful programming language that can be used to quickly create working programs. Both shells handle input from users and shell script programming. Shell scripts can be programmed to prompt users for input, manipulate variables, call utilities, and use programming constructs such as **while, for** and **if then**. Shell scripts can be used to create small programs and to create mock-ups of larger programs that are later written in other languages. This introduction to shell programming provides the foundation for a thorough study of shell programming.

CONCLUSION

11.9   BOURNE SHELL CONTROL STRUCTURES

The if-then Construct

if [*expression*]
then
     command-list
fi

The if-then else Construct

if [*expression*]
then
     command-list
else
     command-list
fi

The case Construct

case *variable-list* **in**
     string)
          command-list
          ;;
     string)
          command-list
          ;;
     *)
          command-list
          ;;
esac

The while Loop

while [*expression*]
do
    command-list
done

The for Loop

for *varname* **in** *word-list*
do
    command-list
done

```
#!/bin/sh

# Program name: menu
# Written by: your name here
# Date: current date here
# Description:
#       This program prints a menu and executes the selected choice.
#       Then it reprints the menu for another selection.
#       This goes on until the user enters the exit option.
#       Choices are:
#             1) Print current working directory
#             2) List all files in current directory
#             3) Print today's date and time
#             4) Display contents of file
#             5) Create backup copies of files
#             x) Exit back to the shell

# start infinite loop . . . exit is in case x
while :

do

clear
# print menu display
cat << ++

                    MAIN MENU

          1) Print current working directory
          2) List all files in current directory
          3) Print today's date and time
          4) Display contents of a file
          5) Create backup file copies
          x) Exit

++
```

FIGURE 11-2.   Listing of menu program

```
# prompt for user input
echo -n "Please enter your selection $LOGNAME: "

# set variable named selection to value of user input
read selection

# start case based on selection
case $selection in

# selection 1 ... print working directory
      1)
           pwd
           ;;

# selection 2 ... list files
      2)
           ls -l
           ;;

# selection 3 . ... display todays day and time
      3)
           date
           ;;

# selection 4 . ...view a file
      4)
           echo -n "Enter a file name: "
           read fname
           if [ -f $fname ]
           then
               echo "The contents of $fname: "
               more $fname
           else
               echo $fname does not exist
           fi
           ;;
```

FIGURE 11-2. Listing of menu program (*continued*)

```
# selection 5 . . . make backup copies of a list of
# user entered files
    5)
        echo -n "Enter file names:"
        read fnames
        for fn in $fnames
        do
          cp $fn $fn.bak
        done
        ;;

# selection x . . . exit
    x)
        exit 0
        ;;

# default case
    *)
        echo "Invalid choice. Try again."
        ;;

# end the case
esac

# pause before redisplaying menu
echo -n "Press Return to continue "
read hold

# end the while
done
```

FIGURE 11-2.   Listing of menu program (*continued*)

·12·

Running Print Jobs

An essential feature of UNIX is printing files. The system is organized so that files can be sent to several different printers attached to one computer. In this chapter you will print files, check the status of a print job request, choose print options, and cancel print jobs.

There are significant differences between the commands to print files on machines running System V and those running BSD UNIX. Both sets of commands are included in this chapter and are listed in the Command Summary at the end of this chapter. Also the differences are summarized in Table 12-1.

TABLE 12-1. A Comparison of System V and BSD Print commands

Sys V Command	BSD Command
lp -d*printer filename*	**lpr -P***printer filename*
lp -d*printer* **-n***number filename*	**lpr -P***printer* **-#***number filename*
lp -d*printer* **-t***title filename*	**lpr -P***printer* **-J***title filename*
lp -d*printer* **-s** *filename*	By default **lpr** does not display the request number. To see the request number use **lpq -P***printer* and look for your job in the list.
lp -d*printer* **-w** *filename*	There is no corresponding option for BSD.
lp -d*printer* **-m** *filename*	**lpr -d***printer* **-m** *filename*
lpstat	To get status information on all print requests (not just yours) for a destination printer, use **lpq -d***printer.*
cancel *printer-jobnumber*	**lprm -P***printer jobnumber*
cancel *printer*	Not possible in BSD

SKILLS CHECK

Before beginning this chapter, you should be able to

- Access and leave the system (Chapter 1, "Touring the System's Features")

- Execute basic commands (Chapter 1)

- Create, display, and print files (Chapter 1)

- Create and modify files using the **vi** editor (Chapter 2, "Basic Editing with the Visual Editor")

- Use the **mail** command to send and receive messages (Chapter 5, "Sending Messages to Other Users")

Upon completion of this chapter, you will be able to   OBJECTIVES

- Start print jobs and use options to alter defaults
- Get status information on your print jobs
- Cancel print jobs

SENDING FILES TO BE PRINTED   12.1

Ask another user or your system administrator for the name of a printer designation that you can use. In this chapter, the printer name *printer* is used in commands. Substitute your printer name for *printer* when you enter each command. If a second printer is available also, get its printer designation, because part of this chapter involves switching a print job from one printer to another.

You have been sending files to be printed by typing one of the following commands (substituting the name of your printer for *printer*):

System V:
lp -d*printer filename*

BSD:
lpr -P*printer filename*

The **-d***printer* and **-P***printer* portions of these commands request a specific printer. The entire command line instructs the line printer program to send a copy of *filename* to the specified printer. Your print job waits in line in a printer queue until its turn to be printed.

1. Create a new small file called *junk1*

Including some text, such as

*This is a test file, and I am going to use
it to try out different print commands.*

Sending More than One File to the Queue

In one command line, you can specify several files to
be printed by listing them all as arguments to the
print command.

1. For instance, to print the two files *junk1* and *practice,*
type the appropriate command line:

System V:
lp -d*printer junk1 practice*

BSD:
lpr -P*printer junk1 practice*

Printing the Output of a Pipeline

As with most other UNIX utilities, you can connect
the output of another command to the input of the
print command using a pipe redirect symbol (**|**). Here
are two examples.

1. You can instruct the system to print the contents of
the current directory without first creating a file.
Have the shell connect the output of **ls** directly to
the input of **lp** or **lpr**. Type one of the following:

System V:
ls | lp -d*printer*

BSD:
ls | lpr -P*printer*

The **lp** or **lpr** utility sends the output of the **ls** command to the printer exactly as if that output had been stored in a file. This piping feature allows you to make hardcopies of on-line information.

2. If your system has the on-line manual, get a hardcopy of the manual pages describing the **sort** utility. Type one of the following:

System V:
man *sort* **l lp -d** *printer*

BSD:
man *sort* **l lpr -P***printer*

3. Modify the previous command to print a copy of the manual pages for the **lp** or **lpr** utilities.

Sending Your Job to a Different Printer

If you have more than one available printer, you can explicitly select a different printer when you issue the print command. If you do not have an alternate printer, go on to the next section.

1. Print the file *junk1* on the printer *printer2*, where *printer2* is the name of the second printer. Type one of the following:

System V:
lp -d*printer2 junk1*

BSD:
lpr -P*printer2 junk1*

These commands allow you to choose your printer. If one printer is down or occupied, you can send your print requests to another.

12.2

USING PRINT COMMAND OPTIONS

The printer programs **lp** and **lpr** are UNIX utilities. You can modify the usage of each by selecting options, identified with the usual minus sign.

Printing Multiple Copies

Suppose you need a copy of your *junk1* file for several of your friends. You can send the file to the printer once for each copy you need, or you can ask for multiple copies by issuing a single command line. For example, request five copies of the file *junk1* by typing one of the following command lines:

System V:
lp -d*printer2* **-n***5 junk1*

The option **-n**5 tells **lp** to print five copies of the file.

BSD:
lpr -P*printer2* **-#***5 junk1*

The option **-#**5 instructs **lpr** to print five copies of the file.

Adding a Title Line to the Banner Page

Each of the jobs just printed was preceded by a banner page, also called a burst-page, containing information about the printer and about the user issuing the request. A title line may be added to this banner page.

1. Add your own title and print the *junk1* file again. Type one of the following:

System V:
lp -d*printer* **-t**"*Escaped Leopard Spotted*" *junk1*

BSD:
lpr -P*printer* **-J**"*Escaped Leopard Spotted*" *junk1*

The two command formats are

System V:
lp -d*printer* **-t***title filename*

BSD:
lpr -P*printer* **-J***title filename*

There is no space between the **-t** or the **-J** and the *title*.

When you use the **-t** option in System V, or the **-J** option in BSD, the title you provide is printed on the banner page preceding your printing job. If your title contains spaces:

- In System V, enclose the entire title in double or single quotes, or precede each space by a backslash character, as in the following examples:

  lp -d*printer* **-t**"*A Title Containing Blanks*" *filename*
  lp -d*printer* **-t**'*A Title Containing Blanks*' *filename*
  lp -d*printer* **-t***A\ Title\ Containing\ Blanks filename*

- In BSD, use quotation marks to include spaces.

Titles are particularly useful for identifying different versions of the same file; for instance

lp -d*printer* **-t**"*23june-4:00 Proposal*" *proposal*

Suppressing Messages to the Terminal

On System V, when you use **lp** to request a print job, the program replies with a message that it has processed your request and assigned a serial number to the job:

```
request id is printer-#
```

1. You can suppress this message by typing

lp -s -d_printer junk1_

The shell prompt is returned to you without the message.

The **-s** option suppresses the "request id" message routinely sent to your terminal.

Because the BSD **lpr** utility does not send a message to your screen upon receipt of your print request, there is no option to suppress the message.

Determining When a Job Is Printed

The "request id" message tells you when the spooler program has queued your print job. (The spooler is explained later in this chapter.) With System V (but not BSD), you can also ask the print utility to notify you when the printer has completed your job.

1. Type

lp -w -d_printer junk1_

You will first see the message

```
request id is printer-#
```

on your terminal. However, this message tells you only that the file *junk1* has been placed in the queue; it does not tell you that the file has been printed.

The following message then appears on your terminal after a few seconds (or a few minutes if your system is busy):

```
lp: printer request printer-# has been
printed on printer name
```

The **-w** option instructs **lp** to write to your terminal informing you when your job has finished printing.

Getting Mail Concerning Print Status

You can instruct the program to send mail to you when the printer has finished your job.

1. On System V, type

   lp -m -d*printer junk1*

   You will first see this message:

```
request id is printer-#
```

Then the shell prompt returns, and you can continue with other activities.

On BSD, type

lpr -m -P*printer junk1*

2. The results are similar for both **lp** and **lpr** commands. After a few minutes, this message appears:

```
You have new mail
```

One of the messages is from **lp** in System V, or **daemon** in BSD. The content of this message is

```
printer request printer-# has been printed on
printer name
```

The **-m** option instructs the spooler to send you mail when a print job is complete.

12.3 CHECKING THE STATUS OF PRINT JOBS

On some systems, print jobs are sent faster than the printer can produce the output. Each new job is added (spooled) to a list of jobs to be done. UNIX lets you check your job, or all jobs in the printer queues.

Collecting the Output from a Printer

The printer programs (**lp** and **lpr**) can handle the queues for several printers. You determine which printer is employed for each job.

1. From the shell, type the appropriate print command:

   System V:
   lp -d*printer junk1*

   BSD:
   lpr -P*printer junk1*

   On System V, after a few seconds, a message will appear on the screen similar to this one:

   ```
   request id is printer-# (1 file)
   ```

   This message indicates that the **lp** program ran successfully and assigned a request ID to your print job (*printer-#*). The *printer* in this ID is the same destination printer name you specified in the command line. The **#** is a sequential number assigned to your print request by the program.

   If you now go to the printer expecting to see your file printed or in the process of printing, you may be disappointed. Your print job could be waiting in line to be printed. Each print job is queued and printed as soon as its turn arrives.

   The *spooler* is the program that administers your print requests. It is the spooler that makes it possible for several users to send several files for printing at the same time.

538 UNIX Made Easy

When you type a print command followed by a printer designation and filename, the spooler processes your request, assigns a request number to the job submitted, and queues it up for printing at the specified destination. If the printer you specify is free, the print request is passed to the printer, and the file starts printing. Otherwise, the job must wait for the printer to be available.

Finding the Status of Your Print Jobs

1. Send the file *junk1* to the printer, using the print command appropriate for your system. Your file *junk1* is now queued for printing, waiting for its turn to be printed.

You can search the printer queue for the status of any job you send (printed, printing, or waiting).

2. Examine the queue by typing one of the following commands:

System V:
lpstat

which stands for **l**ine **p**rinter **stat**us.

BSD:
lpq -P*printer username*

where *username* is the login name of your current account, and *printer* is the selected printer.

3. If few people are using the printer, your print job will be printed immediately upon request. There will be no trace of it in the output of **lpstat** or **lpq**.

4. If your job is queued, you will see screen output something like the following on System V:

```
gutenberg-2232    dave        234   Jan 12 13:02
```

This response tells you the request ID (*gutenberg-2232*), the user who initiated the request (*dave*), the number of characters to be printed (*234*), and the date and time of the print request (*Jan 12 13:02*).
   On BSD, the output is:

```
Rank     Owner    Job   Files      Total Size
1st      javert   237   /etc/motd  545 bytes
```

5. If your job is currently printing, the output of **lpstat** is similar to the following on System V:

```
gutenberg-2232   dave    234   Jan 12 13:02 on guttenberg
```

The final phrase, *on gutenberg,* says this request is currently printing at the printer destination *gutenberg.* On BSD, the response is

```
Rank    Owner       Job   Files      Total Size
active  javert      237   /etc/motd  545 bytes
```

The rank of *active* means the job is currently being printed by the printer.

Listing All Print Requests in System V

The commands in System V that you have used so far report only the print requests you made. You can also get a complete picture of all print requests. This allows you to identify the printer that has the shortest queue, and send your print job to that printer.

1. List all print requests by typing the following:

lpstat -t

The **-t** option on System V gives you a total listing of current events in the spooler.

2. The output of **lpstat -t** looks something like this:

```
scheduler is running
system default destination: gutenberg
device for gutenberg: /dev/lp
device for prnt2: /dev/tty08
gutenberg accepting requests since Oct 16 16:39
prnt2 accepting requests since Jan 6 13:24
printer gutenberg now printing gutenberg-2228.
  enabled since Sep 5 15:29
printer prnt2 is idle. enabled since Jan 6 13:25
gutenberg-
2228 joe 9300 Jan 6 10:57 on gutenberg
gutenberg-2232 dave 21 Jan 6 11:00
```

This display provides you with the following information about print requests for all printers and all users.

Scheduler   The first line indicates that the spooler is currently active and accepting print requests:

```
scheduler is running
```

Default Printer   The second line tells you that the default printer for this system is *gutenberg*:

```
system default destination: gutenberg
```

If a user has not specified a destination printer with the **-d** option, the spooler automatically sends the job to *gutenberg*. Your system may not have a default printer. If not, you will always have to specify the destination for your request.

Ports for Printers   The *device* lines tell you what physical device, or *port,* is associated with each of the printer names:

```
device for gutenberg: /dev/lp
device for prnt2: /dev/tty08
```

Activity Status   The next lines tell you whether each printer is accepting requests and, if so, for how long:

```
gutenberg accepting requests since Oct 16 16:39
prnt2 accepting requests since Jan 6 13:24
```

Printer Status   The printer lines indicate the specific status of each printer, such as whether it is idle or printing, and what it is printing:

```
printer gutenberg now printing gutenberg-2228.
   enabled since Sep  5 15:29
printer prnt2 is idle. enabled since Jan  6 13:25
```

Jobs on Queue   Finally, a list of *all* current print requests is displayed:

```
gutenberg-2228 joe 9300 Jan 6 10:57 on gutenberg
gutenberg-2232 dave 21 Jan 6 11:00
```

In this display, the user *joe* has a request currently printing on *gutenberg*, and the request placed by user *dave* will be printed next. The job size of 21 probably represents only a short wait. Other, longer files may contain hundreds or thousands of characters, resulting in a long delay.

Listing All Print Requests on BSD

On a BSD system you can get a list of all print jobs in the queue of each specific printer. By checking a printer's queue, you can see how busy it is and decide whether or not to send your print job there.

1. Check the queue of *printer* by typing the following:

   lpq -P*printer*

   This command without a specified *username* option outputs printer requests for all users.

2. The **lpq -P** output is similar to the following:

```
Rank      Owner        Job            Files
active    javert    237 /src/sc.h     11545 bytes
1st       mikey     238 /tmp/foo      22000 bytes
2nd       kevan     239 /etc/motd       545 bytes
```

   The commands offered in this and the previous section allow you to observe which other files are queued for printing before yours. If the list is longer than you care to wait for, you may want to cancel the print job.

CANCELING A PRINT REQUEST
12.4

Just as you can send a request to a printer, you can also cancel that request.

1. From the command line, type one of the following commands:

   System V:
   lpstat -t

   BSD:
   lpq -P*printer*

2. If there are no jobs currently queued for *printer*, edit the file *practice* using **vi**, and add enough text so that you have about 500 to 600 lines. Or you could read into *practice* a long system file such as */etc/termcap*. Send the long file to the printer with one of the following commands:

System V:
lp -d*printer practice*

BSD:
lpr -P*printer practice*

On System V, your terminal displays a response message similar to this:

```
request id is printer-1293
```

3. Request the file be printed again:

System V:
lp -d*printer practice*

BSD:
lpr -P*printer practice*

4. Check the status of your jobs.

System V:
lpstat

The output is similar to this:

```
gutenberg-1293 dave 2251 Jan 12 13:32 on gutenburg
gutenberg-1294 dave 2251 Jan 12 13:35
```

BSD:
lpq -P*printer*

The output will resemble this:

```
gutenberg is ready and printing
Rank    Owner     Job   Files       Total Size
1st     kevan     237   practice    12323 bytes
2nd     kevan     238   practice    12323 bytes
```

This report tells you that your requests have been sent to *gutenberg*.

5. Because your first print job is printing, you can remove the second job from the queue. In the following command lines, substitute your printer name for *gutenberg,* and your job number for *1294:*

System V:
cancel *gutenberg-1294*

This command line instructs the spooler to cancel the request *gutenberg-1294.* Even if the job is printing, it will be stopped.

BSD:
lprm -P*gutenberg 1294*

This command instructs the spooler to cancel the request number *1294.* If the job is already printing, it will not be cancelled.

In general, the format for the command to cancel a print request under System V is:

cancel *printer-jobnumber*

In BSD, the format of the command is:

lprm -P*printer jobnumber*

Exercise 12-A

1. What command would you use to send more than one file to the printer for printing?

   _____

2. What command would you use to request three copies of the file *junk1* from the printer?

   _____

3. How would you add a title line to the banner page for the file *junk1* when sending it to the printer?

   _____

4. What command allows you to see if your file is queued for printing?

   _____

5. How would you cancel a print request that is not yet being printed?

   _____

6. How would you instruct the print program to print the file *mail* on the destination *gutenberg,* when you do not want to know immediately the request number for the job, but you do want to see on the terminal and through the mail that the job has finished printing?

   _____

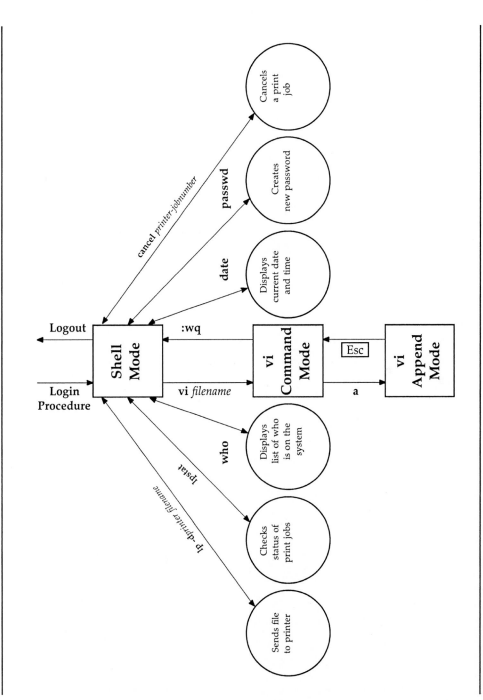

FIGURE 12-1.   System V printing commands

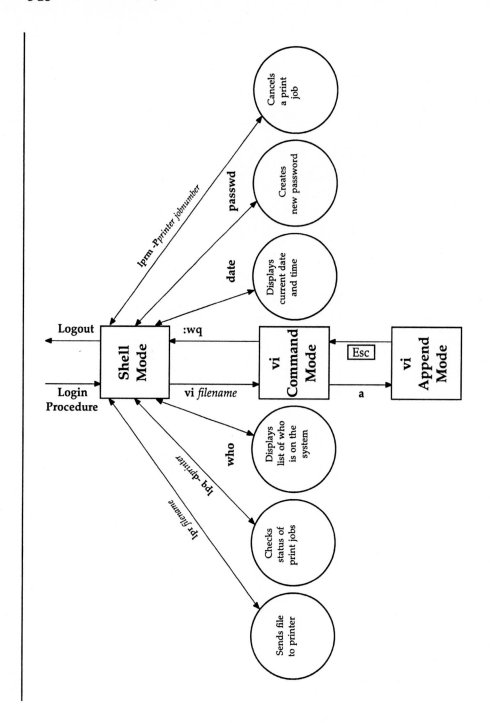

FIGURE 12-2. BSD printing commands

In this chapter you produced hardcopy output of your files using a variety of print commands. Because printer devices are slow when compared with the speed of the computer itself, and because each print job monopolizes the printer, it is necessary to use a job queue to handle printing. The system that manages this print queue is the print spooler. Its command interface includes the utilities **lp**, **lpstat**, and **cancel** in System V, and **lpr**, **lpq**, and **lprm** in BSD. These commands add print jobs to the queue, display status information about the queue, and remove print jobs from the queue, respectively.

At the end of this chapter is a command summary for both System V and BSD. Also, refer back to the conceptual maps, Figure 12-1 and Figure 12-2 that detail how **lp**, **lpr**, and other utilities interact with the shell.

CONCLUSION

COMMAND SUMMARY

SystemV Printing Command Summary

lp -d*printer filename*
Requests that the file *filename* be printed on the destination printer *printer*

utility lp-dprinter **| lp -d***printer*
Sends the standard output of utility lp-dprinter to the destination printer

lp -d*printer* **-n***number filename*
Specifies number of copies to be printed where *number* is the number of copies desired

lp -d*printer* **-t***title filename*
Specifies that *title* be printed on the banner page

lp -d*printer* **-s** *filename*
Specifies that printing of request number information on the screen be suppressed

lp -d*printer* **-w** *filename*
Specifies that **lp** write to the user when the request is finished printing

lp -d*printer* **-m** *filename*
Specifies that **lp mail** a message to the user when the job is finished printing

lpstat
Produces a report on the status of all your print requests

cancel *printer-jobnumber*
Cancels the specified print request (whether printing or not), where *printer-jobnumber* is the *request ID* of the requested job

cancel *printer*
Stops whatever job is currently being printed on *printer*

COMMAND SUMMARY *(continued)*

BSD Printing Command Summary

lpr -P*printer filename*
Requests that the file *filename* be printed on the destination printer *printer*

command | lpr -P*printer*
The output of **command** is piped to the destination printer

lpr -P*printer* **-#***number filename*
Specifies the number of copies to be printed where *number* is the requested number of copies

lpr -P*printer* **-J***title filename*
Specifies the banner to be printed on the banner page

lpr -d*printer* **-m** *filename*
Specifies that the program send the user mail when the requested print job is completed

lpq -d*printer*
Obtains status information on all print requests (not just yours) for a destination printer

lprm -P*printer jobnumber*
Cancels print request if it is not printing

·13·

Using the C Shell History

The basic way you accomplish tasks on UNIX is to type commands from the keyboard. The shell interprets and executes each command as it is entered. Often, you must repeat a series of commands, repeat a specific command, or correct mistyped commands. There are also times when a series of commands that differ only slightly from each other must be entered. In each case, you can spend significant energy and time retyping command lines.

The C shell *history* mechanism is designed to increase your efficiency by making it possible for you to repeat and/or modify previously executed command lines.

SKILLS CHECK

Before beginning this chapter, you should be able to

- Access and leave the system (Chapter 1, "Touring the System's Features")

- Create, display and print files (Chapter 1)

- Execute basic commands (Chapter 1)

- Name, copy, and remove files (Chapter 1)

- Use several shell commands in combination (Chapter 1)

- Access and modify files using the **vi** editor (Chapter 2, "Basic Editing with the Visual Editor")

- Utilize the UNIX directory hierarchy system (Chapter 3, "Using UNIX Directories")

OBJECTIVE

Upon completion of this chapter you will be able to use the history mechanism to

- Repeat commands already executed

- Correct errors in commands already executed

- Add to commands already executed

- Print commands without having them executed

USING THE HISTORY COMMAND

13.1

The C shell can be instructed to maintain a listing of commands that you enter from the shell. This *history list* can be examined; commands in it can be repeated, and previous commands can be modified.

The exercises in this chapter use three files created in earlier chapters: *practice, practice2,* and *journal.* If you do not currently have files by those names, create them. The content of the files is not important; just enter several lines of text in each.

Starting a C Shell

Only the C shell has the history feature described in these exercises. If you are currently using a C shell, proceed to the next section, "Instructing the Shell to Keep a history List."

1. If you are not using a C shell, start one by typing the command:

csh

This command tells your current shell to start up a C shell as a subshell. You will use this new shell to run the exercises in this chapter.

If you get the message:

```
Command not found
```

you probably do not have access to the C shell on your system. If so, you will not be able to do the exercises in this chapter.

Whenever you want to leave the subshell and return to your original login shell, type

exit

Instructing the Shell to Keep a history List

The shell keeps a history list, if you instruct it to do so. Type the command

set history = *20*

This command instructs the C shell to start maintaining a record of each command line that you enter. It also says to keep track of only the last 20 commands.

Inspecting a List of Past Commands Used

The history feature keeps a record of the exact command lines that you enter, in the order that you enter them.

1. Type each of the following shell commands:

   date
   who
   cd
   ls
   cat *practice*

2. Because you started the history mechanism functioning with the **set history**=*20* command, the five
   command lines you just entered are recorded in a
   history list by the C shell. Examine the list by typing

   history

   The output of **history** is similar to the following,
   although the numbers on the left may be quite
   different.

   ```
   2   set history=20
   3   date
   4   who
   5   cd
   6   ls
   7   cat practice
   8   history
   ```

   The last command line on the history list is the last
   command that you entered. All the commands that
   you typed since you set the *history* variable will
   appear on your screen as output from the **history**
   command. If history was already functioning when
   you entered **set** *history* = *20,* previous commands (up
   to a total of 20 commands) are also listed. Each
   command on the list has an associated *event number* on
   the left.

Adding the history Event Number to the Prompt

It is useful to be able to see what event number the
shell is giving to each command as you enter it.

1. From the shell, type the following command to change the shell prompt and have it display the event number of the command about to be entered.

set prompt=" \! % "

Note that there is a space on each side of the percent sign. The ! tells the system to read the last event number from the history list, add one to this number and display it. The backslash instructs the shell to not interpret the ! but pass it to **set**.

This prompt will display each event number until you change the prompt or log out. The setting for the prompt can be made to take effect each time you log in, by modifying the *.login* file, as discussed in a later section, "Permanently Setting the prompt and history Variables."

13.2   REISSUING PREVIOUSLY ENTERED COMMAND LINES

There are several ways to have the shell access the history list and reissue a command. You can request:

- A repeat of the most recently entered command

- The reissuing of a command identified by its event number

- A reexecution of a command by specifying part of the command name

Repeating the Most Recent Command

1. Review the *practice* file by typing the following display command:

   cat *practice*

   This utility moves *downward* through a file. To return to text that you passed by, it is often necessary to repeat the command.

2. When the shell prompt is again displayed, request that the previous command be reissued. Type

   !!

   The file *practice* is displayed on your terminal screen again, because the previous display command was repeated.

   Many UNIX users call the exclamation mark the *bang*. To repeat the last command you entered, type *double bang* or *bang bang*.

Reissuing Long Command Lines

1. The **who** and **grep** utilities can be combined and repeated to reveal how many times a user is logged on to the system. Type the following shell command line:

   who | grep *login*

   where *login* is your login name.

2. The history mechanism repeats complex command lines. When the shell prompt returns, type

!!

The bang bang command is one of the most often used history features.

Executing Commands by Event Number

Several of the remaining exercises use the history event numbers. The numbers that appear on your terminal are determined by the exact commands that you enter. Consult your history list and use the correct event numbers in the exercises.

1. Examine the history list with

    history

2. Select one of the commands to repeat. Place its event number in the following command instead of the *event_number:*

    !event_number

    The shell examines the history list and executes the command with the specified number.

3. Call up your history list again by typing

    history

    The shell does not list commands such as **!!** or *!event_number,* but instead lists the command that was executed.

4. To see if someone new has logged on, repeat the **who** command by using its event number from the history list.

In summary, you can instruct the shell to reissue a command by typing !! to execute the previous command, or !*event_number* for a specific command identified from the history list.

Executing Commands with Beginning Letters

Often users want to repeat a command but cannot recall the event number. You could type **history**, locate the correct event number, and then type !*event_number*. As is usually the case with UNIX, there is an alternate way.

1. To repeat the last **who** command, type the following command:

   !*w*

   This command requests the shell to repeat the last command entered that begins with the letter *w*.

2. Sometimes it is necessary to use more than one letter to correctly specify the correct command. Type the command

   wc *practice*

3. Find out who is logged in by typing

   who

4. To again count the words in the file *practice*, you need to repeat the command line **wc** *practice*. Typing the !*w* command instructs the shell to go back to

the last command that started with a *w*, which is
who. To repeat the last **wc** command, type

!wc

In summary, to reissue a selected shell command
from the shell you must uniquely identify it. Enter
enough of the beginning letters to identify the command.

13.3 MODIFYING COMMANDS PREVIOUSLY ENTERED

In addition to repeating commands, the history feature can be used to modify and reissue the last
commands entered.

Adding to the Previous Command Line

The history feature allows you to add additional
instructions to a previously executed command line.

1. Make sure there are some misspelled words in the
   file *practice* by typing

   who >> *practice*

   The output of **who**, with its many non-English
   words, is thus added to the end of the *practice* file.

2. Have **spell** identify the misspelled words by typing

   spell *practice*

The output appears on the screen.

3. Add to the command line instructing the shell to save the located spelling errors in a new file *sp.-practice*. Type the following command line:

!! > *sp.practice*

The shell starts by reading the last command, then appends whatever you include after the !! to the line. In this case, the !! was **spell** *practice*. Thus, the command line executed is

spell *practice* > *sp.practice*

The **spell** utility examines the contents of *practice* and identifies misspelled words. The shell connected the output of the utility **spell** to the file *sp.practice*. Examine the file *sp.practice* to see the misspelled words.

Adding to Any Previous Command Line

1. To count the number of words in *practice*, type the command

wc -l *practice*

2. To count the words in *journal*, type the command

!*w journal*

This command accesses the history list, finds the most recently executed command that begins with *w*, and appends it to the command line. The command that is executed is:

wc -l *practice journal*

3. Another way to perform this task is to look at the history list and find the event number of the earlier command line. Type

history

Look for the command line for **wc -l** *practice*. Look at its associated event number. The command line to type would then be

!*event_number journal*

4. You just counted the words in the files *journal* and *practice*. The history feature can now be used to create the command line needed to output the word count to the file *count*. Type

!*event_number* > *count*

In summary, to recall and append to a previous command line, type the appropriate recall command followed by the string to be appended.

Correcting Spelling Errors in Command Lines

1. Users often make mistakes. Type the following command, spelzed exactly as written:

spelz *practice*

2. The history mechanism can be used to make corrections. Type the following line:

^z^l^

The ^ (caret) is usually ⌈Shift-6⌉ on the keyboard.

This command line tells history to locate the first occurrence of the letter *z* on the previous command line, substitute the letter *l* for it, and execute the modified command line.

3. The altered command line appears on your screen before being executed:

```
spell practice
```

This option also works with more than one letter or word, and with spaces.

Changing Utilities and Options

The utility to be executed can also be modified.

1. Type the following command line to have the word count utility substituted for **spell**:

   ^spell^wc -l^

2. Often long command lines need only slight modification. For instance, the command **sort** has a variety of options. The most commonly used option, **-d**, requests the utility to **sort** in dictionary order. Type

   sort -d *practice*

3. An alternate option is **-r** for a **sort** in reverse order. To change your **sort** without having to retype the whole command line, type

   ^d^r^

4. A third option to **sort** is **-f**, giving a **sort** in which the lines beginning with uppercase and lowercase letters are folded together. Change your command line to utilize this option by typing

^-r^-f^

Note that the command line **sort** **-r** *practice* contains three occurrences of the letter *r*. The **-r** was specified in the substitution request to specify the particular instance of the letter *r* which you wish to replace with the letter *f*.

Printing the Command Line Without Execution

Often it is useful to look at a previously entered command without having it reexecuted. It is possible to have a command line printed to the screen and added to the history list without executing it.

1. Have the shell display a previous command without executing it by typing

!c:p

The **:p** at the end of the line prints the command on the terminal screen and adds it to the history list.

2. Make a change in this command line using the same command line syntax as the last command, such as

^cat^sort^:p

This printing allows you to confirm that the command is what you want.

3. Execute the command line which you just corrected and printed by typing

!!

The double bang is used to reexecute the last command, even if it previously was only printed on the screen and never executed.

4. Look at the history list. Type

history

The four lines of the output on the terminal screen are

```
28   cat practice
29   sort practice
30   sort practice
31   history
```

The **sort** command appears twice, because the first time you asked for it to print and not execute, and the second time you executed the command using the double bang.

In summary, the **:p** command can be appended to any command line. The **:p** instructs the shell to print the command line to the screen without executing it. The command is also added to the history list, even though it isn't executed.

Making More than One Modification

You have seen how the :p command is useful when you need to make multiple corrections to a single command line. This is especially helpful for long command lines.

1. The number of times a user is logged on can be determined using the *lines* option of **word count**. Type the command

   who I grzp *login* **I WC -l**

   where *login* is your login name.

2. Correct the typing error in the command **grzp**, to make it **grep**, and print it to the screen by typing

   *^zp^ep^*:**p**

3. Correct the case error in the **word count** command, and again print it to the screen to check that the whole command line is correct:

   *^WC^wc^*:**p**

4. Once the command line is correct, tell the shell to execute it by typing

   !!

   In summary, the caret (^) is used in the history utility to make corrections to a previous line. The format for this usage is

*^targetstring^replacementstring^*

Using this procedure to make multiple corrections is rather involved, and is only useful when the command line is long.

Exercise 13-A

1. What command would you use to instruct the shell to print out the last command you entered, but not actually execute it?

   _____

2. What would you type if you wanted to execute the twenty-third command from your history list?

   _____

3. What command will reexecute the last command you entered?

   _____

4. What command could you use to reedit the last file you edited with **vi**?

   _____

5. If you had just run the **spell** command on your file *journal* and wanted to place all misspelled words in a separate file called *journal.errors*, what command would you use?

   _____

13.4 MODIFYING AND EXECUTING ANY COMMAND

You used the caret (ˆ) for substitutions on the previous command. You can also change an earlier command line by combining the **history** command syntax with a *substitute* command syntax.

Using Search and Substitute Command Syntax

1. Use the **history** command to find the event number for the following misspelled command line:

who I grzp *login* **I WC -l**

2. To change the command **grzp** to **grep**, type the following command line (substituting the correct event number for *event_number*):

*!event_number***:s/zp/ep/:p**

The history list command was accessed by the command event number, the substitution made, and the corrected command line **printed** on the screen without being executed. There are two new parts to this command line:

- The colon following the event number acts as a command separator for the history utility. You have already seen it used in the print command, introduced earlier.

- The search and substitute command **s/***zp***/***ep***/** is included. The search and substitute command syntax is the same as was used in the visual editor.

  s/*target***/***replacement***/**

  The **s** instructs the shell to search for the *target* pattern and substitute the *replacement* pattern.

3. Change **WC** to **wc** and print the command line on the screen without executing it. Type

   !c:s/C/*wc***/:p**

4. Make sure the command line is now correct. If it is, execute it by typing

   !!

Using a Selected Argument from the Last Command

Sometimes you may want to use just part of a long command line in a new command. The history mechanism allows you to select parts of a previous command line. The shell assigns an *expansion number* to each word or string of characters delimited by blank spaces or tabs in a command line. It is important to remember that the numbering starts with the number zero (0), not with the number one (1).

1. Type this command:

   spell *practice practice2 journal*

   Table 13-1 shows how this command line appears to the history utility.

TABLE 13-1.   Assigned Expansion Numbers

Expansion Number:	0	1	2	3
Command Line:	**spell**	*practice*	*practice2*	*journal*

2. Suppose the files *practice* and *practice2* did not have any spelling mistakes, but the file *journal* did. You can edit the file *journal* without having to type the filename *journal* again.

   Look back at Table 13-1. The file name is in the location labeled *3* in the previous command. Now type

   vi !!:3

   The *:3* requests retrieval of the third argument of the command line, specified by the **history** syntax preceding it. The shell thus interprets the **vi** command line as follows:

   vi *journal*

3. You can get the same results using the event number instead of the double bang. Exit **vi** and type

   vi !*event_number***:3**

4. To access the file using the beginning letters of the command, exit **vi** and type

   vi !s:3

   This command says to visually edit the third argument of the last command that started with an *s*.

You can use either double bang, the event number, or the beginning letters to access a previous command for modification.

Selecting Multiple Arguments

1. Print the above **spell** command without executing it by typing

   !s:p

2. Suppose you want to look at all the files from this command line, using the **cat** command. You need to access the files *practice, practice2,* and *journal,* which occupy expansion numbers *1* through *3* in the command line. Type

   cat !!:*1-3*

You can access a *range* of arguments from a previous command line. Typing six characters is certainly easier than retyping the filenames in the command line.

Accessing All Arguments

In the above command line, you actually accessed all the expansion numbers except the zero (0), which contains the command name. The special character * (asterisk) is expanded by the shell to be all the filenames in a directory. It can be used in history to specify all expansion numbers other than zero.

1. Type this command:

cat !s:*

The *, better known in UNIX jargon as the *splat* or star, accesses all the words or strings in the specified command line, except the word in the zero position. This method is the simplest way to change only the command in a command line.

Selecting Specific Arguments

1. Use **cat** and the **history** syntax to look at *practice2* and *journal.* Type

cat !s:2-3

NOTE: The following command line would accomplish the same task as the previous one:

cat !s:2-$

The dollar sign $ is a special character which means the last word in the specified command line. Using the $ means that you only have to determine the starting expansion number.

Each word or string in a command line is associated with an expansion number. Using the history mechanism, you can access each word or string by its number, instead of retyping it. This is done by adding :*number* after a **history** command, where *number* represents the expansion number(s) in question. The dollar sign $ symbol can be used to represent the last expansion number.

Selecting the Last Argument

1. If you have not already done so, create the directory *Desk* by typing

   mkdir *Desk*

2. Copy the file journal to the directory *Desk*. Type

   cp *journal Desk*

3. To move to the *Desk* directory, type the following command:

   cd !$

   The !$ means, "take the last word in the previous command line and substitute it here."

4. View the history list to verify that this is, in fact, what happened.

5. Use the **pwd** command to verify that you are actually in the *Desk* directory.

   The !$ can be used to select the last argument, usually the filename in the previous command.

PERMANENTLY SETTING THE PROMPT AND HISTORY VARIABLES

13.5

In the preceding exercises you set the prompt and history variables interactively. When you end this session, these variables die with your shell. To set them permanently, they have to be established in a file that the shell will read every time you log on to UNIX. This can be done in either your *.login* or *.cshrc* file.

1. Move to your Home directory. Type

   cd

2. Call up your *.login* file for editing by typing

   vi *.login*

   If you do not already have a *.login* file, this command will create one.

      You are now going to add to your *.login* file two lines that will permanently set your prompt, and also the history variable that determines how many past command lines the shell will remember. These two lines are identical to the lines you entered interactively earlier in this exercise.

3. The line to set the *prompt* is:

   set *prompt* =" <\!> %"

4. The line to set the *history* variable is:

   set *history* = 20

   You can use whatever value for *history* you want, but the longer the history list, the more time it takes to scan. To modify the *history* or the prompt variable in the future, just edit the *.login* file and make the desired changes.

Exercise 13-B

1. Suppose that you have just entered the command

ls -l / | pg. What command would you give to the shell to substitute another directory for the / ?

_____

2. What command would you execute to increase your history list to 100 commands?

_____

3. What would you type if you wanted to **pg** the second argument from the twenty-third command in your history list?

_____

4. Suppose you have entered the command **cat** _food nip litter_. What would you type if you wanted to use **pg** instead of **cat** and execute it as your next command?

_____

5. Suppose the tenth command in your history list is **pg** _orless_ ; **cat** _nip_. What would you type if you wanted to substitute the **pg** with **cat**? Use the search and substitute feature to edit history.

_____

6. What command would cause the shell prompt to display the event number of each command you enter?

_____

CONCLUSION The history mechanism of the C shell is used to establish how many commands should be recorded, so that you can use the history list to make substitutions in the current command line, to recall commands and arguments, and to edit previous commands without retyping them.

COMMAND SUMMARY

!!
Executes previous command.

!#
Repeats command that was assigned to the number requested (#).

!*letter***
Repeats last command that began with the specified *letter.*

!$
Takes last word in previous command and substitutes it in the current command at the position of this symbol.

!!:p
Prints last command on the screen, but does not execute it.

!!:s*/string1/string2/*
Looks for the first occurrence of *string1* in the last command and substitutes *string2*, then executes the command with the new substitution.

set prompt=*string*
Sets the future shell prompt to *string*. If there is a ! (escaped by a backslash) embedded within *string*, the command number of the command about to be entered will be substituted for it in the prompt.

set history=#
Sets the length of the history list (the number of previous commands to be saved) to #.

!! *string*
Reexecutes the last command with *string* appended to the end of it.

COMMAND SUMMARY (*continued*)

!# string
Reexecutes the command numbered # (from the history list), but with *string* appended to the end of it.

*^string1^string2^*
Looks for the first occurrence of *string1* in the last command, substitutes *string2* for it, and reexecutes.

!#:s/string1/string2/
Looks for the first occurrence of *string1* in the command numbered #, substitutes *string2* in its place, and executes the resulting command.

!#:s/string1/string2/:p
Looks for the first occurrence of *string1* in the command numbered #, substitutes *string2* in its place, and prints the resulting command. It is added to the history list, but it is not executed.

!XX:YY
May be used in a command to pull word number *YY* from previous command number *XX*.

!XX:YY-ZZ
May be used in a command to pull words numbered *YY* through *ZZ* from previous command number *XX*.

!#1:*
May be used in a command to pull all words from previous command number #1.

COMMAND SUMMARY (*continued*)

!XX:YY-$

May be used in a command to pull words numbered *YY* through the end from previous command number *XX*.

!XX:^-YY

May be used in a command to pull words from the beginning of the line through number *YY* from previous command number *XX*.

·14·

Creating Aliases

Small sets of commands frequently issued in the shell command line can be tedious and lengthy to type again and again. With the C shell, you can assign abbreviations, or *aliases,* for commands, thus saving time and mental energy.

We create aliases frequently in our daily lives. When a child calls home and asks for "mom," "mom" is an agreed-upon alias for Ms. Lillian Frank at that address. In UNIX, once an alias is assigned for the name of a command or series of commands, you can use the alias instead of the command or command series.

Aliases can be used in command line features such as piping, and the creation of background processes. The aliases described in this chapter are for the C shell. If you do not have the C shell, you may wish to skip this chapter.

SKILLS CHECK

Before beginning this chapter, you should be able to

- Access and leave the system and execute basic commands (Chapter 1, "Touring the System's Features")

- Create, display, and print files (Chapter 1)

- Name, copy, and remove files (Chapter 1)

- Use several shell commands in combination (Chapter 1)

- Access and modify files using the **vi** editor (Chapter 2, "Basic Editing with the Visual Editor")

- Utilize the UNIX directory hierarchy system (Chapter 3, "Using UNIX Directories")

- Use the **history** mechanism to repeat and edit previous C shell commands (Chapter 13, "Using the C Shell History")

OBJECTIVES

Upon completion of this chapter, you will be able to

- Create and use aliases that abbreviate or rename commands

- Create and use aliases that contain multiple commands

- Create permanent aliases

- Use the original command after it has been aliased

- Remove previously aliased commands

USING TEMPORARY ALIASES FOR COMMANDS

14.1

The simplest use of the **alias** command is to assign new names to commands that already exist. The result is that a command can effectively have multiple names. Often the new name will be an abbreviation for the sake of convenience.

Abbreviating a Command

The **history** command is relatively long in terms of keystrokes entered. It can be abbreviated with an alias.

1. If you are not currently logged in on your machine, do so now.

2. From the shell type the command line

   alias *h* **history**

   You have assigned a new name, **h**, to mean the **history** command.

3. Compare the two commands now available. Type

   history

   and observe the response.

4. Verify that **h** is interpreted the same way by typing

h

The two commands can now be used interchangeably.

Renaming a Command

The alias feature is also useful for renaming commands. Suppose you have been working on a different computer system where there is a command called **dir** that gives you the same information as the shell command **ls**. If you are accustomed to issuing the command **dir**, it would be convenient to have it work on the UNIX system, instead of producing the error message

```
dir: Command not found
```

1. You can create an alias for **ls**, called **dir**, by typing

alias *dir* **ls**

2. From the shell, type

dir

The output is the same as if you had typed the **ls** command. When you typed **dir**, the **ls** utility was executed by the shell.

The basic command line to create a new name for a command consists of three parts:

alias *name* **command**

The *name* becomes a new way to execute the **command**.

Creating an Alias for a Command and Its Options

You can also create an alias that includes options to the command. To use more than a single word as an alias, you must enclose the whole string in single quotes.

1. Type the command line

    alias *ldir* **'ls -l'**

2. Try out the new alias. Type

    ldir

    The alias **ldir** displays a long listing of your current directory, just like **ls -l**.

Passing Arguments to an Alias

Because the shell replaces an alias with its definition, you can pass arguments for the defined command to the alias. Here are two examples.

1. Use the **ldir** alias to display the contents of the /(root) directory. Type

    ldir /

    The shell interprets this command line as

ls -l /

and displays a long listing of the contents of the /
directory.

2. You can use aliases with both arguments and
options. For example, use the **ldir** alias to display all
the dot files in your Home directory by typing

ldir -a ~

The shell interprets this command line as

ls -l -a ~

and displays a long listing of your Home directory,
including the dot files, such as *.login* and *.cshrc*.

Using Command Names as Aliases

It is possible to use the name of a command as the
name of an alias. This is helpful when you habitually
use a specific option with a command. You can
rename the command to include the option.

1. Create an alias for the **rm** command to include the
   -i option, so that you are required to confirm each
   use of the **rm** command. Type

alias *rm* **'rm -i'**

2. Test this new alias by removing your *practice* file.
   Type

rm ~/*practice*

Even though **rm** is the name of a command, the
shell interprets this command line as

rm -i ~ /*practice*

because you redefined **rm** to be the **rm -i** command. You are therefore asked to confirm that you want to remove the *practice* file.

3. Prevent removal of the *practice* file by pressing ⎡Return⎤.

This alias is so useful that some system administrators have it predefined for all users.

Using a Command that Has Been Aliased

Sometimes after using the name of a command as an alias, users want to use the original command.

For example, you just made **rm** an alias for the **rm** command with the **-i** option. If you want to remove many files at once, you will be repeatedly asked if you want to remove each file. One way to sidestep the effects of an alias is to use the complete pathname of the original command.

1. Change to your Home directory, and create a file called *trash* by typing

   cd; who > *trash*

2. Confirm that the file *trash* is listed in your Home directory. Type

   ls

3. Try to remove the *trash* file by typing

   rm trash

4. You are asked if you want to remove the file *trash*. Prevent removal of the file *trash* by pressing Return .

5. Now remove the *trash* file without having to confirm removal by typing

/bin/rm *trash*

6. Verify that the *trash* file was removed. Type

ls

The file is gone. By giving the complete pathname, you instructed the shell to execute a command in the */bin* directory with the name **rm**.

Another way to override an alias is to use the \ character to specifically instruct the shell to escape the alias temporarily.

7. Create another file called *trash* by typing

who > *trash*

8. Examine the contents of *trash*. Type

cat *trash*

9. Escape the **rm** alias and remove the file *trash* by typing

\rm *trash*

10. Try to examine the contents of the *trash* file again with

cat *trash*

You are told that the file doesn't exist. The \ instructs the shell to interpret **rm** as a command and not replace it with its definition.

Listing All Defined Aliases

You can instruct the shell to display all aliases and their meanings.

1. To examine the aliases that have been established, type

   alias

   with no arguments. This displays all of the assigned alias names and their definitions.

2. Examine the list of aliases, which looks something like the following:

```
dir ls
h history
ldir 'ls -l'
rm 'rm -i'
```

   The aliases that you defined are on the list, but there also may be others. Two files in your account are executed each time you log in. These files may contain commands that define aliases. You will learn more about predefined aliases in the section called "Using Permanent Aliases," later in this chapter.

Listing a Single Alias

You can also list a single alias and its definition. By checking an alias you can find out if a command is actually an alias, and you can determine if a desired alias exists.

1. Display the definition of the **dir** alias by typing

   alias *dir*

2. The definition of the **dir** alias is displayed on the screen:

   ```
   ls -l
   ```

Removing a Temporary Alias

Once you create an alias, you can remove it.

1. Remove the alias **dir** by typing

   unalias *dir*

2. Verify that the **dir** alias is gone by typing

   alias

   The alias *dir* no longer appears in the list of aliases.

   You have seen that the **alias** command has a special function when used without arguments: it displays all defined aliases. However, **unalias** without an argument is not valid. Type

unalias

The error message

```
unalias: Too few arguments
```

appears on the screen. The **unalias** command needs at least one argument on which to operate.

Abandoning Temporary Aliases by Logging Off

The aliases you have been using are in your current shell's working memory. For example:

1. You have an alias for **ls** that will print a long listing of files. Type

   ldir

2. Now log out and log back in.

3. Once you are logged in, type

   ldir

   You get the following message:

   ```
   ldir: Command not found
   ```

4. Obtain a listing of defined aliases by typing

   alias

   The aliases that you defined before logging out and logging in again no longer exist.

   When you define an alias from the command line, that alias remains in memory until you log out or delete it from memory. If you log out, the shell you are using dies, and with it all temporary information: hence, the alias disappears.

14.2   USING PERMANENT ALIASES

Each alias you have made so far has been temporary and is eliminated when you log out. You can save aliases so that they are not removed when you log out.

Saving Aliases in a File

You can save each alias you create in a file.

1. Create a file called *.alias* in your Home directory. Type

   cd ; vi *.alias*

   The **cd** command makes your Home directory your current directory, so that the *.alias* file will be listed there.

2. Add the following lines to the *.alias* file:

   alias h history
   alias dir 'ls -l'
   alias t date
   alias a alias

3. Save the file and return to the shell.

   By saving your aliases in a file, you can have the shell reset each alias every time you log in.

4. Log out and log in again.

5. Confirm that the aliases you created earlier are gone. Type

   alias

The resulting display shows you only the aliases that are predefined in your system files. Depending on your system setup, you may see no predefined aliases or many, but none of the aliases *you* created are listed. The aliases you created are in the file *.alias,* but they have not been read by your current shell.

6. Instruct the shell to execute the commands in your *.alias* file. Type

source *.alias*

The **source** command instructs the shell to execute each line in the named file as a shell command. In this case, each line of the *.alias* file is an **alias** command. By executing the file, the shell creates each of the aliases in the *.alias* file.

7. Confirm that the aliases in the *.alias* file exist by typing

alias

The display now contains each of the aliases you created and stored in the *.alias* file. Each time you log in, you can restore these aliases by typing

source *~/.alias*

This command will work if your current directory is Home or any other directory on the system.

Making Aliases Permanent

You have saved your aliases in a file (*.alias*) that you can execute each time you log in. There is an alternative to using **source** *.alias* to explicitly tell the shell to execute the file. Instead, you can modify one of two files so that the *.alias* file is automatically executed each time you log in. The two files are *.login* and *.cshrc* in your Home directory. Ask your local systems administrators if your site expects you to use one or the other. If you use the *.cshrc* file, replace the word *.login* with the word *.cshrc* in the following procedure.

1. Edit the *.login* file in your Home directory with **vi**, adding the following line:

   source *.alias*

2. Save the file and return to the shell.

3. Confirm that the *.alias* file is executed automatically. Log out, then log back in and type

   alias

   Each of your saved aliases and their definitions is included in the list. You can add more permanent aliases to your *.alias* file, and they will also be included.

   You have now created both temporary and permanent aliases. The examples that follow are mostly related to temporary aliases, except where otherwise indicated. The mechanisms used with one are generally the same as with the other. The main difference is that permanent changes are made by modifications to the *.alias* file.

Removing an Alias Temporarily

At this point you have a permanent alias called **h** that represents the **history** command. You can temporarily remove this alias, even though it is a permanent alias.

1. Remove the **h** alias by typing

   unalias *h*

2. Verify that the **h** alias is gone. Type

   alias *h*

   Nothing happens. The **h** alias no longer exists.

Reinstating a Permanent Alias

You can reinstate the **h** alias in two different ways. You can log out and log back in, since the commands in the *.alias* file are now automatically executed each time you log in. Or, you can instruct the shell to execute the *.alias* file, without logging out.

1. Instruct the shell to execute the commands in the *.alias* file as you did before, by typing

   source ~/*.alias*

2. Verify that the **h** alias has returned, with

   alias *h*

   The definition of the **h** alias is displayed on your screen.

3. Alternately, you may reinstate the **h** alias by typing the command that created it:

   alias *h* **history**

Removing an Alias Permanently

You may want to remove an alias defined in your *.alias* file, either because you want to redefine it or because you don't need it any more.

1. Edit the *.alias* file in your Home directory with **vi**.
2. Locate the line where the *dir* alias is defined; then remove it, save the file, and return to the shell.
3. Log out and log back in. You have removed the **dir** alias from the *.alias* file, and you have logged out. The new login shell does not have the **dir** alias.
4. Confirm that the **dir** alias is not available by typing **alias** *dir*

Exercise 14-A

1. What is the simplest use for the **alias** command?

   _____

2. When the command **alias** is used without any arguments, what happens?

   _____

3. What command would you type to create an alias for the UNIX command that displays a list of every file listed in a directory?

   _____

4. What would you type to disable the above alias for **ls**?

   _____

5. In order to create a permanent alias, where should it be entered?

   _____

6. A permanent alias takes effect immediately after you have entered it in your *.alias* file. True or false?

   _____

7. After you have temporarily removed a permanent alias, what command would you type to reinstate it?

   _____

USING COMPLEX ALIASES   14.3

Thus far you have defined aliases for single commands. You can also create and use more complex aliases by replacing a sequence of commands, replacing other aliases, or redirecting output in an alias.

Creating an Alias for a Sequence of Commands

It is useful to use aliases that abbreviate a series of sequential commands.

1. Define a **status** alias by typing

   alias *status* **'history; pwd; ls -l; date'**

   This defines **status** to perform four tasks:

   - Execute the shell command history
   - Print the working directory

- Display a long listing of the directory
- Display the date and time

The semicolon is used to separate commands in the definition. Any number of commands may be used to define an alias. The single quotes tell the shell that the commands listed inside the quotes are all part of the alias definition.

2. Use the new **status** alias. Type

status

and observe the response.

Creating an Alias Using Other Aliases

It is possible to use an alias within an alias.

1. Define the alias **newstat** to include the **h** alias you defined earlier. Type

alias *newstat* **'h; pwd; ls; date'**

2. Confirm that the alias **newstat** works by typing

newstat

Previously defined aliases may be used to define new aliases.

Passing One Argument to a Multicommand Alias

You may want to create an alias in which an argument is needed in the middle of the definition. For example, suppose you want to find a file called *junk,* but you do not know in which directory it is located. You do know it is in a subdirectory of your Home directory.

To do this, you can use the **find** command in the following way:

    find ~ **-name** *junk* **-print**

This instructs **find** to start looking in your Home directory (~) and all subdirectories for a file whose **name** is *junk,* and to **print** its full name when it finds it. This **find** command is long and tedious, so an alias would certainly be appropriate. But an argument is used in the middle of the command line, not at the end of the definition.

1. Define the **where** alias for locating files. Type

   alias *where* '**find** ~ **-name** \!^ **-print**'

   The \!^ tells the shell to place an argument (only one) at this location.

2. Test the **where** alias by typing

   where *lostfile*

   The name of the "misplaced" file is *lostfile.* The shell effectively expands what you entered into this command line:

   find ~ **-name** *lostfile* **-print**

Passing Multiple Arguments

There are many cases in which it would be useful to pass multiple arguments to a command. To accomplish this, the \!* is used much like the \!^ described in the previous section.

Suppose, for example, that instead of removing files with the **rm** command, you would rather move the named files to a special directory called *TRASH*. By doing this, you still have the files on hand, but they have been clearly designated as trash, which you could then throw out occasionally.

1. First create the *TRASH* directory in your Home directory by typing

   mkdir *TRASH*

   We suggest using all uppercase letters for this directory, to clearly indicate that *TRASH* is neither a file nor your ordinary, run-of-the-mill directory.

2. Define a **trash** alias that accepts multiple arguments. Type

   alias *trash* '**mv** \!* ~/TRASH'

   Here the \!* is used to indicate that one or more arguments will be passed to the command.

3. Create two files, *temp1* and *temp2*:

   cp *.practice temp1*
   cp *.practice temp2*

4. You now have two temporary files, *temp1* and *temp2*. Use the **trash** alias to remove the two files by typing

   trash *temp1 temp2*

   The alias accepted two arguments, *temp1* and *temp2*, and moved both files into the *TRASH* directory.

5. Confirm that the two files are no longer listed in your current directory by typing

   ls

6. Confirm that the files are listed in the *TRASH* directory, with

ls *~/TRASH*

Using a Simple Pipe in an Alias

A pipe takes the output of one command and connects it to the input of another command. You can use pipes in an alias in exactly the same way as when you use them in a command line. One way to use a pipe in an alias is to have the alias pipe the output of one command into another.

1. Create an alias called **dispell** that checks a file for spelling errors and sends the output through the **page** or **more** command. If you do not have **spell** on your system, use **wc** and count words. Type

alias *dispell* **'spell \!* | page'**

Now when you use the alias **dispell**, along with any number of filenames, misspelled words in these files will appear on the screen, one screenful at a time.

2. Try the **dispell** alias on several files. Type

dispell *practice .login*

Notice that the non-English words in each file appear on the screen also.

Using a Pipe in the Background

Some commands take a long time, and can be run in the background. You can write an alias so that it runs commands in the background. The ampersand (&) is used at the end of a shell command line to signal the shell to run the job in the background.

1. Create an alias called **prspell** similar to **dispell** that will look for a file's misspellings and print them on a line printer—all of this occurring in the background. Type one of the following:

   System V:
   alias *prspell* **'spell \!* l lp -d***dest* **&'**

   BSD:
   alias *prspell* **'spell \!* l lpr -P***dest* **&'**

   This alias behaves exactly like **dispell**, except that it

- Pipes the output of **spell** to the line printer
- Runs in the background

   It is recommended that you use the \!* or \!^ when using an alias with multiple commands or a set of piped commands. Unless you can guarantee all of the arguments will be placed at the end of the command line, use the \!* and \!^ format, as described in this section.

14.4   AVOIDING AN ALIAS LOOP

A common error is alias looping. An alias loop occurs when an alias definition refers to the alias being defined.

Finding an Alias Loop

So that you can learn how to avoid an alias loop, you must create an alias loop.

1. Make sure that **ls** is not an alias by typing

   unalias *ls*

2. Change the **ls** command to an alias that first prints the name of the current directory and then lists its contents. Type

   alias *ls* **'pwd; ls'**

3. Test the **ls** alias. You get an error message similar to

   `Alias loop.`

   Although both **ls** aliases refer to similar command sequences, you get an error.

Fixing an Alias Loop Quickly

There are two ways to fix an alias loop. One way is to begin the alias definition with the command that causes the loop.

1. Remove the **ls** alias you just created. Type

   unalias *ls*

2. Change the **ls** command to an alias that lists the contents of a directory first, and then prints the name of the directory. Type

   alias *ls* **'ls; pwd'**

3. Test this **ls** alias. Type

   ls

The contents of the current directory are displayed, followed by the name of the directory. Thus, putting the **ls** command first has corrected the loop. A second, preferred, solution is to insist that the **ls** inside the alias be the **ls** utility, not the **ls** alias.

4. Remove the **ls** alias. Type

   unalias *ls*

5. Define the **ls** alias in the original order by typing

   alias *ls* **'pwd; \ls'**

6. Verify that the alias now works correctly, with

   ls

   The backslash instructs the shell to use the **ls** utility, not the alias.

14.5   THE DISADVANTAGES OF ALIASES

There are some minor problems associated with the use of aliases of which you should be aware. Aliases use memory space when their definitions expand. This expansion process can also be time consuming. Aliases also increase the length of the login process, by increasing the time the shell spends reading it each time you log in. However, these drawbacks become unimportant when an alias is used frequently enough to save time.

Occasionally, you might define an alias to have the same name as an already existing shell command (as with **ls**, described above). And you may go about your business, forgetting that the shell command is aliased.

Then when you next issue the command, you realize it has been redefined. To use the original command definition, you must then do one of the following:

- **unalias** the command

- Use the command's entire path

- Escape the alias with a backslash

It is best to define aliases only for frequently used commands. Do not overdo your use of aliases.

Exercise 14-B

1. Suppose the output of the **who** command is almost always more than a screenful, and you want to pipe the output through the **page** command each time you use **who**. How would you construct the alias?

   _____

2. Suppose you have typed the following alias:

   alias *cat* '**pwd; cat**'

   If you tried to use **cat** after entering the alias, would it work?

   _____

3. Suppose you wish to create an alias called **seerm** that first executes **pg** on a file or files, which you supply as an argument, and then executes **rm** on those file(s). What would the **alias** command be? (Keep in mind that you will be supplying at least one argument when using the alias.)

   _____

CONCLUSION

The **alias** command is useful in renaming commands or assigning new names to a series of commands. This renaming ability allows you to create easy-to-remember abbreviations and other terms to identify commands. Arguments may be passed into aliases through the use of the special \!^ and \!* character combinations. Complex aliases can be defined by using such command line constructs as piping and backgrounding.

COMMAND SUMMARY

alias *name* **command**
name is **alias**ed to **command**

alias *name*
Display the alias for *name* if there is one

alias
Display all aliases

alias *name* **'cmd; cmd'**
name is aliased to a sequence of commands

alias *name* **'command \!^'**
name is aliased to a one-argument **command**

alias *name* **'command \!*'**
name is aliased to a multiple-argument **command**

unalias *name*
Remove alias

·15·

Setting the User Environment

The designers and programmers who created UNIX often provided several options to the user, rather than hard coding a specific way of doing things. For example, if you want the visual editor to display line numbers on the screen when you are editing, you can simply make that request. UNIX gives you the power to customize many other aspects of the way the system interacts with you. What features you are able to control depends on which shell and which version of UNIX you are using. The C shell and the Bourne shell have different capabilities, and there are further differences between the C shell on System V and the C shell on BSD. Therefore, you should determine both the shell and the system you are using.

SKILLS CHECK

Before beginning this chapter, you should be able to

- Access and leave the system and execute basic commands (Chapter 1, "Touring the System's Features")

- Create, display, and print files (Chapter 1)

- Name, copy, and remove files and use several shell commands in combination (Chapter 1)

- Access and modify files using the **vi** editor (Chapter 2, "Basic Editing with the Visual Editor")

- Assign and unassign shell variables (Chapter 6, "Command Line Interpretation by the Shell")

- Use local and environment variables (Chapter 11, "Shell Programming")

- Repeat and edit previous C shell commands using the **history** mechanism (Chapter 13, "Using the C Shell History")

- Automate commonly used procedures by invoking aliases (Chapter 14, "Creating Aliases")

OBJECTIVES

Upon completion of this chapter, you will be able to customize your user environment according to your specific needs and capabilities. You will be able to

- Use the initialization file *.login* or *.profile* to set up your system environment when you log in, specifying aliases, variables, and terminal characteristics

- Use the initialization file *.cshrc* to set up your system environment for the C shell

- Use the initialization file *.exrc* to control your interactions with the visual editor

- Use the initialization file *.mailrc* to control your interactions with **mail**

- Establish terminal control characteristics

MAKING PERMANENT CHANGES TO YOUR ENVIRONMENT

15.1

In Chapter 11, "Shell Programming", you examined environment and local variables in the C shell. With the Bourne shell, all variables are local to the shell where they are created, unless **export**ed. For a complete examination of the role of environment variables, see Chapter 20, "Process Monitoring and Control."

Creating Variables in the C Shell

The C shell maintains local variables and environment variables separately.

1. To display the list of environment variables created during this login session, type one of the following commands:

   System V:
   env

BSD:

printenv

The output is a list of environment variables and their values, such as:

```
TERM=dumb
HOME=/lurnix/staff/hyram
PATH=.:/bin:/usr/ucb:/usr/local:/usr/hosts:/etc
USER=hyram
EXINIT=set autowrite number ai magic
```

Most of the environment variables were explored in earlier chapters: *TERM* (Chapter 6), *HOME* (Chapter 3), *PATH* (Chapter 3 and 6), and *USER* (Chapter 11). *EXINIT* is examined later in this chapter.

2. Assign the environment variable *name* to the string *Odysseus Grant* by typing

   setenv *name "Odysseus Grant"*

3. Assign the C shell local variable *name2* to the string *Rob Elee* by typing

   set *name2="Rob Elee"*

4. To confirm these variables' values, type

   echo $*name* $*name2*

5. You can observe the addition of *name2* to the list of C shell variables by typing

   set

6. Examine your list of environment variables by typing one of the following:

System V:
env

BSD:
printenv

Both the local variable *name2* and the environment variable *name* have been assigned their specified strings and are now part of your user environment.

Passing Variables to Subshells

1. To examine the C shell's rules of variable inheritance, start up a subshell by typing

   csh

2. Attempt to display the local variable *name2* that was created in the parent shell. Type

   echo $*name2*

   The output from this command is

   `name2: Undefined variable.`

   The child shell does not have the local variable *name* that was set in the parent shell.

3. Communication is better with the environment variable *name.* Type

   echo $*name*

The C shell displays the string *Odysseus Grant* with no protest. The environment variable *name* was passed on to the subshell, but the local C shell variable *name2* was not.

4. For corroboration, examine the subshell's lists of local and environment variables. On consecutive lines, type

set

followed by one of the following:

System V:
env

BSD:
printenv

Examining What a Parent Shell Is Told About Variables

1. Before you exit this subshell, attempt to modify the environment variable *name*, and create a new environment variable *name3*, by typing, on consecutive lines, the following commands:

setenv *name* "Sean Garrett"
setenv *name3* "Bill Clark"

With these new environment settings in the subshell, you will be able to examine whether it is possible to pass a variable back to the parent shell, or to change an inherited variable's value in the parent shell.

2. Exit the subshell by pressing $\boxed{\text{Ctrl-d}}$. Or type

   exit

   if you have the shell variable *ignoreeof* set.

3. You are now in communication with the parent shell. Examine the list of environment variables to see if the environment variable *name3* that you defined in the subshell, was passed back to the parent shell. Also, note the value of the variable *name* that you confirmed was passed to the subshell. Type one of the following commands:

   System V:
   env

   BSD:
   printenv

   The variable *name3* does not appear in the list of environment variables, because environment variables are only passed to subshells and child processes but not to the parent or calling process. In the same fashion, the value of the variable *name* is not affected in the parent shell by changes that take place in the subshell.

Removing a Variable

It also is possible to remove or unassign environment variables.

1. To remove the environment variable *name* that you created earlier, type

unsetenv *name*

2. To confirm that it has been unassigned, type

echo $*name*

The output is

```
name: Undefined variable.
```

Including Both Local and Environment Variables

In your earlier perusal of the list of local and environment variables, you may have noticed that a number of variables appear in both lists. They include *term* and *TERM, home* and *HOME,* and *path* and *PATH.* The lowercase version of each of these variables is in the list of local variables; the capitalized version is in the list of environment variables. Because UNIX is case sensitive, these are different variables. There can be no misidentification. Confusion could arise if there were local and environment variables of the same name and in the same case.

1. Create a local variable *name* by typing

set *name* = *Will*

Now create an environment variable of the same name by typing

setenv *name Kevin*

2. Examine the value of the variable *name* by typing

echo $*name*

It is the value of the local variable *name* that is displayed. Within the C shell, if there is any conflict between variable names, local variables take precedence over environment variables.

3. The environment variable *name* is still available, though. Type one of the following:

System V:
env

BSD:
printenv

The environment variable *name*, and its value *Kevin*, is listed in the list of environment variables.

Some of the variables that show up in both lists are needed by different utilities within the system. They include:

TERM and *term*
HOME and *home*
SHELL and *shell*

The **set** and **setenv** commands in System V and BSD behave in different ways when used to change the values of these variables. For instance, on BSD only, when you **set** the local variable *path*, the BSD C shell also changes the value of the environment variable *PATH*. On System V, the C shell does not change *PATH*.

To ensure that both local and environment variables are assigned the same value, it is wise to employ both a **set** command and a **setenv** when dealing with any of these variables. For instance, if you got a new vt100 terminal and needed to reset the variable *TERM*, you would type something like this:

set *term = vt100*

followed by

setenv *TERM vt100*

to give both variables the same values.

Passing Variables to Subshells in the Bourne Shell

Passing variables to subshells is different in the Bourne shell, because the Bourne shell maintains only one list of variables.

1. If you are currently running the C shell, start up a Bourne shell to explore how it works. Type

   sh

2. Create two variables, *name1* and *name2*, by typing

   name1 = Robert_Elee

   followed by

   name2 = Odysseus_Grant

Remember, in the Bourne shell, the format for assigning a variable a value is *variable=value* with no spaces on either side of =.

3. Confirm the values assigned to each of these variables by typing, on consecutive lines, the following commands:

echo $*name1*
echo $*name2*

4. To provide for the inheritance of *name1* by all of the current shell's subshells, type

export *name1*

5. Start up a subshell by typing

sh

6. Once the Bourne shell prompt has returned, examine the subshell's list of variables by typing

set

The variable *name1* is in this list, but *name2* is not; *name1* was **export**ed; *name2* was not. Once a variable is **export**ed, it is inherited by all subshells. The variable *name2* was not **export**ed, and thus not inherited.

Attempting to Pass Values to Parent Bourne Shells

1. While in the subshell, create a new variable by typing

name3=Jack_Stonewall

2. Ensure inheritance of this variable by typing

   export *name3*

3. Exit the subshell by pressing $\boxed{\text{Ctrl-d}}$.

4. Once you are back in the parent shell, type

   set

   Both variables *name1* and *name2* remain in the variable list, but the variable *name3*, that you created in the subshell and **export**ed does not appear here. When you **export** a variable, it is passed only to subshells. You cannot pass variables created in a subshell back to the parent shell.

Removing a Bourne Shell Variable

Some Bourne shells have a command like the C shell's **unsetenv** command.

1. To unset the variable *name1*, type

   unset *name1*

2. If your Bourne shell does not provide for the **unset** feature, removal of a variable is accomplished by setting it to no value. Type

   name1 = $\boxed{\text{Return}}$

3. Leave the Bourne shell and return to a C shell.

15.2   EDITING SHELL INITIALIZATION FILES

One of the ways UNIX programs are informed of a particular user's preferred environment is through *initialization files*.

Whenever you log in to the C shell, it looks for two files in your Home directory, the *.cshrc* and the *.login* files. If they exist, the *.cshrc* is read first, and then the *.login* file. All other C shell processes that are created read the *.cshrc* file, but not the *.login* file. This difference allows you to have the login C shell operate differently from other C shells.

The C shell *.login* and *.cshrc* files can be used to set variable values that control values such as *history,* the *path,* or *terminal.* These files can be used to create aliases, and establish visual editor initialization characteristics.

The Bourne shell reads an initialization file at login called the *.profile* file.

In the next section you will insert a variety of commands into your *.login, .profile,* or *.cshrc* files, to tailor your own user environment to meet your preferences.

Examining the *.login* file

1. Begin by examining your *.login* file. Do not make changes to the file until you are certain of the effects of your changes. Type one of the following:

   System V:
   pg *.login*

   BSD:
   more *.login*

---

echo *"your .login is being read"*
setenv *PATH "/bin /usr/bin /usr/local ."*
setenv *EDITOR /usr/ucb/vi*
setenv *EXINIT 'set autowrite ai number'*
setenv *VISUAL /usr/ucb/vi*
setenv *MAIL /usr/spool/mail/$USER*
umask *002*

FIGURE 15-1.   Entries in a sample *.login* file

You may or may not have a *.login* file, depending on how your account is configured. A sample *.login* file is shown in Figure 15-1.

The following is a list of entries from the sample *.login* file, and what effect each will have.

- **setenv** *PATH "/bin /usr/bin /usr/local ."*

  Each directory to be searched is separated by a space. If you add a new directory of commands, or if a new application is purchased and placed on the system, the *PATH* should be changed here to include the directory where the new commands are located.

- **setenv** *EDITOR /usr/ucb/vi*

  This sets up your default editor. A variety of commands allow you to edit files while still running the application. The application will start up a particular editor based on the value of the environment variable *EDITOR*.

- **setenv** *MAIL /usr/spool/mail/$USER*

  This variable sets where the **mail** utility looks for mail for the user account.

- **umask** *002*

  The value for **umask** masks the owner, group, and other permission fields for each file that you create. To select a suitable **umask,** refer to Chapter 7, "Setting File Permissions."

Modifying the *.login* File

If you modify or add to your *.login* file, do it very carefully.

1. Begin by making a backup copy of the working *.login* file, by typing

   cp *.login .login_modified*

2. Make changes to the *.login_modified* file.

   Have your modified version read by the current shell, by typing

   source *.login_modified*

Altering the *.cshrc* File

Figure 15-2 contains a sample *.cshrc* file. The following is a list of entries from the *.cshrc* sample file, and what effect each will have.

- **source** ~/.*aliases*

   This sets up all the aliases that are listed in the .*aliases* file every time you create a subshell.

- **set** *history* = *100*

   This sets the value of the *history* variable to 100. The last 100 of your commands will be saved and can be displayed using the **history** command.

- **set** *ignoreeof*

   With this set, the [Ctrl-d] does not kill a shell or subshell.

- **set** *noclobber*

   Redirecting the output from a utility to an existing file overwrites the file unless the *noclobber* variable is set. When set, the shell produces an error message that the file exists.

 # .cshrc

source ~/.*aliases*
set *notify*
set *noclobber*
set *ignoreeof*
set *mail* = *$MAIL*
set *history* = *100*
set *savehist* = *40*
set *prompt* = *"sub.csh "*

FIGURE 15-2.   Entries in a sample .*cshrc* file

Modifying the *.cshrc* File

If you modify or add to your *.cshrc* file, do so very carefully.

1. Begin by making a backup copy of the working *.cshrc* file, by typing

   cp *.cshrc .cshrc_modified*

2. Make changes to the *.cshrc_modified* file.

Having the C Shell Initialization Files Read Immediately

To have your current shell read the *.login_modified* and *.cshrc_modified* files, type the following lines:

   source *.login_modified*
   source *.cshrc_modified*

1. With the initialization files read, all the changes to the local and environment variables show up in the variable lists you made. Type

   set

   to see the list of local C shell variables.

2. To see the list of environment variables, type one of the following:

   System V:
   env

   BSD:
   printenv

3. If major problems occur, log out with **logout**. When you log in again, the original *.login* and *.cshrc* files will be read. Examine your changes, and try to discover what caused the problems and whether or not you can correct them. Then try sourcing both files again.

4. Once you are satisfied with the changes that you have made and wish to keep them, save the old *.login* and *.cshrc* files by typing

mv *.cshrc .cshrc_old*
mv *.login .login_old*

5. Make your modified files your new *.login* and *.cshrc* files.

mv *.cshrc_modified .cshrc*
mv *.login_modified .login*

Placing set and setenv Commands

C shell users need to decide which file will hold the commands that modify the user environment. Some of the commands belong in the *.login* file, and others belong in the *.cshrc* file.

One method that works well is to place all **setenv**s in the *.login* file, and all the local C shell variable declarations in the *.cshrc* file. This is because your *.cshrc* file is automatically sourced when you create a subshell. The *.login* file, on the other hand, is only sourced once, at login. Placing all the **setenvs** in the *.login* file ensures that the environment variables are set at login and are then passed on to subshells automatically.

Furthermore, placing all **setenvs** in the *.cshrc* file would cause reinitialization of all the environment variables to their original values upon every creation of a subshell. This is a useless exercise, because subshells are automatically passed all environment variables. In addition, local variables such as *history* and *ignoreeof* will be lost during subshell creation unless they are placed in the *.cshrc* file because they are not inherited.

Altering the *.profile* File

The *.profile* file is to the Bourne shell what the *.login* file is to the C shell.

1. To examine the file without making any changes, type one of the following commands:

   System V:
   pg *.profile*

   BSD:
   more *.profile*

2. Be certain to create a backup copy of *.profile* before attempting to modify it.

The following variables can be assigned values and then **export**ed to all subshells. In this way, all the subshells will inherit values for these variables:

PATH=/bin:/usr/bin:/usr/ucb:/usr/local:.
EDITOR=/usr/ucb/vi
EXINIT='set autowrite ai number'
export *PATH EDITOR EXINIT*

As with the *.login* file, the exact arguments for each variable will differ from user to user.

15.3   OTHER USEFUL UTILITY INITIALIZATION FILES

There are initialization files that are used by other UNIX utilities, such as **mail** and **vi**. You can customize these initialization files, too.

Using the Initialization File for mail

The initialization file for **mail** is called *.mailrc*, and it belongs in your Home directory along with the *.cshrc* and the *.login* files. In Figure 15-3 is a sample *.mailrc* file.

1. To begin, create the file by typing

   vi *.mailrc*

2. While in the editor, add the following lines:

---

set *EDITOR=/bin/vi*
set *SHELL=/bin/csh*

set *ask*
set *askcc*
set *autoprint*

set *metoo*
set *nosave*

FIGURE 15-3.   Entries in a sample .mailrc file

set *ask askcc crt=24*
alias *john ucbvax!uunet!lurnix!john*

The first command line appears to be assigning local C shell variables, but this is not the case. These variables are used only by the **mail** utility.

3. After saving these changes, exit **vi** and start a letter to yourself by typing

mail *my_login*

The system will prompt you for a subject heading for this letter. The display will be this:

Subject:

4. Type a subject heading of a few words for this article of mail that you are sending out.

5. Add any number of lines to the letter, and end it with a Ctrl-d, on a line by itself. A new prompt appears:

cc:

The *askcc* variable **set** in the *.mailrc* instructs mail to inquire if you want copies sent. Upon completion of every letter, **mail** will ask you for a list of all users who you want to receive a **c**arbon **c**opy of the letter.

6. For now, just press: Return , and no other users will receive a copy of the letter. In this way, you can send a letter and carbon copy it to any number of other users.

7. The third variable that you set was *crt=24.* To see the effect of this variable, you will need to send yourself a relatively long file. Type

mail *your_login* < */etc/termcap*

8. Check for mail, and start reading **mail** messages by typing

mail

If your letter has not arrived, you will see the message:

No mail.

9. Once this new letter has arrived, type in the message number (it will be 1 unless you have other messages). The long letter is displayed one screenful at a time, because the variable *crt* was assigned the value of 24. This is the length of a

normal screen. The letter will be displayed 24 lines at a time, with a prompt for input after every screenful.

10. The second line that you added to the *.mailrc* file is an alias for a long, complicated mail address. Now, instead of typing in the long address, all you have to type is:

mail *john*

The **mail** utility looks in the *.mailrc* file and expands the alias to the actual address, and mails the letter off to that address.

Exercise 15-A

1. What command lists your environment variables and their values for the current session?

   _____

2. In the C shell, how would you assign the value *vt100* to the environment variable *TERM,* and the value *Jones* to the local variable *name?*

   _____

3. Assume the settings in question 2, what value would *TERM* and *name* have if you created a new C subshell?

   _____

4. In the Bourne shell, what command would you use to ensure that subshells inherit the variable *deptname?*

_____

5. In the C shell, in which file would you place all assignments of (a) environment variables and (b) local variables?

_____

6. In the C shell, what command would you use to have the system reread the *.login* file immediately?

_____

7. What is the name of the file for customizing your interaction with **mail**?

_____

The Initialization File for the Visual Editor

The initialization file for the **vi** editor is the file *.exrc.* When the visual editor is started up, it reads the *.exrc* file (if there is one) in the *current* working directory. For that reason, you can have different initializations for individual directories, when different editing features are needed. In Chapter 9, "Advanced Visual Editing," you learned commands to modify the editing environment. Those commands may be placed in the *.exrc* file.

In Figure 15-4 is a sample *.exrc* file. If you see

---

set *nu*
set *ai*

ab *inc incomprehensible*
ab *irs Internal Revenue Service*

map @ O*1600 Pennsylvania Ave, Washington DC*

FIGURE 15-4.   Entries in a sample *.exrc* file

anything that you don't understand, look it up in Chapter 9.

1. In your Home directory, type

   vi *.exrc*

2. Now add these lines to the file

   map @ O*1600 Pennsylvania Avenue, Washington DC*
   ab *inc incomprehensible*

   The first command maps the @ sign, creating a new line (with the O) and entering the address of the White House. The second command creates an abbreviation for the word *incomprehensible*.

3. Exit the editor after saving the changes, and immediately create a new file. Type

   vi *testfile*

4. While in **vi** command mode, type

   @

The command that was mapped to this keystroke opens a new line and adds text to it.

5. Move into append mode and type

this is inc [Esc]

The editor expands the abbreviation *inc.*

All the commands within **vi** discussed earlier (Chapter 9) can be placed in the *.exrc* file. When you begin an editing session, the commands in the *.exrc* file in your current directory are interpreted. Whatever abbreviations the commands call for will apply to the editing session (except if you override them by keying in further commands that override them during the session).

15.4 USING STTY TO SET INPUT AND OUTPUT OPTIONS ON A TERMINAL

You often modify the terminal display using keys such as [Ctrl-h] for backspace, or signal a program interrupt with [Ctrl-c]. These and other *keystroke functions* can be changed through the use of the **stty** utility. This feature of UNIX is particularly useful in situations where you are used to one keyboard configuration but must work on another. Both versions of **stty**, for System V and BSD, are examined in this section.

Setting Terminal Control Characters in BSD

You can examine the current terminal settings by typing

stty all

The output of this command will be similar to the following:

```
new tty, speed 9600 baud; -tabs
crt nohang
erase kill werase rprnt flush lnext susp   intr quit stop   eof
^H    ^X   ^W     ^R    ^O    ^V    ^Z/^Y  ^C   ^\   S/^Q  ^D
```

The last two lines of the display show the names of eleven commands that are special to the terminal. These keyboard characters are mapped or bound to the commands shown below the command names. It is possible to remap the commands to any key. In the following exercises, you will remap (rebind) keys in some rather strange ways, but when you log out and log back in, the original bindings will return.

The first function in the list is the *erase* command. This command erases the character to the left of the cursor and is usually mapped to the [Backspace] key. The following exercises help you practice mapping the commands from the **stty** list to the number keys [2] through [0].

1. To map *erase* to the [2] key, type

   stty *erase* 2

Try out your new *erase* key by typing

   ls -al[2][2][2][2][2][2]

2. The next function is the *line-kill* command. This command erases the entire input line that was typed in. To map *line-kill* to the ③ key, type

stty *kill 3*

Try out your new line-kill key by typing

more */usr/dict/words* ③

3. The *rprnt* command reprints the entire command line that has been typed in so far. To map it to ④, type

stty *rprnt* 4

Once again, experiment with this change by typing

cat */etc/passwd* ④

4. The *flush* command flushes the system's output buffer. To map it to ⑤, type

stty *flush 5*

This command is of no immediate use to an ordinary user. It is helpful for controlling a program's output. Flushing the output buffer will display all of its contents immediately.

5. The *lnext* command forces a literal interpretation of the **next** character that is typed. If the next keystroke (or combination of keystrokes) is a special command usually interpreted by the terminal, like Ctrl-d or Ctrl-c, the *lnext* command forces literal interpretation and simply displays it. To map *lnext* to ⑥, type

stty *lnext 6*

Observe this change by typing

echo 6 Return

The Return , which usually signals the end of a command line, is masked out in this instance. Press Return again to issue the command.

6. The *suspend-job* command is used for job control (Chapter 10, "Running Multiple Commands"). To map *suspend-job* to 7 , type

stty *susp 7*

Now suspend a job by typing

cat */usr/dict/words* Return
7

7. The *delay-suspend-job* command is also used for job control. To map it to 8 , type

stty *dsusp 8*

To try this change out, type the following commands in quick succession:

pg */etc/termcap* Return

Then after the prompt to display the next page appears, type the following in quick succession:

Spacebar 8

The result of the *delay-suspend* can thus be observed. The **pg** job will be suspended after two pages have been displayed, instead of stopping immediately, which is the result of a *suspend-job* command (as in Step 6).

8. The *end-of-file* command is used to end input, such as letters sent with the **mail** utility, and often to log off a system. It is usually the Ctrl-d. To map it to 9, type

stty *eof 9*

Try out this modification by sending **mail** to yourself. Type

mail *your_login*
This is a test.
9

9. When the *intr* key is pressed, an interrupt signal is sent to the running process. It is often Ctrl-c. To map it to 0, type

stty *intr 0*

Try to interrupt a process by typing

cat */usr/dict/words*
0

All of the preceding examples make one change to each terminal command at a time. It is also possible to combine all of the previous commands into one long command. An example would look like this:

stty *erase* Ctrl-h *intr* Ctrl-c *eof* Ctrl-d

The basic syntax of the preceding command line is

stty *command command_key command command_key* . . .

10. After trying out all of the preceding exercises, most of your keyboard commands are now mapped to rather unusual keys. To set the keyboard back to normal, either reset them or simply log off and log back on if it is easy to do this on your system.

Thus far you have examined the **stty** command and command arguments in BSD. Later on in the chapter, you will explore a number of options that exist both in BSD and in System V.

Setting Terminal Control Characters in System V

To begin, type

stty -a

The output of this command is

```
speed 1200 baud; line = 1; intr = DEL; quit = ^|; erase = ^h;
kill = @; eof = ^d; eol = ^'; swtch = ^'
-parenb -parodd cs8 -cstopb hupcl cread -clocal -loblk
-ignbrk brkint ignpar -parmrk -inpck istrip -inlcr -igncr icrnl -iuclc
ixon -ixany -ixoff
isig icanon -xcase echo echoe echok -echonl -noflsh
opost -olcuc onlcr -ocrnl -onocr -onlret -ofill -ofdel tab3
tdcd = 0; tact = 0
```

The part of this display that is of most interest is the first two lines, which specify the characters that carry out terminal commands. These lines are similar to the columns you saw earlier in the BSD version of the **stty** output. In System V, it is also possible to remap the commands to any key.

1. The *erase* command erases the character to the left of the cursor. To map *erase* to the ⟨2⟩ key, type

   stty *erase 2*

   Try out your new *erase* key by typing

   ls -al⟨2⟩⟨2⟩⟨2⟩⟨2⟩⟨2⟩⟨2⟩

2. The next terminal command we will explore is the *line-kill* command. This causes the entire input line to be erased. To map it to the ⟨3⟩ key, type

   stty *kill 3*

   Try out this modification by typing

   ls -al */bin* ⟨3⟩

3. The *end-of-file* command is used to end letters that are sent using **mail**, and also to exit from your login shell. To map *end-of-file* to ⟨4⟩, type

   stty *eof 4*

   Explore this change by sending **mail** to yourself. Type

   mail *your_login*
   This is a test.
   ⟨4⟩

4. The *intr* command sends an interrupt signal to any running process. To map it to ⟨5⟩, type

   stty *intr 5*

Try out this change by typing

cat */usr/dict/words*

⑤

5. You have now modified most of the terminal command keys to rather unusual settings. To set them back to the original keyboard assignments, simply log off and log back on again, or type

stty *sane*

The echo Option to stty

One useful option to **stty** is **echo**. If **echo** is set, your terminal will **echo** each character to the screen as you type it. This is the normal setting when you log in.

1. In this section, you will unset the **echo** option. But before you do, establish a safety net. If you are using the C shell, create a one-letter alias to set **echo** because you won't be able to see your typing once **echo** is unset. Type

    alias *r* **'stty echo'**

2. Now, to prevent the echoing of your input, type

    stty -echo

    Your prompt returns, and everything seems normal. However, your next input will not be visible when you type it.

3. Slowly, type

    who ⌷Return⌷

You don't see the letters **who** appear on the screen, but the output of the **who** command is displayed on the screen as usual.

4. Now type the command

   date Return

   Again the input is not displayed, but the output appears on the screen.

5. To have your input echoed again, type one of the following commands:

   C shell:
   r Return

   Bourne shell:
   stty echo

6. You did not see the commands **date** and **who** when you entered them. Now, in the C shell type

   history

   The commands **date** and **who** do show up in the history list—even though they were never displayed on your screen. The **history** feature keeps track of all of the commands received by the system, regardless of whether or not they were displayed on the screen.

   One example of the use of **-echo** is when you are prompted for a password at login. The password is not echoed when you type it in. This prevents people from seeing your password and gaining access to your account.

The Raw and Cooked Terminal Modes

Your terminal connection to UNIX has several different modes, one of which is the *raw* mode. In *raw* mode, everything you type at the keyboard is passed along to the application without any sort of input processing by the terminal driver program. This is useful when you are running programs that need to handle all keyboard inputs, such as **vi**.

The opposite to *raw* is the *cooked* mode, which is the normal (default) condition. If, when you exit from a program or simulation, you notice your terminal behaving in an unusual way, such as ignoring the control keys, you might be in *raw* mode. If this happens, type

stty *cooked*

Exercise 15-B

1. What command would you place in which file to allow the use of the abbreviation *org* for the word *organization* in the visual editor?

    _____

2. What command would you use to change the interrupt key to ⎡@⎤ ?

    _____

3. What command would you enter to discontinue echoing of input characters to the terminal?

    _____

CONCLUSION

In this chapter you have customized many aspects of your user environment; You set up various initialization files (*.login, .profile, .cshrc, .mailrc, .exrc*). These files and the commands you have learned allow you to customize

- What aliases you have

- How various variables are set

- How you interact with the visual editor

- How you interact with **mail**

One of the strong points of UNIX is the flexibility you have in setting up your customized environment.

COMMAND SUMMARY

set
Display current variables with their values.

set *name = value*
Set the variable *name* to the value *value* (C shell).

name = value
Set the variable *name* to the value *value* (Bourne shell).

unset *name*
Delete the variable *name* (C shell and many Bourne shells).

set *name =*
Same effect as **unset** (Bourne shell).

env
For System V, display current environmental variables with their values.

printenv
For BSD, same as **env**.

setenv *NAME value*
Set the environmental variable *NAME* to the value *value*.

unsetenv *NAME*
Delete the environmental variable *NAME*.

source *filename*
Read and execute the commands in *filename* without starting up a subshell, then continue reading and executing commands from standard input.

alias *name command*
Make *name* an alias for *command*.

COMMAND SUMMARY (*continued*)

stty *all*

For BSD, display various terminal information, such as baud rate and the keyboard characters that will perform various actions like deleting characters.

stty -a

For System V, similar to stty *all*.

stty *action character*

Change the keyboard character used to perform various actions like deleting a character.

stty *raw*

Tell the terminal driver program to pass all characters along without interpreting them.

stty *cooked*

Tell the terminal driver program to interpret certain characters (this is the normal mode).

stty echo

Tell the terminal driver to echo each character typed to the screen.

stty -echo

Tell the terminal driver not to echo each character typed.

Shell Variables Summary

HOME

Home directory of user.

PATH

List of directories searched when looking for command files requested on a command line.

COMMAND SUMMARY (*continued*)

SHELL
Pathname and filename of the user shell.

TERM
Terminal type (for instance, vt100).

USER
Login ID of user.

EXINIT
Initialization commands for **vi**.

·16·

Using a Network
of UNIX Machines

Computers are often connected in a network so that
users on different machines can communicate and
exchange information. Some UNIX machines, like
those in an office, are connected to each other in a
small local network and communicate with one another almost constantly. Other machines are connected to large nationwide (and sometimes
worldwide) networks, but communicate rarely. In
either case, there are specific UNIX commands that
allow users to communicate via networks.

In this chapter you will be accessing machines
connected to a local network. Check with your system
administrator to see if your machine is connected to a
network, if you have access to the network, if the

network is working, and if your network system is derived from Berkeley. If you don't have access to a network, you will not be able to do the exercises with this chapter.

SKILLS CHECK

Before beginning this chapter, you should be able to

- Access and leave the system (Chapter 1, "Touring the System's Features")
- Execute basic commands (Chapter 1)
- Create, display, and print files (Chapter 1)
- Rename, copy, and remove files (Chapter 1)
- Access and modify files using the **vi** editor (Chapter 2, "Basic Editing with the Visual Editor")
- Send and read electronic mail using the mail program (Chapter 5, "Sending Messages to Other Users")

OBJECTIVES

Upon completion of this chapter, you will be able to

- Find out what machines are on your local network
- Get information about users on other machines
- Communicate with users on other machines
- Access accounts on other machines
- Execute commands on other machines
- Transfer files between accounts on different machines

GETTING INFORMATION ABOUT LOCAL MACHINES

16.1

Machines are connected on a local network so that users on different machines can access files, share programs, and otherwise work together. There is a UNIX utility that will report the names and other statistics about machines on your local network.

1. Find out the status of every machine on your network by typing

ruptime

2. If the computer responds with the message

```
No hosts!?!
```

or

```
ruptime: not found
```

ask your systems administrator for help.

Normally, the computer responds with a list of computers on your network and the status of each, the output is similar to the following:

```
vanilla    down  4+02:34
chocolate  up 13+18:28,  1 user,  load 0.25, 0.24, 0.00
strawberry up  2+08:33,  0 users, load 0.33, 0.26, 0.01
rocky-road up     2:44,  0 users, load 0.24, 0.24, 0.00
pistachio  up  5+22:10, 15 users, load 8.13, 6.17, 4.19
```

The components of the **ruptime** output are as follows:

host	In the left column are the names of the various computers. These computers are called *hosts*, and they are given names so that users can identify them.
status	Whether the host is up or down (operational or not).
time in status	The time it has been in the current state (format: days+hours:minutes).
users	The number of users on this host.
load	A number that indicates how busy the host is. The three numbers following *load* give the machine's load average over 1 minute, 5 minutes, and 10 minutes—the larger the number, the busier the machine.

To be able to report this list, **ruptime** maintains a data file. Every minute, each host on the network sends out a message to all of the other hosts describing its status. If any host is not heard from for five minutes, it is listed as being down.

By knowing the status of the hosts on your network, you can use it more efficiently. For example, if you have a task that requires a lot of system resources, an unloaded machine is best. You can use **ruptime** to find out which host is least loaded.

16.2   FINDING INFORMATION ABOUT USERS ON THE NETWORK

You have determined what machines are on your network. On each of the machines are users. There are

UNIX utilities that provide information about these users.

Determining Who Is Logged on to Local Machines

The **who** command lets you find out which users are logged on to your machine. It is also useful to find out which users are on other machines on your network.

1. Find out what users are on your local network by typing

   rwho

2. If the listing is long, you might want to pipe the output through the **page** or **more** command. Type

   rwho | page

   The output is a list similar to this:

```
smith     chocolate:ttyp0   Jun 27 10:22
root      pistachio:console Jun 27 10:14
roberts   pistachio:ttyh2   Jun 27 10:20
salinger  pistachio:ttyh3   Jun 21 18:11
bronte    pistachio:ttyh5   Jun 27 09:41
guest-1   pistachio:ttyh6   Jun 26 08:47 :15
orwell    pistachio:ttyi0   Jun 27 10:06
robbins   pistachio:ttyi2   Jun 27 10:49
kevin     pistachio:ttyi3   Jun 27 09:06 :01
mitchell  pistachio:ttyi7   Jun 27 08:25
maugham   pistachio:ttyie   Jun 23 16:00
guest-4   pistachio:ttyj1   Jun 27 08:51
guest-1   pistachio:ttyp0   Jun 27 09:40
guest-3   pistachio:ttyp1   Jun 27 09:07 :24
```

Each line of the output is in the following form:

```
user machine_name :tty_port login_date login_time
```

The first column lists the users on machines connected to the network. The middle column names the machine and terminal the user is logged onto. The last column shows when the user logged on and, if the user has been idle for more than a minute, the amount of idle time. Users who are idle for more than an hour are not listed at all. Note that some of the tty's (terminals) being used are in the form ttyp*X* or ttyq*X*. Terminal names beginning with ttyp or ttyq are *network ports*, which are used by the **rlogin** utility discussed later in this chapter.

The **rwho** command can be helpful when you need to communicate with another user. By using **rwho**, you can find out whether users are logged in, where they are logged in, and how long they have been idle.

Checking Who's Logged on a Specific Machine

The **rwho** command displays the logins of users who are on all of your local systems. This might be too much information to sift through if you want to find a specific machine. Fortunately, there is also a UNIX utility that will display who is on a specific network machine.

1. Type the following command:

finger

The output is a display similar to this:

```
Login           Name      TTY     Idle      When        Office
root        Super User     co      11    Tue 10:14     767-2676
matt        Matthew Adams  h2            Tue 10:20
smith       Jean Smith     h3      19    Wed 18:11
sam         Sam Silver     h5            Tue 09:41
guest-4     ???            j1            Tue 08:51
guest-1     ???            j2            Tue 09:40
guest-3     ???            j4       1    Tue 09:07
```

The **finger** command displays all users logged into your machine, their "real" names (if known), terminals, idle times, and login times.

You can also check a network machine by specifying the name of the machine.

2. Pick a machine (*machine_name*) on your network and find out who is logged on it by typing

   finger *@machine_name*

   You get an output similar to the earlier output for **finger.**

   The *@machine_name* address tells **finger** to check for users on the machine named *machine_name,* instead of on your machine.

Finding Out How Recently a Specific User Logged On

Besides using **finger** to check who is logged in, you can use it to find information about a specific user.

1. To find out when the user *root* (who has an account on every system) last logged on your system, type

finger *root*

The output will be similar to this:

```
Login name: root                        In real life: Super User
Directory: /                            Shell: /bin/csh
Last login Mon Jun 26 18:41 on console
No Plan.
```

There are four lines in the display. The first line tells you the login ID and real name of the user of the account. The second line tells you the account's Home directory and default shell. The third line says when *root* last logged in, and which tty port *root* used. (If *root* is logged in, this line says when *root* logged in and which tty port *root* is using.) The last line says that *root* doesn't have an optional file called *.plan*. The *.plan* file usually contains a short description of the account's purpose as conceived by the owner.

2. If you know the login IDs of friends on your system, use **finger** to determine when they last logged in.

You can also check this same information for a user on another system by specifying the user and the machine.

3. Pick a machine, and find out when the user *root* last logged in by typing

finger   *root@machine_name*

where *machine_name* is the name of the machine. This output tells you when *root* last logged onto that machine.

As before, the *@machine_name* address tells **finger** to check the specified network machine named *machine_name,* instead of your machine. In this way, @ is a special character that separates the login ID from the machine name. The general form for **finger** is

finger   *user@machine_name*

This will either tell you that a user is logged in or when the user last logged in.

Finding an Account Belonging to a User

Not only can you find the name of a user of a given login ID, and when that user last logged in, but you can also often determine the login ID for a user, given the user's real name.

1. If you have a friend with an account on another machine, type

   finger   *friend_name@machine_name*

   where *friend_name* is either the first or last name of your friend.

2. The computer either displays your friend's login ID and **finger** information, or the following:

```
Login Name: friend_name    In real life &: ???
```

which means that **finger** couldn't find the login ID matched with *friend_name*.

The **finger** command checks both the login ID list, and the real name list. If **finger** finds a name in the real name list, it will display the information for the login ID matching that name.

16.3   COMMUNICATING OVER A NETWORK

For users on different machines to work together effectively, they have to be able to send messages and data back and forth.

Sending Mail to Users on Other Machines

Electronic mail is one of the basic ways that users communicate with one another. You have already sent mail to users on your machine by using the **mail** *login_ID* command. You can also send mail to users on other machines, as long as you know their login IDs and machine names.

1. If you do not have the login of a friend on another machine, send mail to the user */dev/null* on another machine by typing

   mail */dev/null@machine*

   where *machine* is the name of a machine besides your own.

2. Type the following:

   Hi,
   I'm trying mail.
   Could you please answer this.
   Thank You.

   and then press $\boxed{\text{Ctrl-d}}$.
       Don't expect an answer. On some machines, this mail will be thrown away. On other machines, you will get a reply saying that the user */dev/null* doesn't exist.

3. Try sending mail to a friend with an account on another system. If you don't know the login ID, use **finger** to find it out.

   In general, to send a message to a user on another machine, you have to type

   mail *login_ID@machine_name*

   where *login_ID* is the user's login ID, and *machine_name* is the name of the machine where the user's account is located.

Talking to Users Logged on to Other Machines

Using **mail** is not the fastest way to communicate. You have to type an entire letter, send it, and wait for a reply. Sometimes it is necessary to **talk** to another user (like using a telephone). There is a UNIX utility that allows you to **talk**, by typing, to another user.

1. Try **talk**ing to a friend on another machine. Type the following command:

   talk *friend@machine*

   where *friend* is your friend's login ID, and *machine* is your friend's machine name. If your friend is not logged on, try a different user, or try this command at another time.

2. If your friend is logged on, the **talk** command clears your screen and divides it into two parts. Meanwhile, your friend's terminal gets beeping messages like this:

   ```
   Message from Talk_Daemon@machine at 12:23...
   talk: connection requested by login_ID@machine
   talk: respond with: talk login_ID@machine
   ```

   When the connection is established, whatever you type appears on the top half of your screen and on the bottom half of your friend's screen, and vice versa. This is just like talking on the telephone, except that you are typing instead of talking.

3. Either you or your friend can end the **talk** by pressing Ctrl-d or Ctrl-c.

The general form of the **talk** command line is

talk *user@machine*

Notice that the *user@machine* part of this command is exactly the same as using **mail** and **finger**. The *user@machine* part is the *address*. It tells **finger** what information you want to check, **mail** where you want to send mail, and **talk** where the login is located.

Exercise 16-A

Examine the following questions as a review before proceeding with this chapter.

1. What command displays the names of the machines on your local network?

   _____

2. What is the main difference between the **rwho** and **finger** commands?

   _____

3. How would you send mail to the user *strawberry* whose account is on the machine *red*?

   _____

4. What do you do to leave **talk**?

   _____

16.4   ACCESSING AN ACCOUNT ON A SECOND SYSTEM

Before beginning the rest of this chapter, ask your system administrator, "Do I have an account on any other host(s) besides the one I normally use?" If the answer is no, ask, "Can I get one?" Be sure you know the machine name, the login ID, and the password of the new account.

By having access to more than one account, you can be more efficient by working on a system that isn't as busy as your normal system.

Logging in to a Remote System

You can log in to an account on another system, called a *remote machine,* from your account, called the *local account,* by using the **rlogin** utility.

1. Try to log in to a remote machine by typing

   rlogin   *machine_name*

   After a short wait, the machine replies with:

   ```
   Password:
   ```

   The system doesn't ask you for the login ID, because **rlogin** assumes that the account you are logging into has the same login ID as your local account.

2. If the account you are logging into has the same login ID as your local account, enter the password.

3. If the account you are logging into has a different login ID, press [Return].

The system now prompts you with this message:

```
Login:
```

4. Enter the correct login ID and then the password, just as you would if you were logging onto your local machine.

You can also log onto a different account by using the **-l** option of **rlogin** like this:

rlogin *machine_name* **-l** *login_ID*

where *login_ID* is the login ID of the account you are logging into.

Executing Commands

Now that you are logged into an account on a remote machine, you can execute commands just as if you were on your own local machine.

1. Create or modify a file called *.rhosts* in your Home directory with the **vi** editor.

2. Add a line to the *.rhosts* file like this:

your_machine_name:your_login_ID

where *your_login_ID* is the login ID of your local account, and where *your_machine_name* is the name of your local machine.

3. Now **write** and **quit** the file.

You will use the *.rhosts* file in the next section.

Logging Out

Now that you have finished using this other account, you need to log out. To log out from an account on a remote machine, go through the same process, as if you were logging out from your local account.

1. Log out from this other account by typing

logout

2. Press **pwd** to confirm that you are back at your local machine.

16.5   EXECUTING PROGRAMS ON A SECOND SYSTEM

Sometimes it's useful to execute a command on a remote machine without actually logging in. This way you can do work on your machine, while another machine is also doing work for you.

Running Programs

1. Execute the command **cal** on the remote account you have been using. Type

   rsh *machine* **-l** *login_ID* **cal**

   After a short while, the machine displays the current month. (Notice that you are not asked to type the password. This will be explained in Step 2.)

   In general, to use the **rsh** command, you type

   rsh *machine_name* **-l** *login_ID* **command**

   where **command** is the name of the shell command line you want to execute on the remote machine.
   Just like the **rlogin** command, **rsh** assumes that the account name on the remote machine is the same as your local account. If the account name is different, you must use **rsh** with the **-l** *account_name* option, where *account_name* is the name of the account you want to log into.

2. Examine the file *.rhosts* that you just created (or modified) on a remote account earlier. Type

   rsh *machine* **-l** *account* **cat** *.rhosts*

   where *machine* is the name of the remote machine, and *account* is the name of the account.
   Again, **rsh** did not prompt you for a password. The *.rhosts* file on the remote account contains a line with your machine name and your account name. You can remotely log in or execute commands *without providing a password.* Your local account is

*rhost*ed for the remote account. Most versions of **rsh** require that you be *rhost*ed on the remote account.

3. Test this out. Change the name of the *.rhosts* file on the remote account to the name *rhosts.copy* by typing

   rsh *machine* **-l** *account* **mv** *.rhosts rhosts.copy*

4. Now that you are no longer *rhost*ed, try to look at the file *.login* on the remote account by typing

   rsh *machine* **-l** *account* **cat** *.login*

   If the machine prompts you for a password, you can execute the **rsh** command by entering the password for the account on the remote machine. If it doesn't, you cannot execute the **rsh** command. However, you can still use **rlogin** to access the account.

5. Log into the account you have been using on the remote machine. Type

   rlogin *machine* **-l** *account*

   and enter the password.

6. Copy the name of the file *rhosts.copy* back to *.rhosts* so that you can use **rsh** again. Type

   cp *rhosts.copy .rhosts*

7. Log out from the remote account. Type

   logout

8. You are now *rhost*ed again. Go ahead and try again to look at the file *.login* on the remote account. Type

   rsh *machine* **-l** *account* **cat** *.login*

This time you are able to access the file.

Using rsh Without a Command

So far, you have given **rsh** a command to execute, for example, **cat**.

1. Try **rsh** without a command:

   rsh *machine* **-l** *account*

2. Notice that **rsh** just logged you into the named *machine*. If you enter **rsh** without a command, you are given a **remote sh**ell on the remote machine by executing the **rlogin** program.

COPYING FILES FROM AN ACCOUNT ON A SECOND SYSTEM   16.6

Sometimes you and other users need to exchange files. One way to exchange files would be to **mail** them, but this is slow and doesn't work for binary files. There is a UNIX utility similar to the **cp** program that allows you to copy files across a network.

Copying Files from a Remote Account to a Local Account

1. Make a copy of the file *.rhosts* from the remote account you have been using, and call it *rhosts* on your local account. Type

rcp *machine.login_ID:rhosts.copy temp*

where *machine* is the name of the remote machine, and *login_ID* is the login ID of the remote account.

Instead of using *login_ID@machine* as the remote address, **rcp** uses the form *machine.login_ID* for addresses.

2. Take a look at the copy, *temp.* It is exactly the same as the file *rhosts.copy* on the remote account.

The command **rcp** copies files over the network. (It makes **remote copies**.) To use **rcp** to copy a file from a remote account to your local account, use this command format:

rcp *machine.login_ID:remotename localname*

where *machine* is the name of the remote machine, *login_ID* is the login ID of the account, *remotename* is the name of the file you want to copy, and *localname* is the name you want to call the new copy. Just like the **rsh** command, in most cases **rcp** requires that your account be *rhost*ed on the remote account.

You can now use **rcp** to copy files from another account into your account, if permissions on the remote file allow it.

Copying Files from a Local Account to a Remote Account

You have used **rcp** to copy files from another account into your account. You can also use **rcp** to put copies of files from your account into another account.

1. Copy your file *practice* to the remote account and call it *old.practice* by typing

   rcp   *practice machine.account:old.practice*

2. Now check that the file is there by typing

   rsh   *machine* **-l**   *account*   **cat**   *old.practice*

   To make a copy of a file from your account to a remote account, type

   rcp   *localfile   machine.account:copyfile*

   where *localfile* is the name of the file on your local account that you want to copy, *machine* is the name of the remote machine, *account* is the name of the account where you want to put the copy, and *copyfile* is the name you want to give the new copy.

   Now that you can copy files both ways, you can exchange files between accounts on which you are *rhost*ed.

USING FTP COMMANDS TO COPY FILES ON A REMOTE ACCOUNT

16.7

You have used **rcp** to copy files between accounts. To use **rcp** you must to be *rhost*ed in the remote account. Another way to copy files over a network is to use the **ftp** interactive copying program, which doesn't look at the *.rhosts* file. Unfortunately, the program requires you to transfer files using the **INTERNET**. If your machine is not on the **INTERNET**, these exercises will not apply to you.

1. Start up **ftp** by typing

   ftp

   You now get a prompt that looks like this:

   `ftp>`

   This is the **ftp** prompt, which tells you that you are in the **ftp** program and can execute **ftp** commands.

2. Find out what **ftp** commands are available by typing

   help

3. There are many **ftp** commands, but you will only need to know a few of them to copy normal files. If you want to get a short synopsis of a command, type

   help *command_name*

   where *command_name* is the name of a command.

Logging In

Before you can use **ftp** to copy files between your account and a remote account, you need to log in or connect to the remote machine.

1. Log onto the remote machine that you have been using by typing

   open *machine*

where *machine* is the name of the remote machine that you have used throughout this chapter. The **open** command tells **ftp** to open a connection between your machine and the remote machine.

2. Enter the account name and password. This tells **ftp** what account you want to access.

Logging in with **ftp** is not the same as using **rlogin**. Although you are connected to the remote machine, you cannot execute shell commands on the remote machine. You can only execute **ftp** commands.

Finding What Files You Can Copy

Before you can copy a file using **ftp**, you need to know what files you can copy.

1. Get a list of files by typing

   ls

2. The screen displays a single column listing of all files in the Home directory of the remote account.

The **ftp** command **ls** is exactly the same as the **ls** UNIX shell command, except that it doesn't have any options.

Getting Copies from a Remote Account

One way to make copies of a file is to obtain the copy from the remote account.

1. Pick a file on the remote account. Copy it by typing

   get *filename*

   where *filename* is the name of the file you are **get***ting*.
   The **get** command copies files from the remote account into your account.

2. Make sure that the file has been copied. Type

   !ls

   You get a listing of all the files in your current directory on your account.
   The **!** command tells **ftp** that you want to run a shell command (**ls**) from your local account.

3. You can also specify the name you want to give the copy. Pick a different file on the remote account and copy it by typing

   get *filename filename.copy*

   where *filename* is the name of the file you are copying from the remote machine, and *filename.copy* is the name you want to give the copy on the local machine.

4. Now check what files are listed in your account by typing

   !ls

   Note that the file *filename.copy* is in the listing.

   In general, to copy a remote file with **ftp**, you type

get *remote_original local_copy*

where *remote_original* is the name of the file you want to copy, and *local_copy* is the name you want to call the copy.

Putting Copies into a Remote Account

You have used the **get** command to copy files from a remote account into your account. You can also use **ftp** to copy files from your account into a remote account.

1. Choose a file to copy over to the remote account. Copy it by typing

   put *filename   filename.copy*

   where *filename* is the name of the file that you want to copy, and *filename.copy* is the name you want to give the copy.
   The **put** command copies files from your account into the remote account.

2. Check that the copy was made. Type

   ls

   This time you get a list of all the files in the Home directory of the remote account; the copy has been added.
   In general, to copy a file from your local account to a remote account with **ftp,** you type

   put *local_original   remote_copy*

where *local_original* is the name of the original file, and *remote_copy* is the name you want to call the copy.

Changing Directories

Users often keep files in directories for better management. When looking for files to copy, users often need to change directories to find the file.

1. Move to the parent directory of the remote account by typing

   cd ..

   The **ftp** command **cd** *directory_name* allows you to change directories on the remote machine.

2. Just like on your account, you sometimes need to know the path to your current directory. Type

   pwd

   The output of **pwd** is the path to the remote account. In **ftp,** the **pwd** command works exactly the same as it works with the shell.

   Now that you know how to move around remote directories, and find what directory you are in, you can explore the directories on the remote account and copy files into your account.

Logging Out of ftp

Eventually, you will want to leave **ftp**.

1. Type the following command to leave **ftp**:

   bye

2. You are now back in the shell on your local machine. The **bye** command tells **ftp** to close the connection to the remote machine, and return to your regular shell.

   Copying files with **ftp** is often easier than using **rcp**. There are other **ftp** commands that you can experiment with. You can use the **help** command to investigate these further.

Exercise 16-B

Answer the following questions:

1. How would you log onto the account *vanilla* on the machine *shake* from your account?

   _____

2. What command would you enter from your account to look at the file *work* in the account *siamese* on the machine *kitten*?

   _____

3. What happens when you try to **rsh** to an account without being *rhost*ed?

_____

4. What command would you enter to copy the file *television* from your account to the remote account *green* on the machine *grass,* naming the copy *radio?*

_____

CONCLUSION

You have now learned how to take advantage of a network through communication with others, expansion of your machine resources, and exchanging of files. By using the network, you can expand your resources and productivity.

COMMAND SUMMARY

ruptime
Displays statuses of all machines on the local network

rwho
Displays users logged into machines on the local network

finger @*machine_name*
Displays all users logged into the machine named *machine_name*

finger *user@machine_name*
Displays when *user* last logged into the machine named *machine_name*

mail *login_ID* @*machine_name*
Sends mail to the user with login ID *login_ID*, whose account is on the machine named *machine_name*

talk *login_ID* @*machine_name*
Sends a talk request, which might or might not be answered, to the user with login ID *login_ID*, whose account is on the machine named *machine_name*

rlogin *machine* **-l** *login_ID*
Log into account with login ID *login_ID*, on the machine named *machine*

rsh *machine* **-l** *login_ID* **command**
Executes a **command** through the account with login ID *login_ID*, on the machine named *machine*, without logging into the account

rcp *original machine.login_ID:copy*
Makes a copy named *copy* into an account on the machine named *machine* with login ID *login_ID* of the file *original*

rcp *machine.login_ID:original copy*
Makes a copy named *copy* into your account, of the file named *original*, from an account on the machine named *machine* with login ID *login_ID*

COMMAND SUMMARY *(continued)*

ftp Command Summary

open *machine*
Opens a connection between your account and the machine named *machine*

user *login_ID*
Attempts to log on to the connected machine using the account with login ID of *login_ID*

help
Displays the list of available **ftp** commands

help *command*
Displays a brief synopsis of the **ftp** command named *command*

get *original copy*
Copies the file *original* from the remote account into a file named *copy* on the local account

put *original copy*
Copies the file *original* from your local account into a file named *copy* on the remote account

·17·

Using the X Window System

UNIX is a multitasking operating system, allowing you to do more than one job at the same time. In previous exercises, you ran programs in the background, enabling you to get several jobs done at once. Running multiple commands simultaneously lets you schedule your efforts and your computing time intelligently and efficiently. Unfortunately, programs that require access to the terminal display or keyboard cannot be run in the background. While running such programs, you may find yourself staring at the screen, waiting, when you could be doing something else.

To solve this problem, *window systems* were developed. The terminal screen is divided into regions called windows. A single terminal screen can display several windows. A mouse is used to select windows. In each window, you can issue commands, create files, and examine output. By opening multiple windows, you can have a number of programs running at the same time, including those needing access to the terminal display or keyboard.

The **X Window** system is rapidly becoming a standard for window systems in the UNIX computing environment. Many terminals, computers, and workstations are available that use the **X Window** system. When you use **X Window** you can use the multiprocessing abilities of UNIX more efficiently, and take advantage of the large library of **X Window** system application programs available.

This chapter is based on the **X Window** system, Version 11, Release 3. Even if your computer does not have access to the **X Window** system, you may want to read this chapter, but you will be unable to complete the exercises.

SKILLS CHECK

Before beginning this chapter, you should be able to

- Access and leave the system (Chapter 1, "Touring the System's Features")

- Create and display files (Chapter 1)

- Execute basic shell commands alone and in combination (Chapter 1)

- Access and modify files using an editor (Chapter 2, "Basic Editing with the Visual Editor")

Upon completion of this chapter, you will be able to

- Start the **X Window** system on your workstation

- Make selections with the mouse

- Modify the size and location of a window

- Use the cut and paste features to copy text between windows

- End an **X Window** session

STARTING X WINDOW — 17.1

In this chapter we describe only the standard method of starting the **X Window** system. There may be an alternate method if your machine is configured differently. Additionally, you can define a personalized **X Window** setup in a control file located in your Home directory. When this control file exists, the information it contains is used for starting **X Window**. If your system logs you immediately into **X Window**, you have such a startup. It is still useful to read this section; however, omit the exercises.

By dividing the screen into many independent, possibly overlapping displays or *windows*, the **X Window** system lets you use many different programs simultaneously. Each of the windows acts as an independent terminal display. You can edit a file, maintain a **talk** session with another user, and read **mail** while running other application programs.

1. Log in to your account.

2. After the prompt appears, type

xinit

This command starts up the **X Window** server, which is the program that controls the window system. The screen clears, and the entire display of your workstation becomes a grey rectangle. This is the *root window*. All of your other windows are put on top of this root window.

A mouse cursor appears, and a little later, a single window appears in the upper left corner. **X Window** has started and is now ready to communicate with you. Once the cursor is moved to the window, it is ready for input. This first window functions as an independent terminal and is called the *console window*.

The console window is the control center for the **X** application programs you run. Keep this window in the upper left corner to distinguish it from any other windows you might create. Logging out from this window will not only kill **X Window** but will also end the processes running in all of your other windows.

Moving the Cursor

When you move the mouse along the table or the *mouse pad*, the large X or *mouse cursor* moves on the screen.

1. Move your mouse around on your desktop or mouse pad, and notice the corresponding movements of the mouse cursor on the screen.

2. Move the mouse cursor into your console window.

3. Move it back out of the console window.

When the mouse cursor is within the bounds of a window other than the root window, three things happen:

- The mouse cursor changes shape from an X to an I beam.

- The *window cursor* changes from an outline to a solid box.

- The window border is highlighted.

When the mouse cursor is in the large screen (or root window), the cursor is a large X. In the window currently available, it is the shape of an I, or the cross section of an I beam. The cursor can also take other shapes, which will be discussed later in the chapter.

Using a Terminal Emulator Window

1. Move your cursor into the console window.

The console window functions like a terminal, running the C shell (or whatever shell is set up for your account). When the mouse cursor is in the console window, it is the I beam, and characters typed on the keyboard are sent to the shell running within that window.

2. Type several UNIX commands, such as **date, who,** and **ls -l**.

3. Request a report on the processes currently running, by typing

ps

Because this window interacts with you as though it were a terminal, it is called an **xterm** (**X term**inal) emulator window.

17.2   STARTING THE WINDOW MANAGER

For any window system to be of value, it must allow you to move windows, change their size, change their stacking order, and make them into representations. The program that provides these functions is called the *window manager*. The most common window manager for the **X Window** system is called **uwm**, or the universal window manager.

1. Start up **uwm** *in the background* by placing the mouse cursor anywhere in the console window and typing

   uwm &

   Nothing appears to have happened, but the window manager is now running. A beep sounds to tell you **uwm** is ready for input. Once **uwm** is running, all future **X** applications and other **X** programs will be managed by **uwm**.

2. Reexamine the process table with **ps** to confirm that the manager is running.

Starting a Default-Size Terminal Window

1. Start up another **X** terminal emulator (**xterm**) window by typing

   xterm &

After a few seconds, the top left corner of the new window appears on the screen under the mouse cursor.

2. Press and hold the *left* mouse button. Note that a "ghost" outline of the new window appears.

3. Holding down the left button, use the mouse to move the new window to a remote portion of the screen.

4. Release the *left* button to place the window.

5. Activate the new window by moving the mouse into it.

6. Using **ps**, check on the processes to see what is running from this window. Notice that both **uwm** and the new terminal emulator program were run in the background, permitting you to continue entering commands from the console window.

The new window you created is composed of 24 lines, each with 80 characters. If you use the *right* mouse button to place a window on the display, you will produce an **xterm** window 80 characters wide, with its length running from the mouse cursor position to the bottom of the screen.

Starting a Variable-Size Terminal Window

1. Establish another **xterm** window by typing this command in the console window:

xterm &

2. Wait until the top left corner of the **xterm** window is on the screen. Then do the following:

  - *Hold* down the *center* mouse button

  - *Drag* the cursor *down and to the right*

  - *Release* the button when the new window is approximately two-thirds the size of the root window

Keeping the Root Window Exposed

When creating windows, always make sure that some of the root window remains exposed. You will need to access the root window with the mouse to complete many functions described in the exercises of this chapter. If you should completely cover your root window, you will need to kill one of the windows that obscures it. If this happens, do the following:

1. Make sure that the window to be killed is not the console window.

2. Move the cursor into the window to be killed.

3. Tell the window to "die" by typing
   exit

Leaving X Window

The **X Window** features that you are using are programs running in the shell.

1. Move the cursor into the console window to make that window your active window.

2. Type
   exit.

When you type **exit** in your console window, you kill **X Window** and all of the associated window processes.

Running an X Application

The major appeal of the **X Window** system is that it provides a standard window interface for application programs. A properly written and installed **X** application can run on any machine running the **X Window** system.

One of the basic **X** applications provided on most systems is the **clock** program.

1. To start up a **clock** application window, move the mouse cursor into an **xterm** window and type the following:

   xclock &

   A "ghost" outline of the **clock** window materializes. The ghost window can be moved using the mouse.

2. Position the **clock** ghost window in a corner of the screen, and press the *left* mouse button to place it. Your **clock** program, which is running in the background, is now displayed on the screen.

An application can be manipulated in the same manner as an **xterm** window. The application display can be positioned in its default size with the left mouse button. Or, use the middle mouse button to determine the size of the application window before placing it.

3. Practice making a window the size you want it. Create another **clock**, and make it very small.

17.3   MANIPULATING WINDOWS WITH THE WINDOW OPTIONS MENU

Now that you have used **uwm** to place windows on the screen, you might wonder what can be done if a window is too big or poorly positioned. There are only so many windows you can put on a display, even if you make each window very small.

You can call routines to manipulate windows using the mouse, mouse buttons, and a menu called **WindowOps** (**Window Options**).

1. Move the cursor into the root window (the window all the others are on top of).

2. Press and hold down the middle mouse button. The **WindowOps** or menu appears.

3. Without releasing the middle button, use the mouse to move the cursor up and down in the menu listing. Unless your system has been modified by a system administrator or manufacturer, you will see the following entries:

```
NewWindow
RefreshScreen
Redraw
Move
Resize
Lower
Raise
CircUp
CircDown
AutoIconify
LowerIconify
NewIconify
Focus
Freeze
Unfreeze
Restart
KillWindow
Exit
```

4. Move the cursor out of the menu, and then release the button. The menu goes away.

Creating a New Window

Previously, you created a new **xterm** using the **xterm** shell command. **xterm** windows can also be created using the **WindowOps** menu.

Create a new **xterm** by completing the following:

1. Move the mouse cursor into the root window.

2. Press and hold down the middle mouse button.

3. Move the cursor down the list of options listed. Highlight the **NewWindow** line of the menu.

The **X Window** system places large demands on the memory, networking capabilities, and processing power of your machine. As a result, the display reactions to mouse movement and button presses are often delayed. Consequently, you may not be doing what you think you are doing. If you accidently select an incorrect window option, move the mouse to the root window again, and press any mouse button. This cancels the command.

4. Release the middle button while the **NewWindow** option is highlighted. This creates a blinking outline of the new window's left corner at the current cursor position.

5. Press and hold the left button, positioning the window outline so it slightly overlaps another window. Again, be certain to leave some of the root window showing.

Refreshing the Screen

When many windows are on the screen, or when the computer becomes busy, the **X** *server* sometimes draws application program windows improperly on the display screen. Windows may be drawn incompletely or as blank rectangles. At such times it is best to *refresh* or redraw the entire display.

1. Bring up the **WindowOps** menu, and drag the cursor down the menu list until the **RefreshScreen** option is highlighted.

2. Release the mouse button. The entire display is redrawn.

Redrawing a Window

You have seen what happens when the entire terminal screen is refreshed. **X** also provides you with the capability to *redraw* only one window.

1. Bring up the **WindowOps** menu, and choose the **Redraw** option. Notice that the mouse cursor has changed. It now looks like a closed hand with an index finger pointing to the left. This pointer is how the mouse cursor looks when **uwm** is waiting for you to *select* a window.

2. Move the *mouse pointer* into the window you want to redraw.

3. Press any of the mouse buttons to tell **uwm** to redraw the window.

Moving Windows

Some of the windows you have created may have been awkwardly placed. In cases like this you need to be able to move the windows to another portion of the display.

1. From the **WindowOps** menu select the **Move** option. The cursor changes to a pointing finger.

2. Move the pointer into the window you want to move.

3. Press and hold down the center mouse button.

4. Use the pointer to drag the window to a new location.

5. Release the button when the window is in the desired location.

6. Practice rearranging your screen by placing windows in useful locations, remembering to always leave a portion of the root window visible.

Changing Window Size

There are several reasons why you may want to change the size of a window. Perhaps the window does not display enough lines of your text or, conversely, it takes up more screen space than is warranted. Using the **WindowOps** menu, you can make a window either larger or smaller.

1. Select the **Resize** option from the **WindowOps** menu.

2. Place the mouse pointer in the **clock** window on the corner that is closest to the center of the root window.

3. Press and hold down the middle mouse button. A grid appears superimposed over the window.

4. Still holding down the middle mouse button, move the mouse cursor toward the center of the terminal screen. The grid and the window grow larger. As you are changing the size of the **clock** window, a small highlighted window appears in the display. It reveals the new size of the clock window.

5. Watch the displayed size of the window, and continue moving the mouse cursor until the window grows to approximately 10 × 10.

6. Release the mouse button. The **clock** window has now been changed to a size of 10 characters high by 10 characters wide. The clock within the window has also been scaled accordingly.

7. Following the same procedure, resize at least two other windows. Again, make certain that a portion of the root window remains visible.

Iconifying Windows

In the **X Window** environment with the **uwm** window manager running, windows may obscure each other. If you imagine that each window is a piece of paper, you can see that a terminal display with many open windows looks a lot like a cluttered desk. Papers are strewn about, and it is hard to discern more than one complete piece at a time.

On a desk, you can temporarily file less important or unneeded papers in folders, and then label the folders by their contents. The desk becomes less cluttered, because the folders take up less space and can be stacked. In the **X Window** system, the analogue to the file folder is the *icon.*

AutoIconify

Iconify a window by completing the following steps:

1. Move the mouse cursor into the root window, and bring up the **WindowOps** menu.

2. Hold down the middle mouse button, and move the cursor down the menu until the **AutoIconify** option is highlighted.

3. Release the mouse button. The **AutoIconify** option is now selected, and the cursor is now the pointing hand.

4. Move the pointer into a terminal window that is obscuring another window, and press any mouse button.

    The window changes into a small rectangle titled with the name of application **xterm**. This rectangle is the *icon* for the **xterm** window. When you changed the window to the icon, you *iconified* the window. The window beneath the obscuring window is now more visible.

Manipulating an Iconified Window

1. Move the icon to a free space in the root window, using the **WindowOps Move** command. (*Icons* accept all the **WindowOps** commands except **Resize**.)

    Since the area of iconified window is so small, be sure the mouse cursor is actually in the icon when you are issuing mouse button signals. The center of the X and the I beam and the tip of the index finger on the pointer are called the *hot spot* of the mouse cursor. Normally, all keyboard and mouse button input is sent to the window that is directly under the hot spot of the cursor.

De-iconifying a Window

Pick one of the iconified windows and transform it back to a window by doing the following:

1. Select the **AutoIconify** command from the **WindowOps** menu.

2. Move the mouse pointer into the iconified window.

3. Press any mouse button to de-iconify the selected window. The window reappears in its former size and position.

NewIconify and LowerIconify

Despite their different names, **NewIconify** and **LowerIconify** are the same commands on most machines.

1. Move the mouse cursor into the root window, and bring up the **WindowOps** menu.

2. Press and hold the middle mouse button, and move down the menu list until the **NewIconify** option is highlighted.

3. Release the button to select the **NewIconify** option. The cursor is now a hand pointer.

4. Choose a window other than the console window, and move the mouse cursor into the window.

5. Hold down any mouse button to iconify the selected window.

6. As long as you continue holding down the mouse button, you can move the iconified window by moving the mouse.

7. Release the mouse button to place the iconified window. **NewIconify** and **LowerIconify** are a combination of **AutoIconify** and **Move**.

8. De-iconify the window. To do this, you may use either **NewIconify** or **LowerIconify** in the **WindowOps** menu.

9. After the mouse cursor has become the pointer, move it into the iconified window, and hold down any mouse button.

   The window now appears, concentric with the center of the mouse cursor. You can continue to move the window about the display as long as the mouse button remains depressed.

   Had you used **AutoIconify** to de-iconify the window, rather than **NewIconify** or **LowerIconify**, the window would have reappeared in its former position.

10. Experiment with different combinations of **AutoIconify**, **NewIconify**, and **LowerIconify**.

Raising a Window That Is Obscured

You have just iconified and de-iconified windows. Using the cluttered desk metaphor again, iconifying is a useful way of uncluttering the desk. But usually you need to look at only one particular piece of paper at a time. More often than not, that piece is buried under a stack of paper, or in this case, under several windows. Thus, rather than iconifying a stack of windows, you want to be able to pull the needed window to the top of the pile.

You can raise a selected window to the top of the window stack.

1. Move the mouse cursor into the root window.

2. Bring up the **WindowOps** menu and select the **Raise** option.

3. Move the cursor into the window you want to raise and press the middle mouse button. The window is raised above the obscuring window and is fully visible.

Lowering a Window

The function opposite to **Raise** is **Lower**, which lowers the selected window to the bottom of the window stack.

1. Bring up the **WindowOps** menu, and select the **Lower** option.

2. Move the cursor into the window you just raised, and press any mouse button. The window is lowered to the bottom of the window stack.

Shuffling Window Order

You have raised and lowered individual windows. But what if the window you need to use is completely obscured by other windows? You could lower all the windows, or iconify as many of the obscuring windows as required and then raise the window. Alternatively, you can rotate the window stack to change its order.

1. If you do not have at least one window stack, create one with several windows.

2. Move the mouse cursor into the root window, and bring up the **WindowOps** menu by holding down the middle button.

3. Drag the cursor down the options until the **Circup** (**Circulate Up**) option is highlighted. Whatever window was at the bottom of the stack is now raised to the top.

   Try rotating windows the other way:

4. Move the mouse cursor into the root window, and bring up the **WindowOps** menu by holding down the middle mouse button.

5. Drag the cursor down the options until the **Circ-Down** (**Circulate Down**) option is highlighted. Any window that was on the top of the stack is moved to the bottom.

6. Shuffle the windows with the **CircUp** and **Circ-Down** options a few times.

Focusing on One Window

While typing in an **xterm** window, it is easy to bump the mouse and move the mouse cursor, unnoticed, out of the window. All keyboard input while the mouse cursor is out of the window is typed into the wrong window, or lost altogether. If you expect to be typing in one particular window for extended periods, you may want to redirect the inpact *focus* to that window until you are finished typing.

A window has the *focus* when it is the window that receives keyboard input. **X Window** shows that a window has the input focus by highlighting the border of the window. Normally, the focus is on the window in which the mouse cursor is located. Hence, a window becomes highlighted when you move the cursor into it.

You can redirect input focus to a single window, regardless of mouse cursor position, as follows:

1. Bring up the **WindowOps** menu, and select the **Focus** option. Once again, the mouse cursor changes to a pointer.

2. Focus on one window by moving the cursor to the desired window.

3. Press any mouse button.

This causes the input focus to remain in the selected window. The window border is highlighted and remains so even if you move the mouse cursor out of the window.

4. Move the mouse cursor out of the window, and type a command. Notice how all keyboard input goes to the focused window, regardless of the mouse cursor's location.

5. Return to the default focus by selecting the root window as the focus window.

Freezing and Unfreezing Windows

During the execution of some graphics applications, you may need to stop or freeze the display of new keyboard input.

1. Bring up the **WindowOps** menu and select the **Freeze** option. All keyboard input processing is now frozen.

2. Move the mouse cursor into an **xterm** window and type

   ls

   Notice that nothing appears in the window.

3. Move the mouse cursor into another **xterm** window and type

   ps

   Again, no text appears.

4. Move the mouse cursor into the root window and type

   who

5. Move the mouse cursor into a noninteractive application window, such as the **clock** window, and type

date

Freeze has stopped the processing and display of all keyboard input.

6. To see what happened to your typing entries, you will need to unfreeze your windows. Select the **Unfreeze** option from the **WindowOps** menu.

   The **ls** and **ps** commands you typed while the mouse was in **xterm** windows now appear and are executed in their windows. The input typed in the root window and in the **clock** window is lost.

Restarting Your Window Manager

The **Restart** option of the **WindowOps** menu is rarely used. **Restart** kills the current **uwm** process without otherwise affecting your **X** environment. **Restart** then causes the **uwm** startup file

/usr/lib/X11/uwm/system.uwmrc

and any *.uwmrc* file in your Home directory, to be interpreted. These *.uwmrc* files perform a function similar to the one performed for the C shell by your Home directory and system *.cshrc* files.

   The **uwm** program usually runs with a default configuration file that dictates how **uwm** looks and works. Using a *.uwmrc* file, you can add and alter menus and change the function of mouse buttons. **Restart** is particularly useful when testing personalized *.uwmrc* files. Read the UNIX manual entry for **uwm** to see how to write a custom *.uwmrc* startup file.

Killing a Window

You can exit and kill an **xterm** window just as you do when you log out of a normal terminal. From within the window, type **exit**, and you are "logged out" of the **xterm** window, which then disappears.

Alternatively, you can use the **Kill** option in the **WindowOps** menu:

1. Call up the **WindowOps** menu and select the **KillWindow** option. The mouse cursor changes to the pointing hand.

2. Move the pointer to the window you want to kill. Make sure you do not choose the console window. Killing the console window will cause the **X Window** system to shut down, killing all the processes you started in **X Window**.

3. Press and release the middle button. The window vanishes. Any processes running in that terminal window are killed.

Exiting

There are times when you need to kill the window manager, **uwm**. For example, you may want to switch window managers. One way to kill **uwm** is to use **ps** to find the **pid** (process **id**entification number), and then use **kill** to kill the process. (See Chapter 20, "Process Monitoring and Control.")

The **uwm** program itself provides a much simpler method to exit. Simply bring up the **WindowOps** menu, and select the **Exit** option. You will hear the dying beep of the **uwm** program as it exits.

MOVING TEXT BETWEEN WINDOWS

17.4

The **X Window** system allows you to select and then copy text within the same **xterm** window, or between **xterm** windows, using the mouse cursor and buttons. This technique is called *cutting and pasting*.

Pasting Text with the Middle Mouse Button

The **X Window** cut and paste features are used in a variety of ways. The most common uses are to repeat a command in the same or a different window, or to copy text within or to an editor.

1. To practice using the cut and paste features, first open your *practice* file by typing

   vi *practice*

2. Make sure the editor's **autoindent** feature is turned off; in the editor, type

   :se noai

   The **autoindent** text formatting feature of **vi** automatically indents the lines that follow a line beginning with a space or tab. If **autoindent** is turned on, the window text you paste into the editor will not be copied properly.

3. Move the editor cursor to the end of the *practice* file and enter the **vi** append mode by typing

   G

   o

4. Begin the cut and paste process. Move the mouse cursor to the beginning of any line in your *practice* file.

5. Hold the left mouse button down, and move the mouse to the right. Then, move the mouse cursor up some. The region of the screen you have thus outlined, or *cut*, is highlighted.

6. Still holding the left button down, move the cursor to the end of any word within the original line (the line used in Step 4).

7. Release the button.

   You have now copied the highlighted portion of the text into the *cut buffer*. If you made a mistake positioning the mouse cursor, don't worry—just start over again. The cut buffer is a storage space that **X Window** uses to hold a region of text. Initially, it holds nothing. Once you cut a piece of text, the cut buffer holds that piece of text and continues holding it until you either exit **X Window** or cut a new region of text.

8. Now copy the text from the cut buffer by *pasting* it into a new position in the same window. With the mouse cursor anywhere within the same window, push the middle mouse button.

   The region that you cut is copied, or pasted, into position as though it were normal typed keyboard input. If you cut and pasted the text all the way to the end of the line, you copied not only the visible text but also the carriage return as well. When you paste such text into the **xterm** window, the carriage return is included.

Cutting and Pasting into a Different Window

1. Move the mouse cursor into an **xterm** window.

2. Type in the command

   who | sort

3. Use the left mouse button to highlight and select the whole command line.

4. Move the mouse cursor to a new window and press the middle mouse button.

   The command is placed in the second window next to the cursor and executed. When pasting into a terminal window, the text copied from the cut buffer will always be pasted into the position where it would have been displayed had you typed it, regardless of where the answer is located in the window.

Cutting Words with the Left Mouse Button

You can also cut and paste single words:

1. Move the mouse cursor to the middle of a word in your *practice* file.

2. Press the left mouse button twice in quick succession. The entire word from your mouse cursor to the next blank space is highlighted. The *double click*

(two quick left mouse button presses) cuts from the mouse cursor to the end of the word.

3. Paste the word with the middle button.

Cutting Lines with the Left Mouse Button

To cut and paste an entire line:

1. Move the mouse cursor to the middle of a line in your *practice* file.

2. Press the left mouse button three times in quick succession (*triple click*).

   The entire line is highlighted and is now in the cut buffer.

3. Paste the buffer into the desired location.

   Quadruple clicking turns off the highlighting and so nothing will be cut.

Extending Text with the Right Mouse Button

You can cut and paste several lines of text by marking both ends.

1. Move the mouse cursor to a letter in the middle of a line in your *practice* file.

2. Select the letter by pressing and releasing the left mouse button.

3. Move the mouse cursor over another character some distance to the right of the first.

4. Press the right mouse button.

   The section of text from the position of the left mouse button press to the right mouse button press is highlighted. This section has now been copied to the cut buffer. Pressing the right button *extended* the copied region from the single letter to the point of the right button press.

5. Paste the text by pressing the middle mouse button.

   It is a good practice not to copy more than five or six lines at a time because the buffer is limited in size.

6. Leave the **vi** append mode by pressing [Esc].

7. Write and quit the file with the **:wq** command.

8. Check the *practice* file contents using the **more** command.

   In Summary, the mouse buttons have the following meanings in an **xterm** window:

- The left mouse button is used to *save* text into the cut buffer.

- The middle mouse button is used to *place* the saved text into a window.

- The right mouse button is used in conjunction with the left mouse button to *extend* the saved text before it is stored in the cut buffer.

17.5 SOME HELPFUL FILES

For additional information concerning the **X Window** system, consult the manual pages on the following subjects:

uwm	a window manager
X	an overview of the **X Window** system
xclock	the clock program
xinit	the **X Window** system startup program
xset	program that sets **X Window** system options
xsetroot	program that sets root window display options
xterm	the **X** terminal emulator program
xwininfo	program that prints the settings for an **X Window**

17.6 CLEANUP AND EXITING

1. When you exit **X Window**, any unfinished jobs will be killed and their information lost. Therefore, before going further with this exit procedure, make sure you have resolved all pending jobs in all windows. First, type **ps** in one of the windows.

2. Resolve any important unfinished processes—for example, quit editors; wait for sorts and program compilation to run to completion.

3. Move the mouse cursor to the console window and type

exit

The console window and any other **X** applications disappear, and you are returned to the full screen display of your terminal. You have now exited the **X Window** system.

Exercise 17-A

1. What program is usually run to start up the **X Window** system?

_____

2. What program manages look, layout, and functioning of windows in the **X Window** system?

_____

3. What shell command calls up a terminal emulator window?

_____

4. How do you select a command from the **Window-Ops** menu?

_____

5. What is the **WindowOps** menu command that allows you to iconify and move a selected window?

_____

6. What is the easiest way to cut and paste a line of text from one **xterm** window to another?

_____

CONCLUSION

The importance of the **X Window** system is that it provides a standard and extensible graphic interface for modern large screen displays. A standard interface ensures that applications written under the **X Window** system will function in the same manner on any machine running **X**. An extensible interface assures that **X** will be able to incorporate technological improvements as they occur to meet your changing computing needs.

COMMAND SUMMARY

exit
Exits the **X Window** system when typed in the console window. Otherwise, exits the individual window.

xterm
Opens a new **X term**inal emulator window.

xclock
Starts the **clock** application program.

uwm
Starts the **universal** window **manager**, which handles how the windows can be manipulated and displayed.

xinit
Starts an **X Window** session and creates the console window.

xset *arguments*
Modifies how the **X Window** environment works while **X** is running.

xsetroot *arguments*
Modifies the characteristics of the root window while **X** is running.

The Window Options Menu

New Window
Creates a new **xterm** terminal emulator window.

RefreshScreen
Redraws the entire display.

Redraw
Redraws a selected window.

COMMAND SUMMARY *(continued)*

Move
Moves the selected window.

Resize
Changes the size of a selected window.

Lower
Moves the selected window to the bottom of the window stack.

Raise
Moves the selected window to the top of the window stack.

CircUp
Moves the window at the bottom of the window stack to the top.

CircDown
Moves the window at the top of the window stack to the bottom.

AutoIconify
Changes the selected window to an icon, and changes a selected icon to a window. The icon appears concentric with its window. The window appears in its former position.

NewIconify/LowerIconify
A combination of **Iconify** and **Move**. Iconifies a selected window. While the button is held down, the icon may be moved freely about the display without affecting the window's original position. When the icon is selected and the mouse button held down, the iconified window can be moved to a new position.

Focus
Shifts the input focus to a selected window. All keyboard input is processed by that window until the focus is shifted to the root window.

COMMAND SUMMARY *(continued)*

Freeze
Stops the processing of all keyboard input to all windows.

Unfreeze
Restarts the processing of keyboard input to the windows.

Restart
Kills the **uwm** window manager and then restarts it, rereading the system **uwm** startup file and any **uwm** startup file in the user's Home directory.

KillWindow
Kills the selected window.

Exit
Exits the **X Window** system, killing the **X** server, all windows, and any associated processes.

·18·

Basic Text Formatting

The UNIX text processing features are used to format a wide range of documents—from simple memos to complex books. With the UNIX utilities, files created on one system can be transferred to another for modification or printing. By placing specific formatting instructions in a text file, you tell the formatter to start paragraphs, underline words, center text, double space, adjust line length, and so forth.

In this chapter you will use formatting commands to create several basic documents for line printers, as well as for typesetting machines and laser printers. You will also create simple tables, mathematical expressions, and line drawings. The basic formatting program available on UNIX systems is the **nroff** (for **new run off**) utility. The corresponding typesetter program is the **troff** (for **typesetter run off**) utility.

SKILLS CHECK

Before beginning this chapter, you should be able to

- Access and leave the system and execute basic commands (Chapter 1, "Touring the System's Features")

- Create, display, and print files (Chapter 1)

- Create, access, and modify files using the **vi** editor (Chapter 2, "Basic Editing with the Visual Editor")

OBJECTIVE

After completing this chapter, you will be able to

- Use the formatter to accomplish basic formatting of documents, such as skipping lines, indenting, centering text, and changing margins

- Change fonts and point sizes

- Use some basic macros, especially for formatting paragraphs

- Include simple tables in your documents

- Create simple pictures and numeric equations in documents

CASH MEMO   Phone : 506369

আইডিয়াল লাইব্রেরী   **IDEAL LIBRARY**

১৮০/৮১ ঢাকা নিউ মার্কেট   180/81 Dhaka New Market

ঢাকা-১২০৫   Dhaka-1205

No. 52   Date 7. 2. 91.

Name ... ...

Address ... ...

Qnty	Description	Amount	
		Taka	Ps
1'	unit mod easy —	650/	=
		650/	=
	TOTAL		

Books once sold are not taken back.

Any overcharge through error or ignorance is refundable.

Signature

Qty	Description	Taka	Ps
		555	
		535	

TOTAL

FORMATTING A FILE USING NROFF   18.1

The formatting process consists of entering instructions into a text file, and then sending the file to the formatter to have the commands read and executed. The UNIX text formatter, **nroff**, scans text files for formatting commands and performs the actions indicated. The formatter takes some actions by default, that is, in the absence of specific instructions.

Sending a File to the Formatter

1. Log in to your UNIX account.

2. Review the file *practice*, which you created in an earlier chapter. From the shell, type one of the following commands:

   System V:
   pg *practice*

   BSD:
   more *practice*

   The output is simply the file, as you created it, with text lines of varying length.

3. Even though there are no formatting instructions included in the *practice* file, you can still have it formatted using **nroff**'s default formatting operations. Type one of the following shell command lines:

   System V:
   nroff *practice* **I pg**

BSD:
nroff *practice* **| more**

This command line instructs the **nroff** formatter to format the contents of the file *practice*. The output from **nroff** is then sent to the **pg** or **more** utility for screen display.

Examining the Default Format

With the formatted file *practice* displayed on your screen, several operations completed by **nroff** are demonstrated.

Line Length   By default, **nroff** outputs lines that are 6.5 inches long, leaving one-inch right and left margins on 8.5-inch paper.

Filled and Justified   The output no longer has an uneven right margin. The formatter reads the first input line, and then adds as many words as possible from the next input lines (it *fills* the line). Spaces are added between the words in the line to produce output that has a straight right margin (the formatter adjusts or *justifies* the line).

Blank Lines   If you included any blank lines in the input file, there are corresponding blank lines in the output.

Full Page Display   The formatter produces output for whole pages. If there are only a few lines of text, the rest of the page is filled with blank lines. Because the output is a full page and will not fit on the screen, the top of the page will scroll by your screen if you do not pipe the output to **pg** or **more**.

PLACING BASIC FORMATTING COMMANDS IN A FILE

18.2

Examine the input file in Figure 18-1. Formatting commands are interspersed with text in the file.

1. Create a new file named *sample.* Type

    vi *sample*

2. Enter the text, complete with **nroff** commands, from the sample in Figure 18-1.

3. Save the file and exit **vi** with the **:wq** command.

All **nroff** formatting commands are located on lines by themselves and begin with a period in the first character position on the line. This distinctive format allows them to be identified in surrounding text.

When a file is sent to the **nroff** formatter, the formatting instructions are followed. The output is a copy of the file formatted according to the embedded instructions.

In the next few sections of this chapter, you will be comparing the input and output of **nroff**. It is best if you print out exactly what you have included in the specified files as you go along. If you do not have access to a printer, there are printouts included in this chapter.

.ce
Sample nroff Paper
.sp
by John Doe
.br
August 15, 1989
.sp
.ti 5
There are a few rules in using nroff commands.
The command must be
.ul
at the beginning of a line
and it must be the only thing on the line.
The default line length for nroff is 6 1/2
inches leaving 1 inch margins on the left
and right.
The default output is filled and right adjusted,
like this.
.sp
.na
You can also have the output filled but
not adjusted.
This paragraph is filled but not adjusted
by using the .na command.
Notice that the right margin is not completely smooth
though the lines have
been filled.
There may be times,
such as in indented paragraphs of quotes,
where you will want to use this format.

FIGURE 18-1.   Sample paper input file

.sp
.ll *4i*
The line length command, .ll,
changes
the length of the lines of output.
The above command sets the line length at 4 inches.
The no adjust and line length commands will stay in effect
until you change their value
with the same command or with a macro.
.nf
.sp
You can also have the
output formatted the same
as the input by using
the .nf command for no
fill.
This will leave the lines
broken where they are broken in the
input file.
.sp
.fi
You can also
add tables and equations and pictures.

FIGURE 18-1.   Sample paper input file *(continued)*

4. Print out an unformatted copy of the file *sample* by
   typing one of the following commands:

   System V:
   lp -d*dest sample*

BSD:
lpr -P*dest sample*

5. Create a formatted paper version of the file, with one of the following:

System V:
nroff *sample* **I lp -d***dest*

BSD: **nroff** *sample* **I lpr -P***dest*

Figure 18-2 shows the formatted *sample* file.

18.3 FORMATTING LINES

Formatting a document occurs on several different levels. The formatter manipulates individual words and lines. You can also give instructions to format large blocks of text or even the whole document. The next few sections examine commands used to format specific lines in a file.

Centering One Line

One essential formatting feature centers text, such as titles, on a page. Instead of counting characters and inserting spaces yourself, you can have **nroff** center lines for you.

1. Look at the first two lines of the unformatted *sample* document (Figure 18-1). The first line is

.ce

This command **c**enters the next line of text. In formatted output (Figure 18-2) the first line of text is centered on the page.

```
                    Sample   nroff Paper

by John Doe
August 15, 1989
        There are a few rules in using nroff commands.  The  command
must  be at the beginning of a line and it must be the only thing
on the line.  The default line length for nroff is 6  1/2  inches
leaving 1 inch margins on the left and right.  The default output
is filled and right adjusted, like this.

You can also have the output filled but not adjusted.  This para-
graph is filled but not adjusted by using the .na command.  No-
tice that the right margin is not completely smooth though the
lines have been filled.  There may be times, such as in indented
paragraphs of quotes, where you will want to use this format.

The line length command, .ll, changes
the length of the lines of output.  The
above command sets the line length at 4
inches.  The no adjust and line length
commands will stay in effect until you
change their value with the same command
or with a macro.

You can also have the
output formatted the same
as the input by using
the .nf command for no
fill.
This will leave the lines
broken where they are broken in the
input file.

You can also add tables and equations
and pictures.
```

FIGURE 18-2.   Sample paper output

If you have a particularly long title that spans several lines, you can center all the lines by giving the **.ce** command a number argument, such as

.ce *3*

This command centers the next three lines of the input file that follow the command.

Skipping Lines

There are times when you need to include blank lines in output, such as in displays or between paragraphs. One way to produce blank lines in **nroff** output is to leave blank lines in the input file. You can also explicitly instruct the formatter to include blank lines, with the following command:

.sp

The **skip** command (or **space** command, for vertical spacing) instructs **nroff** to leave a blank line at that point in the text.

1. Look at the third line of the unformatted *sample* file. Compare it to the formatted output. There is a blank line after the centered title.

   To skip more than one line at a time, add an argument to the **.sp** command, such as:

   .sp *3*

   This command will skip three lines instead of one.

2. Add this command to the *sample* input file:

   .sp *4*

You will be adding **nroff** instructions to the *sample* file as you go through this section. You may want to format *sample* occasionally, and pipe the output to **pg** or **more**. This will give you the chance see the effect of the **nroff** instructions as you make them.

Breaking Between Lines

1. Find the **.br** command early in the *sample* input file. Notice in the output file that the next line after the **.br** is on a new line. The **.br** tells **nroff** to break the formatting, that is, start a new line. If the first character on a line is a space, a break will also occur.

2. Add a **.br** somewhere in your input file *sample.*

Indenting One Line

The default for left and right margins for **nroff** are set at one inch. There are several ways to indent text from the margins in a document. One way is to indent one line.

1. Examine the input file's fourth line, just after the **.sp** command. This line contains the following **nroff** command:

   .ti 5

The formatted output for the next line is indented five spaces. This **.ti** command temporarily indents only the next line five spaces from the left margin. It operates only on the next line of output. It does not indent the whole paragraph. The second line following the **.ti** command starts at the default margin.

2. Add a new paragraph to the end of the *sample* file, formatting it with **.sp** and **.ti** *5* commands.

Underlining Text

There are several ways to draw attention to text. One way is to use underlining.

1. In the unformatted *sample* file, find the formatting command

   .ul

   Compare this part of the input with the formatted output. Notice where the underlining begins and ends. The line following the **.ul** command is underlined in the formatted output. To underline more than one input line, give the **.ul** command a number argument, such as

   .ul *3*

   This command instructs the formatter to underline the next three lines from the input file.

2. Add additional underlining to your *sample* file.

The **.ul** command results in italics when the output is formatted for some machines.

FORMATTING BLOCKS OF LINES   18.4

The **nroff** commands examined thus far operate on one or more specific lines from the input file. The commands that follow are settings that apply to all text from where they are invoked to the end of the file, or until the settings are changed.

Stopping Line Adjustment

The output from **nroff** is by default filled and right justified. The right margin is a straight line. You can change this.

1. Find the following command toward the middle of the unformatted text:

   .na

   Examine the formatted output, and notice the difference in the right margin before and after the command. Following the **.na** command, the lines are filled, but the right margin is left uneven. This command, **n**o **a**djust, instructs **nroff** not to add spaces to smooth the right margin after filling the text.

2. Pick a place several lines after the **.na** command and type the **.ad** command. This command instructs the formatter to begin adjusting again.

Changing Line Length

You can modify the length of lines that are output by the formatter.

1. Look at the input (unformatted) version of *sample* and find this line:

    .ll *4i*

    This command changes the line length of lines begun after the command to be four inches. Examine the formatted version. The length of the lines (begun after this command) is changed to four inches.

    The value you set for line length remains in force until you change it with another command. The argument *4i* tells **nroff** to change the line length to four inches, but you can also use other units of measure. You can set the value in inches (3.5i), points (38p), centimeters (11c), ens (5n), ems (3m), or Picas (22P).

2. Change the line length of the last paragraph in *sample* to 3.5 inches, by typing

    .ll *3.5i*

Filling and Not Filling Text

1. In the unformatted file, find the commands .nf (nofill) and .fi (fill).

In the output the text between these commands occurs exactly as it was typed in the original file. The **.nf** halts filling, and the **.fi** command restarts it. Because no filling occurs, adjustment is turned off too.

Using Other nroff Commands

The **nroff** formatter accepts a wide set of commands. At the end of this chapter is a summary of **nroff** formatting commands.

1. Try each **nroff** command, individually and in combination, in your *sample* file; become familiar with how they work. Be sure to use the **page offset** (**.po**), line spacing (**.ls**) and **in**dentation (**.in**) commands.

Examining When Formatting Commands Take Effect

Each **nroff** command that you enter instructs the formatter to accomplish a specific action: center, indent, fill, stop filling, and so on. When the commands take effect can sometimes be confusing. Here are some guidelines:

After a **.ce** instruction, the next line is centered.

After a **.ul** instruction, the formatter underlines (or italicizes on a typesetter) the next line read from input. If the next line is one word long, only that word is underlined.

If you instruct the formatter in the middle of a document to change line length (.ll) to seven inches, the formatter first completes filling the line it has started and then begins creating new lines with the new line length.

1. To examine how .ll works, type the following into a file called *format.temp*:

   .ll 3i
   This is a test
   .ll 6i
   that's being entered
   into a file for formatting.
   The question is "When
   does the 6i line length
   take effect?"

2. Have this file formatted and sent to the screen with one of the following commands:

   System V:
   nroff *format.temp* **| pg**

   BSD:
   nroff *format.temp* **| more**

   As the formatter begins to process a line of output, it checks on the variable for line length. In this case, the first line in the file (.ll 3i) sets the line length to three inches. The formatter then reads the next line from the input file. It is text so the formatter starts formatting a line of three inches in length.

After the words *This is a test* are added to the three-inch line, the formatter reads the next line of input, which is an instruction to change the line length to six inches. The variable for line length is then changed to six inches. Additional input lines are read and formatted until the current three-inch line is completed. When the next line of output is started, the line length for that new line is set to six inches.

The same process occurs for indentation and line spacing. The formatter first completes the output line. Then, it checks for new values of the formatting variables (such as indent, line length, and line spacing) before beginning the next line.

Obtaining Paginated Output

If you have sent a file more than one page long to the formatter, there are no header or footer margins in the output. It is just one long page. To paginate output send the output to the **pr** utility.

1. Paginate the *sample* file with one of the following commands:

   System V:
   nroff *sample* **| pr | lp -d***dest*

   BSD:
   nroff sample **| pr | lpr -P***dest*

Exercise 18-A

1. To leave three blank lines between two blocks of text in your file, which **nroff** command would you use?

   _____

2. What is the **nroff** command for changing the line length from five inches to two inches?

   _____

3. To center one line of text in your file, which **nroff** command would you use?

   _____

4. To center three lines of text in your file, which **nroff** command would you use?

   _____

5. Which **nroff** command instructs the formatter to print a block of text exactly as you typed it in?

   _____

6. If you wish to indent one line of text five spaces, which **nroff** command would you use?

   _____

7. When used, what will the **.ul** command underline?

   _____

8. What command line will allow your file *practice* to be formatted and sent to a printer?

   _____

9. When do formatting commands take effect?

_____

USING THE MS MACRO PACKAGE   18.5

The **nroff** commands you have seen so far will accomplish most formatting tasks, but they are limited. There are several features, called *macros*, that combine **nroff** commands in useful ways and add other features not found in **nroff** alone. Macros will do on one line what it would take several **nroff** commands to do. The two most popular macro packages distributed with UNIX are the **mm** and **ms** packages.

Placing Macros in a File

For this section, you will create a short file containing formatting macros.

1. Open a file called *mac_sample* by typing the following command:

vi *mac_sample*

2. Enter the text from Figure 18-3 into the *mac_sample* file.

3. Close the file with **:wq** and print out a formatted copy of this file with one of the following commands:

System V:
nroff -ms *mac_sample* **l lp -d***dest*

.SH
Example of Using Macros to Create Paragraphs
.PP
This is a standard paragraph
produced by .PP.
One line is skipped before it and
the first line is indented.
.LP
This is a left block paragraph produced by .LP.
One line is skipped before it and the first line is not indented.
.LP
The following is a quoted paragraph:
.QP
In UNIX almost everything is treated
as a file.
This includes directories and devices.
.LP
The following is a display listing
of some special features of
UNIX that you have learned about:
.DS
aliases
history
pipes
redirection
.DE
.LP
The following block of text
shifts the display margin to the
right using .RS and .RE.
.RS
UNIX is said to be the most universal operating system.
This means it is on more different computers than any other
operating system.
.RE
.LP
And that's all for this example.

FIGURE 18-3.   Sample macro input file

BSD:

nroff -ms *mac_sample* **l lpr -P***dest*

The **-ms** option tells **nroff** to process the file while interpreting all **ms** macros. All normal **nroff** (lower-case) commands are still interpreted. The output should look like Figure 18-4.

The **-ms** macros provide for headers and footers, so output is in pages. The default line length is changed to six inches.

Creating a Section Header

The **.SH** macro creates a simple, unnumbered heading.

1. Find the **.SH** macro and the line that follows it in the input file. In the corresponding output, the header is underlined and on a separate line.

Defining Paragraphs Using ms Macros

There are several **ms** macros available that produce different styles of paragraphs.

In an earlier section of this chapter, you produced a standard paragraph with **nroff** by typing in the following commands:

.sp
.ti 5

These commands told the formatter to skip one line and then indent the next line of text five spaces. To accomplish the same output using **ms** macros, you need only one command:

.PP

Example of Using Macros to Create Paragraphs

     This is a standard paragraph produced by .PP. One line
is skipped before it and the first line is indented.

This is a left block paragraph produced by .LP. One line is
skipped before it and the first line is not indented.

The following is a quoted paragraph:

     In UNIX almost everything is treated as a file.
     This includes directories and devices.

The following is a display listing of some special features
of UNIX that you have learned about:

       aliases
       history
       pipes
       redirection

The following block of text shifts the display margin to the
right using .RS and .RE.
     UNIX is said to be the most universal operating system.
     This means it is on more different computers than any
     other operating system.

And that's all for this example.

FIGURE 18-4.   Sample macro output

This macro instructs the formatter to skip a line, and to indent five spaces the first line of text that follows the command.

Macro commands follow the same syntax that **nroff** commands follow: each command must begin with a period and be on a line by itself. Like **nroff** commands, some macro commands can accept arguments.

1. Find one of each of the following macros in the input file: **.PP** (Standard Paragraph), **.LP** (Left Block Paragraph), and **.QP** (Quoted Paragraph).

2. Find the corresponding command in the command summary, read its description, and check the result in the output. Pay special attention to differences in the indentation of the paragraphs, depending on which paragraph formatting command you use.

Making Displays

The **ms** macros **.DS** and **.DE** mark the beginning and end of a display.

1. Find the block of text between the **.DS** and **.DE** macros in the input file. Notice the spacing before and after the output display. Displays are not filled or justified, and are kept on one page.

Indenting Blocks of Text

1. In the input file, find the **.RS** (Relative Start or Right Shift) and **.RE** (Relative End) macros. The lines between these macros are indented in the output. These macros may be used to create nested lists.

Using Other ms Macros

1. At the end of this chapter is a table of commonly used **ms** macros. Try each of them in your *mac_sample* file to become familiar with how they work.

Defining Strings

The **ms** macro packages help you format headers and footers.

1. Insert the following lines at the very beginning of the *mac_sample* file:

   .ds RH *History 101*
   .ds CF *Copyright 1990*

   CAUTION: The **define string** (**.ds**) command must be typed in lowercase to distinguish it from the **Display Start** (**.DS**) macro.

2. Format and print the file, using one of the following:

   System V:
   nroff -ms *mac_sample* **| lp -d***dest*

   BSD:
   nroff -ms *mac_sample* **| lpr -P***dest*

The **define string** command is used to specify text in headers at the left (**.ds LH**), center (**.ds CH**), and right (**.ds RH**) and in footers at the left (**.ds LF**), center (**.ds CF**), and right (**.ds RF**).

The string definitions can be changed in the middle of a document. Any change will take effect at the beginning of the following page.

Using Number Registers to Control Formatting

1. Add the following line as the first line in the input file, preceding the string definitions:

.nr *LL 4i*

2. Add some text after the string definitions and before the first paragraph call (**.PP**).

3. Format the file again.

The **.nr** *LL 4i* command does *not* reset the value of the line length variable. The **.nr** *LL* command resets only the value of a **number register** named *LL*. When the first paragraph call is made, the number registers are read, and all appropriate variables such as **ll** (line length) are reset. For that reason, files usually include the **.LP** immediately after the number register lines to read the number registers and reset the variables.

If a file includes the command **.nr** *LL 2i* but no paragraph calls, the number register *LL* is set to two inches, but the line length variable remains at the default six inches set by the **ms** macros.

4. Examine the "ms Macro Strings and Number Registers" section of the Command Summary. Several other number registers are described. Include each and examine their effects.

Comparing ms with Other Macro Packages

There are several different macro packages available with UNIX. The macro packages you are most likely to have are **ms** and **mm**.

This chapter primarily focuses on the **ms** macro package partly because it is relatively easy to use. However, the complexity of the **mm** macro package is balanced by its strength in assisting you to create memorandums because you can easily structure lists and distinguish headings at different levels.

Although each package has its own strengths, some of the tasks that they address do overlap. For example, the **.P** and **.P 1** macros of **mm** are equivalent to the **.LP** and **.PP** macros of **ms**.

To use the **mm** macro package, you type a command line similar to what you enter to call the **ms** package. Use one of the following:

System V:

nroff -mm *filename* **I lp -d***dest*

BSD:

nroff -mm *filename* **I lpr -P***dest*

18.6   TYPESETTING WITH UNIX TROFF

The **nroff** utility works well for sending output to the screen or a line printer. You can also typeset a document, using the related utility **troff**.

With **troff** you can change line spacing, fonts, and type sizes in documents. Unlike **nroff**, the **troff** utility does not send output to standard output, but to a specific typesetter. Therefore, you do not need to redirect the output to a separate spooler such as **lp** to print a file.

1. Print the file *sample* using **troff** by typing the following command:

troff -ms *sample*

   Specific sites often modify this command. Check with an experienced user or your system administrator for the exact syntax at your site.

   This command tells **troff** to process *sample* using the **-ms** macro package, and to place the output in the queue for the typesetter or laser printer.

   If you do not have the **troff** processing package installed on your system, you may receive an error message like this:

```
troff: Command not found.
```

   If you do not have a typesetter or a laser printer, you can send **troff** output to a line printer, but the output will not be significantly different from that of **nroff**. On some systems, you can specify a particular device by adding a **-T***dest* option to the **troff** command. The *dest* represents the destination printer (or typesetter), just as it does in the **lp** or **lpr** commands.

Determining Point Size

The main advantage of a typesetter or laser printer is that you can change the size and type of the font, as well as the spacing between lines, at any point in a document. Although there are default values for many parameters—such as margins, line length, distance between paragraphs, point size, and vertical spacing—you can change the defaults using **number registers**.

1. Open the file *sample,* and set the size of type using the **Point Size** number register. Add the following line at the top of the file:

    .nr PS *12*

    With this line at the beginning of a document, each paragraph call resets the point size to 12 points. Depending on your printer, you can set the number register point size to as large as 48 or 80 points, or even larger.

2. Another value set with a number register is the **Vertical Spacing** of a document. While you have the *sample* file open, type the following line after the point size number register entry:

    .nr VS *14*

    This sets the number register for vertical spacing of the document to 14 points. As a rule of thumb, vertical spacing should be set two points larger than the type size. The **ms** default values are 10 points for type size and 12 points for vertical spacing.

3. Add at least 20 words of text after the **.nr** entries and before the next macro call.

4. Process the file and send it to the typesetter with the appropriate command, such as:

    troff -ms *sample*

5. Compare the new **troff** output with the old **nroff** output for *sample*. Notice that the point size is larger (12 instead of 10) after the first paragraph call. The point size variable that is read when the formatting begins is the default set by **ms**, 10 points. The first paragraph macro resets the point size variable to the same value to which the point size number register is set (12 points). Only after the paragraph reset is the point size actually changed.

Changing Type Font

There are a number of ways to change fonts in a document.

1. Using the **vi** editor, create the file *samplefonts* containing the following:

.nr PS *12*
.nr VS *14*
.nr LL *3i*
LP
.sp
This is an example of
how to change from
.ft B
bold to
.ft I
italics to
.ft R
roman.
Everything stays in the specified font
until the next font command.

.sp
You can also change fonts
within an input line
from \fB*bold to* \fI*italics to* \fR*roman.*
.sp
Or you can specify the font
for an individual word such as
.B *bold*
or
.I *italics*
if you wish.

2. Process the file and send it to the typesetter with the following command:

troff -ms *samplefonts*

The output looks something like this:

This is an example of how to change from **bold to** *italics to* roman. Everything stays in the specified font until the next font command.

You can also change fonts within an input line from **bold to** *italics to* roman.

Or you can specify the font for an individual word such as **bold** or *italics* if you wish.

3. Find the **.ft B, .ft I,** and **.ft R** commands in the input. These instruct the formatter to change fonts. The **.ft**

stands for font, and the **B, I,** and **R** stand for Bold, Italics and Roman, respectively.

4. Find the **\fB, \fI,** and **\fR** commands in the input. These are similar to the **.ft B, .ft I,** and **.ft R** commands, except that they do not have to occur on separate lines. You can change fonts within words using these commands because they change fonts instantly. For example, the input:

\fBn**\fR**umber **\fB**r**\fR**egister

generates

number **r**egister

in the output.

   All of these font-changing commands remain in effect until the next font command.

5. Find the **.B** and **.I** commands in the input. They only change the font of the word following them on the same line. Notice in the output that words on other lines are unaffected by the **.B** and **.I** commands.

   There are usually several fonts available on most systems.

Changing Size Locally

There are two command formats for changing point size that are similar to the command formats for changing fonts. Point size changes and font changes and their different command formats may be intermixed.

1. Using **vi**, create a file called *samplesizes* that includes the following:

   .nr PS *12*
   .nr VS *14*
   This is a sample page
   of how to change **\s+4***point size* **\s-4** *within a line*
   or even within a **\s+6w\s-6***ord.*
   .LP
   This line follows a paragraph call.
   .sp
   .ps *14*
   .vs *16*
   It also illustrates how to
   change point sizes for a block of lines
   until the next paragraph or size change command.
   .LP
   So there is more than one way to
   change point size.

2. Print the *samplesizes* file by typing the command:

   troff -ms *samplesizes*

   The output looks something like this:

This is a sample page of how to change point size within a line or even within a Word.

This line follows a paragraph call.

It also illustrates how to change point sizes for a block of lines until the next paragraph or size change command.

So there is more than one way to change point size.

As you can see, the output changes point size several times. Note these characteristics of the input:

- The default value of the point size is set by **ms** to be 10 points.

- **.nr PS** *12* sets the **P**oint **S**ize **n**umber **r**egister to 12 points. There is no paragraph call; the point size variable has not been reset.

- The first three lines from the input file are set in 10-point type.

- The **.LP** resets the point size variable to the value in the number register, 12 points.

- The next input line is set in 12-point type.

- The **.ps** *14* command changes the point size from its current value to 14 points.

- The text is set in 14-point type until the .LP command resets the point size to the value in the number register, 12 points.

3. The point size is also modified by using the \s + *number* and \s − *number* commands in the input. The \s command adjusts the point size of the subsequent text larger (+) or smaller (-) by the specified number of points.

In summary, point size can be changed using **.ps** *number* macros in the text, **\s+***number* and **\s-***number* for relative changes in line, and **.nr PS** for the number register. A frequent mistake is to forget to modify the vertical spacing whenever point size changes are made.

18.7   CREATING TABLES

One way to spice up a letter or presentation is to display information in a table. Tables are created by sending the file to a preprocessor called **tbl**, which creates **nroff** or **troff** instructions from the table code. The output is then sent to **nroff** or **troff**.

1. Using **vi**, create a file called *table* with the following contents:

   .nr PS *12*
   .nr VS *12*
   .LP
   .ce
   Table 1
   .sp *2*

```
.TS
tab(+);
l c c
l c n.
.sp
\fBDescription + Quantity + Cost\fR
.sp .5
=
Frame + 1 + $200.00
Wheels + 2 + $39.50
Seat + 1 + $18.95
.sp
\fBTotal\fR + + $297.95
.TE
```

2. Enter the following command for a printout of the table:

tbl *table* **| troff -ms**

The table that is output looks like the following:

Description	Quantity	Cost
Frame	1	$200.00
Wheels	2	$39.50
Seat	1	$18.95
Total		$297.95

Examining Table Formatter Code

The following table explains each line of formatter code for the example table.

.TS
This macro tells the **tbl** preprocessor where to start table interpretation.

tab(+);
The default field separator for **tbl** is Tab , which is not easily identified in printed versions of the code. This line changes the field separator to a + character.

l c c
This instruction tells the formatter to format the first line of data with the first column against the left edge, the second column centered, and the third column centered. If this were the only field specification line and had a period at the end, all table entries would be formatted according to this instruction.

l c n.
Format all remaining lines as left, center, and number. Numbers are aligned on the decimal point. The period is essential. It indicates that this is the last field specification line.

.sp
Regular **nroff** commands are followed. In this case, include a blank space (line).

\fB*Description*+*Quantity*+*Cost***\fR**
The first line of data (column headings) is to be bold and consist of the three specified words. They will be positioned at the **l**eft, **c**enter, and **c**enter according to the specification **l c c** above.

.sp *.5*
Leave one half-space.

=
Include two lines the width of the table.

Frame+*1*+*$200.00*
Enter a table entry of three fields with the data provided. The number of entry records is not limited. In this case, three records (Frame, Wheels, and Seat) are included.

.sp
Place a blank line after the body and before the Total line.

\fB*Total***\fR**+ +*$297.95*
Place *Total* in the first column, nothing in the second, and *$297.95* in the third.

.TE
This last macro tells **tbl** to stop processing input until the next **.TS** command.

18.8   FORMATTING EQUATIONS

To format mathematical equations, another preprocessor called **eqn** is used.

1. Using an editor, create a file called *equation* containing the following lines:

   .EQ
   x= {-*b* + − sqrt {*b* **sup** 2 - 4 *a* *c*}} **over**
   2*a*
   .EN

   This is the **eqn** input for the quadratic equation.

2. Print this equation with **troff** by typing the following command line:

   eqn *equation* **| troff -ms**

   Like **tbl**, the command **eqn** preprocesses a file to
   output **troff** commands for math equations. The
   output from **troff** looks like the following:

   $$x = \frac{-b \pm \sqrt{b^2 - 4ac}}{2a}$$

Subscripting and Superscripting

To create subscripts and superscripts in equations, use
the operators **sub** and **sup**. Find

b **sup** 2

in the input. This results in the output:

b^2

Using Square Roots

The square root is formatted using the instruction **sqrt**. Whatever follows the **sqrt** is enclosed in the square root radical.

Grouping Symbols Together

Symbols may be grouped together with curly brackets. Find the symbols

$\{b \ \textbf{sup} \ 2 - 4 \ a \ c\}$

in the input. These symbols occur together in the output under the square root radical. If they had not been grouped with the { }, only the first symbol would have been under the square root radical.

Including Mathematical Symbols

Mathematical symbols may be represented in **eqn** equations. Find **+-** in the input. The output is

$\pm$

Other mathematical symbols allowed in equations include **inf** (**infinity**), **int** (**integration**), **inter** (**intersection**), **prod** (**product**), **sum**, **union**, and **times**. Greek letters are also available, such as *alpha, beta, chi, mu, omega, pi,* and *psi.*

Putting One Part Over Another

The word **over** in **eqn** instructions refers to the line that separates the top part from the bottom part of a fraction. Find the **over** symbol in the input. Notice that it becomes a line in the output. The resulting fraction looks like this in the output:

$$\frac{-b \pm \sqrt{b^2 - 4ac}}{2a}$$

Brackets are used to identify the symbols included in both the numerator and denominator.

18.9   DRAWING PICTURES

As programs are developed using the new window systems (see Chapter 17, "Using the X Windows

System"), creating diagrams with UNIX is becoming easier. Even if you do not have a diagramming or drawing program, you can still create basic drawings with the **pic** preprocessor to **troff**.

Making Objects

The **pic** utility allows you to create three types of objects simply by naming them: the **box**, **circle**, and **ellipse**.

1. Using **vi**, create a file called *sampledraw* containing the following:

```
.PS
box
circle
ellipse
.PE
```

2. Enter the following command to obtain a formatted output of *sampledraw:*

pic *sampledraw* **| troff**

The output looks like Figure 18-5.

3. The three objects you named, **box, circle**, and **ellipse**, are output left to right.

Labeling Objects

It is useful to be able to label the objects you create.

FIGURE 18-5.   Result of making three objects

1. Using **vi**, add the following labels to the objects in *sampledraw*:

   .PS
   box *"box" "one"*
   circle *"circle" "two"*
   ellipse *"ellipse" "3"*
   .PE

2. Print out the result. The objects are labeled as shown in Figure 18-6.

3. The text placed in quotes after an object name in the input file is output as a label inside the object. If more than one quoted string is given for an object, the strings are stacked on top of each other inside the object.

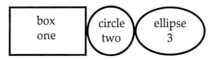

FIGURE 18-6.   Result of labeling three objects

Controlling the Size of Objects

The default sizes of **pic** objects are as follows:

- Box height = .50 inches

- Box width = .75 inches

- Circle radius = .25 inches

- Ellipse height = .50 inches

   These are the sizes of the objects you produced, because you did not specify any changes in their values. You can, however, change the width and height of boxes, the radius of circles, and the height of ellipses. This is done by setting the variables *boxwid*, *boxht*, *circlerad*, and *ellipseht*.

1. Using an editor, add the following to *sampledraw*:

```
.PS
boxwid = .40
boxht = .40
box "box"
circlerad = .20
circle "circle"
ellipseht = .40
ellipse "ellipse"
.PE
```

The new output looks like Figure 18-7. Notice that the objects in the new output are a little smaller than the earlier objects. Also, the box is now a square, because the width and height are equal.

FIGURE 18-7. Result of making three objects smaller

Placing Objects on the Page

Objects may be positioned on the page by moving up, down, to the right, and to the left.

1. Using **vi**, add the following picture to *sampledraw* and print it out:

   .PS
   box *"box"* *"1"*
   move right *1* **from last box**
   box *"box"* *"2"*
   move down *1* **from last box**
   box *"box"* *"3"*
   .PE

   The new picture looks like Figure 18-8.

2. In the input, find the command:

   move right *1* **from last box**

   Notice in the output that box 2 is to the right of the first. The distance between the boxes is one inch, as specified in the **move** command.

Connecting Objects with Arrows and Lines

It is possible to connect **pic** objects with lines and arrows. The commands to do this are **line** and **arrow**.

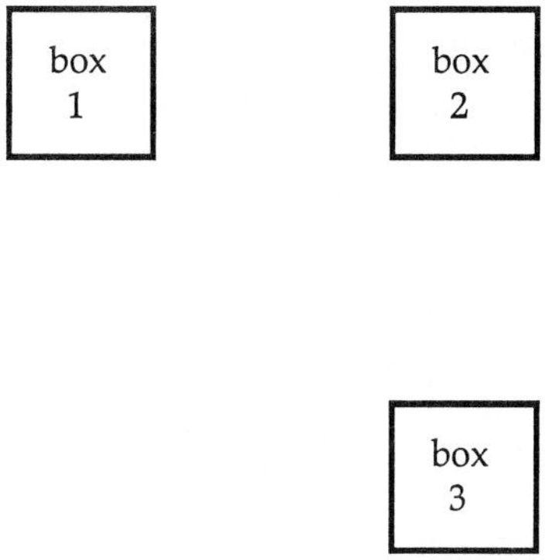

FIGURE 18-8.   Result of placing three boxes on a page

1. Using **vi**, add the following to *sampledraw,* and then print the result.

.PS
box *"box" "1"*
move right *1* **from last box**
box *"box" "2"*
move down *1* **from last box**
box *"box" "3"*
line from right of 1st box to left of 2nd box
arrow from bottom of 2nd box to top of 3rd box
arrow from bottom of 1st box to left of 3rd box
.PE

The new picture should look like Figure 18-9.

The new lines in the input

arrow from bottom of 2nd box to top of 3rd box
arrow from bottom of 1st box to left of 3rd box

request an arrow (a line with an arrowhead on it)

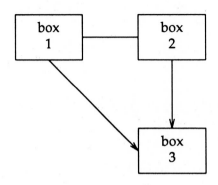

FIGURE 18-9.   Result of connecting three boxes with lines and arrows

going from the bottom of box 2 to the top of box 3 and from the bottom of box 1 to the left of box 3.

Exercise 18-B

1. What macro would you use to create a paragraph with one blank line preceding it, and with no indentation?

_____

2. What dot command would you use to change to bold font?

_____

3. What is the command to change the point size within a line to four sizes larger?

_____

FIGURE 18-10.   Two connected ellipses

4. How would you describe the equation $c^2 = a^2 + b^2$ to **eqn**?

_____

5. How would you describe the picture in Figure 18-10 to **pic**?

_____

In this chapter you have been introduced to some of the basic tools available to you for formatting documents. Some of the tools, such as **pic** and **eqn**, take time to really master. Others like **nroff** are easily learned, and let you create professional-looking documents with relative ease. The use of macro packages can improve productivity and text preparation. Several books are available, as well as manuals that instruct you on advanced use of these programs.

CONCLUSION

COMMAND SUMMARY

Shell Formatting Utility Commands

lp -d*dest filename*
Sends *filename* to the printer for printing without formatting. (On BSD, use **lpr** instead of **lp**.)

nroff filename **| pg**
Formats *filename* and displays it on the screen. (On BSD, use **more** instead of **pg**.)

nroff *filename* **| pr | lp -d***dest*
Formats *filename* and sends it to **pr** for page breaks, and then to the printer for printing. (On BSD use **lpr** instead of **lp**.)

troff *filename*
Formats *filename* and sends the output to a printer (best when printer is a typesetter or a laser printer).

nroff Line Formatting Commands

.sp#
Skips the next # number of lines, leaving them blank. Default is one line.

.br
Breaks between lines.

.ti #
Temporarily indents the following line of text # number of spaces. No default value. Resets to default margin on next line following the indented line.

.ce #
Centers the next # number of lines. Default is one line.

.ul #
Underlines the next # number of lines. Default is one line.

COMMAND SUMMARY (*continued*)

nroff Page Formatting Commands
.po
Controls the page offset. The command **.po** 2*i* offsets the page by two inches from the left edge (default is left edge).

.ls
(Lowercase l) Controls the spacing of the paper. The command **.ls** 2 double-spaces the text (default is single-space).

.in
Indents # number of spaces, beginning with next line, until indent is reset.

.ll
Establishes line length. For instance, **.ll** 5*i* creates five 5-inch lines (default is 6.5 inches).

.nf
Stops filling of text. Must have a **.fi** to resume filling.

.fi
Resumes filling text (normal **nroff** mode).

.na
Stops the adjustment of lines, leaving right margin ragged.

.ad
Starts the adjustment of lines (default mode).

The ms Macros
.SH
Section Heading: using **nroff** underlines headings and places them on separate lines. Using **troff** places heading in bold on separate line.

.PP
Standard Paragraph: skips one line and indents next line five spaces.

COMMAND SUMMARY (*continued*)

.IP
Indented Paragraph: skips one line and indents the entire left margin five spaces.

.LP
Left block Paragraph: skips one line, no indenting.

.QP
Quoted Paragraph: indents equally on both margins.

.DS
Display Start: starts a display with spacing before and after.

.DE
Display End: ends a display started by **.DS**. Keeps display on one page.

.RS
Right shifted Start: starts indented text. Remains indented until **.RE**.

.RE
Right indent End: cancels one **.RS** indent command. Must accompany **.RS**. Placed at the end of display.

.KS
Keep Start: keeps the text between the **.KS** and the **.KE** on the same page. If the page would normally break within the surrounded text, the text is moved to the next page.

.KE
Keep End: ends the Keep Start.

.UL *word*
UnderLines the *word*. Only accepts one word per **.UL**.

.BX
Puts the *word* in a BoX.

COMMAND SUMMARY (*continued*)

ms Macro Strings and Number Registers

.ds LH *string*
Sets the Left Header to be *string*.

.ds CH *string*
Sets the Center Header to be *string*.

.ds RH *string*
Sets the Right Header to be *string*.

.ds LF *string*
Sets the Left Footer to be *string*.

.ds CF *string*
Sets the Center Footer to be *string*.

.ds RF *string*
Sets the Right Footer to be *string*.

.nr FM *value*
Sets the bottom or Foot Margin register to *value*.

.nr HM *value*
Sets the top or Head Margin register to *value*.

.mr LL *value*
Sets the Line Length register to *value*.

.nr PS *value*
Sets the Point Size register to *value*.

.nr VS *value*
Sets the Vertical Spacing register to *value*.

COMMAND SUMMARY (*continued*)

Font Changing Commands

.ft I

Changes the font to **I** until a similar command changes it.

.I *word*

Changes the font of *word* without affecting other text. To change more than one word, surround with quotes (**.I** *"another word"*).

\fI

Changes font to **I** until a similar command changes the font. Unlike the commands above, this command can be used within a line or even within a word.

NOTE: For the three commands above, **I** (for Italics) could be replaced by **B** (for Bold) or **R** (for Roman).

Point Size Changing Commands

/s+*number*

Sets the point size to the current point size plus *number*.

/s−*number*

Sets the point size to the current point size minus *number*.

·19·

Using the UNIX
Reference Manual

The great power of the UNIX system is directly
reflected in the large number and diversity of UNIX
utility programs, application programs, and programming support libraries available to the user. These
diverse UNIX facilities are too mumerous to remember. Consequently, the UNIX Reference Manual is an
indispensable part of the UNIX system. It contains
detailed documentation of the use and function of all
standard utility programs, many application programs and libraries, as well as information on UNIX
system files and system programming libraries. The

Reference Manual also contains supplementary information on related special files and commands for each entry. In addition, examples and error conditions are often provided.

A hardcopy version of the Reference Manual is provided with most systems and can usually be found in terminal rooms or work areas. On many systems, the entire UNIX Reference Manual is available on-line.

SKILLS CHECK

Before beginning this chapter, you should be able to

- Access and leave the system (Chapter 1, "Touring the System's Features")

- Execute basic shell commands (Chapter 1)

- Use several shell commands in combination (Chapter 1)

- Use simple regular expressions with **grep** (Chapter 4, "Using Basic UNIX Utilities")

OBJECTIVES

Upon completion of this chapter, you will be able to

- Display the on-line manual pages for commands and files

- Search for specific on-line manual pages by keyword or regular expression

- Find related manual entries through cross-referencing

- Use the permuted index found in many hardcopy versions of the Reference Manual

ACCESSING THE ON-LINE MANUAL   19.1

On-line Reference Manual pages can be displayed on your terminal screen just as they would appear in hardcopy form. If your system does not have the on-line manual, you may want to skip this first section.

Displaying a Manual Entry

From the shell, you can request that individual manual entries be written on the terminal screen.

1. Examine the on-line manual entry for the **cat** utility by typing

man *cat*

2. A portion of the first page of the output is shown here:

```
CAT(1)          UNIX Programmer's Manual          CAT(1)


NAME
   cat - concatenate and print files

SYNOPSIS
   cat [ -u ] [ -n ] [ -s ] [ -v [-e] [-t] ] file  . . .

   . . .
```

On most systems, the **man** command displays each manual entry one screenful at a time. If your system does not provide a screen-by-screen display of the manual, you can explicitly include the appropriate utility necessary for this function by typing

System V:
man *cat* | **pg**

BSD:
man *cat* | **more**

Examining the Entry

Every manual entry follows the same basic organization. The top line of the output includes the name of the utility, followed by a number enclosed in parentheses that refers to the section of the manual where the entry is located. Then capitalized words such as NAME and SYNOPSIS introduce the various sections of the entry.

1. Advance the display for **cat** to the next page by pressing [Spacebar].

2. Observe that additional headings and text are presented. Continue to examine the manual entry.

   Because **man** utilizes either the **pg** or **more** utility to display its output, all of the pattern search and display capabilities of **pg** and **more** are available to you.

3. You may be familiar with the **dir** command from the DOS world. To see if UNIX has a similarly named command, type

man *dir*

The **man** command responds with this message:

```
No manual entry for dir
```

This message does not necessarily mean there is no **dir** command. It does mean there is no entry in the manual for **dir**.

To search for and display a manual entry with the title *title* type

man *title*

If there is no manual entry with a title *title* you entered, you will get an error message. For commands the *title* is the command's name.

4. Examine the manual entries for a few of the commands you have used, such as **date**, **who**, **vi**, and **cp**.

Entries in the manual tend to follow the structure of a newspaper story: Usually the most important information comes first. By reading just the first few portions, you can find out most of what you need to know about that utility.

Examining the Sections of the Manual

Manual entries are grouped into a number of categories, called sections. There are eight standard sections
numbered 1 through 8, plus a few optional sections
that may be on your system such as *n, l,* and *x* for *new,
local,* and *experimental,* respectively. Descriptions of
the most common sections are summarized in Table
19-1.

Accessing Manual Entries from a Specific Section

Sometimes an entry appears in more than one section
of the UNIX Reference Manual.

1. Examine the manual entry for **chmod** by typing

   man *chmod*

   Among the entries listed under SEE ALSO is *chmod(2).*
   This refers to a listing for **chmod** in Section 2 of the
   Reference Manual. Section 2 contains the descrip-
   tion of UNIX system calls.

2. Try to examine the second entry for **chmod**. Type

   man *chmod*

   The **man** command again displays only the first
   manual entry for a utility. An additional argument
   is needed to instruct **man** to display the other
   chmod entries.

TABLE 19-1.   UNIX Reference Manual Categories

SECTION	SYSTEM V	BSD
1	Basic utilities to be invoked by users or programs at command level interpretation	Basic utilities to be invoked by users or programs at command level interpretation
1C	Commands for communication with other systems	Commands for communication with other systems
1G	Commands used primarily for computer graphics or computer aided design	Commands used primarily for computer graphics or computer aided design
1M	Basic administration utilities	
2	System calls, the C language interface, error numbers, and signals	System calls, the C language interface, error numbers, and signals
3	The subroutine libraries available, usually in /lib /usr/lib	C Programming Language library functions
3C	C Programming Language Libraries	
3S	Standard I/O routines	Standard I/O routines
3M	Mathematical library routines	Mathematical library routines
3N	Networking support library	Internet library functions
3X	Specialized libraries	Minor libraries and miscellaneous run-time facilities
3F	FORTRAN Programming language libraries	FORTRAN programming language libraries
4	File formats	Special files and hardware support
4N		Network interfaces
4P		Protocol usage
4F		Protocol families
5	Miscellaneous facilities	File formats
6	Games	Games
7	Special files	Miscellaneous documentation
8	System maintenance procedures	System maintenance and operations
8C		Network related services
8V		Device dependent procedures
L		Locally installed software
N		New software
X		Experimental software

3. To look at the Section 2 entry for **chmod,** type

man 2 *chmod*

The entry describing the system call **chmod** appears on your screen.

In summary, the command to look up an entry in a specific manual section is:

man *section title*

where *section* is the section number and *title* is the title of the entry.

Determining What a Manual Section Contains

Most sections (and some subsections) of the manual include a special entry that describes the contents of the section.

1. To find out what Section 1 of the manual contains, type

man 1 *intro*

2. You will see output like this:

```
INTRO(1)       UNIX Programmer's Manual       INTRO(1)


NAME
  intro - introduction to commands

DESCRIPTION
  This section describes publicly accessible commands, listed
  in alphabetical order. Certain distinctions of purpose are
  made in the headings:

  (1)  Commands of general utility.

  (1C) Commands for communication with other systems.

  (1G) Commands used primarily for graphics and computer-aided design.
  . . .
```

This entry is the *intro*duction to Section 1 of the manual. The *intro* entries are written in the same format as other manual entries. They contain descriptions of the section and any of its subsections, along with references to other useful information.

Not all sections (or subsections) will have an *intro* entry. The inclusion of an *intro* for an on-line manual section is most often determined by the space considerations on your machine.

DESCRIBING THE ELEMENTS OF MANUAL PAGES

19.2

In this section you will examine a manual entry in depth.

1. Display the manual entry for the **cat** utility again by typing

man *cat*

2. Examine the output:

```
CAT(1)            UNIX Programmer's Manual            CAT(1)


NAME
    cat - concatenate and print file

SYNOPSIS

    cat [ -u ] [ -n ] [ -s ] [ -v [-t] [-e] ] files . . .

DESCRIPTION
    Cat reads each file in sequence and writes it
    on the standard output. Thus cat file displays
    the file on the standard output, and cat
    file1 file2 > file3 concatenates the first
    two files and places the result in the third.

    If no input file is given, or if the argument -
    is encountered, cat reads from the standard
    input file.

OPTIONS
    -b   Used with the -n option;  omits the line
         numbers from blank lines.

    -e   Used with the with the -v option;  displays
         a $ character at the end of each line.

    -n   Displays the output lines preceded by line
         numbers, numbered sequentially from 1.

    -s   Deletes multiple adjacent empty lines so
         that the output is displayed single-spaced.
```

```
    -t    Used with the -v option;   displays
          tab characters as ^I.

    -u    Makes the output completely unbuffered.

    -v    Displays non-printing characters so
          that they are visible.  For example,
          CTRL-X is printed as ^X;  the delete
          character (octal 177) is printed as ^?.
          Non-ASCII characters (with the
          high bit set) are printed
          as M- (for meta) followed by the
          character of the low 7 bits.

 WARNING
   Command formats such as
     cat file1 file2 >file1
   will destroy the original data in file1
   before it is read.

 SEE ALSO
   cp(1), ex(1), more(1), pr(1), tail(1)
```

The headings (NAME, SYNOPSIS, etc.) are generally in the order shown in this section, but there may be some variations in your system.

The Header

The first line of the output is the header. Its exact format varies among UNIX installations. However, the header usually includes the name of the manual entry, and a number enclosed in parentheses that indicates the manual section from which the entry was taken.

In our example manual entry you see the header line:

```
CAT(1)      UNIX Programmer's Manual      CAT(1)
```

NAME Line

Look at the first heading following the header line:

```
NAME
  cat - concatenate and print file
```

This line consists of the primary name of the command, and then any alternate name of the command, followed by a brief description of the command's function. This line is the table of contents entry from the hardcopy version of the manual.

SYNOPSIS Section

The SYNOPSIS section summarizes the *usage* of the command described by the entry.

```
SYNOPSIS
  cat [ -u ] [ -n ] [ -s ] [ -v [-t] [-e] ] files...
```

In the case of a command like **cat**, the usage is the proper method of entering the command, including any valid arguments the command may take.

Throughout the manual, the square brackets [ ] are used to denote optional arguments. If a command has many options, the word *options* appears in the brackets instead of a list of the actual options.

Following the options is the word *file. . .* or *files,* indicating that one or more filenames may follow the **cat** command at that position.

Some manual entries are for important system files. In these cases, the SYNOPSIS consists of the full pathname of the file. For example:

1. Look at the entry for the *termcap* database in Section 5 of the manual by entering

   man 5 *termcap*

   The SYNOPSIS section for *termcap* consists of this line:

   /etc/termcap

   If the entry is a programming library function, the SYNOPSIS may include the file that contains the entry and any additional information you need to use the file.

2. Examine the UNIX C Programming Language library routine **rmdir**, by entering

   man 2 *rmdir*

   The **rmdir** function is the C language subroutine equivalent of the UNIX **rmdir** shell utility. You see:

```
RMDIR(2)       UNIX Programmer's Manual       RMDIR(2)

  NAME
    rmdir - remove a directory file

  SYNOPSIS
    rmdir(path)
    char *path;
    . . .
```

The SYNOPSIS consists of the proper method of using the function from within a C program.

DESCRIPTION Section

Return to the manual entry for **cat** and examine the next heading, DESCRIPTION. This section of the manual entry is invariably the longest, and discusses the entry in detail. In this case, DESCRIPTION outlines the correct methods of using the **cat** command and the expected results.

OPTIONS Section

The OPTIONS section describes the function and use of each option available to a given utility. In this example, you can see that **cat** accepts the **-n** and **-s** options. These options are used together, in the following:

cat -ns */etc/termcap*

This command asks **cat** to display the */etc/termcap* file, with the lines numbered and separated by, at most, a single blank line.

On some systems, the list of command options will appear under DESCRIPTION.

WARNINGS Section

There are often dangerous aspects of utilities. In the example of **cat**, the WARNINGS section cautions users about using **cat** with re-direction:

```
Command formats such as
  cat file1 file2 >file1
will destroy the original data in file1 before it
is read.
```

The WARNINGS section contains information on common usage mistakes, and tips for avoiding difficulties.

SEE ALSO Section

Here you will find references to other related entries in the manual, and occasionally to technical papers, journal articles, or books. For the **cat** entry there are cross-references to the entries for *cp(1)* and *pr(1)*, among others. As you saw in the heading for **cat**, the number enclosed in parentheses following each of these referenced entries indicates the manual section containing that entry.

FILES Section

The FILES section lists the names of files associated with the entry. It sometimes includes a short description of each file's use. For example, the manual entry for the **at** utility lists the files */usr/lib/atrun* and */usr/spool/at* in its FILES section.

DIAGNOSTICS Section

This section describes the more unusual diagnostic messages a utility may produce.

BUGS Section

Information about the known bugs and deficiencies of the utility or command, and occasionally a method of correcting the problem is listed in this section. Because the material covered in the WARNINGS and BUGS sections is topically similar, on many systems the two sections are combined under the BUGS heading. On systems that use both headings, the information presented in each section is determined by intent. WARNINGS deals with problems of improper usage (or sometimes improper design) of a command. BUGS deals with program design deficiencies, and describes where a program can deviate from its expected behavior.

Other Sections

Most manual entries contain just the following headings:

Name
Synopsis
Description
Options
Examples
Files
See Also
Diagnostics
Warnings
Bugs

Occasionally you will encounter other topic headings, which will be self-explanatory.

USING THE SYSTEM V HELP UTILITIES   19.3

System V UNIX provides interactive assistance for the on-line manual pages. Like an experienced teacher, the System V **help** facilities provide assistance for all levels of users—from novice to expert.

Getting Started with help

The **help** utility is not a single command, but an *environment* in which you may access the various on-line user assistance databases.

1. To enter the System V UNIX on-line help environment, type

   help

   The screen clears and displays the following:

   ```
   help:   UNIX System On-Line Help

   choices    description
      s        starter:  general information
      l        locate:   find a command with
                          keywords
      u        usage:    information about commands
      g        glossary:  definitions of terms

      r        Redirect to a file or a command
      q        Quit
   ```

   ```
   Enter choice >
   ```

   This is the top-level **help** menu. From this menu the full repertoire of help choices is accessible. The help user interface is *menu-driven*. The possible commands and arguments in the help environment are presented in a list at each level of **help** menu. Entering the appropriate letter or word at the *Enter choice* > prompt displays information about the corresponding command, command option, or argument.

2. At the menu prompt, type

   q

   You exit **help** and are returned to the shell.

Using the starter

The **starter** utility offers the novice UNIX user a guide to helpful on-line information about the UNIX system.

1. To initiate the **starter** from the top-level help menu, type

s

You see the following information:

```
starter:  General UNIX System User Information

    starter provides general information for
    system users.  Enter one of the choices be-
    low to proceed.

        choices      description

          c          Commands and terms to learn first
          d          Documents for system users
          e          Education centers for UNIX
                     System training
          l          Local UNIX System information
          t          Teaching aids available on-line

          r          Redirect to a file or a command
          q          Quit

Enter choice >
```

2. Examine the entry for *Commands and terms to learn first* by typing

c

You see:

```
Commands & Terms to Learn First

    The most basic UNIX system commands and terms
    are listed here.  You should understand these
    commands and terms before continuing.

        UNIX Commands       |       UNIX Terms
                            |
        cat   ed    mv      |       argument   password
        cd    grep  pwd     |       command    path name
```

```
chmod  ls    rm    |    directory  program
cp     mail  who   |    file       shell
date   mkdir       |    file system syntax summary
                   |    login       UNIX system

For information about a command or term,
     type: q    to quit.
     type: usage UNIX_command or glossary UNIX_term
     where: UNIX_command and UNIX_term come from
            the lists above.

-----------------------------------------------------------
Choices:  s (restart starter), r (redirect), q (quit)
-----------------------------------------------------------
```

3. Restart the **starter** utility by entering

s

4. Examine the other subject headings for the **starter**.

5. Quit the **starter** by typing

q

    You can also begin the **starter** directly from the shell, by typing

help *starter*

or

starter

Finding the Usage for Utilities

1. Reenter the help environment with

help

2. Start the **usage** command from the top-level **help** menu by entering

u

The system displays the following:

```
usage:  Information about Commands

  usage provides information about specific UNIX
  System commands.

    Within usage, double quotes " " mark options or literals,
  and angle brackets < > mark argument variables.

    You should see starter for basic UNIX system commands and
  terms before going on to anything else.

  Enter one of the choices below to proceed.

      choices         description

   UNIX_command     Obtain usage information
                    for a command

       p            Print a list of commands

       r            Redirect to a file or a
                    command
       q            Quit
Enter choice >
```

3. Examine the usage of the **cat** command, by entering after the prompt:

cat

The **usage** command responds by displaying:

```
cat:  Description

Syntax Summary:  cat [-su] [ -v [-et] ] [file_name . . .]

        where:  file_name is the name of a file.

Description:
    cat is shorthand for "concatenate."  Use cat to send the
    contents of a file to standard output.  If more than one
    filename is used, cat prints each file in sequence on
    the standard output.  cat echos standard input if
    you do not list a filename or if you use "-" as an argument
    See also: cp(1), pg(1) and pr(1) for commands with
    functions similar to cat.

-------------------------------------------------------------------
Choices:  o (options), e (examples), UNIX_command, p (print list),
r (redirect), q (quit)
-------------------------------------------------------------------
```

This is followed by the prompt

```
Enter choice >
```

The **usage** command prints an abbreviated description of the chosen command. This description is similar to the DESCRIPTION, SEE ALSO, and SYNOPSIS sections of the manual entry. The usage display gives the correct form for calling the command, the command's options, and a brief description of what the command does. To produce a complete list of options to the command, enter the **e** command. To display sample uses of the command, enter **o** at the prompt while usage is displayed.

4. Investigate the usage of the **sort**, **help**, and **usage** utilities by typing the name of each utility at the prompt.

5. Examine the examples and options for these commands. For example, to see a list of the utilities documented by the **usage** utility, enter

   p

   The usage utility prints out all of the commands that are in the **help** database.

6. Quit the **usage** utility.

   You can also access the **usage** utility from the shell by entering

   help *usage*

   or

   usage

Getting Definitions from the Glossary

As new ideas and inventions appear in our culture, names are designed to identify each new artifact. Frequently a name is borrowed from an existing language; sometimes a new word is created to explain the idea or invention. Either way, the English language is extended. No human endeavor is immune to the creation of specialized languages or *jargon*.

   The computer sciences suffer particularly from an overabundance of jargon. Read any piece of UNIX documentation, and you will find at least one term that is not from standard English. To explain the vagaries of "UNIX English," System V provides an on-line **glossary** of UNIX terms.

1. Restart the **help** utility.

2. From the top-level help menu, start the **glossary** by entering

g

The screen displays the following:

```
glossary:  UNIX System Terms & Symbols

     Enter any of these terms to obtain its definition.  Within
  each definition, important terms defined elsewhere in the
  glossary are enclosed in double quotes ("") and footnoted
  on the bottom of the screen.
  " "                                    #
  $                                      &
  ⊥                                      .
  ?                                      ▯
                                         "
  |                                      3B2
  3B20                                   3B5
  ASCII                                  ASCII collating sequence
  CPU                                    CPU priority
  EOF                                    $HOME
  HOME                                   HOME directory

  ----------------------------------------------MORE--------------
  Choices: UNIX_term (from list), r (redirect), q (quit), n (next pg)
  ----------------------------------------------------------------
  Enter choice >
```

The list of terms defined in the **glossary** spans many pages.

3. You can step through the pages of entries by typing

n

after each prompt in the **glossary** menu.

4. Examine the entry for *manual page,* which is one of the *UNIX terms* in the list. From the **glossary** menu, type *manual page*

Or enter from the shell:

help glossary *manual page*

or

glossary *manual page*

The **glossary** displays the following information about the term *manual page:*

```
 manual page:  section number

A manual page is a page or pages from the UNIX System User's,
Programmer's,  or Administrator's Reference Manual that
describes a command and lists its "arguments"*.  These
manuals are divided into sections.  Each section has a
section number and the numbering is continuous from one
manual to the next.  Commands are commonly referred to
by name and section number.  For  example, profile(2) refers
to the manual page for profile in section 2 of the manual.
If no section number is listed, you should assume section 1.

* defined in the glossary


---------------------------------------------------------------
Choices: UNIX_term (from list), g (restart glossary),
         r (redirect), q (quit)
---------------------------------------------------------------
Enter Choice >
```

Notice that the **glossary** entry for *manual page* refers you to another entry *argument* in the on-line **help** database, the *asterisk* (*) character.

5. Examine the entry for *argument* by typing the *UNIX _ term:*

argument

Not only does the **glossary** contain information about UNIX terminology, but also general information about computer technology, system hardware, and explanation of UNIX special characters such as *, ! , and ^ .

Restarting the **glossary** will redisplay the **glossary** list from the beginning. You can also access the **glossary** from the shell by entering

help glossary

or

glossary

19.4   SEARCHING THE MANUAL DATABASES FOR KEYWORDS

The on-line manual consists of a number of files in the */usr/man* directory (and in the case of System V, the */usr/lib/help* directory). On many systems you can have the computer search the on-line manual database for all entries containing a keyword of your choice. Like any reference book, it is easier to search the manual's table of contents than to search the entire book for a specific piece of information.

Using Keywords to Search the Manual

UNIX provides a utility for referencing manual entries through keyword pattern matching. Descriptions of each entry in the manual's table of contents, or in a special on-line **help** database, are searched for occurrences of the keyword. All entry descriptions that contain a match for that keyword are returned for inspection. This process is similar to that of the **grep** utility. This capability is not available on all systems.

Examining the Keyword Search Process

1. Suppose you forgot the command to send a file to the printer. Do a keyword search for the word *printer* to see which entries relate to printers. Type one of the following:

   System V:
   locate *printer*

   BSD:
   apropos *printer*

   or

   man -k *printer*

   Among the entries listed, you will find either the **lp** command for System V, or the **lpr** command for BSD. Both commands send files to a line printer for printing.

2. Do similar searches using the keywords *move, help,* and *file.*

3. If you are using System V UNIX, search the table of contents for all lines containing the word *copy* by typing

locate *copy*

You see something like the following:

```
Commands found using copy:

The cp (copy) command
The cpio (copy in, copy out) command
The mv (move) command
The tee command
```

The System V **locate** command looks for *copy* in a special on-line database of keywords. Each entry in the manual has a set of keywords associated with it. For example, the **cp** command has the following set of entries in the database:

key = 'copy'   echo 'The cp (copy) command'
key = 'move'   echo 'The cp (copy) command'
key = 'duplicate' echo 'The cp (copy) command'
key = 'link'   echo 'The cp (copy) command'
key = 'rename'   echo 'The cp (copy) command'

In all cases, the pattern match must be exact. For instance, the command **locate** *cop* will not produce the same output as **locate** *copy.* Consequently, you must be careful to use complete words.

4. On BSD systems, search the table of contents for the word *copy* by typing

man -k *copy*

or

apropos *copy*

You will see:

```
arff, flcopy (8)            - archiver and copier for floppy
bcopy, bcmp, bzero, ffs (3)- bit and byte string operations
cp (1)                      - copy
dd (1)                      - convert and copy a file
fork (3F)                   - create a copy of this process
rcp (1C)                    - remote file copy
uucp, uulog (1C)            - UNIX to UNIX copy
```

Each of these table of contents entries contains the word *copy,* either in the title or in the brief description that follows. You will find the output from the search to be familiar; the lines are taken from the NAME section for each of the returned entries. Both the **man -k** and **apropos** commands perform a pattern-matching search of the NAME section for each related entry in the on-line manual.

On BSD systems, the keyword may be any combination of letters. Notice that the first two entries do not contain *copy* as a separate word; instead, *copy* is part of the title word. When doing a keyword search, **apropos** searches for all instances of the string *copy,* whether or not it is a word.

Titles separated by a comma indicate shared entries. If you examine the entry for *arff,* you also see the entry for *flcopy,* and vice versa. The two commands are identical in all respects except name.

Using More Than One Keyword

You may use more than one keyword argument during a keyword search of the table of contents.

1. Search for a utility that identifies duplicated or repeated lines (the two words are interchangeable). Type one of the following commands:

System V:
locate *duplicate repeat*

BSD:
apropos *duplicate repeat*

You get a display similar to the ones shown here.

On System V:

```
Commands found using duplicate repeat:

The cp (copy) command
The crontab (chronological table) command
The echo command
The ln (link) command
The tee command
The uniq (unique) command
The xargs (execute arguments) command
```

On BSD:

```
dup, dup2 (2) - duplicate a descriptor
uniq (1)      - report repeated lines in a file
yes (1)       - output string repeatedly
```

All manual entries that have any of the keywords you specified associated with them appear in the output. In System V, a separate data base is searched. In BSD, the NAME section is searched. This is particularly useful in a search for a keyword with common synonyms. In the above examples, you can see the **uniq** utility finds repeated lines in a file. If you had searched only for the keyword *duplicate,* you would not have found **uniq**.

In summary, to do a keyword search, type the appropriate command:

System V:
locate *keyword(s)*

BSD:
apropos *keyword(s)*

Exercise 19-A

1. What command displays the manual entry for **man?**

_____

2. There are three entries titled **sleep** in Sections 1, 3, and 3F respectively. How would you examine the entry in Section 3?

_____

3. What command would you enter to search the table of contents for all lines containing the word *file?*

_____

19.5   DETERMINING PROPERTIES OF KEYWORD MATCHING

You can perform more complex keyword searches by combining a keyword search command with other utilities.

Searching for Combinations of Keywords

You can use either **man -k** or **apropos** on BSD systems, or **locate** on System V machines, to search for lines containing one keyword, but you cannot search for a specific line containing several keywords. However, on BSD systems, by sending the output of a search to the **grep** utility, you can retain only the lines that contain several keywords.

1. Find all lines in the table of contents that mention either the word *receive* or the word *send* by typing one of the following:

   System V:
   locate *send receive*

   BSD:
   apropos *send receive*

   The lines in the table of contents containing the words *send* or *receive* appear on your screen.

2. On BSD systems, you can distill the **apropos** output further by sending the output of the multiple keyword search to the **grep** utility to find the lines

containing both words. To search the table of contents for lines containing *both* the words *receive* and *send,* type

apropos *receive* **| grep** *send*

The **apropos** and **locate** commands produced all entries with descriptions containing the pattern *receive.* The output of the **apropos** utility is then sent to the **grep** utility, which retains only those descriptions containing the pattern *send.* Hence, only the lines that contain both the word *send* and the word *receive* are selected. Here is a sample output:

```
binmail (1)   - send or receive mail among users
mail (1)      - send and receive mail
```

On BSD, to perform a keyword search for lines containing a combination of keywords, use this command:

apropos *keyword1* **| grep** *keyword2* **| grep** *keyword3* . . .

As with any other UNIX shell command, the usefulness of the BSD manual searching utilities can be enhanced with the many powerful UNIX text processing utilities, such as **awk, sed** and **grep**.

Because of the way System V performs its keyword search, the keywords do not appear in the output of the **locate** utility. Therefore, further keyword searches may not be possible in System V.

Searching a Specific Manual Section on BSD

On BSD systems, you can search one specific section of the manual by using **grep** and regular expressions.

1. Search the table of contents for lines containing the word *system,* and restrict the output to lines from Section 1. Type

apropos *system* **| grep** *"(1.*)"*

2. The output is similar to the following:

```
hostid (1)    - set or print identifier of
                current host system
hostname (1) - set or print name of current host system
msgs (1)      - system messages
sendbug (1)   - mail a system bug report to bugs@isi
sysline (1)   - display system status on status line
                of a terminal
time (1)      - print a command's elapsed, system and user times
tip, cu (1C) - connect to a remote system
uptime (1)    - length of time system has been up
users (1)     - compact list of users who are on the system
who (1)       - who is on the system
```

This output is considerably shorter than what would be produced by a keyword search through the entire table of contents for the word *system.*

To limit a search to a specific section of the manual, use the command:

apropos *keyword(s)* **| grep** *"(section.*)"*

where *section* is the on-line manual section you want to search.

Avoiding Long Keywords on BSD

You have learned how the **man** utility can be used to do keyword searches through the table of contents. You have also seen how the pattern-matching capabilities of **grep** can be used to augment the simpler search capability of **man**. But even this method can miss certain entries that ought to be included in the pattern.

1. Try a keyword search for *unique.* Type

apropos -k *unique*

2. Observe that the UNIX utility **uniq** does not appear in the output:

```
gethostid, sethostid (2) - get/set unique identifier
                           of current host
mktemp (3)               - make a unique file name
```

This keyword search for *unique* did not include the utility **uniq** among the matches, because the word *unique* does not appear anywhere in the table of contents line for **uniq**. The word *uniq* does appear, as the name of the utility, but the keyword search only identifies the exact match between the keyword and the text in the table of contents line. Therefore, if you had used *uniq* as the keyword you gave **man,** then the entry for **uniq** would have matched and thus been included in the output.

On BSD systems, use as short a keyword as possible. You may have to scan through more output, but you will have a better chance of finding what you are looking for.

19.6   BROWSING THROUGH THE ON-LINE MANUAL

The **man** utility can be used for looking randomly through the Reference Manual. Investigating the manual this way can uncover remarkable relationships between utilities. This is one of the best ways to increase your knowledge of the UNIX system.

1. Look up the manual entry for the **grep** utility in Section 1. Type

   man *1 grep*

2. Scan through the entry and look for the SEE ALSO header. One of the entries there is *sed(1)*.

3. Examine the manual entry for **sed** in Section 1 by typing

   man *1 sed*

   The **sed** utility is a stream editor that copies standard input into standard output. Its most common use is pattern search and replacement.

4. Look for the SEE ALSO header again. One entry listed is *awk(1)*.

5. Look up the entry for **awk** in Section 1. Type

man *1 awk*

You will find that **awk** is a pattern scanning and processing language. Each of the entries you have looked at has mentioned *process scanning.* Continue to browse, and you are referred to a utility called **lex**, and then to a compiler generator called **yacc**.

To browse through the manual, first consult an entry for a familiar utility, and then look up the entries listed under the SEE ALSO header.

USING THE HARDCOPY MANUAL AND THE PERMUTED INDEX   19.7

Originally, the hardcopy version of the manual contained the eight numbered sections in one volume. Some recent versions have split the manual into three volumes:

- The *Users Reference Manual* contains information about the standard UNIX commands, utilities, application packages, and games.

- The *Programmer's Reference Manual* contains information on the programming libraries, system calls, protocols, and special files.

- The *System Administrator's Manual* consists of procedures, files, application packages, and commands useful to system administrators.

806 UNIX Made Easy

The hardcopy manual contains the same manual pages as those displayed by the **man** utility. In the hardcopy version, the entries are sorted alphabetically into the eight sections described earlier. This makes searching for entries somewhat tedious, because if you don't already know in which section to look, you must search several sections to find the entry you want.

Fortunately, the hardcopy manual comes with an index. Sometimes the index is a *permuted index*, also known as a *keyword-in-context index*. A permuted index allows you to do keyword searches similar to those done automatically by **man -k** or **apropos**.

Describing a Permuted Index

Suppose you have the following book titles:

The Golden Gate
Interview With The Vampire
One Hundred Years of Solitude

The keywords for this list of titles are the words *Golden, Gate, Interview, Vampire, One, Hundred, Years,* and *Solitude.* A permuted index of these titles is an alphabetized listing of certain rotated versions of the titles.

Gate, The Golden
Golden Gate, The
Hundred Years of Solitude, One
Interview With The Vampire
One Hundred Years of Solitude
Solitude, One Hundred Years of
Vampire, Interview With The
Years of Solitude, One Hundred

Specifically, in the preceding permuted index

- Each title appears exactly once for each keyword it contains.

- Each entry has had its words cyclically shifted until it begins with a keyword.

- Each keyword in a title appears at the beginning of a shifted version of that title.

- No duplicate entries appear.

- The shifted titles appear in alphabetical order.

In the hardcopy version of the manual, the permuted index of command names and titles appears in this equivalent, but easier-to-read form:

The Golden	Gate
The	Golden Gate
One	Hundred Years of Solitude
	Interview With The Vampire
	One Hundred Years of Solitude
One Hundred Years of	Solitude
Interview With The	Vampire
One Hundred	Years of Solitude

Using the Permuted Index

1. Suppose you want to find the title of a book that contains the keyword *Vampire.* If you scan along the words to the right of the wide center space in the preceding list (it is sorted alphabetically), you will find the entry:

   Interview With The Vampire

2. Now look at the permuted index for the hardcopy manual. Search for entries with the word *editor* in them. You will find something similar to the following:

```
screen-oriented (visual) display  editor based on ex vi(1) ............ vi(1)
               ed(1) red(1) text  editor .............................. ed(1)
                     ex(1) text   editor .............................. ex(1)
                  sed(1) stream   editor .............................. sed(1)
             users) edit(1) text  editor (variant of ex for casual .. edit(1)
```

There are references to five editors: **vi, ed, ex, sed,** and **edit.** By looking at the permuted index, you can find the entry you are looking for.

Exercise   19-B

1. What command would you enter to find all entries containing the keyword *directory?*

   _____

2. What part of a manual entry refers to other manual entries?

   _____

3. While searching a permuted index for a particular word or phrase, which column do you look at?

   _____

In this chapter you consulted the on-line or hardcopy manual for assistance with UNIX utilities. If your system allows, you can also search the table of contents to find an appropriate entry relating to your question. If you cannot search the on-line table of contents, you can use the permuted index of the hardcopy manual to search for entries relating to a topic. By using the manual, you can get descriptions and instructions for commands, or find the right command to perform a task.

CONCLUSION

COMMAND SUMMARY

System V Command Summary

man *section title*
Displays the on-line manual entry titled *title* from Section *section*.

glossary *term*
Displays the definitions of common technical *terms* and symbols.

help *command(s)*
Displays general information about *commands*.

locate *keyword*
Displays all UNIX commands with descriptions containing the *keyword*.

starter
Starts the UNIX system **help** facility for beginning users.

usage *entry(s)*
Prints the SYNOPSIS section of an entry from the UNIX Reference Manual.

BSD Command Summary

man *section title*
Displays the on-line manual entry titled *title* from Section *section*.

apropos *word(s)*
Displays all lines in the table of contents containing any word listed in *word(s)*.

man -k *word(s)*
Same as **apropos**.

·20·

Process Monitoring and Control

UNIX is a multiuser, multitasking computer environment. At any given moment several users may be on UNIX, each having different operations underway. One user may be editing a file in the foreground and at the same time performing a database update in the background, while other users are running the same or different programs. The system is also running tasks in the background to handle scheduling of print jobs, delivering mail, and a variety of other functions.

In this chapter, you will investigate how the hardware and software execute utilities via *processes*. Whether you are a novice user or a guru, knowledge about the execution of a process will help you monitor and control the system more effectively, write useful and efficient shell scripts, and troubleshoot system problems.

SKILLS CHECK

Before beginning this chapter, you should be able to

- Utilize the UNIX directory hierarchy system (Chapter 3, "Using UNIX Directories")

- Use the shell to issue complex commands (Chapter 6, "Command Line Interpretation by the Shell")

- Employ permissions to specify access to files and directories by the owner, groups of users, and all users on a system (Chapter 7, "Setting File Permissions")

OBJECTIVES

Upon completion of this chapter, you will be able to

- Display process information and identify problems with processes

- Terminate processes that are creating a problem

- Describe the major components of a process

- Trace the events that occur when a process is created

20.1   EXAMINING THE LIFE CYCLE OF PROCESSES

When you enter a command line at the shell prompt and press the [Return] key, the shell executes the utilities specified in the command line. The system follows instructions located in a file, performing an action or set of actions for you. Most of the commands you have used in this book, such as **vi**, **cat**, and **mail**, are utilities. The shell, too, is a utility.

Whenever a utility is executed, computer memory is addressed, the central processing unit (CPU) performs calculations, information is written back to memory, and output is passed to a destination—a *process* is underway. When a utility such as **vi** is being executed by several users (or several times by the same user), each execution of the program is a separate process. When UNIX was designed, multitasking was a primary objective, to allow several tasks to be accomplished at the same time. Processes were the solution.

When you are working on the system, you are interacting with processes. If a utility does not respond as you expect it to, you may need to request and examine a listing of current processes. The next step may be to kill or restart processes.

A process consists of the data exchange, CPU activity, memory accesses, and other events associated with an instance of the execution of a program. Some processes last only a short time; others, often called daemons, run continuously. All processes, however, go through a life cycle that begins with their creation (spawning) and ends with their death (exiting).

Identifying Your Processes

Log onto your system. A shell process has begun.

When you enter commands to the shell, it executes the commands you typed in. It generally stays in operation for as long as you are logged on.

1. Display information about all of your currently running processes with one of the following commands:

   System V:
   ps

   BSD:
   ps -g

   The output shows at least two processes running The numbers shown in the PID, TTY, and TIME columns will certainly be different in your output.

   For System V:

   ```
   PID   TTY  TIME   COMMAND
   8464  2    1:20   csh
   9512  2    0:05   ps
   ```

   For BSD:

   ```
   PID   TTY  STAT  TIME   COMMAND
   8464  2    S     1:20   csh
   9512  2    R     0:05   ps -g
   ```

2. Using the output displayed on your terminal from the **ps** command, complete the following chart:

PID	TT[Y]	TIME	COM[MAN]D

In this example, two processes are listed. You recorded three pieces of information for each process: PID (pronounced "P. I. D." rather than "pid"), TIME, and a COMMAND.

PID   The numbers in the PID column are **P**rocess **ID**entifiers. As each process is created, it is assigned a PID, somewhat like customers who receive a number when they enter a busy bakery. The numbering of PIDs begins with 0. Thus, if 1207 were the PID of your **ps** process, it was probably the 1208th process started on your system since your system was rebooted. Each system has a maximum PID number. When this number is reached, the numbering starts again from the first available number greater than 1 in System V, or greater than 2 in BSD.

TIME   CPU time used by the process.

COMMAND   The items listed in this column (**csh** and **ps**) are the names of the utilities associated with each of the two running processes. In the Bourne shell, **sh** is listed, rather than **csh**.

Examining Processes as Temporary Entities

All processes have definite beginnings and ends.

When you ran **ps** in the previous exercise, one of the listed processes was **ps**. The **ps** utility was running. It listed all the processes that were running. It therefore listed itself.

1. Run the **ps** utility again, using one of the following commands:

System V:
ps

BSD:
ps -g

Complete the following chart based on the new output.

PID	COM[MAN]D

Compare the PIDs for the shell process in this table and the one for the previous exercise. It is the same shell process. However, compare the PIDs for the **ps** process in the two tables. They are different. This instance of executing the **ps** utility is a new one.

When you start a utility at the shell prompt, a process is created to carry out the instructions contained within the utility. It dies upon completion of its task. If you then enter the same command name again (as you just did with the **ps** command), a new process is created, with a new PID.

Examining the Life Cycle of a Shell Process

Most processes live short, happy lives—they simply execute a utility. They complete their function, usually successfully, and then die.

1. Log out now, and then log back in.

2. Once you are logged in again, get a list of the processes you are running. Type one of the following commands:

   System V:

   ps

   BSD:

   ps -g

3. Compare the PID of your current shell with the PID of your previous shell, as noted in the tables in previous exercises. You are now in a new shell process. It has a new PID. When you logged out, you killed the old one.

The shell process that you are currently utilizing was created when you logged in. It cycles through the following steps until you log out:

- Print a prompt
- Wait until the user enters a command line
- Interpret the command line
- Execute the utility(s) named in the command line
- Wait for the utility(s) to complete
- Issue a new prompt and start all over again

(The third step in the list, interpret the command line, was examined in detail in Chapter 6, "Command Line Interpretation by the Shell.")

When you enter the command **logout** (or **exit**, or Ctrl-d), the shell process does what all processes finally do—it dies. Shell processes go through the same life cycle as other processes. They also have a special role in starting (spawning) other processes, as examined in a later section.

Communicating Between a Process and a Terminal

A process is more than just the instructions in the utility being executed. A process consists of information about itself, about the user, and about how the system is executing the process. The first part of the information, which you have already examined, is the

Process Identifier (PID). The **ps** utility also gives you the associated terminal identifier (or *tty*).

1. Examine the processes you are currently running, by entering one of the following:

   System V:
   ps

   BSD:
   ps -g

   Notice the values displayed under the TTY or TT column heading of the output. They are the same for all the processes you just executed. The *tty* corresponds to the port on the computer where your terminal is attached. Each *tty* can have a number of processes attached to it.
   Most user processes need to read input from and write output to a terminal. Thus, most user processes must know the terminal to which they are attached. This data is stored with each process and is displayed as part of the output from the **ps** command.

Creating a Process

Earlier, a utility was defined as a set of instructions stored in a file. A process is an instance of the execution of these instructions. This does not explain, however, where utilities and processes are located, or why a process is called a process. The answers to these questions are based on the functions performed by three important pieces of hardware: the *disk*, the *main memory*, and a *CPU*. Figure 20-1 and the following chart describe each of these components and their relationship.

disk	Magnetic storage devices that are relatively slow to read and write, but are permanent. All files, including utilities, are stored on a disk.
CPU	The **Central Processing Unit** is the computer logic chip that executes instructions.
main memory	A collection of computer chips that temporarily store information. Instructions contained in a utility are transferred from the disk to main memory, and then executed by the CPU.

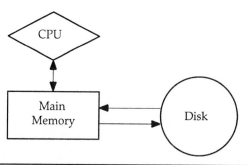

FIGURE 20-1. The disk, main memory, and CPU

The sequence of events in the life of a process is as follows:

- The shell process is running. It displays a prompt on the screen.

- A user types a command line that begins with the name of the utility that is to be run and presses the [Return] key.

- The shell interprets the command line, and instructs the system to execute the utility. The shell process then sleeps.

- The system creates a process and loads the instructions that make up the utility from disk into main memory, for use by that process.

- The system lists the process on a table or queue and waits for the CPU's attention.

- The CPU executes the instructions now in main memory.

- After the CPU reaches the end of the instructions, the process dies and informs the shell that the process is finished. The locations in main memory occupied by the process are freed for use by other processes.

- The shell process wakes up, displays the prompt, and is ready to receive input.

In summary, a process is an instance of a running program, the instructions of which are loaded from the disk to main memory and executed by the CPU.

20.2   USING PS TO OBTAIN DATA CONCERNING PROCESSES

You can obtain extensive information about processes. In both System V and BSD, **ps** gives you a display that tells you if a process is running, along with other information.

1. To generate a long listing of your processes, type one of the following commands:

   System V:
   ps -l

   BSD:
   ps -lg

   Additional fields are displayed. Locate the four fields explained below and fill in the chart:

F	S[TAT]	SZ	COM[MAN]D

   F   The **F** field is the Flags field, which contains a number indicating what flags are set for the process. In this example, the rightmost digit is a 1, indicating that the process is in memory. Identify which of your processes are in memory. Among them are **ps** (it must be in memory when it is running and performing its function) and probably your login shell (**csh** or **sh**).

S[TAT] The State field contains a capital letter indicating the state of the process. This field is labeled **S** in System V and **STAT** in BSD. The two most common states are **Sleeping** and **Runnable**. A runnable process is currently on the run queue and can be run whenever the CPU is free. Another state for processes is **Idle**, which on System V indicates that the process is being created. In BSD, **I** indicates that the process has been sleeping for longer than 20 seconds. If it has been sleeping for less than 20 seconds, on a BSD system, the flag is set to **Sleeping**. If the process is stopped by a signal from the process that created it (parent process), in System V, it is in the Traced state.

SZ The Size field contains a number that indicates the **SiZe** of the process in memory. If you can read hexadecimal (base 16), you can use this field to determine the relative sizes of processes.

COM[MAN]D — This is the actual command being run by the process. It is abbreviated to **COMD** in the **ps**
output for System V.

Identifying the Parent Process

In addition to instructions for the CPU, other important data is associated with each process. This includes the terminal (*tty*) it is attached to, a list of open
files that the process can write to or read from, and
other pertinent information. When you create a process, it inherits most of this information from the
parent process, that is, the process that issued the
command to create it.

1. Enter one of the following commands to explore
   how each process obtains the information or data it
   needs:

   System V:
   ps -l

   BSD:
   ps -lg

2. Fill in the following table using information displayed by the **ps -l** or **ps -lg** command:

PID	PPID	TT[Y]	COM[MAN]D

Each process has an associated **PPID** (Parent Process **ID**entifier). All processes (except for the great grandparent process, with the PID of zero) are created (or *spawned*) by a previously existing process—its parent. In the table you just created, the PPID associated with the **ps** process is identical to the PID associated with the shell process (**csh** or **sh**). The shell process is the parent of the **ps** process. When the PID of a process matches the PPID of another process, the former process is the parent of the latter.

Processes inherit information (data) from their parent process. When you log onto the system, your first process (usually either **csh** or **sh**) is started up by the **login** program. From then on, every utility or executable filename that you type in is executed by a process that is a child (or nth grandchild) of your shell process. The exceptions are certain shell built-in programs (see Chapter 6, "Command Line Interpretation by the Shell"). Because each new process is a child process, it inherits data (such as your terminal *tty*, user ID, and current directory) from the parent process.

Displaying a Long Listing of Data About Your Process

1. Enter one of the following commands:

System V:
ps -lf

BSD:
ps -l

This command displays all the process data fields usually output by either one or both of the options. On System V, the two options can be combined to generate a long list of fields for your processes displayed by **ps**. Regardless of which options are used, all **ps** commands display the PID, TTY, TIME, and COMMAND fields. On BSD, the **-1** option alone provides the long listing.

Table 20-1 indicates which fields are displayed by the **-1** and **-f** options on both System V and BSD.

The fields of Table 20-1 are defined as follows:

F   The **F**lags field indicates what (fl)ags are set for the process. The rightmost digit **1** indicates that the process is in memory.

TABLE 20-1.   Fields Displayed by **ps-1** and **ps-f** on System V and BSD.

System	Column Heading											
	Option	F	S STAT	UID	PPID	C	STIME	PRI	NI	ADDR	SZ	WCHAN
System V	-f			x	x	x	x					
	-1	x	x	x	x	x		x	x	x	x	x
BSD	-1	x	x	x	x	x		x	x	x	x	x

S[TAT]	The **S**tate of the process. The two most common states are **S**leeping and **R**unnable.
UID	The user name (**-f**) or number (**-l**) of the process.
PPID	The **P**arent **P**rocess **ID**entifier of the process.
C	A number used by the system scheduler to schedule processes.
STIME	The **S**tarting **TIME** of each process.
PRI	The **PRI**ority of the process, with higher numbers indicating a lower priority.
NI	The **NI**ce value of the process as set by the **nice** command. (The **nice** command is used to alter the priority of a given process, allowing more critical processes to execute more quickly.)
ADDR	The memory **ADDR**ess (in hex) of the process.
SZ	A hex number that indicates the **SiZe** of the process in memory.
WCHAN	The event for which the process is waiting.

20.3   RUNNING SCRIPTS TO EXAMINE PROCESSES

In this section, you will create a C shell script and run it in three different ways to examine how processes are created.

1. Create a shell script called *display*, containing the following commands:

   System V:
   #!/bin/csh
   ps -f
   sleep *10*

   BSD:
   #!/bin/csh
   ps -lx
   sleep *10*

   The first command line causes this script to be interpreted by a C shell, and the second line instructs the C shell to execute the **ps** command to display a list of processes on your screen. The third command causes the script to wait for ten seconds before exiting.

2. Make this file executable by typing

   chmod +x *display*

Spawning a Shell Script That Displays How It Is Executed

1. Run the shell script by typing

   display

2. Complete the following chart:

PID	PPID	COMMAND

In System V, notice that the command you entered, **display**, is listed as

```
/bin/csh display
```

On BSD you either get

```
display
```

or

```
(csh)
```

This command is the parent of the **ps** command, and the child of your original (login) shell. When you enter a command consisting of the name of a shell script, your login shell creates, or *forks*, a child shell, which interprets the shell script. This child shell then forks other processes for each utility in the script.

The default method of running a script is to have a subshell interpret it. This is often referred to as *spawning* a subshell to interpret a script. Spawning a subshell makes sense for two reasons:

- Your login shell is immune to changes performed by the script.

- After the script is complete, control is returned to your login shell.

There are, however, occasions when spawning a subshell has important disadvantages. For this reason, there are two alternative methods of running a script.

Running a Script with exec

One disadvantage of spawning a subshell is that it creates an extra process. Heavily used systems frequently run more slowly because of excess processes. Also, all systems have a maximum number of processes that can exist at any given time—known as the number of *process slots*—the default is 70. (This number can be changed using an advanced procedure that is not discussed in this book.)

It is not that unusual for a system to run out of process slots. Fortunately, it is possible to run a script without creating an extra process.

1. Examine your current processes with one of the following commands:

System V:
ps

BSD:

ps -g

and write down the PID of your **csh** process here:

PID of the **csh**: _____

2. Enter the following command, which will log you off the system:

exec *display*

Note the PID associated with the **csh** process running your *display* script.

The PID of the **csh** process running your *display* script has the same PID as your login shell. After the script runs, you are logged out. How does this work? The **exec** command causes your login shell to **exec** a new shell directly, without **fork**ing. The process executing your login shell is now running a new shell; thus, no child process is created. The subshell has the same PID as your login shell, and this new shell then runs your script. When the script is completed you are logged out, because there is no login shell left to return to. It has been overlaid by the new shell that it **exec**ed.

This method of running a script is useful when the script is a menu, or when you are calling a script from within a script. In both of these situations there is no need to return to the original shell, and spawning is wasteful because it creates an unneeded process. Because all systems have a limited number of process slots, unneeded processes are to be avoided.

Running a Script with source

You have learned that spawning a subshell makes sense because your login shell is immune to changes performed by the script. However, sometimes you will want your script to affect your login shell.

1. Type the command:

source *display*

Here there is no new shell, no getting logged out. The **source** command instructs the current shell to interpret the contents of the specified script.

In Chapter 15, "Setting the User Environment," you used the command line:

source *.login*

The file *.login* is actually a shell script that is **source**d when you log on. When you change this script, you want it to be reread by your login shell so that it is informed of any changes; therefore, you **source**d it. The **source** command is used in situations where you want the current shell to be affected by the contents of a script.

20.4 DISPLAYING INFORMATION PERTAINING TO ALL PROCESSES

Thus far, you have been using **ps** to display information concerning the processes that are owned by you.

You can also display information about every process running on your system.

1. Type one of the following commands:

System V:

ps -e | pg

BSD:

ps -axg | more

This command is useful for finding out if any unexpected processes are running on your system, or if any expected processes are not present. For example, the printer spooler program should be running. In System V, look for **lpsched**; in BSD, look for **lpd**. Likewise, if mail is to be handled, the **sendmail** program must be running.

There are utilities that run in the background all the time, waiting for someone to send mail or a file to the printer. They are begun when the system is booted and are called *daemons*. Such processes are not attached to a terminal.

Processes only need a *tty* attached to them when there is a need for input or output. Many system processes belonging to *root*, such as **init, scheduler**, and **sendmail**, do not need a *tty* attached to them.

Obtaining Detailed Information on All Processes

Options to **ps** can be combined to display extensive information about every process on your system. These commands are important tools used by the system administrator.

1. Type one of the following commands:

   System V
   ps -ef | pg

   BSD:
   ps -axlg | more

2. To identify all processes that have 1 as the parent process, type one of the following commands:

   System V:
   ps -ef | awk '$3 == 1'

   BSD:
   ps -axlg | awk '$4 == 1'

   In the output, look for PPIDs that match other processes' PIDs, and note the relationships.

Limiting Output to Processes of a Specific User

The long listing of processes provides a wealth of information about currently running processes, regardless of owner. In the previous section you saw that all processes are associated with some user, usually the one who initiated the process. It is possible to display data about all of the processes associated with a specified user.

1. Use the **who** command to identify a user who is currently logged onto your system.

2. Type one of the following commands (replacing *user* with the user name you identified in Step 1):

System V:

ps -fu *user*

BSD:

ps -aux | grep *user*

A **fu**ll listing of all processes associated with the specified *user* is displayed on your screen.

Identifying Your Terminal

The next several steps require you to be logged onto two terminals. While remaining logged on through your current terminal, log onto another terminal.

1. At the new terminal, identify the terminal port where you are logged on. Type

tty

The name of the port through which your terminal is connected is displayed on your screen. The name is in this form:

```
/dev/tty22
```

All ports are listed in the */dev* directory or one of its subdirectories. All port names begin with *tty,* and the number (or letter and number) that follow *tty* uniquely identify your port. This is the port number.

Write down the number displayed for your current terminal port in this space:

New terminal port number: _____

Identifying Processes Associated With a Specified Port

Follow the next few steps using both the terminals where you are logged on.

1. On the new terminal, type

   vi *trashfile*

   and leave the editor active.

2. Return to your original terminal and enter one of the following commands:

   System V:
   ps -ft22

   BSD:
   ps -lt22

   Replace 22 with the port number from the new terminal that you wrote into the space provided earlier.
   The **-t** option tells **ps** to look for processes that are associated with a particular terminal number. The output from **ps** includes the **csh** and the **vi** that you left running on the second terminal.

3. Complete the following table with your results:

UID	PID	PPID	TT[Y]	COM[MAN]D

Note that **vi** is a child of **csh**, and they both are connected to the same *tty* and have the same UID.

4. You can now log out of the new terminal.

Exercise 20-A

1. Suppose that you log into a terminal and enter the **who** command (which is located in */bin*). Describe the life cycle of the resulting process.

_____

_____

2. Imagine the following scenario: You log into your system on tty23. The system starts a **csh** for you that has a PID of 1056. Then you start a shell script (PID of, say, 1080) that in turn executes **mail** (PID of 2020). In this scenario:

What is the PPID of the **mail** process?

_____

What is the PPID of the shell script?

_____

With what *tty* is the **mail** process associated?

_____

3. What command would you use to get a long listing of *all* processes on the system?

_____

4. Suppose that a user with the login name *them* is logged onto terminal tty13, and has been editing a file for some time. In System V, how could you determine exactly when the user began editing this file?

_____

20.5   DISTINGUISHING THE THREE COMPONENTS OF A PROCESS

Examine Figure 20-2. It shows the relationships between the three major components of a process.

text region	Instructions to be followed by the CPU.
system data	Data that is needed about the system. Much of this data can be displayed using the **ps -l** command, and includes a UID, PID, PPID, cumulative execution time, priority, and the *tty* to which the process is attached. System data is used by the system to manage a process.

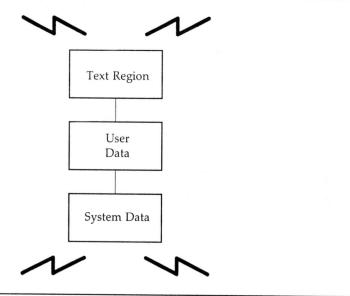

FIGURE 20-2.   Image of a process

user data	Data that is used by the processes themselves. All utilities contain variables as part of their code. When a utility is loaded into memory, a local data area is created to store the values of these variables.

EXAMINING HOW PERMISSIONS WORK   20.6

System data is a part of a process. The UID (user identification) is part of the system data for each process. With the UID the system can determine whether a user has permission to perform a requested action.

1. While logged in as a regular user (a user who is not the superuser), type

   vi */etc/passwd*

   The password file is displayed on your screen.

2. Now make a change to this file, and type

   :wq

   The message:

   ```
   Permission Denied
   ```

   or

   ```
   File is read only.
   ```

   is displayed on your screen.

3. Quit this file now by typing

   :q!

   The system allowed you to read the file, but not to write it.

Examining Information About Access Permissions

The file data that the system uses to determine access permissions is available to users.

1. Type the command

ls -l */etc/passwd*

The display is similar to the following:

```
-rw-r--r--   1 root system 9356 Mar 16 14:01 /etc/passwd
```

The owner and group fields indicate that this file is associated with the user *root* and the group *system*. The permissions fields at the beginning of the line indicate that the file can be written only by its owner, but is readable by the owner's group, as well as by all other valid users of your computer. (If you are not sure about how to read this line, you may want to review Chapter 7," Setting File Permissions".)

Examining How Process Information Is Used to Determine Access Permissions

The next exercise again requires you to be logged onto two terminals.

1. While remaining logged in through your current terminal, log into a second terminal such as the one you used previously as your "new" terminal.

2. On the new terminal, type

   vi */etc/passwd*

3. Return to your original terminal and type the following:

   ps -lt*xx*

replacing *xx* with the port number of the new terminal (you recorded it in the earlier exercise). The output from **ps** looks something like the following:

```
UID   PID   PPID C    STIME TTY TIME COMMAND
640 24444   1    7 12:07:01 4   0:14 csh
640 26628 24444 0 13:09:13 4    0:05 vi /etc/passwd
```

Note the UID associated with your **vi** process.

4. You can now log out of the new terminal you logged into for this exercise.

Examining How File Permissions Are Determined

A file has both permissions and an owner associated with it; a process has an owner associated with it. Examine Figure 20-3. Determining whether a process has permission to access a file is accomplished in three steps.

- If the UID of the process matches the UID of the file, the system checks the owner permission bits of the file to see if the action (reading, writing, or executing) is permissible.

- If the GID of the process matches the GID of the file, the system checks the group permission bits of the file to see if the action (reading, writing, or executing) is permissible. (The GID of a process is stored with the process but not displayed by **ps**.)

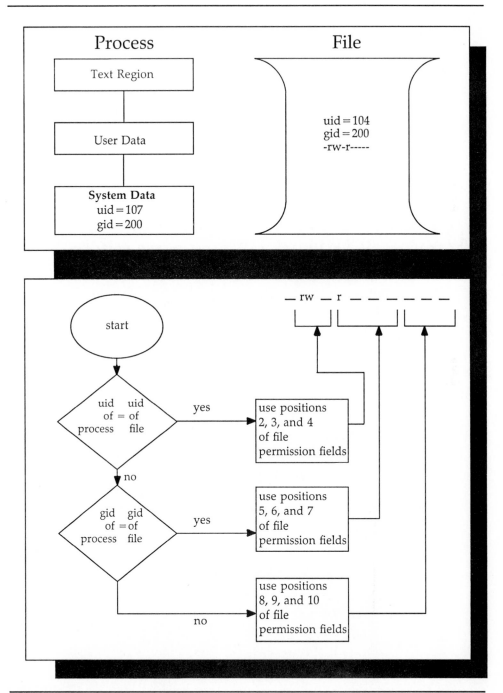

FIGURE 20-3.   Determining permissions

- If neither the UID nor GID of the process matches the UID or GID of the file, the system checks the other permission bits of the file to see if the action (reading, writing, or executing) is permissible.

The permissions stored with a file do not determine who can access the file, but rather which *processes* can access the file.

20.7 DESCRIBING THE RELATIONSHIP BETWEEN UTILITIES AND THE KERNEL

Figure 20-4 illustrates the relationships between the UNIX operating system's four functional components that are involved in process creation: the shell, other utilities, the kernel, and the operating system hardware.

Each layer represents a UNIX environment component that is responsible for performing a type of function. You have used the shell and utilities; indirectly, you have also used the two other components of the operating system:

- The kernel is the *master control program* of the UNIX operating system. It performs the general low-level functions of mediating between the UNIX system utilities and the system hardware. This mediation includes locating program and data files on disk, loading program and data files into main memory, scheduling processes to be worked on by the CPU,

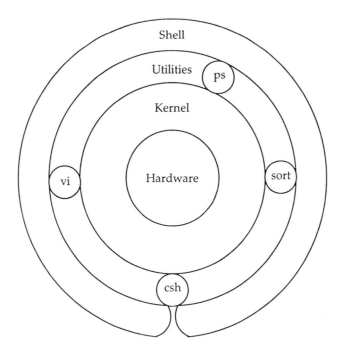

FIGURE 20-4.   Relationship between shell, utilities, kernel, and hardware

reading user input from terminals, and writing output to terminals and printers.

- The hardware includes the CPU, which manipulates information; main memory, which serves as the work area for the CPU; the disk, which stores information; printers, which produce hardcopy information; and terminals, which can be used for both input and output.

Describing Communication Between Components

Communication occurs between adjacent layers of the system. Users communicate with the shell, the shell communicates with the utilities, the utilities communicate with the kernel, and the kernel communicates with the hardware.

The instructions contained in a utility file include *system calls*, which are commands the system utilities give the kernel. A system call asks the kernel to perform one of its functions, such as locating a disk file. One set of system calls results in the creation of processes.

Examining How Processes Are Created

Process creation requires mechanisms for achieving two primary goals:

- Processes must inherit system data from their parents.

- The instructions to be followed by the CPU must be loaded from disk into main memory.

A shell process also requires a mechanism for starting other processes, waiting for these processes to complete, and finding out when its children have completed, so that it knows when to print its prompt for the user.

Examine Figure 20-5. The generation of a new

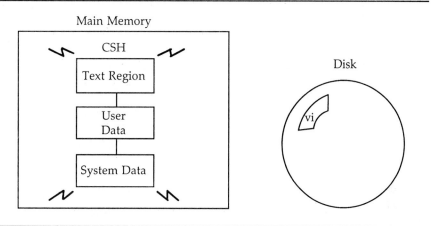

FIGURE 20-5.   Process creation

process begins with a **csh** process already in memory,
ready to go to work. The user enters the command
and presses the [Return] key. The shell process interprets the command line, and invokes a system call
(**fork**) to create a child process to perform the requested task. Figure 20-6 illustrates that this child
process is, at first, nothing but a duplicate of the shell
itself—instructions, user data, system data, and all.

As indicated in Figure 20-7, the shell then executes
the **wait** system call. The parent shell quietly waits
(sleeps) as the child process begins its task.

The first step in the child's task is to invoke the
system call **exec**, which instructs the system to find a
utility file, such as the one named **vi**. This command
file contains the instructions and variables the child
process needs. The **exec** call tells the kernel to load
these instructions into memory. The new instructions
overlay the child process' copy of the shell instructions and user data that it inherited from its parent,

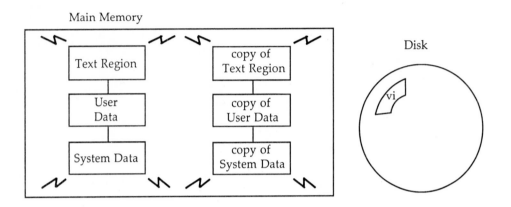

FIGURE 20-6.   Creation of child process

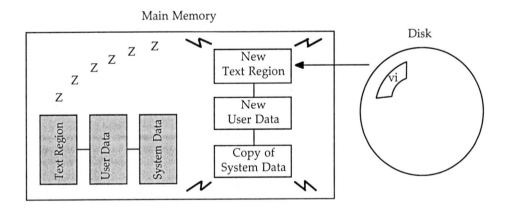

FIGURE 20-7.   Execution of child process

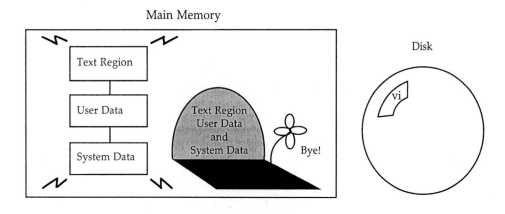

FIGURE 20-8.   Exiting a child process

but preserves the child's copy of its parent's system data.

The CPU then follows the instructions contained in the child's text region, using the child's user data region as its workspace. The CPU draws on the child's system data to make decisions about things like what terminal to write to, who the process belongs to, and so forth.

Finally, as illustrated by Figure 20-8, when the child has completed its work, it executes the **exit** system call. This system call signals to the parent that the child has either succeeded or failed at its task, and then quietly fades from memory. The parent, in this case the shell, hearing this signal, awakens and prints a new shell prompt.

Describing Information Exchange Between Parents and Children

Computing is made up of calculations and communication. The communication is two-way: information is passed from a parent to its child process, and a limited signal is passed from a child to its parent.

The child process uses a copy of the parent's system data. The parent process can communicate through environment variable values passed to the child process. By having the child use a copy, rather than the parent's system data itself, the designers of UNIX avoided the possibility of a child process ruining the parent's environment. This feature is called *parental immunity*. In fact, the only information that a child can communicate to its parent is its exit status.

Because each process initializes its own user data, the methods are limited by which a parent can pass data to its children. In fact, the only method by which it is possible to pass data from parent to child is by *binding* the data to the process' *environment*. The environment is a small set of variables stored with a process. This data is essentially part of the system data, because it is passed from parent to child, as is the system data.

The C shell binds the value of all environment variables (variables set with **setenv**) to a C shell process' environment. The Bourne shell binds the value of all **exported** variables to a Bourne shell process' environment.

HAVING A PROCESS PAUSE   20.8

The **sleep** utility tells a process to pause for a specified duration. This command can be entered from the command line.

1. Type the command:

sleep *10*

This command illustrates the function of the system call **wait**. When you enter this **sleep** command, your shell **forks** a child process that **execs** the command **sleep**. As the **sleep** process is being executed, your **csh** process **wait**s.

Examining the Effect of Backgrounding

1. To run the **sleep** command in the background, type the command:

sleep *10* **&**

Your shell immediately prints the PID of this process, followed by a shell prompt, indicating that your shell is awake and ready for instructions.

When you enter this command, your shell **fork**s a child process that **execs** the command **sleep**. Because you used the **&** character to run this command in the background, your shell does not **wait** for **sleep** to complete before printing a new prompt.

Putting the wait Back

Even when you run a command in the background, it is possible to issue a **wait** to your shell.

1. Type the following two commands in close succession:

sleep *10* **&**
wait

The **wait** command causes the shell to wait for the completion of all backgrounded processes.

This command is also useful in shell programming, when you have run a command in the background but then have to invoke a command that cannot be run until the completion of the backgrounded process.

Exercise 20-B

1. Which component of a process is used to determine the access permissions of files?

_____

2. Which component of a process varies in size based on the number of variables set?

_____

3. What are the four system calls used when a shell is requested to spawn a new process?

_____

4. For each of the following items, determine whether the task falls primarily to the **Kernel**, **Shell**, or Utility layer of UNIX, and circle the correct letter:

(a) Keeping track of the available blocks on the disk: **K   S   U**

(b) Printing a list of the currently logged-on users: **K   S   U**

(c) Interpreting the character *: **K   S   U**

(d) Editing a file: **K   S   U**

(e) Loading a utility from the disk into memory: **K   S   U**

KILLING PROCESSES THAT ARE UNDER WAY

20.9

Generally, once a process is under way, it runs until it is finished. Or, you may end the process by issuing an interrupt control character such as Ctrl-c , or by logging out. You can also instruct the process to die by issuing a specific **kill** command.

1. Type the command:

sleep *200* &

2. Examine the list of current processes with the command:

ps

3. Identify the PID of the **sleep** process, and kill the process. Type the following command, replacing *PID* with the appropriate process ID for **sleep**.

kill *PID*

Processes can be stopped using the **kill** command in one of these three basic forms:

kill *PID*
kill -1 *PID*
kill -9 *PID*

Each sends a different **kill** signal to the process. These signals are explained in the next section.

4. Try Steps 1 through 3 again, using **kill -1** *PID* and **kill -9** *PID.*

Examining How Signals Work

Signals are used to communicate special instructions to processes, much like traffic signals are used to communicate special instructions to drivers. The **kill** command is used to send one of three specific signals to a process. The following table shows the correspondence between various forms of the **kill** command and the signal that is sent to the specified process.

Command	Signal Sent
kill *PID*	terminate
kill -1 *PID*	hangup
kill -9 *PID*	kill

Of the three **kill** signals, **kill -9** is the most powerful. It stops the process immediately, without allowing any time to let the process clean up after itself. If the stopped process has any child processes or open file descriptors, this abrupt termination causes these now orphaned child processes and open file descriptors to remain on the system, taking up process slots and entries on the system open file table. This is a waste of system resources. The **kill -1** command simulates a hangup, like logging out. The system attempts to kill all related child processes and to close all open file descriptors. Just plain **kill** generates an interrupt (like pressing Ctrl-c), allowing for complete, orderly ending of the specified process.

When you practice using the **kill** command, you should start by using it with no option or with the **-1** option. Different signals have different effects. Try them out in a sequence of increasing power, because programs respond to specific signals in specific ways. Many programs are designed to ignore certain signals.

Because the signal generated by **kill -9** is not interpreted, captured, or *trapped* by intervening processes, it is the most certain to work (it cannot be ignored). It is also the most certain to make the utility exit without cleaning up. The safest way to proceed when killing a process is to first enter **kill** with no options. If this does not work, enter it with the **-1** option. Finally, if this does not work, use the **-9** option.

Killing the Child Processes First

The process with the highest PID (most recently spawned child process) should be killed first, because there are two negative outcomes that are possible when you **kill** a parent process before you **kill** its child process:

- The parent and child will both die, when killing only the child process would have been sufficient. For example, if a user's application is hung and you kill their shell, they will be logged out. Instead of killing their shell, you may solve the problem by simply killing the application.
- The parent process will die, and the child will become a defunct process, as explained in the next section.

Eliminating Defunct Processes

One of the most troublesome and mysterious events on a UNIX system is the *defunct process*. A defunct process is listed as <defunct> or <exiting> under the COMMAND column of the output from **ps**.

Defunct processes occur when the parent process dies but the child does not die with it. If you are unable to kill a process by the techniques described earlier, it is probably a defunct process. You may wish to bring the defunct process to the attention of the system administrator who may do one of the following:

- Run special software that kills defunct processes.
- Reboot the system (see Chapter 21, "System Administration Utilities" for more information).
- Ignore the problem.

Because defunct processes cannot be killed using the **kill** command, ask for help in eliminating them. Or if you are the system administrator, you may reboot the system.

Exercise 20-C

1. You are the system administrator, and a user tells you that a terminal is completely hung. After observing the situation, both physically and with **ps**, you confirm that the terminal is indeed hung and that the only processes associated with the terminal are a **csh** and a **vi**. What do you do?

   _____

2. What would happen if you entered the following sequence of commands to your shell?

   who > */dev/null* **&**
   sleep *100* **&**

mail *kevan* < */etc/motd* **&**
wait

_____

3. What would happen to a group of child processes if their parent process is **kill**ed with the **-9** option?

_____

4. If a defunct process will not exit, even after a **kill-9** command, how would you eliminate the process?

_____

CONCLUSION

In this chapter, you have used the **ps** command in some new variations that are valuable tools for system management and troubleshooting. You have also examined the composition of processes and how processes come into being. This knowledge is essential for system startup and shutdown, system diagnostics and troubleshooting, and shell and C programming.

COMMAND SUMMARY

ps
Lists all processes that you own. (In BSD it does not include the shell process.)

ps -g
Lists all processes that you own, including the shell process in BSD.

ps -1
Generates a long listing of processes that you own.

ps -f
Outputs a full listing of processes that you own (System V).

ps -u *login*
Lists processes that are owned by the user whose login ID is *login* (System V).

ps -u
Prints a user-oriented output (BSD).

ps -t*xx*
Lists processes associated with the *tty* whose last two ID characters are in *xx*; as in */dev/ttyxx*.

ps -e
Prints information about all processes (System V).

ps -a
Prints information about all processes with terminals (BSD).

ps -x
Prints information about processes not associated with a terminal.

COMMAND SUMMARY (*continued*)

kill *PID*
Terminates a process.

kill -1 *PID*
Hangs up a process. Does not work on background processes.

kill -9 *PID*
Kills a process. Usually the last form of **kill** to try. Cannot be ignored, but may not allow the utility to clean up.

·21·

System Administration Utilities

A UNIX system can operate for long periods of time without much human attention. Many programs run constantly in the background, performing essential tasks such as print spooling and mail delivery. However, several essential functions need to be handled by a system administrator.

This chapter is an introduction to some of the system administrator's functions: communicating with all users, adding users, creating backups, checking the filesystem, and shutting down and restarting the system. If you are on a large, multiuser system, an experienced person probably handles system administration. If you are not that person, only the first section—on making tape or backup copies of files— will be of use to you. The rest of the chapter describes the administrator's job. You might read these sections to increase your understanding. You might also ask the system administrator to let you observe these tasks the next time they are performed.

If you are running a single-user system, complete the tape archive section under your own login name, then log in as **root** to complete the remainder of the chapter. You will need access to your machine's manuals.

SKILLS CHECK

Before beginning this chapter, you should be able to

- Access and leave the system and execute basic commands (Chapter 1, "Touring the System's Features")

- Create, display, and print files (Chapter 1)

- Name, copy, and remove files, and use several shell commands in combination (Chapter 1)

- Access and modify files using the **vi** editor (Chapter 2, "Basic Editing with the Visual Editor")

- Utilize the UNIX directory hierarchy system to properly allocate system space for all users (Chapter 3, "Using UNIX Directories")

- Set file permissions to specify users' capabilities (Chapter 7, "Setting File Permissions")

OBJECTIVES

Upon completion of this chapter, you will be able to

- Make tape copies of files

- Describe superuser powers
- Add user accounts
- Delete users
- Make backups
- Shut down and reboot the system

USING TAR TO CREATE AND USE ARCHIVE TAPES

21.1

It is common practice to transfer files on magnetic tapes between UNIX sites. The information placed on the tapes must be in the same format for both machines. The most common format is **tar** (**t**ape **ar**chive utility). The **tar** utility is used to *archive* (store with a specific format) one or more directories or individual files on magnetic media using the **tar** format. Making **tar** tapes is useful both for system administrators and ordinary users. Many users need to transfer files between systems, or to make their own file backups.

With **tar** you can create tape archives, append files to an existing archive, display a listing of the contents of an archive, and extract files from archives. The **tar** utility is particularly useful because you can transfer files between machines running any version of the UNIX operating system.

Creating an Archive Tape

1. Read your system hard copy manual entry for using the tape drive, to see how to put a tape in the drive of your system.

2. Put a blank tape in the drive.

3. Change to a directory containing a file to be archived, such as your Home directory, where the file *practice* is located.

4. To create an archive copy of *practice* on tape, type

tar c *practice*

The options to **tar** are not preceded by a dash (-).
   This command instructs **tar** to create an archive copy of your *practice* file on the cartridge tape in the default tape drive.

   The format for the command to create a new archive of a file is

tar c *filename*

where *filename* is the name of the file located within the current directory. The **c** option instructs **tar** to create an archive.

Listing the Contents of a Tape

1. To instruct **tar** to output a list of the contents of the tape in the default drive, type

tar t

The **t** option asks for a listing of the table of contents of the archive tape in the tape drive. Your *practice* file is listed. If it is not, the **tar** command line did not function properly, and you will need to consult your system administrator or manuals.

Once a cartridge tape contains an archive copy of your file, you can take the tape to another machine and unload it. Let's practice this; the next step instructs **tar** to unload the file in a different location on your present machine.

2. Begin by creating a new subdirectory and changing to the new directory:

mkdir *Storage1;* **cd** *Storage1*

3. Retrieve your file from tape by typing

tar xv

The x option tells **tar** to extract all files from the archive tape. The **v** option tells **tar** to be verbose during the process (**tar** will display detailed information while extracting). The screen output looks like the following:

```
x   ./practice  1234  bytes,  3  tape  blocks
```

The file is written into the current directory, because the full pathname on the tape begins with a dot, for current directory.

4. Confirm that the file has been extracted by examining the contents of the current directory. Type

ls -l

You have now successfully extracted the file *practice* from your archive tape into the *Storage1* directory.

Adding to an Existing Tape

One way to add a file to an archive is to create a brand new archive, with the old and new files writing over the existing tape. A simpler method is to append a new file to the archive tape.

1. Add *practice2* to the tape by typing

tar r *practice2*

The **r** option tells **tar** to append the named file or files to the **r**ear of the existing archive, rather than to overwrite.

2. Verify that the addition was successful by getting a detailed table listing with

tar tv

Putting Several Files on Tape

To create an archive of many files, simply include new filenames as options in the command line.

1. Add new files to the tape, with filenames such as the following ones from your current directory:

tar r *users_on names first_file*

2. Check the contents of the tape with

tar t

Several files can be listed as arguments to the **tar** command when creating, adding, and extracting files.

Archiving All the Files in a Directory

You can archive whole directory trees using the **tar** utility by specifying the directory at the top of the tree.

1. Change to the parent directory of your Home directory, by typing

   cd
   cd ..

2. Make a **tar** archive of *directoryname* (your Home directory) and all its subdirectories, by typing

   tar c *directoryname*

   This command instructs **tar** to archive all of the files in your current (Home) directory. The archive will contain not only the files from your Home directory, but all the files from its subdirectories, as well. The **tar** archive will include all files and directories *below* the specified directory.

3. Obtain a listing of the **tar** archive, with

   tar tv

   Observe that each file pathname includes the directory name explicitly.

Archiving the Current Directory

1. Return to your Home directory.

2. To archive all of the files in your current directory, type

tar c .

All files are **tar**red to the tape.

3. Confirm the preceding action by getting a listing. Notice that this time each file is listed as *./filename*.

If your current directory is root (/), and you execute the **tar c .** command, you create an archive containing every single file and directory on your system. The only exception is that **tar** will not archive an empty directory.

Using Filename Expansion with tar

It is possible to use the shell metacharacters in *file-list*. For example, the command

tar c *p******

creates an archive copy of all files in the current directory that begin with the letter *p*.

The basic command syntax to create an archive is

tar c *file-list*

where *file-list* is the name of a single file, or a directory (including .), or a list of several files and/or directories.

1. Obtain a listing of the contents of the archive table:

tar tv

2. Observe that the output names the files using the current directory notation, as in this example:

```
./practice
```

Although it is possible to name the files to be copied by using each file's absolute pathname (such as */usr/staff/john/practice*), it is not always advantageous to do so. In the preceding example, when **tar** extracts the file *practice* from the tape, the file will be archived with exactly the same pathname. If you then try to move the file to another system that does not have the directories */usr/staff/john,* **tar** will not be able to extract the file *practice.* This is because **tar** needs to put *practice* in the same path from which it is extracted—that is, */usr/staff/john.* It is therefore prudent to work from the directory containing the file that is to be archived, so that the path given to **tar** will be *./practice*; this enables extraction of the file into any other current directory.

Extracting a Subset of an Archive

To extract a subset of the archive and not its total contents, simply ask for the file by name.

1. Extract the file *practice* by typing

tar xv *./practice*

As the file is extracted, a message to that effect is displayed on your screen because of the **v** option.

CAUTION: You cannot use shell metacharacters when *extracting from* an archive tape.

2. Try it; change to a different directory and type

tar xv *./prac**

You are most likely to get an error message indicating that there is no match. This is because the shell expands the characters *prac** by looking for files that start with *prac* in your current directory, *not* on the archive tape. Quoting the * does not work either because the **tar** utility does not do file expansion.

Using a Nondefault Cartridge Tape Device

To use a cartridge tape drive (or a nine-track drive if you have one) that is not the default drive, you must specify the device to be used. You will need to consult with the system administrator or manuals to obtain the correct device information.

1. For example, to copy all files in your current directory into an archive on the second cartridge drive, type the following command:

tar cf */dev/device* .

where *device* is *rct1* on BSD, and something like */rmt/c0d0v* in System V. The **f** option says to use the file following this command as the target for the archive, instead of the default cartridge tape drive. (Everything on line is treated like a file.)

2. If you wish to list the table of contents or extract files from this archive, you must also use the **f** option:

tar tvf */dev/device*

or

tar xf */dev/device*

where *device* is your selected drive.

Exercise 21-A

1. What is **tar** used for?

_____

2. Who uses **tar**?

_____

3. What is the command to list the contents of a tape that is in the system's default tape drive?

_____

4. What is the command for appending a file named *people* to an existing tape?

_____

5. When can you use metacharacters in filenames for a **tar** command?

_____

21.2   SUPERUSER TASKS AND RESPONSIBILITIES

The system administrator must have the power to add and remove users, change users' Home directories from one place to another, back up all files on tape or disk, and reconfigure the system. All these tasks require **root**, or *superuser* powers. The superuser is able to read, write, or execute any file in the system and can modify the system's configuration. Superuser status is reserved for specific people to use only for these system administration tasks.

Once you become a superuser, the entire system is under your control. As a superuser, you can

- Access any directory
- Modify permissions on all files
- Access any group
- Execute any file that is executable by anyone

Figure 21-1 describes the differences between **root** and other users in terms of Home directories and powers.

You should only become a superuser when you need to perform superviser tasks. As soon as you have carried out these tasks, you should step back into the phone booth, exit superuser status, and become a regular user. This avoids accidental abuse of superuser powers.

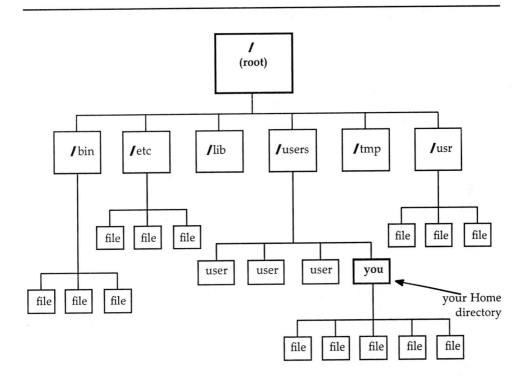

FIGURE 21-1.   Root and user Home directories and powers

Root Powers

Access to any directory

Read and write permis-
sions on all files

Access to any group

Execute permissions on
all executable files

Your Powers

Selective directory access
depending on permissions

Selective file access
depending on permissions

All limits based on individual
and group permissions

Becoming the Superuser

There are two ways to become the superuser: by logging in as **root**, or by changing to superuser after logging in as a regular user by invoking the **su** (substitute user) utility.

In this chapter you will learn to become the superuser with the **su** utility. It is a good habit to use the **su** utility rather than logging on as **root**. One reason is that the utility **su** keeps a record of the names of users who invoke it. If a user logs into the system as **root**, there is no record of that user's name.

Another security reason for using **su** is to protect the system from a fake login program that a system cracker may have left running at a terminal. This program emulates the login banner of your system and waits for an unsuspecting user to try to log in. The program then prompts the user for the password, saves the login and password in the cracker's files, and dies. The authentic login banner is then displayed, prompting the user to try logging in again, thinking he or she has made a typing error. In this way, your password can be stolen. Moreover, if you log in as **root**, this will give the cracker the password to **root**, and thus total control of your system. If you log in as yourself and not as the superuser, the only password that can be compromised is your own.

1. To become the superuser, type **/bin/su**

2. Provide the correct password

Using Full Pathnames for Utilities

Another security precaution for the superuser is to always type the full pathname to any command. As the superuser, instead of typing **ls**, type **/bin/ls**. This explicitly executes the **ls** program in **bin** and prevents you from running any program that a system cracker may have left in a directory in the superuser *PATH*.

For example: if the superuser *PATH* includes the directory */usr/local* before */bin*, a cracker can leave a modified copy of a utility such as **ls** in */usr/local*. Then, when the superuser enters **ls** *testfile*, the first executable file called *ls* found in the *PATH* and executed is the one in */usr/local*, instead of the one in */bin*. This may mean that security has been compromised.

A wise precaution is to never include the current working (dot) directory or any nonsystem directory in the superuser's *PATH* environment variable. The shorter the superuser's *PATH*, the better. A suitable *PATH* for the superuser would be */bin /usr/bin*.

Exiting from Superuser Status

Once you have carried out the tasks that needed superuser status, it is wise to immediately exit from it.

1. If you used **su** to become superuser, exit by typing

   exit

SECURITY CONCERNS IN SETTING SYSTEM DIRECTORY PERMISSIONS 21.3

One matter of importance for UNIX system administrators is the setting of appropriate permissions for all system directories and system files.

It is impossible to list all files and all of their permissions in this section; however, certain principles can be followed to ensure system security.

The first rule is to close off certain system directories to ordinary users who do not need access to them. This includes directories such as */usr/spool/at* and */usr/spool/uucp*. Other directories must be accessible and readable, but not writable, such as */usr/include* and */usr/spool/mail*.

The same care should be taken with files. Files in the */bin* directory should only be executable, and neither readable nor writable by anyone other than **root**. The directory */bin* itself should only be readable and executable, but not writable — to prevent potential breaches by system crackers replacing utilities with modified versions of their own.

21.4   COMMUNICATING TO ALL USERS ON THE SYSTEM

As a superuser, there are times when you need to communicate to everyone on the system. One of those times is when you are bringing the system down. If the system's users are given fair warning of the system going down, they can exit from whatever programs they are using and not lose any of their work.

1. First, type

/bin/su

2. Type in the superuser password.

3. When your shell prompt returns, type one of these commands:

System V:
/etc/wall

BSD:
/bin/wall

The command **wall** is an acronym for **write all** users. Observe that the shell prompt does not return; the **wall** program is waiting for input. Everything you type after the command is transmitted to all users currently on the system.

4. Type

This is a test.
This is simply a test.
Ctrl-d

Ctrl-d must be on a line by itself. It is the end-of-file (EOF) signal that ends the transmission.

After you've typed in Ctrl-d, you see a message something like this one:

```
Broadcast message from isis!root (ttyp). . .
This is a test.
This is simply a test.
```

On some systems, the **wall** utility can be accessed by all users. If a user terminal has its access turned off (**mesg n**), only the superuser can write to the terminal. When the superuser uses **wall**, all terminals receive the messages, regardless of terminal permissions. Some system administrators set the permissions for **wall** so that only the superuser can use it.

When you run this utility as the superuser, you add legitimacy to your message. Part of the **wall** output informs users of the message sender. For example, a message from the superuser saying that the system is going down in five minutes will be given more credence than one from an ordinary user. It is therefore advisable that only the superuser run this utility.

Using wall with an Argument File

You do not always have to type in your message when you use the **wall** utility. Instead, you can use redirection and specify an existing input file.

1. First, create a file using **vi**. Type one of the following commands:

   System V:
   /usr/bin/vi/*wall _file*

   BSD:
   /usr/ucb/vi/*wall_file*

2. In **vi**, type an appropriate message such as the "This is a test" one used previously.

3. Save the file and exit **vi**.

4. To broadcast the message type one of these commands:

System V:
/etc/wall < /*wall_file*

BSD:
/bin/wall < /*wall_file*

The utility reads its input from *wall_file* and transmits it to all users on the system.

CREATING A NEW LOGIN ACCOUNT IN BSD

21.5

If you are on a BSD system, all administrative duties must be carried out from the shell by the superuser. The next few sections describe how to perform these duties on a BSD system. The final section of the chapter presents the System V system administration menu and the tasks that it accomplishes. Even if you are on a System V machine, you will want to read the following sections to see what must be accomplished in performing system administrator tasks.

This section describes how you as a superuser can create a new account from the command line. There may also be an **adduser** utility or shell script present for adding a new user on your BSD system.

If your system is distributed on a network, speak to your system administrator before attempting any of the changes mentioned here.

1. First substitute user to the superuser.

2. Determine which group the new user will belong to. Type

    /usr/ucb/more */etc/group*

    and select a suitable group for this user. Make a note of that group's number *(gid)*.

3. To add a user, you must edit the password file. Type

    /etc/vipw

    When the utility **vipw** is invoked, a lock is placed on the file */etc/passwd,* so that no one else can edit the file while you are doing so. It also edits on a temporary file, */etc/ptmp,* which prevents destruction of the password file if the editor is accidentally killed.

4. Normally, you add new users to the end of the password file and assign the next available user number (**uid**). An easy way of adding a new entry is to **yank** the last line of the password file and copy it immediately after itself. While on the last line of the file, type

    yy
    p

5. Now you can edit the **yank**ed line for the new user. Our example line looks something like this:

```
leroy:7Pgqtc:340:101:Leroy Page:/users/leroy:/bin/csh
```

- The first field is the login name. Change it to the new login name.

- Everything between the first and second colons is the password field; delete all of it.

- The third field is the *uid*. Change it to the next available user ID.

- The fourth field is the *gid*. Set that to the group that you selected in Step 2.

- Change the next field to the new user's name. If you wish, you can leave this field blank.

- The next field, */users/leroy*, refers to the user's Home directory. Change it to what the new user's Home directory will be called.

- The last field refers to the shell that this new user will use. If it is to be the Bourne shell, change this field to */bin/sh*.

The new entry for the user James Lee should now look like this:

```
james::341:101:James Lee:/users/james:/bin/csh
```

6. Save the changes and exit the editor.

7. While you are still the superuser, give the new account a password by typing

   passwd *james*

8. After typing in and verifying the new password, look through the file */etc/password*. Notice that in the new user's entry, the second field is no longer empty and contains the encrypted version of the password you entered.

9. Next, create the Home directory of this user, with an appropriate directory pathname:

mkdir */users/james*

10. The new user will need a *.login* file, and either a *.profile* or a *.cshrc* file. Copy the system templates of these files into the newly created Home directory.

11. Change the ownership of these directories and files to the new user. Type

chown *james /users/james/.login*
chown *james /users/james/.cshrc*
chown *james /users/james*

The new account has now been set up.

21.6   REMOVING A USER FROM A BSD SYSTEM

Occasionally, it is necessary to remove a user from your system. A user may resign from the company, or perhaps an abusive user is discovered.

1. Log in as a superuser using the **su** utility.

2. If you wish to save a backup copy of the files belonging to this soon-to-be-obsolete login, do so using the **tar** utility.

3. Once all backups have been made, change into the Home directory of the user by typing

cd ~*old_login*

where *old_login* is the user's login.

4. Make sure that you are in the correct directory by typing

pwd

5. Remove all the files from this directory and all related subdirectories by typing

/bin/rm -rif *

6. Once all the files have been deleted, change to the parent directory and remove the obsolete login's Home directory with the **rmdir** utility.

7. Edit the password file with **vipw**. Delete the entry for this particular user.

BACKING UP A FILESYSTEM IN BSD   21.7

BSD provides a utility that makes incremental back-ups of the filesystem. The syntax of the command that calls it is

dump *key filesys*

Determining the dump Level

The first argument, *key*, is a code consisting of two or more option characters. The first character is a digit, 0 through 9, which is the **dump** level. The **dump** level tells the utility which files to **dump**. All files created or modified since the last **dump** of a lower-numbered level will be **dump**ed to tape. (The file */etc/dumpdates* is used to keep track of **dump** dates.) Thus, a **dump** level

0 backs up all the files in the filesystem (this is known as a full dump). A level 1 **dump**s all files changed since the last level 0 **dump**, a level 2 **dump**s all files since the last level 1 **dump**, and so forth.

Specifying a level other than 0 produces an *incremental backup* (a backup containing recently modified files). If a level 1 backup is done a day after a level 0 backup, all files modified in the last day are backed up. If a level 9 backup is done a week after a level 8 backup, all files modified in the last week are backed up. This arrangement of **dump** levels enables the system administrator to set up a regular system of quarterly, monthly, weekly, and daily backups.

Keeping Track of Backup Files

The second character of the *key* may be the letter **u**, which tells **dump** to update the */etc/dumpdate* file. This ensures that future **dump**s at the same or higher level will not **dump** the same files, unless they have been modified.

Specifying the Device for Backup

The argument *filesys* represents the name of the device you are **dump**ing. Get the name of the file-system to be backed up from the manual or your system administrator. So that */etc/ddate* can accurately keep track of **dump**s, the same name must be used each time a given filesystem is backed up. Because filesystems may be referred to by various names, be sure to find out which name to use from the manual or your system administrator.

Running the **dump** command with these two arguments will **dump** the indicated filesystem, at the indicated level, to the default **dump** device. This device is usually the top cartridge tape drive.

Using a Different Tape Device

If you wish to **dump** to a tape that is not the default drive, such as a nine-track tape drive, you must include the *f* character in your *key* argument. Type the command

dump *0uf devname filesys*

where *devname* is the name of the tape drive you wish to use.

CAUTION: Each tape drive has several different names (for example, */dev/rmt0* and */dev/fsrmt0* both name the nine-track drive). Again, look in the manual or ask your system administrator.

Examining dump Options

Here are the options available with the **dump** command:

f Place the result of the **dump** on the next argument file, instead of on a device. If the name of the file is - (dash), **dump** writes to standard output.

u Write the date of the beginning of the **dump** in the file /etc/dumpdates if the **dump** completes successfully. (The file /etc/dumpdates records a date for each file-system and each **dump** level.)

W Display what filesystems need to be **dump**ed, using the information in the files /etc/dumpdates and /etc/fstab.

s Inform **dump** that a nonstandard tape length is being used.

n Instruct **dump** to notify all the operators in the group operator, by means similar to the **wall** utility, whenever the program or equipment needs attention such as replacing tapes.

b Specify the density of the tape. Default is 1600 bits per inch.

In summary, the command line

dump 0ufsbn /dev/fsrmt0 3600 512 filesys

writes a level 0 **dump** of the filesystem filesys onto a 3600-foot tape located on the nine-track tape drive, with a tape the density of 512.

Ask your system administrator to explain how your site utilizes the **dump** command, and to which devices the files are **dump**ed.

Interacting with dump

1. Once you have typed the appropriate **dump** command, you receive several messages on the console:

```
Phase I: Tape and Disk files opened successfully.
Phase II: Deciding which files to dump.
    Estimating amount of tape needed.
    Estimated xxxx blocks on x 450 foot tape(s).
Phase III: Dumping the directories of /dev/xx.
Phase IV: Dumping the files of /dev/xx.
```

2. If the system tells you that a second tape is required, unmount the first tape (when prompted to do so) and mount a second one. Repeat this as necessary for a third tape, a fourth tape, and so on.

3. Be sure to label each tape when you put it in the drive. The second tape should be labeled the same as the first, except that it is tape #2.

4. If your terminal screen goes blank during the **dump** procedure (due to the terminal's screen-save feature), it is advisable to use the [Spacebar] rather than the [Return] key to redisplay screen data. This prevents inadvertently telling the **dump** program to proceed with the **dump** on a second tape (which may not have been loaded yet).

5. When the **dump** is finished (indicated by the message DONE), follow the same procedure to **dump** any additional filesystems.

Restoring Files from a dump Tape

Obviously, tape copies of important files are useless unless you have some means of retrieving them. The way to extract a file or files from a **dump** tape is with the **restore** command.

The basic syntax of the command is

/etc/**restore** *key [name]*

If you were about to **restore** a file from a **dump** tape, you would type a command line that would look something like:

/etc/**restore** *i*

The keys available with **restore** include

i This mode allows an interactive restoration of files from the tape. It is one of the more useful options. Within this mode, the command **help** lists a summary of available commands within this interactive shell.

r With this option, the tape is read and loaded into the current directory.

CAUTION: This option will overwrite existing files.

x This option extracts the named files from the tape. If the name matches a directory, it extracts the entire directory and all of its subdirectories.

The optional *name* argument refers to the tape drive where the backups are situated. If no *name* is provided, **restore** expects the default tape drive to contain the backup tape.

Restoration of files and/or filesystems from backups can be a tricky and dangerous procedure. This is because it is possible for files to be overwritten with older copies from the backup tapes. For this reason, **restore** is typically performed only by the system administrator.

BRINGING DOWN THE SYSTEM IN BSD USING SHUTDOWN

21.8

As a superuser, there are times when you need to shut down the system for some reason, including software installation, filesystem backups, and maintenance. The BSD system provides you with a useful utility called **shutdown**. All of the following information about the shutdown process is system dependent, so before you use **shutdown**, speak to your system administrator. Ask for the exact command to bring the system back up to multiuser mode, and arrange for your system administrator to be available to aid you in case of problems.

1. To shut down the system, first log in as the superuser. Type

   /bin/su

2. Bring the system to a complete halt by typing

   /etc/shutdown *+15*

   This command brings down the system in 15 minutes. The amount of lead time can be modified by changing the argument.

3. Using the system's clock, you can specify an exact time for the system to be shut down. Type

   /etc/shutdown *15:00*

   The 15:00 argument to **shutdown** means that the system will be shut down at 3:00 in the afternoon (based on a 24-hour clock).

Examining the shutdown Options

The command syntax for the **shutdown** command is as follows:

shutdown *[-option] time message*

There are a number of useful options to **shutdown**.

-k   When this option is specified, the system sends your *message* to all users on the system, but does not shut the system down. This is useful when the superuser needs to end all use of the system without actually bringing the system down.

-h   This option tells the system to execute the **halt** utility that writes all contents of main memory to the disk, stops the processor, and does not allow reboot, even if the reboot switch is set on the machine.

-r   This option executes the utility **reboot** that brings the system back up after it has been shut down. This is useful when you have modified system software and you wish to test it out.

Rebooting After shutdown

Once **shutdown** has been executed without the **reboot** option, the system is usually placed in a single-user mode called *monitor*. From here, typing the command **boot** will reboot the system into multiuser mode.

USING FSCK IN BSD TO CHECK THE FILESYSTEM

21.9

In BSD, the UNIX filesystem can be checked for damage and then repaired using the file system check (**fsck**) utility.

   The procedures in this section require that you be logged in as the superuser and will render the system unavailable to others at various points. If you are on a multiuser system, be sure to clear these activities with your system administrator.

Unmounting a Filesystem Before Running fsck

Filesystems that are accessible to users are *mounted.*

1. Before beginning to check and repair a filesystem, you must *unmount* it. For example, to unmount the */dev/xyz* filesystem, type the command

   umount */dev/xyz*

   Once you *unmount* a filesystem, the files are inaccessible for normal input/output operations.

Running fsck on a Single Filesystem in Check-Only Mode

The **fsck** utility normally checks and repairs filesystem damage at the same time. It is possible, however, to run **fsck** in check-only mode. This mode allows you to check the filesystem for damage, but does not permit **fsck** to attempt to fix anything.

1. To run **fsck** in check-only mode, type the command:

   fsck -n */dev/***xyz**

   The */dev/xyz* specifies which filesystem to check, and the **-n** option tells **fsck** to answer **no** to all changes.

2. At this point, **fsck** may tell you:

   ```
   Need scratch file.
   ```

If so, you are being asked to provide the name of a file in which **fsck** can do its work. This file must not be in the filesystem that you are checking and should not already exist because it will be removed when **fsck** exits. If you are asked for this file, give the utility a filename something like

/tmp/scratch

The utility **fsck** will report all errors to you and also inform you that each phase of the checking procedure is being performed.

Remounting a Filesystem That fsck Has Checked

Now that you have perused the text produced by **fsck**, you can make the filesystem accessible again by remounting it. Type

mount */dev/xyz* */z*

The filesystem is again accessible to other users.

Running fsck in Check-and-Repair Mode

1. Unmount the filesystem.

2. To run **fsck** in check-and-repair mode, type the command

   fsck */dev/xyz*

3. You will probably be prompted for a scratch file. Type the full pathname, such as */tmp/scratch2.*

Without the **-n** option, **fsck** not only reports any errors to you and informs you about each phase of its checking procedure but also asks you for help if it encounters any problems.

Removing Troublesome Files

The **clri** command can be used to remove a damaged file or directory that has been identified by **fsck**, but that cannot be removed with **rm**. This command removes the disk listing associated with the problem file, while leaving its directory entry intact. After **clri** is used, **fsck** must be rerun to deal with the directory entry for the file.

21.10 THE SYSTEM V MENU INTERFACE FOR SYSTEM ADMINISTRATION

Under System V, UNIX provides a menu interface to help the superuser in performing system administration. It is possible to assign a password to this menu interface program. Consult the manual or your system administrator if you are prompted for a password.

The interface provides a series of menus with many useful utilities for each group of functions. This section examines several essential entries in the main menu and submenus.

To start up the menu system, type

/etc/sysadm

Here is the main menu:

```
SYSTEM ADMINISTRATION
1  diagnostics     system diagnostics menu
2  diskmgmt        disk management menu
3  filemgmt        file management menu
4  machinemgmt     machine management menu
5  packagemgmt     package management menu
6  softwaremgmt    software management menu
7  syssetup        system setup menu
8  tapemgmt        tape management menu
9  ttymgmt         tty management menu
10 usermgmt        user management menu
```

The main menu makes it possible to accomplish the following series of functions.

diagnostics   Gives you access to system diagnostics utilities used to identify and repair problems within the system.

diskmgmt   Permits you to manage removable disks, including formatting, copying, and mounting them.

filemgmt   Allows you to prevent loss of files on the hard disk by copying them onto other media. If data loss does occur, you can copy the files from the other media back to the hard disk.

machinemgmt	Provides tools to operate the machine firmware, including turning it off, rebooting the machine, and going into monitor mode.
softwaremgmt	Permits you to install and test new software.
syssetup	Allows the superuser to modify system utilities, including the system clock and the system nodename, and also to modify and assign system passwords.
usermgmt	Allows the superuser to add, remove, and list the users on the system; add and remove groups on the system; and change users' passwords and login shells.

Adding a New User

To add a user to the system, select the **usermgmt** option from the main menu. From the **usermgmt** submenu, select the option **adduser**. The utility then steps you through this addition. It asks a series of questions about the new user and then makes the new entry. Once you are finished with this procedure, the new account is ready to be used.

Removing a User

To remove a user from the system, select the **usermgmt** option from the main menu. From the secondary menu, select the **deluser** option. This removes the user's login entry from the file */etc/passwd* and also deletes all of the user's files. None of these files can be reaccessed. Therefore, it is wise to **tar** the files before deleting the account.

Ensuring Filesystem Integrity

To inspect a filesystem, first select the **diskmgmt** option from the main menu. In the secondary menu, select the **checkfsys** option; this begins the check on the filesystem for errors. If there are errors, **checkfsys** attempts to repair them.

Making System Backups

To make backups, select the **filemgmt** menu. In the secondary menu, select the **backup** option. This utility makes backups from the integral hard disk to floppy disks or tape. It carries out two kinds of backups: complete and incremental. A complete backup copies all files and is used in case of serious file damage. An incremental backup only copies files changed since the last backup, like the BSD **dump** utility discussed earlier in this chapter.

Shutting Down and Restarting the System

To shut down or restart the system, select the **machine-mgmt** option. Useful options from this menu include

powerdown	This stops all running programs and turns off the machine.
reboot	This stops all running programs and reboots the machine.

Exercise 21-B

Answer the following questions:

1. In BSD, what is the command to bring down the system in ten minutes?

   _____

2. What is the name of the file to which you add new users?

   _____

3. What is the command for giving a password to a user with the login *sam?*

   _____

4. When removing a user from the system, how would you eliminate all of that user's files? What would you do first?

   _____

5. What is the difference between a level 0 and a level 1 **dump?**

   _____

6. What is the command for checking (but not repairing) the */dev* file system?

   _____

In this chapter, you examined superuser responsibilities and tasks that are handled by the system administrator. The system administrator is responsible for the filesystem, adding and removing users, making backups, and restoring files. This chapter introduced these skills. The manuals for your machine will be useful for the specifics of your site.

CONCLUSION

COMMAND SUMMARY

tar *filename*
Creates an archive copy of *filename* on the tape in the default tape drive without rewinding the tape.

tar c *filename*
Creates an archive copy of *filename* in the default tape drive at the beginning of the tape.

tar r *filename*
Appends *filename* to the tape in the default drive without rewinding the tape.

tar t
Lists the table of contents of an archive tape on the default tape drive.

tar x
Extracts all files from the archive tape on the default drive.

tar xv
Extracts all files from the archive tape on the default drive in verbose mode.

tar cf */dev/filename* .
Makes an archive copy of all files in the current directory onto a tape in another drive.

wall
Sends a message to all writable terminals. If run by superuser, a message is sent to all terminals. End the message with Ctrl-d on a line by itself.

/etc/sysadm
Starts up the System V menu interface for system administration.

/etc/shutdown *+15*
(BSD only) This brings the system down in 15 minutes.

COMMAND SUMMARY*(continued)*

/etc/shutdown *15:00*
(BSD only) Shuts down the system at 3:00 p.m.

/etc/shutdown -h *15:00*
(BSD only) Shuts down the system at 3:00 p.m. Executes the **halt** utility that writes all information to the disk, and does not allow reboot, even if reboot switch is set.

/etc/shutdown -r *15:00*
(BSD only) Shuts down the system at 3:00 p.m. Executes the **reboot** utility to bring the machine back up after shutdown.

/etc/vipw
(BSD only) If run by superuser, this starts up an editing session of the *//etc/passwd* file, to add or delete a user or to modify a user's entry.

dump [*dumplevel*][*optioncharacters*] *filesystem*
(BSD only) Makes a backup of the *filesystem*. The key is made up of the *dumplevel* and the *optioncharacters*.

/etc/restore [*irx*] [*filename*]
(BSD only) Restores a filesystem from a **dump** tape. The *filename* is specified if the **dump** tape is not on the default device.

umount */name*
Unmounts a filesystem. Normally used before performing a filesystem check using **fsck**.

fsck */name*
(BSD only) Runs a **filesystem check** and makes all necessary changes.

mount */name*
Mounts an unmounted filesystem.

·A·

Utility Information Pages

The following Utility Information Pages (UIP) are designed to provide you with an easy way to look up information about each utility discussed in Chapter 4, "Using Basic UNIX Utilities," which explores how a variety of basic utilities work by leading you through example exercises. The UIP provides a transition between the tutorial focus of this book and the UNIX Reference Manuals available with most systems.

Each entry describes how a certain utility works and includes the following:

- The function of the utility
- Sample commands with explanations of how they work
- A list of key options, including the syntax and function of each
- Warnings, notes, and other useful information

awk

EXAMINING DATA WITH awk

The **awk** utility has two functions: it scans a file for a specified pattern and then carries out an associated action.

Sample Commands

awk '/*pat*/ {print}' *file1*
This **awk** command line searches the file *file1* for all lines containing the pattern *pat* and outputs the selected lines. Because the output has not been redirected, it is sent to the screen.

awk 'length >*40* {**print**}' *file1*
Displays all lines from the file *file1* that are longer than 40 characters.

awk '{ print $3 $2 $1 }' *file1*
Searches all lines and then outputs the first three fields in 3, 2, 1 order.

awk '*/hello/,/goodbye/* {**print**}' *file1*
Displays every group of lines from the file *file1* where
the first line in each group contains the string *hello*,
and the last line in each group contains the string
goodbye.

awk -f *prog_file file1*
Executes the **awk** command listed in the file *prog_file*
on the input file *file1*.

Options

-F*char*	Change the field separator character from the default to whatever *char* you enter after the **F.**
-f *file1*	Follow instructions in the file *file1*.

Command Format

All **awk** commands are in this format:

awk '*pattern* {**action**} '

If no pattern is given, the default pattern of every line
is used by **awk.** All lines are a match. If no action is
given, the default action, {**print**}, is evoked. Selected
lines are output.

Patterns

Each pattern statement given in an **awk** command relates to a sequence of characters. The following are possible pattern statements:

/string/ Perform **action** on all lines containing the string of characters in *string*.

/string1lstring2/ Perform **action** on all lines containing either *string1* or *string2*.

$n ~ /string/ Perform **action** on all lines in which the *n*th entry matches the string of characters in *string*.

$n !~ /string/ Perform **action** on all records in which the entry in field number *n* does not match the string of characters in *string*.

variable relation value For example, *NR> =5* performs an action on all lines that have a record number of *5* or greater. Perform **action** on every line where the *variable* has the given *relation* to the given *value*. Variables include *NR* (the current record or line number), *NF* (the number of fields in the current line), *$n* (the contents of the *n*th field of the current line), and *$0* (the contents of the current line). The *variable* portion can also be a function such as **length,** which is the length of the

current line. The *relation* can be one
of the following:

= =	equals
!=	does not equal
<	less than
< =	less than or equal to
>	greater than
> =	greater than or equal to
~	equal to string
!~	not equal to string

The *value* can either be a string, a
number, or another variable.

pattern1,   Execute **action** on all lines between
pattern2   and including the two lines satisfy-
ing the pattern statements in *pattern1*
and *pattern2*. A comma separates the
two patterns.

BEGIN   Perform the following **action** before
reading the first input line.

END   Perform the following **action** after
reading the last line of input.

Actions

All actions are enclosed by curly brackets, as in {**print**
$3}. Multiple actions can be separated by semicolons

on a single line or by new-line characters if in an **awk** program file. Available actions include, but are not limited to, the following:

print	Print the line.
print $field	Print the given *field*.
foo= *value*	Set the variable *foo* to the given *value*. (The *value* may be another variable or function.) You can set your own variables. The two separator variables *FS* (the field separator character) and *RS* (the record separator character) can only be set in a **BEGIN** statement.

Warnings

All single **awk** command statements should be enclosed in single quotes to prevent interpretation by the shell. White space in the input is not kept in the output when fields are involved.

Notes

The name **awk** is derived from the authors of the utility, Aho, Weinberger, and Kernighan. Consult the UNIX Reference Manual or other documents for information about other **awk** features.

DISPLAYING THE CONTENTS OF FILES WITH cat

cat

The **cat** utility can be used to create files, display the contents of files, and to merge files.

Sample Commands

cat *file1*
The **cat** utility reads the contents of the file *file1* and writes it to the screen.

cat *file1 file2* > *file3*
Instructs **cat** to read *file1* and *file2* and place the output in *file3*. Concatenates the two files.

cat -v *file1*
Outputs the entire content of *file1*, including the nonprinting characters.

cat -v -e *file1 file2*
Outputs both files *file1* and *file2*, marking the end of each line with a $ character.

Options

-v   Display nonprinting characters, such as control and meta characters, by preceding control characters with a ˆ and meta characters with a **M-**.

-t	Display the tab character as ^I for the key [Ctrl-i]. In System V, **-t** must be used with the **-v** option.
-e	Display the end-of-line character as a **$**. In System V, **-e** must be used with the **-v** option.
-s	On System V, instructs **cat** not to notify you about nonexistent files. On BSD, causes **cat** to ignore all but one of adjacent empty lines, making the output look single-spaced.
-n	Print each line with its line number (BSD only).
-nb	Print each non-blank line with its line number (BSD only).

Warnings

Beware of overwriting files.

Notes

The name **cat** is short for **cat**enate or, if you prefer, con**cat**enate. The **cat** utility reads standard input and writes to standard output.

COMPARING THE CONTENTS OF TWO FILES WITH comm

comm

The **comm** utility compares the lines of two sorted files.

Sample Commands

comm *file1 file2*
Compares both files and produces a three-column output: lines that are only in *file1*, lines that are only in *file2*, and lines that are in both files.

comm -3 *file1 file2*
Outputs the lines that are unique to each file, leaving out the lines common to both files.

comm -12 *file1 file2*
Leaves out unique lines and outputs the lines that both files have in common.

Options

-1	Suppress printing of the first column (lines unique to the first file).
-2	Suppress printing of the second column (lines unique to the second file).
-3	Suppress printing of the third column (lines in both files).

Notes

The options for the **comm** utility can be combined.

cut

SELECTING FIELDS FROM A FILE WITH cut

The **cut** utility displays portions of each line or *record* in a file specified either by a column of data, called a *field*, or by a character position in the line.

Sample Commands

cut -c1-40 *testfile*
Prints the first 40 characters of each line in *testfile*.

cut -f1,3 *testfile*
Prints the first and third fields (which are separated by tabs) of each line in the file *testfile*.

cut -d: -f2-4 *testfile*
Prints the second, third, and fourth fields of each line in *testfile*. The **-d:** specifies that the fields are separated by the colon character. Any character may be specified.

Options

-c*list*   Display the characters in positions specified by *list*. The list is a series of entries separated by commas. A list entry may be a single number representing a character position, or two numbers separated by a dash (-) representing all characters from the first position to the last. For example, the list *2,5-10,13* instructs **cut** to output the second character, the fifth through tenth characters, and the thirteenth character.

-f*list*   Display the fields (or columns) specified by *list*, and lines that contain no field separation character. Fields are normally separated by tabs.

-d*char*   Specify the field separation character to be *char* (used only with the **-f** option).

-s   Suppress printing lines that do not contain a field separation character (used only with the **-f** option).

Warnings

You must specify either the **-c** or **-f** option, or you will receive an error. Lines must be no longer than 1023 characters.

dc

CALCULATING WITH dc

The **dc** (short for **d**esk **c**alculator) utility is an on-line reverse-notation (postfix) calculator. On this calculator, the notation for six plus three is 6 3 + rather than 6+3.

Sample Commands

To execute the calculator, type

dc

Like **vi** and **mail**, **dc** is an interactive utility. After you enter **dc**, you are in communication with the **dc** utility, not the shell. You enter **dc** commands like these:

1 7.216 + **p**

Takes 1 and 7.216, adds the two numbers together, and **p**rints the answer.

_3 67 * **p**

Multiplies -3 by 67 and prints the answer. The _ in front of the 3 is an underscore, not a minus sign. Negative numbers must be preceded by an underscore.

q

Quits the **dc** utility and returns to the shell.

Operations

number	Places the number *number* on top of the stack.
+	Removes the top two arguments on the stack, adds them, and pushes the answer onto the stack.
-	Removes the top two arguments on the stack, subtracts the second from the first, and pushes the answer onto the stack.
*	Removes the top two arguments on the stack, multiplies them, and pushes the answer onto the stack.
/	Removes the top two arguments on the stack, divides the first argument by the second one, and pushes the answer onto the stack.
^	Removes the top two arguments on the stack. The answer, the first number to the power of the second, is pushed onto the stack.
v	Removes the top argument on the stack, takes the square root of it, and pushes the answer onto the stack.
c	Removes all arguments from the stack.

p	Prints the top argument of the stack.
f	Prints all arguments on the stack.
q	Quits the **dc** utility and returns to the shell.

Warnings

As noted above, negative numbers must be preceded by an underscore (_). The minus sign (-) is interpreted as the command to subtract the last two numbers.

Notes

The **dc** makes use of a stack. During an arithmetic operation, the number of arguments needed is popped from the stack, the operation is performed, and the answer is placed on top of the stack. The UNIX Reference Manual entry for **dc**, as well as other system documents, examines additional features. There is also a programming language for **dc**, called **bc.**

diff

FINDING DIFFERENCES BETWEEN FILES WITH diff

The **diff** utility compares the lines in two files and reports any differences between them.

Sample Commands

diff *file1 file2*
The **diff** utility reports the differences between the files *file1* and *file2* by displaying output similar to the following:

```
1,2c1,2
< This is a line from file1
< Humpty Dumpty sat on a wall.
---
> This is a line from file2.
> Humpty Dumpty sat on a gate.
6c6
< This ends file1.
---
> This ends file2.
```

The lines from *file1* are preceded by a < symbol, while the lines from *file2* are preceded by a > symbol. The numbers and letters (*1,2c1,2* and *6c6*) denote the positions of the lines in the first and second files.

Options

-b   Ignore blanks (spaces and tabs) at the end of a line and evaluate other strings of blanks as equal.

-h	Request a fast but incomplete job. Works only if the files are very similar, with only short stretches of differences that are far apart; otherwise, **diff** reports false differences. This is recommended for long files.
-i	Ignore the case (upper or lower) of letters when searching for differences (BSD only).

Warnings

If the last line of a file is missing a new-line character, it may be reported as different from a line in the other file that is otherwise identical.

grep

SEARCHING THROUGH FILES WITH grep

The **grep** utility examines input for lines containing specified target strings of characters.

Sample Commands

grep and *testfile*
Outputs each line of *testfile* that contains the string *and*, whether as a word or part of another word.

grep -vi *'and then'* *file1* *file2*

Instructs **grep** to print all lines of *file1* and *file2* that do not contain the phrase *and then*, regardless of case.

grep -l *'[D,d]ictionary'* *

Prints the names of all files in the current directory that contain either the string *dictionary* or *Dictionary*.

Options

-c	Print the number of lines containing the pattern.
-i	Ignore upper- and lowercase when searching for a pattern.
-l	Output the names of the files that contain the pattern.
-n	Include line numbers with each output line.
-s	Do not output error messages.
-v	Output all lines in which the pattern is not found.

Regular Expressions

grep, awk, and **sed** use the following regular expressions in pattern matching:

.	Stands for any character. For example, the pattern *'t..'* targets the letter *t* followed by any two characters.
*	Stands for any number of repetitions of the previous character. For example, the pattern *'a*m'* targets a string of zero or more letter *a*'s followed by the letter *m*.
[*pat1,pat2*]	Locates either pattern *pat1* or *pat2*. For example, the pattern *'[hi,hello]'* refers to both patterns *'hi,'* and *'hello,'*.

Warnings

Output lines longer than 256 characters are truncated.

Notes

You must enclose patterns containing blanks or regular expressions in single- or double-quotes to avoid having the shell interpret them. With multiple files, the filename is printed before each line.

join   COMBINING FILES WITH join

The **join** utility combines lines of two sorted files by matching the values of entries in designated fields.

Sample Commands

join *file1 file2*
The **join** utility examines the first field (column) of each line in the sorted files *file1* and *file2*. It combines those lines with matching values in the first field. The resulting output line consists of the matching field, followed by the remainder of the line from *file1*, and the remainder of the line from *file2*.

For example, if the contents of *file1* are

```
Clark William
Downs Kelly
Lee Mike
Smith Jane
Witt Kate
```

and the contents of *file2* are

```
Clark 555-1234
Evans 555-2345
Lee 555-3456
Smith 555-4567
Zoe 555-5678
```

the joined output is

```
Clark William 555-1234
Lee Mike 555-3456
Smith Jane 555-4567
```

join -j 2 **-t:** *file1 file2*
Joins lines using the second field from both files where the fields are separated by colons.

join -j1 2 **-j2** 1 *file1 file2*
Joins lines by matching entries in the second field of the first file with entries in the first field of the second file.

join -o 3.2,2.1 *file1 file2*
After joining the lines, **join** outputs the third field of the second file, followed by the second field of the first file.

Options

-a*n*	In addition to paired lines, output each unmatched line from the *n*th file.
-j*n m*	Use the *m*th field of the *n*th file to compare for joining.
-o *list*	Output only the fields listed in *list*. The list is of the form *entry1,entry2,* and so on. Each entry of the list is *n.m*, where *n* represents the file number (1 or 2), and *m* represents the field number.
-t*char*	Specify the character *char* as the field separator instead of blanks.

Warnings

Each field that is being examined for joining must be
sorted in ASCII order.

PUTTING LINES TOGETHER WITH paste

paste

The **paste** utility combines lines from files.

Sample Commands

paste *file1 file2*
The **paste** utility outputs lines consisting of each line
in files *file1* and *file2* side by side (in two columns on
the same line, separated by a tab).

paste -d"*n***"** *file1 file2*
Combines the files *file1* and *file2* so that the output is
one column of lines that alternate between a line from
file1 and a line from *file2,* like this:

First line from *file1*
First line from *file2*
Second line from *file1*
Second line from *file2*
and so on. . .

paste -s -d" *n***"** *file1*
Combines adjacent pairs of lines in the file *file1* into
single lines.

Options

-d_list_   Change the column separation character from tab to the characters in _list_. Each character in the list separates its respective columns.

For example, if _list_ were +$, the first and second columns would be separated by the character +, and the second and third columns would be separated by a $. If there are too many columns for a list, the list is recycled. So, for the list of +$, the third and fourth columns would be separated by a +, the fourth and fifth columns would be separated by a $, and so on.

The list may contain these following special escape sequences: \n (newline), \t (tab), \\ (backslash), and \0 (empty string, not a null character). Lists that include spaces or escape sequences must be enclosed in double-quotes, as in the preceding examples 2 and 3

-s   Print each line from a file as a column.

Warnings

A maximum of 12 input files at a time may be combined without using the **-s** option. Output lines are truncated if longer than 511 characters.

EXAMINING FILES WITH pr

pr

The **pr** utility **pr**ints, paginates, and formats files.

Sample Commands

pr *file1*
The **pr** utility outputs each page of *file1* with the date, time, filename, and page number as a header.

pr +*5* **-h** *Mine file1*
Prints the file *file1* starting from the fifth page and replaces the filename *file1* in the header with the title *Mine.*

pr -s$ -m *file1 file2 file3*
Prints the contents of the files *file1*, *file2*, and *file3* side by side, with each column separated by $ characters.

pr -m -w40 **-l**24 *file1 file2*
Prints the two files *file1* and *file2* side by side, using a page width of 40 characters, and a page length of 24 lines.

Options

+*page*	Begin printing on page number *page*.
-*cols*	Print in columns, using *cols* number of columns.
-h *header*	Replace the filename in the page header with *header*.
-m	Print multiple files side by side, using one column for each file.
-s*char*	Substitute the default column separator (tab) with *char*
-w*width*	When printing multiple columns, set page width to be *width*, instead of the usual 72 characters.
-l*length*	Set the page length to *length*.
-f	Use a form-feed character, instead of several line-feeds, at the end of a page. (This is only useful when sending to a line printer.)
-t	Suppress printing of the five-line header at the beginning of a page, and the five-line footer at the end of each page.
-d	Print the output in double-spacing (System V only).

-ncx

Number each line, using x spaces for the numbers, separating the lines from the line numbers by the character given in c. The separation character c can be any nonnumeric single character. If c is not given, a tab is used to separate the lines from the line numbers (System V only).

-ecx

Output tab characters from the input as white space, from the starting character position to the next tab end character position. The tab end character positions occur at the character positions x, $2x$, $3x$ and so on. If x is not given in the command line, the default value of x is 8. Define input tab character to be the character given in c. If c is not given, use tab $\boxed{\text{Ctrl-i}}$ as the tab character (System V only).

-icx

Where possible, replace white space from the input with tabs in the output. Tabs are expanded as in the explanation for **-e**cx. Again, if x is not given, the default value of 8 is used. Define input tab character to be the character given in *c*. If *c* is not given, use tab $\boxed{\text{Ctrl-i}}$ as the tab character (System V only).

-p   Pause after each page until told to go on (System V only).

-r   Do not report any errors if a file cannot be opened (System V only).

Warnings

Sending messages to the terminal using the **write** command is not permitted when **pr** is executing.

sed   MAKING CHANGES TO INPUT WITH sed

The **sed** utility (short for **stream editor**) allows you to make changes to a file or input without an editor.

Sample Commands

sed '*4,7* **d**' *file1* > *file2*
The **sed** utility uses *file1* for its input and executes the command *4,7* **d,** which deletes the fourth through seventh lines. The output is placed in the file *file2*.

sed '*s/vanilla/rocky-road*/**g**' *file1* > *file2*
Replaces all occurrences of the word *vanilla* in *file1* with the word *rocky-road,* storing the output in *file2.*

who I sed '*s/ */ /***g**'
The output of **who** is piped to **sed,** which replaces all instances of one or more spaces with one space.

sed -e '*1,5* **d**' **-e** '*s/parakeet/parrot*/**g**' *file1* > *file2*
Deletes the first five lines of *file1* and replaces all occurrences of the word *parakeet* with *parrot,* storing the output in *file2.*

sed -f *sedscript file1* > *file2*
Executes the **sed** commands in the file *sedscript,* taking input from *file1,* and storing the output in *file2.*

Options

-n	Suppress the default output.
-e *command*	Execute the **sed** command given in *command.* (Allows you to execute multiple commands on a single **sed** command line.)
-f *script_file*	Execute the **sed** commands in the file *script_file.*

Command Format

All **sed** commands are in this format:

location **action**

The *location* portion can be in the form of a string of characters or a line number. Character strings are enclosed by slash characters, like this: */string/*. The *location* can be a range of locations, separated by a comma. For example, the location 4,7 denotes the fourth through seventh lines. If no location is given, the action is performed on all lines.

Actions

The **action** portion is any set of editing commands, including but not limited to the following:

p	Print the line.
!p	Do not print the line.
d	Delete the line.
q	Quit printing.
i *text. . .*	Insert *text* above the given line.
a *text. . .*	Append *text* below the given line.
w *filename*	Write the line to the file named *filename*.
s/*word***/***replacement***/**	Substitute the first occurrence in a line of the string *word* with *replacement* string.

s/*word*/*replacement*/**g**   Substitute all occurrences in a line of the string *word* with *replacement* string (global substitution).

Warnings

All **sed** command strings must be enclosed in single-quotes to prevent the shell from interpreting any special characters.

Notes

All **sed** commands are also **ed** commands (**ed** is the line editor). There are many other **sed** commands. Consult the UNIX Reference Manual and other system documents.

ORDERING THE LINES OF A FILE WITH sort   sort

The **sort** utility reads all lines from input and then sorts the lines according to one of several schemes. The sorted lines are the output.

Sample Commands

sort *file1*
The **sort** utility sorts the lines of *file1* in ASCII order (symbols first, then numbers, followed by upper- and then lowercase letters). The output is then displayed on the screen.

sort *file1 file2*
Reads the lines of both files *file1* and *file2*, sorts the lines of both files together in ASCII order, and then displays the sorted lines on the screen.

sort -m *file1 file2*
Tries to merge the lines of both files *file1* and *file2* into sorted order, without first sorting both files. If either file is not sorted, then the merged output will not be sorted.

sort +*1* -*2 file1*
Arranges the lines of *file1* by sorting on the second field. Fields are separated by blanks.

Options

-c	Print nothing if the input file is sorted. Otherwise, output the first line that is out of order.
-m	Merge the lines of input files without sorting them. (Assumes that the input files are already sorted.)

-u   Make all lines unique by print-
                 ing only one of a set of duplicate
                 lines.

-o *file*   Send output to *file* instead of to
                 standard output, as long as *file* is
                 not an input file, too.

-d   Sort in "dictionary" order, com-
                 paring only blanks, letters, and
                 numbers.

-f   Sort by treating uppercase letters
                 as lowercase.

-i   Sort, including only ASCII char-
                 acters in the range 040 to 176 in
                 non-numeric comparisons. This
                 is useful if a file is cluttered with
                 line noise from a modem.

-n   Sort real numbers in numeric
                 order, smallest to largest.

-r   Sort in reverse order.

+*field-1* **-***field*   Arrange the lines by sorting on
                 the entries of the field number
                 given by *field*. The field number
                 listed after the **+** is one less
                 than the number of the field on
                 which you want to sort. The
                 field number listed after the **-** is
                 the number of the field on

which you want to sort. See "Sample Commands." Fields are normally separated by blanks (spaces and tabs).

f*char*   Specify the field separator character to be the character given in *char*, instead of the default space character.

-M   Treat the first three non-blank characters as uppercase, and sort in month order (JAN, FEB, MAR, and so on; System V only).

Warnings

Very long lines are truncated without any error message.

Notes

When an error is discovered, **sort** notes it and exits without doing any sorting. This occurs under a number of conditions, including disorder found with the -c option. You can also sort on multiple fields of different types. To do so, consult the UNIX Reference Manual.

STORING OUTPUT BEING PASSED IN A PIPELINE WITH tee

tee

The **tee** utility writes its output to a file and to a standard output, which maybe connected to the terminal or the input of another utility.

Sample Commands

who l tee *file1*
The **tee** utility reads its input (in this case, the output of the **who** utility) and writes to both the given file, *file1*, and the standard output (in this case, your terminal). The file *file1* will contain a copy of the output of the **who** utility.

cat *file1 file2* **l tee** *file3* **l sort**
The **tee** utility reads its input (which is connected to the output of the **cat** command) and writes output to the file *file3*, and to standard output, which is connected to the input of the **sort** utility.

who l tee -a *file1* **l sort**
The **tee** utility reads its input and writes its output to the standard output connected to the input of sort, and also appends (**-a**) its input to the file *file1*.

Options

-a	append the output to a given file instead of overwriting the file.
-i	Ignore interrupt signals.

Warnings

Beware of overwriting existing files.

tr

CHANGING CHARACTERS WITH tr

The **tr** utility searches for all examples of specific characters and translates each into another specified character.

Sample Commands

tr *A a* < *infile* > *outfile*
The **tr** utility scans each line from the input, in this case, the file *infile*. It changes all uppercase *A*'s to lowercase *a*'s and writes to the output file *outfile*.

tr -d *aAtT* < *infile* > *outfile*
Deletes all instances of the characters *a*, *A*, *t*, and *T* from the input (taken from the file *infile*). The changes are written to the output (the file *outfile*).

tr *hi ih* < *infile* > *outfile*
Changes all occurrences of *h* to *i*, and all occurrences *i* to *h*. The input is taken from the file *infile*, and the output placed in the file *outfile*.

tr "[*A-Z*]" "[*a-z*]" < *infile* > *outfile*
Changes all of the uppercase letters to lowercase letters.

Options

-**d**_string_   Deletes all instances of each character in _string_.

Warnings

Be careful about overwriting existing files. Strings with special characters should be enclosed in quotes to prevent the special characters from being interpreted by the shell.

Notes

You can specify a group of characters by enclosing the characters in brackets and separating the characters by a -. For example, [_c-y_] stands for all characters from _c_ to _y_. To specify characters like [ ] and \ and -, you must precede each with a backslash (\).

REMOVING DUPLICATE LINES WITH uniq

uniq

The **uniq** utility examines adjacent lines and removes all but one instance of identical lines. To get only unique lines the input file should be sorted.

Sample Commands

uniq *file1*
All the lines from *file1* are output with only one
instance of repeated lines. For instance, if the contents
of *file1* were

```
Hello
Hello
Hello
123
123
456
123
```

then the output of the above command would be

```
Hello
123
456
123
```

uniq -c *file1 file2*
Stores in *file2* all of the lines from *file1*, including the
number of times each line is repeated. Assuming *file1*
contained the lines in sample command 1, the contents of *file2* would be

```
3 Hello
2 123
1 456
1 123
```

Options

-d	Display only lines that are repeated.
-u	Display only lines that are not repeated.
-c	Display the number of times a line is repeated.

COUNTING THE WORDS IN A FILE WITH wc   WC

The **wc** (word count) utility counts the number of lines, words, and characters in a file.

Sample Commands

wc *file1*
The **wc** utility outputs the number of lines, words, and characters in the file *file1*, each separated by a space.

wc -w *file1*
Displays only the number of words in the file *file1*.

Options

-l	Display only the number of lines in the file.
-w	Display only the number of words in the file.
-c	Display only the number of characters in the file.

·B·

Answers

Answers to Exercise 2-A:

1. **h**
2. */Admin*
3. **dd**
4. Anywhere on the line
5. *8***dd**
6. *3***dw**
7. Enter **:q!** to exit without rewriting the original.

Answers to Exercise 2-B:

1. a

2. Press ⌈Esc⌉.

3. vi command mode

4. I

5. press ⌈Esc⌉ :w *room*
   press ⌈Esc⌉ :q!

6. u

7. .

Answers to Exercise 2-C:

1. r

2. cc

3. C

4. :set number

5. b

6. 23G

7. z6.

3

EXERCISES

Answers to Exercise 3-A:

1. **mkdir** *Proposals*

2. **cd** *Proposals*

3. **cd**

4. **pwd**

5. **ls -F**

6. *Projects*

7. The files exist in different directories.

8. **mv** *florence Proposals*

Answers to Exercise 3-B:

1. **cd** *Proposals/Education*

2. **vi** *Proposals/kirby*

3. First enter **cd** *Proposals*; then enter **mkdir** *Rejected* or **mkdir** *Proposals/Rejected.*

4. **cp** *selquist Proposals/Education*

Answers to Exercise 3-C:

1. **find** ~ **-name** *atlantis* **-print**

2. **cd ..**

3. **cd** ~*/Marilyn*

4. **cd** *..*/*Letters*

5. **mv** *eakins* ~

6. **rmdir** only removes empty directories while **rm -r** removes a directory and all of the files inside of it.

4

EXERCISES

Answers to Exercise 4-A:

1. pr *sample sample.2* **| lp -d***dest* (or **lpr**)

2. The **-d** option

3. The **sort** command outputs the lines of a file in ASCII alphabetical order.

4. The **wc** utility outputs the number of lines, words, and characters in a file.

5. This command line will concatenate the files *lions, tigers,* and *bears,* into a new file called *oh.my.*

6. comm and **diff**

Answers to Exercise 4-B:

1. pr -n *joy* for System V, or **cat -n** *joy* for BSD.

2. The command paginates and prints the files *red* and *yellow* side by side on the screen, using a width of 50 characters, a page length of 22 lines, and a header title named *two_files.*

3. The **comm** utility only works on sorted files, while the **diff** utility works on unsorted files. The **comm** utility displays the lines that are common to both files and the lines that differ between each file, while the **diff** utility displays the differing lines and their location in their respective files.

4. grep *color green*

Answers to Exercise 4-C:

1. paste and **pr**

2. cut -d# -f1-3 *data_base*

3. Make sure that the two files are sorted.

4. tr + - < *add*

5. Both **sed** and **awk** must be given special commands in addition to options and files.

6. *7 12* **+ p**

EXERCISES   5

Answers to Exercise 5-A:

1. mail *user1* **<** *letter1*

2. Ctrl-d

3. Mail the contents of a file called *form.letter* to users whose login IDs are *andy, fred* and *joe.*

Answers to Exercise 5-B:

1. No. Your mailbox is checked periodically while you are logged in, and you are informed of any new mail at the next shell prompt.

2. mail

3. Type **p**.

4. Type **h** from the command mode of **mail**.

Answers to Exercise 5-C:

1. s

2. **mail -f** *letters*

3. x

4. r

5. Allows you to edit the file through the **vi** editor

6 ## EXERCISES

Answers to Exercise 6-A:

1. **date ; who**

2. **sort** *contacts* **>** *sorted.contact* **&**

3.

- **sort** is the utility being called.
- **-r** is the option to **sort** that requests the output to be in reverse order.
- *contacts* is the name of the file to be sorted.

4. *chapter1, chapter2, chapter3* and *newchapter1,* but not *chapter, chapter2a* or *intro.*

5. **ls ~**

Answers to Exercise 6-B:

1. **noclobber**

2. **>** redirect output into a file

< redirect input from a file or utility

>> append output to an existing file

>& redirect standard error

3. mail *terry* < *letter*

4. who I sort

5. In C shell: **set** *city* = *Boston* or **set** *city=Boston*
   In Bourne shell: *city=Boston*

6. set *datem* = `` `date` ``

7. set

Answers to Exercise 6-C:

1. *\~*abc.*

2. echo *"it's mine"*

3. ' *"$20"* '

4. echo' *"$20"* '

5. The commands are executed one time for each (**foreach**) file.

Answers to Exercise 6-D:

1. *.cshrc* contains environment commands interpreted each time a shell starts (C shell).
   .login contains special initialization commands to be interpreted only at login (C shell).
   .profile is same as *.login* (Bourne shell).

2. *PS1* in Bourne shell. Prompt in C shell.

3. Terminal driver

4. Shell sets up redirection; shell creates and clobbers files; shell expands filenames

5. The utility

7 EXERCISES

Answers to Exercise 7-A:

1. ls -l

2. Read and execute permission for the user, but not write permission

3. chmod 700 *filename*

4. -rwx------ (read, write, and execute permissions)

Answers to Exercise 7-B:

1. Owner may list the contents, add/remove files, **cd** into the directories, and execute files. Group may list contents, **cd** into the directories, and execute files. Others may list contents only.

2. umask 022

3. umask 066

8 EXERCISES

Answers to Exercise 8-A:

1. cd /

2. */dev*

3. */bin* **and** */usr/bin*

EXERCISES   9

Answers to Exercise 9-A:

1. **vi** *+50 practice*

2. **vi** *+/help practice*

3. **view** *filename*

4. Ctrl-w

5. **:set** *list*

Answers to Exercise 9-B:

1. **:***1,33* **w** *report.10*

2. **:***29,200* **w!** *report*

3. **:***36,74* **w** *>>* *report1*

4. **vi** command mode

5. **:***17,93* **move** *$*

6. **:***118,$* **d**

7. **:***32,57* **move** *0*

Answers to Exercise 9-C:

1. **:***4* **r** *report2*

2. **vi** *practice1 reminders practice2*

3. **:n**

4. **"a3yy**

Answers to Exercise 9-D:

1. :!ls

2. :sh

3. :r !date

4. :q

5. :n *other*

10   EXERCISES

Answers to Exercise 10-A:

1. ps &

2. fg %3 or fg %-

3. kill %4 or kill %+

4. jobs

11   EXERCISES

Answers to Exercise 11-A:

1. #!/bin/sh

2. You use the $ symbol to indicate that the following string should be evaluated as a variable.

3. With the **read** command.

4. **cat** <<**tag**
   input
   tag

Answers to Exercise 11-B:

1. **case**, a condition statement, and **esac**.

2. **while**

3. Use **echo** to prompt users to press a key to continue, and **read** to wait for their input.

4. To signify the default condition

5. Separate each alternative with a I pipe.

6. **fi**

Answers to Exercise 11-C:

1. The : is a condition that always evaluates as true.

2. **exit**

3. Proper indentation, sensible variable names, and useful comments.

4. Yes

5. C shell

EXERCISES _____ 12

Answers to Exercise 12-A:

1. System V: **lp -d***printer file1 file2 file3*
   BSD: **lpr -P***printer file1 file2 file3*

2. System V: **lp -d***printer* **-n**3 *junk1*
   BSD: **lpr -P***printer* **-#**3 *junk1*

3. System V: **lp -d***printer* **-t***title junk1*
   BSD: **lpr -P***printer* **-J***title junk1*

4. System V: **lpstat**
   BSD: **lpq -P***printer*

5. System V: **cancel** *printer-jobnumber*
   BSD: **lprm -P***printer jobnumber*

6. System V: **lp -d***gutenberg* **-s -w -m** *mail*
   BSD: **lpr -P***gutenberg* **-m** *mail*
   The **-w** option invoking notification to you that the print job is complete is not available on BSD. The *-s* function has a different function on BSD.

13   EXERCISES

Answers to Exercise 13-A:

1. **!!:p**

2. **!22**

3. **!!**

4. **!vi**

5. **!!** > *journal.errors*

Answers to Exercise 13-B:

1. **^/^~^**

2. **set history=100**

3. **pg !22:2**

4. **^***cat***^***pg***^** or **pg !!:***

5. **!10:s/***pg***/***cat***/**

6. **set prompt="<\!> % "**

EXERCISES ———————— 14

Answers to Exercise 14-A:

1. Assigning new names to commands that already exist

2. A list of all **alias** names and their definitions is displayed.

3. **alias** *ls* 'ls -a'

4. **unalias** *ls*

5. In your *.alias* file

6. False

7. **source** ~/.*alias* or recreate the alias using the **alias** command

Answers to Exercise 14-B:

1. **alias** *who* 'who | pg'

2. No, it would not. It would be an alias loop.

3. **alias** *seerm* 'pg \!*; rm \!*'

EXERCISES ———————— 15

Answers to Exercise 15-A:

1. System V: **env**
   BSD: **printenv**

2. setenv *TERM vt100*
   set *name=Jones*

3. *TERM* would equal *vt100*
   name would be undefined

4. export *deptname*

5. a) *.login*
   b) *.cshrc*

6. source *.login*

7. *.mailrc*

Answers to Exercise 15-B

1. ab *org organization* in the file *.exrc.*

2. stty *intr @*

3. stty -echo

16   EXERCISES
_____

Answers to Exercise 16-A:

1. ruptime

2. rwho displays all users on every machine connected to the network, while **finger** displays users on a specific machine

3. mail *strawberry@red*

4. Press Ctrl-d or Ctrl-c

Answers to Exercise 16-B:

1. rlogin *shake* **-l** *vanilla*

2. rsh *kitten* **-l** *siamese* **cat** *work*

3. The machine either doesn't allow you to use **rsh** or prompts you for a password.

4. rcp *television grass.green:radio*

EXERCISES ———————————— 17

Answers to Exercise 17-A

1. xinit

2. the window manager

3. xterm

4. With these steps:

- Move the mouse cursor into the root window.

- Hold down the middle mouse button to bring up the **WindowOps** menu.

- Drag the cursor down the menu until your choice is highlighted.

- Release the mouse button.

5. NewIconify or **LowerIconify**

6. With these steps:

- Move the mouse cursor to the beginning of the selected line.

- Triple click with the left mouse button to select and highlight the entire line.

- Move the mouse cursor into the window where you are pasting in the line.

- Paste the text by pressing the middle mouse button.

18   EXERCISES

Answers to Exercise 18-A:

1. .sp *3*

2. .ll *2i*

3. .ce

4. .ce *3*

5. .nf

6. .ti *5*

7. The next line in your file (**nroff** only)

8. **nroff** *practice* | **lpr -P***dest*

   or

   nroff practice | **lp -d**dest

9. *Only* when the text is passed through the formatter (**nroff**)

Answers to Exercise 18-B:

1. .LP

2. .ft B

3. \s+4

4. .EQ

   c **sup** *2* = *a* **sup** *2* + *b* **sup** *2*
   .EN

5. .PS
   ellipse *"E1"*
   move right *1* from last ellipse
   ellipse *"E2"*
   arrow from right of 1st ellipse to left of 2nd ellipse
   .PE

EXERCISES   19

Answers to Exercise 19-A:

1. **man** *man*

2. **man** *3 sleep*

3. System V: **locate** *file*
   BSD: either **man -k** *file* or **apropos** *file*

Answers to Exercise 19-B:

1. System V: **locate** *directory*
   BSD: either **apropos** *directory* or **man -k** *directory*

2. The part under the heading SEE ALSO

3. Search the column to the right of the blank center column.

20 EXERCISES

Answers to Exercise 20-A:

1. The file **/bin/who** exists on the disk. You type in the **who** command. The system loads the utility from the disk into main memory. The CPU executes the instructions in main memory, causing a list of users currently logged in to be printed on your terminal. When the last name is printed (the instructions are finished), the process dies, and the space in main memory taken up by the process is freed for use by other processes.

2. *1080, 1056, 23*

3. System V: **ps -elf**.
BSD: **ps -axlg**.

4. System V: **ps -ft** *13* or **ps -fu** *them*
BSD: **ps -lt | 3** or **ps -aux | grep** *them*

Answers to Exercise 20-B:

1. The system data component

2. The user data component

3. **fork, wait, exec** and **exit**

4. (a) K   (b) U   (c) S   (d) U   (e) K

Answers to Exercise 20-C:

1. Kill the **vi** (child) process using **kill** with no option or the **-1** option.

2. The **who** utility would execute, but its output would disappear. User *kevan* would receive a copy of the message of the day in his **mail**, and your prompt would be returned in roughly 100 seconds.

3. All of the related child processes would then become defunct processes, and they would have to be **kill**ed individually.

4. To eliminate the defunct process, reboot the system.

EXERCISES
21

Answers to Exercise 21-A:

1. Archiving one or more files or directories on magnetic tape

2. Superusers and ordinary users

3. **tar t**

4. **tar r** *people*

5. When archiving, but not when extracting

Answers to Exercise 21-B:

1. **/etc/shutdown** +*10*

2. */etc/passwd*

3. **passwd** *sam*

4. **cd** ~*username;* **/bin/rm -rif** *

5. Level 0 **dumps** all the files of a filesystem. Level 1 **dumps** all the files modified since the last level 0 or level 1 **dump**.

6. **fsck -n** */dev*

Index

988   Index

RESOURCES

After completing this book, you may wish to use it as a reference to locate information such as the best utility to use for a particular function, or the correct syntax for a command. The following portions of the book will be excellent resources for these tasks.

1. **Utility Information Pages—UIPs (page 903)** These pages contain information on 16 UNIX utilities. The UIPs explain each utility's function, syntax, and options, as well as examples of commands, and warnings when special care is needed.

2. **Index (page 961)** The Index contains entries for

   - Actions (such as combining, counting, extracting, and listing)

   - Commands (such as **join, wc** and **cut**)

   - Command components (such as options and arguments)

   - Objects (such as files, directories, and jobs)

   - Other topics (such as command interpretation and dictionary order)

3. **Command Summaries (at end of most chapters)** These Summaries contain the commands and command formats (and their functions) that are relevant to each chapter. Command Summaries let you quickly find the command you want, and its function.